Praise for *The Hated Cage*

"In Britain, American military cemeteries dot the landscape, none more forgotten or haunting than the one at Dartmoor, with 271 American sailors from the War of 1812. Guyatt has written a stunning, revealing history of one of the darkest and most inhumane outposts of the British empire, hidden in plain sight and historical memory in southwest England. The book is a withering tale of race and the suffering fate of seamen in the age of sail. It is also a brilliant reminder of why we do research and why we remember."

—David W. Blight, Sterling Professor, Yale, and
author of *Frederick Douglass: Prophet of Freedom*

"Nicholas Guyatt's absorbing story of the early nineteeth-century Dartmoor prison 'massacre' asks who was an American and could Black men, detained as British as prisoners of war, be citizens? Told by way of archival sleuthing and exacting analysis, *The Hated Cage* is a fascinating study of how ideas about racism and the state became fused to one another in the early American republic. It is a must-read for anyone concerned with the origins of the anti-Black thought of our own time."

—Martha S. Jones, author of *Vanguard*

"In Guyatt's truly extraordinary recovery of Americans imprisoned long ago, he has excavated a most disturbing racial as well as carceral past, one that will feel disturbingly familiar, and one that underscores on every page the imperative of finally reckoning with white supremacy if there is to be a different future."

—Heather Ann Thompson, Pulitzer Prize–winning author of *Blood in the Water: The Attica Prison Uprising of 1971 and Its Legacy*

"In this brilliant book, Nicholas Guyatt tells the fascinating story of a long-forgotten massacre of American sailors in a British prison. While that tale on its own is gripping, *The Hated Cage* uses this prison drama to unlock a range of insights about life and death across the nineteenth-century Atlantic world. A must-read work."

—Kevin M. Kruse, professor of history, Princeton University

"This is history as it ought to be—gripping, dynamic, vividly written, and altogether brilliant in its interpretation. Nicholas Guyatt has liberated a motley crew of American sailors from the double darkness of Dartmoor Prison and our own poor historical memory."

—Marcus Rediker, author of *The Slave Ship: A Human History*

"Mostly set in a prisoner-of-war camp located on an otherworldly English moor, Nicholas Guyatt's *The Hated Cage* is history at its most beguiling. Guyatt expertly synthesizes critical maritime and prison scholarship to give us a unique window into war, repression, racial violence, and incarceration in early modern American history. Anyone interested in exploring the meaning of the American Revolution would do well to lay off its founding fathers and read Guyatt's account of long-ignored, tellingly so, events in Dartmoor's 'Black Prison.'"

—Greg Grandin, Peter V. and C. Vann Woodward
Professor of History, Yale University

THE
HATED
CAGE

THE
HATED
CAGE

AN AMERICAN TRAGEDY IN
BRITAIN'S MOST TERRIFYING PRISON

NICHOLAS GUYATT

BASIC BOOKS

New York

Basic Books
Hachette Book Group
1290 Avenue of the Americas, New York, NY 10104
www.basicbooks.com

Printed in the United States of America

First Edition: April 2022

Published by Basic Books, an imprint of Perseus Books, LLC, a subsidiary of Hachette
Book Group, Inc. The Basic Books name and logo is a trademark of the Hachette Book
Group.

The Hachette Speakers Bureau provides a wide range of authors for speaking events. To
find out more, go to www.hachettespeakersbureau.com or call (866) 376-6591.

The publisher is not responsible for websites (or their content) that are not owned by the
publisher.

Print book interior design by Amy Quinn

Library of Congress Cataloging-in-Publication Data has been applied for.

ISBNs: 9781541645660 (hardcover), 9781541645646 (ebook)

LSC-C

Printing 1, 2022

CONTENTS

LIST OF FIGURES

INTRODUCTION

THERE WERE DEAD AMERICANS IN THE YARD. IT WAS DARK now and Frank Palmer didn't know how many.

Dartmoor prison, perched on high moorland in southwest England, was a place where even the British thought the weather was bad. The morning of 6 April 1815 had felt like the first day of spring, but the rare opportunity to spend time outdoors had only exposed the prisoners' restiveness. The War of 1812 had been over for two months, and more than five thousand Americans were still locked within Dartmoor's massive walls. In the afternoon, hundreds of them had started an impromptu fight, throwing mud at each other and then at the British soldiers who were guarding them. The commotion made it easy to miss the smaller crowd of prisoners who were trying to punch a hole in the inner wall between the prison yard and the barracks building. Surely they didn't think they could escape from Britain's most fearsome prison? After the winter just gone, the guards believed the Americans capable of anything. When the 'sport' in the yards led to the breaching of the prison's inner wall, the situation deteriorated rapidly.

The shooting started after six in the evening. Frank ran back to his prison block and cowered for an hour or more, listening helplessly to the screams. As British soldiers moved through the yard, prisoners fell in all directions. Crowds of Americans ran to the prison blocks and thrashed against the locked doors. The guards fired on them, too. Frank's estimation of 'British humanity' had never been high. During the eighteen months he'd spent as a prisoner of war—in Bermuda, Canada, and now in Britain—he'd recorded terrible things in his diary. But nothing had prepared him for the guards firing *into* the prison blocks, through the doors and narrow windows, 'killing and wounding without mercy' even those Americans who had tried to shelter from the trouble.[1]

When the shooting stopped, the wounded were too afraid to emerge from the blocks and cross the yard to the prison hospital. Men lay bleeding and groaning all around Frank's hammock until the prison's governor, who was known as 'the agent', sent word that the injured should be brought out for treatment. The agent was a Royal Navy captain named Thomas Shortland, who lived with his wife and children in a house at the front of the prison. When he had taken over at Dartmoor in December 1813, the Americans had viewed him as a good man. But survivors of the massacre were adamant: it was Shortland himself who had ordered the guards to fire, who had led the rampage through the yards, and who had 'stamped on those who were already dead—or nearly'. The Americans had lost their faith in Shortland's decency during the bleak winter just past, and Frank had little trouble believing the reports. By the light of a candle on the evening of 6 April he summarised the day's horrors. 'Is this not a sufficient proof of British barbarity?' he wrote in his journal. 'The blood of the murdered will ever stimulate us to vengeance. WE CRY FOR VENGEANCE.'[2]

Nathaniel Pierce, another prisoner who kept a diary of his time in Dartmoor, blamed the British turnkeys for locking the prison block doors and denying inmates any respite from the slaughter. He accused Agent Shortland of sending 'scouting parties' to kill prisoners who were hiding in the corners of the yard and of ordering the execution of one American who was carrying a wounded man on his shoulders. 'It is an impossibility for me to describe the barbarity of this Captain Shortland,' Pierce wrote. The killings had been like 'firing into a hencoop among a parcel of fowls'. Americans knew all about British brutality; they had fought the Revolutionary War to escape it. But what Pierce saw that evening reminded him of the darkest day of America's founding struggle: 'This is worse than the massacre at Boston in the year 70,' he wrote.[3]

On 5 March 1770, a crowd of Americans protesting the British occupation of Boston had been fired upon by a line of Redcoats guarding the Custom House. Five Americans were killed. The grisly episode became a touchstone for the independence movement, from Massachusetts to Georgia, and the Boston Massacre became a key part of America's founding mythology. Nathaniel Pierce assumed that the Dartmoor Massacre would be no less enduring. Six Americans were already dead; another three would succumb to their injuries in the following days, and nearly three dozen had been gravely wounded. The terrible scene would be 'long remembered by all true Americans,' Pierce told his journal. Frank Palmer felt the same way. 'Enough cannot be said on this subject,' he wrote. 'Never (so help me God) will I make Peace with the English until I revenge the blood of my countrymen.'[4]

When news of the killings reached the American papers later that spring, editors and publishers jockeyed to secure eyewitness testimony and pour opprobrium on Britain. How could so many unarmed Americans have been killed in a British prison? What were they even doing there months after the War of 1812 had ended? As newspapers and congressional representatives pressured the administration of President James Madison, the survivors of the massacre awaited news of compensation—from the British, or at least from their own government. Americans and Britons had been at odds with each other for more than half a century, since the successful conclusion of the Seven Years' War in 1763 had prompted British politicians to demand more money from the American colonists to pay for the upkeep of the empire. The Dartmoor prisoners were only the latest American victims of 'British Barbarity', in Frank Palmer's phrase, and they surely would not be the last.[5]

Palmer was wrong about that. Although he and Nathaniel Pierce couldn't possibly have known it, the nine men who lost their lives in the Dartmoor Massacre were the last Americans to be killed in wars between Britain and the United States. The half century of hostilities that had preceded the massacre gave way to more than two centuries of peace between the old enemies. As a consequence, Dartmoor—like the War of 1812 itself—was marooned by history. The Boston Massacre retained its power in American memory because it explained why independence was necessary. The Dartmoor Massacre, on the other hand, became an awkward anachronism. James Madison had no appetite for reopening the war in May 1815, when news of the killings at Dartmoor reached his desk. Instead, he and his diplomatic representatives carefully steered the controversy into a siding. The prisoners had learned at Dartmoor not to place much hope in their government, but they were amazed at how completely their cause would vanish from view.

AS A HISTORIAN OF THE UNITED STATES WHO TEACHES IN BRITain, I'm embarrassed to admit that I found out about the Dartmoor Massacre entirely by accident. On vacation in Devon, a picturesque coastal county on England's southern shore, I dragged my family into the car to tour the bleak uplands of Dartmoor National Park. An hour later, I more or less drove into the prison. For a portion of the nineteenth century and nearly all of the twentieth, Dartmoor was a high-security facility: it was home to political prisoners and hardened criminals, and it became a byword for remoteness and despair. Most Britons would be surprised to learn that Dartmoor had been built during the Napoleonic era to serve as a war prison—a strangely transitory purpose for a huge granite building. The graves of 271 American POWs outside the prison reveal its true origins and the heavy cost paid by those Americans who were brought to Dartmoor between 1813 and 1815.[6]

I resolved when my vacation was over to plug the gaps in my knowledge, but I found that very little had been written about the Americans at Dartmoor. Their ordeal had inspired a few articles and chapters, but the massacre was mostly where James Madison had hoped it would end up: in obscurity. I wanted to tell the story of what happened but also to understand why such an extraordinary episode vanished from American history. The prison, which was opened in 1809, was the largest and, by all accounts, most feared detention facility in the world. More than six and a half thousand Americans passed through the stone archway which bordered its main gate, the largest single contingent of American POWs held overseas before World War II. For the first year of their stint in Dartmoor, Americans were outnumbered by French prisoners, who taught them a good deal about how to survive. After Britain made peace with France in 1814, Americans had the place to themselves. In early 1815, Dartmoor would have constituted the twentieth-largest city in the United States, if it hadn't been on blasted moorland in the southwest of England.

In its physical scale, and in the extent of suffering within its walls, Dartmoor was an exceptional place. It also cast a long shadow. Prisons are a relatively recent invention, a product of late-eighteenth- and early-nineteenth-century debates on both sides of the Atlantic about the power of incarceration to rehabilitate the fallen. Although prisoners of war were not criminals, Dartmoor's inmates rehearsed or invented nearly every prison cliché. They wore bright yellow uniforms with a diagonal arrow. They bribed the guards for advice on how to escape and slipped money to local tradesmen in return for favours or equipment. (A shiv was discovered inside one of the loaves of bread sent to the prison.) They played games—including one that looked a lot like baseball—and staged their own entertainment: Shakespearean tragedies and fashionable farces, dancing and boxing lessons, relentless gambling. Of course they tried to dig their way out, piling up dirt and paranoia as their secret tunnels inched towards the moorland beyond the prison walls.

One reason these remarkable stories failed to gain traction within the United States is that the Dartmoor prisoners were on the margins of American society. Virtually all of them were sailors and civilians rather than navy personnel. Thomas Jefferson and

James Madison, who held the presidency across four terms from 1801 to 1817, had decided against building up the (tiny) US Navy despite their fears that the United States would be dragged into another conflict. When Congress finally declared war on Britain in 1812, private vessels were outfitted with guns and directed to prey on British merchant shipping. These 'privateers' became the front line of the American war effort, which meant that ordinary sailors rather than soldiers or US Navy personnel were spilled into Britain's sprawling prison system.

Sailors were young—the average age of Dartmoor prisoners was around twenty-five—and necessarily mobile. To their compatriots on shore, they could seem rough and rootless. Around 10 percent of sailors on American ships were foreign nationals, and the maritime world acquired a reputation (not always fairly) for harbouring misfits and lowlifes. 'The crew were a motley set indeed, composed of all nations,' wrote the Dartmoor prisoner George Little of the sailors he had served with before his capture. 'They appeared to have been scraped together from the lowest dens of wretchedness and vice.' Although many sailors were fiercely patriotic, others were accustomed to a life in which they would sail under the flags of other countries and spend long years away from the United States. Thousands had been forcibly recruited into the Royal Navy, an experience which occasioned both sympathy and suspicion from their compatriots. When the Americans at Dartmoor were released after the massacre of 1815, most could not afford to spend months on shore advancing their claims for recognition and compensation. Instead, they went back to sea, taking their experiences and grievances with them. The itinerant nature of sailors' lives meant that the US government could ignore them just as easily as it had taken them for granted.[7]

The War of 1812 has been styled for two centuries as a 'second war for independence.' It lives on in American culture partly through the national anthem, written by the Maryland lawyer Francis Scott Key during the abortive British attack on Baltimore in the fall of 1814. Key had actually witnessed the assault on the city from an enemy warship: he had been trying to negotiate a prisoner exchange with British commanders and had felt a rush of relief when the Star-Spangled Banner continued to wave despite the Royal Navy's bombardment. But Key's mission had been to secure the release of a friend of his, and more importantly a friend of James Madison. While Key was working to free this well-connected captive, American prisoners were piling up in Dartmoor by the thousands. Throughout the fall and winter of 1814, American POWs were marched into the prison with no prospect of release before the war's end. Then, to their horror, they were not permitted to leave even when the war was over. Dartmoor presented a very different view of American power and persistence from the one popularised by Francis Scott Key. The men trapped there were forced to conclude that their government had abandoned them.[8]

ONE FURTHER STRAND OF THE STORY HELPS US TO SEE WHY DARTmoor was largely forgotten. Of the six and a half thousand Americans who were detained in the prison, around a thousand were men of colour. Native Americans, African Americans, and people from throughout the African diaspora were drawn to the sea as a place of possibility, even escape. Black people who had been born free, alongside those who had been manumitted or had escaped from slavery, could be found on virtually every American vessel. After being captured by the British during the War of 1812, they were cast into Dartmoor alongside the white men they had served with aboard merchant ships and privateers. But then, a few months after the first Americans arrived in April 1813, the British agent received an unusual request from the white American prisoners: Could they be moved away from their Black compatriots? After a short correspondence with his superiors in London, the agent agreed. Far from home, thrown into a monumental prison by a common enemy, white sailors had chosen to divide their community by race rather than to stand together as Americans. Dartmoor became the first racially segregated prison in American history.

But this wasn't the end of it. In the spring of 1814, when Britain's long war with Napoleon came to an end, the French prisoners were released and American POWs were transferred to Dartmoor from British prisons in India, South Africa, the Caribbean, and Canada, among other places. Black prisoners were given an entire block to themselves. There were seven of these blocks at Dartmoor; Prison Four, which Black Americans had previously shared with the French, now became the focal point of social and economic life for Black and white prisoners alike. With thousands more Americans arriving in the fall of 1814, white prisoners slept in the other prison blocks but spent a huge amount of time in Four. It was home to Dartmoor's preeminent theatre, along with its best boxing school and most charismatic preacher. High-rollers and penniless addicts convened nightly to play cards and spin the roulette wheel. (The French prisoners had smuggled a roulette wheel into the prison— we'll get to that.) The 'Black Prison' was at the heart of everything, and at the heart of Four was the only Dartmoor prisoner whose name would linger in American memory: King Dick.

'He is by far the largest, and I suspect the strongest man in the prison,' insisted the first published account of King Dick's reign over Prison Four, which appeared in 1816. 'This black Hercules commands respect, and his subjects tremble in his presence.' On the rare occasions that American writers chose to remember Dartmoor, Dick emerged as a powerful but elusive figure. He had been born in Salem, Massachusetts, or perhaps in Virginia or Maryland. He had served aboard an American privateer, or perhaps a French ship, or maybe he had been press-ganged into the Royal Navy. He was six feet two inches in height, or perhaps six-five, or maybe seven feet. He prowled the corridors of Prison Four with two young boys— white boys—and a huge club, which he swung liberally and without warning to maintain absolute order within his prison. 'If any of his men are dirty, drunken, or grossly negligent,' went that 1816 account, 'he threatens them with a beating, and if they are saucy, they are sure to receive one.' Fascinated by King Dick, white writers reached the same conclusion about his role at Dartmoor: he may have been a despot, but only a despot could bring order to a Black community.[9]

This image of Dick as a necessary tyrant seems so palpably racist it's amazing it has lingered among the relatively small number of writers and historians who have noted the American experience at Dartmoor. One reason for its persistence is that our sources for what happened in the prison are hugely skewed. Around fifty American prisoners left a significant trace in the archive: a letter to a family member, perhaps, or a petition to the American or British government. Around two dozen prisoners left narrative accounts of their captivity, but many of those are very short. A dozen or so prisoners left something more substantial: the journals of Frank Palmer and Nathaniel Pierce, among others, and published memoirs of prisoners written years or decades after the War of 1812. Not one of these accounts was written by a person of colour.

We can't escape the limits of our sources. White people monopolized the story of Dartmoor, and the archive privileges their perspective even as it narrows our view of what really happened inside Prison Four. My approach has been to think carefully about how white journals and diaries—the accounts that were scratched out in real time within the prison's walls—tell a different story from the one sculpted in memoirs and reminiscences published long after the fact. I've also mined the massive body of prison records in the National Archives in London, along with the extensive correspondence on prisoners and sailors held at the State Department's archives in Maryland. And then there's the prison register: an unusually detailed database of every American prisoner, all 6,553 men who were processed by the prison's clerks in the two years after the first arrivals in April 1813.[10] Early in the process of researching this book I decided to transcribe the five heavy volumes of the register into a spreadsheet that would allow me to cross-reference the claims made by published accounts about the identity and exploits of individual prisoners. In the process I came to know more than any previous historian about the thousand or so Black prisoners who found their way to Four. And I came to doubt whether the stories told by white people about Dick had any relation to what really happened at Dartmoor.

I've tried to drag Dick out of mythology and into the real world in the pages that follow, but I'm resigned to the truth that he can't be fully tied down—the myth and the man have become inseparable. What we know of Dick, however, vividly illuminates a key question in American history. During the first and second decades of the 1800s, as Black sailors took their place among crews up and down the American seaboard, the United States was convulsed by debates over slavery. Alongside the ethical and economic issues— was slavery immoral? could the republic survive without it?—white and Black Americans debated the kind of society which might exist in the United States on the other side of emancipation. Would Black people live alongside white people in freedom, as most African Americans assumed? Or should they live apart from white people in a colony or nation beyond the United States, as both Thomas Jefferson and James Madison fiercely believed? Prison Four became an accidental testing ground for these questions. After the new republic of Haiti, which had secured its independence from France (and from white enslavers) in 1804, Prison Four was one of the largest self-governing Black communities outside of Africa. But it was also a place to which white people couldn't stop returning, despite the prejudices that had created this community in the first place. In this respect, as in so many others, Dartmoor is an unmistakably American story.

PART I

KING DICK AT VIENNA

AFTER WHAT HAPPENED AT DARTMOOR, PLENTY OF PEOPLE would tell stories about King Dick. He may have told some himself, though we know him entirely through the things white people said about him: partial, contradictory, outlandish. Of his early years we know almost nothing, though after his capture near Bordeaux in the spring of 1814 on an American schooner—or was it French?—he was asked to give his name, age, and place of birth. The British clerk who surveyed the new prisoner wrote 'Richard Crafus' in the first column. He judged Dick's height to be six feet, three and a quarter inches, remarkable even for a man who hadn't spent his career among the diminutive breed of sailors. Dick was twenty-three years old, or so he said, which would place his birth around 1790—just after George Washington became the first president of the United States. And Dick told the clerk he was from Vienna, a small town in Dorchester County on Maryland's Eastern Shore.[1]

We don't know if Dick was born into slavery or freedom, though the former is much more likely. In 1790, the year of the first federal census, around 90 percent of Maryland's Black inhabitants were enslaved. Although the state's free Black population increased in subsequent decades, the Eastern Shore remained tightly in slavery's grip until the Civil War. It also produced two of the greatest abolitionists in American history. Frederick Douglass grew up in Talbot County, around thirty miles north of Vienna. Harriet Tubman spent her childhood just twenty miles to the west of Dick's hometown. Born a generation later, in 1818 and 1820, Douglass and Tubman became famous not only for their courage but also for their mobility. After her daring escape from Maryland to Philadelphia in 1849, Tubman made at least nineteen subsequent visits to the South to smuggle out friends, relatives, and strangers—hundreds of people in total. Douglass, who fled from Maryland to New England in 1838, was in constant motion as an antislavery lecturer and activist.[2]

Given their spectacular careers, it's easy to overlook the fact that Douglass and Tubman came from a desperately confining place. In their early years, they were separated from their closest family members, hired out among the relatives and associates of their owners, and beaten for their acts of defiance and self-expression. When he paid a visit to Baltimore in 1877, a lifetime away from his brutal youth, Douglass cheerfully performed the role of native son: 'I am an Eastern Shoreman,' he told the crowds. 'Eastern Shore corn and Eastern Shore pork gave me my muscle.' But Americans knew from his speeches and his celebrated narratives that the Eastern Shore had been a hard training ground. It was a place from which most enslaved people would never escape and to which runaways would never return.[3]

In Vienna, at least, Dick saw many comings and goings. The Nanticoke River brought ships up from the Chesapeake and the vast oceans beyond. Captains presented their credentials at the Custom House, emptying cargoes and collecting tobacco from the surrounding plantations. A small shipyard sat on the river's edge, launching sloops and schooners into the thriving coastal trade. Most African Americans in and around the town were employed in manual labour: picking tobacco, tending livestock, building and loading ships. The seasonal nature of work meant that children would be hired out long before they became adults. Some were sold to new masters, though the terrors of being cast into the expanding cotton belt of the lower

South were a greater threat to Douglass's and Tubman's generation than to Dick's. An African American born into slavery in Vienna in 1790 might have expected to end her life in the same situation, inhabiting a world in which the colour line was indelible. But this would not be Dick's story.

When Frederick Douglass described his early life, he recalled the dread that accompanied a child's realisation of what slavery really meant. He remembered the cold: with no shoes, trousers, or jacket, he would steal a sack used for carrying corn, crawl into it, and sleep with his head and legs poking out of the bag. (His feet were so cracked from the cold 'that the pen with which I am writing might be laid in the gashes'.) Like Douglass, the young Dick would have seen the casual violence which was never far from the surface of slavery. He would also have settled into a worldview in which white people presided easily and inexplicably over Black. But in the fall of 1796, something remarkable happened in Vienna which challenged the grim certainties of Dick's world. The region had produced a record crop of Indian corn, a mainstay of the coastal trade and one of the commodities which fuelled American trade with Europe. There was so much of the stuff in Vienna that word had spread throughout the Chesapeake that corn could be had at a good price there. One sea captain from Massachusetts, recently arrived in Norfolk, Virginia, decided to investigate. He had never seen Vienna before, and no one in Vienna had ever seen anything quite like him. His name was Paul Cuffe.[4]

As Cuffe's ship, the *Ranger*, moved slowly up the Nanticoke River, people near the shore looked on with astonishment. It was no surprise to see Black sailors on a schooner; African Americans were a mainstay of merchant crews during the early decades of the United States. But an observer on the banks of the Nanticoke would have noticed a great many Black sailors aboard the *Ranger*. In fact, the ship was entirely crewed by Black people, including its captain. 'A vessel owned and commanded by a black man,' Cuffe later wrote, 'and manned with a crew of the same complexion, was unprecedented and surprising.' As Cuffe remembered it, the white population of Vienna was 'filled with astonishment and alarm'. Surely, an all-Black crew would not risk a journey into the maw of slavery simply to find a bargain. Were they lost? Had they come to start an uprising among the enslaved people of the region?[5]

Paul Cuffe would become one of the most celebrated African Americans in the early United States. His father, Kofi, had been enslaved in Ghana in the 1720s, sold to a Quaker merchant in Massachusetts, and eventually freed in the mid-1740s. Cuffe's mother, Ruth Moses, was a Wampanoag Indian from Martha's Vineyard. Kofi and Ruth had fallen in love and were married in 1746, then built a life for themselves on Cuttyhunk Island, a small strip of land between the Vineyard and the mainland. Kofi and Ruth owned and managed property, but their principal interest was the sea: they repaired boats, ferried people and goods from the islands to the shore, and became modest players in the coastal trade. All ten of their children—four sons and six daughters—took up the family business, though Paul Cuffe, born in 1759, stood out from the rest. As a child he learned to repair and then to build boats, and when he was old enough he went to sea himself. After voyaging to Newfoundland, the West Indies, and Mexico, Cuffe realised that he could be more than just a sailor. He wanted to be a captain, and more than that—he wanted to own the ships he commanded.[6]

Cuffe and his siblings did well in the American Revolution, running daring raids through the British blockade which had severed the Quaker communities of Nantucket and the Vineyard from the shore. But Cuffe wanted to expand the Revolution's promise to encompass equality for everyone. In 1780, when a state tax collector appeared at the Cuffe residence, Paul and his brother John reminded him that they were currently barred from voting in state elections, despite the cries of 'no taxation without representation' which had animated the Revolution. The collector, inflicting 'many vexations' on the Cuffes, eventually forced them to pay up. Paul and John then presented a petition to the state legislature arguing that if Massachusetts expected free Blacks to pay taxes it must grant them 'all the privileges belonging to citizens'. The battle for Black citizenship in the United States was just beginning. When Cuffe died in 1817, the 'privileges' he had claimed under the banner of the American Revolution were far from secure even in Massachusetts. But Paul Cuffe never limited himself to reminding white people of their inconsistencies or pleading with legislators and neighbours for equal treatment. As he bought and sold ships and recruited sailors of colour to crew them, he was determined to shape his own destiny.[7]

Although the white residents of Vienna had never seen a ship crewed entirely by Black people, images of Black empowerment were a mainstay of their nightmares. In 1791, in the French Caribbean colony of Saint-Domingue, hundreds of thousands of enslaved people had risen up against white enslavers whose grip on power had previously seemed unshakable. In a matter of weeks, Saint-Domingue's towns were under attack and its sugar fields were ablaze. Hundreds of planters fled—many with their enslaved people—to American cities along the Eastern Seaboard. White people throughout the United States fretted about revolutionary contagion from these 'West Indian slaves'; in towns like Vienna, Haiti posed troubling questions about the stability of a slave system which had previously seemed secure. In the 1790s, every slave state passed a ban on the external slave trade, convinced that the numbers and proportion of enslaved people on the American mainland were dangerously high. Rumours of insurrection moved throughout the waterways of the Chesapeake, disrupting the harsh calm on which enslavers had previously relied. Paul Cuffe knew that his arrival in Vienna would stun the locals, but he made the trip anyway. He had long since decided that he would live his life on his own terms.[8]

The white residents of Vienna initially refused to let the *Ranger* tie up at the wharf. As Cuffe remembered it, they were 'struck with apprehensions of the injurious effects which such circumstances would have on the minds of their slaves, suspecting that [Cuffe] secretly wished to kindle the spirit of rebellion and excite a destructive revolt among them.' Understanding their anxieties, Cuffe chose to 'combine prudence with resolution'. He presented his paperwork at the Custom House and announced his desire to trade. He then returned to his ship, ordering the crew to behave with 'a conciliating propriety' while they waited for Vienna to choose profit over prejudice. Within a few days, he was permitted to sell his goods and inspect the town's impressive store of Indian corn. Within a week or two, he was receiving invitations to dinner from local notables, who treated him and his crew 'with respect and even kindness'. After three weeks, Cuffe had emptied his hold and restocked the *Ranger* with three thousand bushels of corn. He sailed back to Norfolk, cleared a thousand dollars in profit, and further expanded his maritime empire.[9]

In 1796, the six-year-old Dick would have been among the first enslaved people to encounter Paul Cuffe's remarkable example of Black self-reliance. The *Ranger* and its successors in Cuffe's fleet would become a regular sight off the coast of the mid-Atlantic in the late 1790s and 1800s, and Cuffe's thoughts soon turned to an even bigger prize: trade with the new Black colony of Sierra Leone, on the west coast of Africa. But when he wrote up his experiences in 1811, he lingered on the sensation he had created among Vienna's white population. For the Black onlookers who crowded the banks of the Nanticoke River and gawped at the *Ranger* and its crew, the effect was no less profound. Enslaved people saw in Paul Cuffe possibilities which seemed unthinkable before his arrival. At some point in the ensuing years, Dick broke away from Vienna and did what Paul Cuffe had shown him Black people could do: he went to sea.

1.

A Seafaring Life

O N A GLOOMY APRIL MORNING IN 1813, THE AMERICAN SAIL- ors held prisoner aboard the British prison hulk *Hector* awoke to what should have been good news: they were ordered to pack their belongings and leave the ship. The *Hector* was moored on the outskirts of Plymouth on Britain's south coast, one of the busiest and most important naval bases in the empire. Some had been in British custody for six months already, captured at sea soon after the United States declared war on Britain in June 1812. The *Hector* had served Britain with distinction during the American Revolution and the first years of the conflict with Napoleon Bonaparte. Since 1806, it had been lashed to the shore in its current spot, filling up first with French prisoners and now with Americans. When the weather allowed, the prisoners might spend some of their days on deck before being counted back in the hold of the ship at nightfall. When it rained, which it often did, the prisoners huddled in the gloom of the ship's hold, wondering when (or if) they would ever be released. The 250 Americans on the *Hector* were delighted to be leaving, until they realised the British were sending them some- where even worse.[1]

After gathering their belongings, the prisoners were called for- ward by name, handed an allowance of bread and fish, and given a pair of new shoes. They were then ferried by launches to New Passage, close to the centre of Plymouth and not far from where the *Mayflower* had set sail for New England nearly two hundred years earlier. On the shore to greet them were hundreds more British soldiers, a lavish escort reflecting Plymouth's military importance, and a crowd of curious locals. (Some of the latter were surprised that the prisoners spoke English.) The Transport Board, the arm of the British government which oversaw the prison system, would not give these Americans even the slightest opportunity to slip through their clutches and into the busy naval yards. Instead, they were mustered again, paired up with their escorts, and ordered to march north. They had a lot of ground to cover before nightfall.[2]

The Americans were mostly young—in their teens or twenties—and came from across the Union, from New Orleans to New Hampshire and everywhere in between. Several were born outside the United States: in Denmark, France, Germany, Ireland, and even Britain. The oldest prisoner, Edward Johnstone, had been born in Darlington in northeast England in 1745; he would turn seventy before his release in 1815. Twenty-two of this first complement of prisoners were Black; all of them told the British they'd been born in the United States save for John Newell and James Lawson, respectively, the cook and the steward of their vessels, who gave their birthplace as 'Africa'. Most had been captured aboard American privateers, commercial vessels which had been retooled after the declaration of war with Britain to complement the (tiny) US Navy. But dozens of the prisoners had been fighting for the other side when the war broke out. These men had been 'impressed' into the Royal Navy, seized and bundled onto British ships to serve His Britannic Majesty.[3]

The War of 1812 had thrown all of these sailors together, but their diverse backgrounds and pathways to captivity complicated the matter of solidarity. Was every prisoner a loyal American? Now that they'd found their way into the sprawling British prison complex, were they all on the same side? Those questions had already been asked aboard the *Hector*, and they would emerge repeatedly in the months and years ahead. For now, though, on this damp and grey morning in Plymouth, they would have to wait. At half past ten, the prisoners were told to begin their march northward, through the western reaches of the city and out into the countryside. Any prisoner who stepped out of line would be killed, or so went the threat from the British commander. Buildings gave way to fields and hedgerows, and the pace was unrelenting. The party made one stop around eight miles into the journey, and the prisoners rushed to finish the bread and fish they'd been given in the morning. Then they began the march again, and the hedgerows and fields were replaced by a bleak and treeless moor.[4]

As the rutted road became steeper, snow appeared on the barren land to each side. For the Americans, the emptiness of the terrain was disconcerting. This was, one later wrote, 'the Devil's Land, inhabited by ghosts and sundry imaginary beings. Rabbits cannot live there, and birds fly from it.' Nearly a century later, when Arthur Conan Doyle wrote about the same corner of southwestern England in *The Hound of the Baskervilles*, Sherlock Holmes shared the sentiment: 'Avoid the moor in those hours of darkness when the powers of evil are exalted.' With the light beginning to fade, more than sixteen miles into their march, the prisoners finally glimpsed their destination. A vast circular wall, fifteen feet high and a mile in circumference, enclosed seven massive prison blocks and a cluster of smaller buildings. The road from Plymouth ended in a huge, turreted gate. 'Nothing could form a more dreary prospect than that which now presented itself to our view,' wrote one prisoner. 'Death itself, with the hopes of a hereafter, seemed less terrible.' Nearly a year after the war with Britain had begun, American captives had found their way to Dartmoor prison.[5]

NEARLY ALL OF THE SIX AND A HALF THOUSAND AMERICAN PRISoners who would make it to Dartmoor were sailors. In the first half of the nineteenth century, maritime work was the second largest occupation in America (after farming). Sailors were easily the most numerous and visible American presence overseas. In 1800, no American newspaper employed a correspondent in a foreign capital and the United States retained consuls in barely a dozen countries. (The State Department had ten employees in total.) Although American missionaries would spread across the globe by the 1830s, virtually none worked beyond North America before the War of 1812. At that point more than a hundred thousand Americans were already sailing on the open ocean. It was through sailors that peoples of other nations came to know something about Americans. And, in turn, American sailors became a crucial conduit for delivering stories about the wider world to the new republic.[6]

Americans became sailors for many reasons. The most obvious was proximity to the sea. A young boy with a father or uncle in the merchant marine had immediate connections to the trade and a role model who was likely to act, sometimes inadvertently, as a recruiter. George Little, who would eventually become prisoner no. 1367 at Dartmoor, was born just outside Boston in 1791. His father was a sailor in the infant United States Navy. George later remembered how, as a boy, he'd been gripped by his father's stories of 'the scenes he had witnessed in foreign lands' and 'the wonders of a seafaring life'. When he realised that George was rapt, his father would abruptly try to 'throw a somber aspect over the whole picture' and play up the 'perils and privations' of the ocean. But George had other sources of inspiration. A local gardener who had once been a sailor quickened George's pulse with his own catalogue of 'thrilling incidents' at sea. 'If I had twenty sons,' he told George, 'I would make them all seamen.' George's family tried to kill his enthusiasm by apprenticing him to a merchant in New Hampshire, but by 1807 the sixteen-year-old had talked his way to a position at a counting house close to the wharves in Boston. Now just a few steps away from the life he'd been dreaming of, George would be on the ocean before the year was out.[7]

Benjamin Morrell, another sailor who would end up in Dartmoor, also went to sea in defiance of his family's wishes. Morrell was born in 1795 in Rye, a coastal town near the New York–Connecticut state line. Morrell's father worked for a shipbuilder, struggled to start his own business, and took to sea when his fortunes were low. In his absence, the young Morrell felt enveloped by 'marvelous stories' about 'the wonders of the mighty deep and the curiosities of foreign climes'. His mother and father refused to let him sail, so at the age of seventeen Morrell left home for New York without 'intimating my purpose to a single soul' and joined a merchant vessel bound for Lisbon. It was March 1812, and Morrell knew he'd done the right thing. 'I cannot describe my sensations on finding myself afloat on the mighty ocean,' he wrote. 'My soul seemed to have escaped from a prison or cage.'[8]

For many sailors who would later write about their experiences, the ocean was a source of boundless possibility. Joseph Bates, another Dartmoor prisoner, was born in 1792 near the busy town of New Bedford on the Massachusetts coast. Like George Little, Bates became infatuated with sea stories and told everyone that his 'most ardent desire was to become a sailor.' His mother hoped that the obsession would pass; when it didn't, she sent Bates to stay with an uncle in Boston, hoping that a bout of homesickness would crush his romance with the sea. The plan backfired. When he saw the ocean, Bates knew that the world of New England was not enough for him: 'I wanted to see how it looked on the opposite side.' On his first crossing of the Atlantic, as a fifteen-year-old cabin boy, Bates befriended a fellow crew member who insisted that he had signed up for the voyage to London solely 'to obtain a certain book which could not be obtained at any other place.' For most men, the appeal of the sea was more basic. It provided a means of employment, and for all its dangers it offered a measure of security and progression. Novices like Joseph Bates, George Little, and Benjamin Morrell—'green hands,' as they were known on board—were promised only a tiny cut of the profits at the end of the voyage. But if they returned safely, they could expect a bigger share on their next outing. Experience and skill trumped every other consideration in the merchant marine, which is why so many sailors remained in the profession even after experiencing its cruellest misfortunes.[9]

The physical demands of shipboard work suited younger recruits. But some green hands had lived many lives before they went to sea. Henry Van Meter was born into slavery about a decade before the outbreak of the American Revolution. His enslaver, Thomas Nelson Jr., was one of Virginia's leading planters and a signatory of the Declaration of Independence. The British promised freedom to enslaved Virginians who crossed over to fight for George III, but as a personal servant to Nelson—who became Virginia's governor in 1781—Van Meter's opportunities for escape were limited. If he actually fought on the Patriot side, he didn't mention this to the biographers who caught up with him at the end of his long life. But he claimed to have encountered George Washington on several occasions, as the momentous events of independence and war swept through his household.[10]

Van Meter was in his mid-twenties in 1789 when Nelson died, and he was sold and resold to a series of enslavers in Kentucky who treated him with unremitting cruelty. Resolving to break the cycle, Van Meter stole one of his master's horses, raced it to the Ohio River, and then (with the help of 'some benevolent white people') sailed the river to Cincinnati, a tiny outpost in what was then the Northwest Territory. Van Meter soon found himself in the middle of the United States's first major war with Indigenous people: the so-called Western Confederacy of Indigenous nations committed to halting the US advance into the southern Great Lakes region. In 1791, the Western Confederacy inflicted a stinging defeat on the US Army expedition which had been sent to suppress them—still the most bloody loss, proportionally speaking, in the history of the American military. Van Meter, destitute and on the run from slavery, volunteered to fight in the replacement force directed by Congress to restore the honour of the republic. Van Meter got to know General Anthony

Wayne, the force's famously obstreperous commander, and helped to secure victory for the American republic at the Battle of Fallen Timbers in 1794. The defeat of the Western Confederacy allowed US settlers and officials to expedite their colonization of what is now the Midwest.[11]

Many of the soldiers who fought at Fallen Timbers made their futures on the land they had stolen. Van Meter, though, journeyed back to the coast—this time to Philadelphia, where he came to the attention of a group of local Quakers who paid for him to attend one of their schools. Van Meter was nearly forty years old when he finally learned how to read and write, and then his trail runs cold until he turns up in Dartmoor prison. We don't know why he decided to go to sea in his forties. Philadelphia harboured one of the liveliest free Black communities of any American city, along with an energetic (if decidedly paternalistic) community of white philanthropists promoting gradual emancipation and Black uplift. But it was also a place of rising prejudice towards Black people, and it may not have been easy for a man like Van Meter—recently educated but lacking relatives or connections—to obtain a steady position. The sea was always an option if a would-be sailor could convince a captain that he was willing and able. At some point between 1805 and 1814, when he was anywhere between forty and fifty years old, Henry Van Meter decided that the next chapter of his extraordinary life would take place on the ocean.[12]

PEOPLE OF COLOUR WERE A MAINSTAY OF AMERICAN CREWS IN the late eighteenth and early nineteenth centuries. Some were Native American. The Indigenous communities along the coast of southern New England and Long Island—Wampanoags, Mohegans, Pequots, Narragansetts, and others—had been sailors since before the arrival of Europeans. Instead of being pushed west by Euro-American settlement, they adapted and persisted in their ancestral lands. At sea, they mobilized their expertise to forge new roles as commercial brokers between the British and Dutch empires in the seventeenth century, and between British North America and the rest of the world in the eighteenth. On land, Native nations discovered that settler colonialism might be kept in check through the judicious playing of one empire against another. The sea offered parallel possibilities for resisting settler supremacy and creating new fronts of Indigenous power. By the middle of the eighteenth century, coastal Indian communities were supplying thousands of sailors to the merchant marine.[13]

Meanwhile, Native women met, worked alongside, and fell in love with the Black mariners who were also integral to the region's maritime life. Two of the most famous Black Americans in the late colonial and early national periods—Crispus Attucks, martyr of the 1770 Boston Massacre, and Paul Cuffe, the celebrated sea captain—each had an Indigenous parent. The Native identity of these mixed-race sailors was typically obscured by the tendency of white Americans to flatten racial identity into a simple binary. Some Native sailors may have been able to pass as white; others, even those with two Indigenous parents, were categorized as Black. We'll revisit these questions when we reach Dartmoor, where the question of racial identity became an urgent challenge not only for the British but also for American sailors themselves. For now, we need to remember that Native Americans formed an important component of the American merchant marine, even if they were sometimes hard to see.[14]

Although the slave trade—and especially the Middle Passage between Africa and the Americas—has fixed an image of Black people as cargo rather than crew, Black sailors were central to the Atlantic maritime world. Historians have estimated that between 15 and 20 percent of the more than one hundred thousand American sailors in the early nineteenth century were African, African American, or from the broader African diaspora. (This figure includes mixed-race Native-Black sailors like Paul Cuffe.) The overwhelming majority of these sailors were free men. Some had been born free; others had won freedom through manumission, state or judicial action, or their own flight from slavery. Paul Cuffe, who owned his own ships and hired exclusively Black and Native-Black crews, was an exceptional figure. Most Black sailors worked as ordinary seamen for white owners and captains.[15]

Racial prejudices hardly evaporated when white men took to sea, but a maritime career was attractive to many people of colour. Sailors were paid by ability and experience, which usually meant that Black sailors could receive the same pay as white sailors with comparable skills. Black and white sailors lived and ate together below-decks, where ordinary seamen of any race were subject to the same sharp discipline of the captain. Narratives, letters, and memoirs attest to a professionalism and even a camaraderie which developed across the colour line. A racial ceiling meant that Black sailors were rare among the petty officers of a merchant vessel, and even rarer among sea captains. Black sailors were also keenly aware of the dangers of enslavement or (for manumitted or emancipated people) re-enslavement. White sailors clumsily compared the threat of the British press gang with the horrors of racial slavery; Black sailors worried about both.[16]

The sea connected the many parts of the Black diaspora throughout the Atlantic world, bringing African Americans into contact with political communities in which the status of Black people varied wildly. This was usually true even within a particular empire or nation. In 1772, the British judge Lord Mansfield declared that a Black 'servant' named James Somerset could not be held against his will in London by his West Indian master. The Somerset decision electrified the nascent antislavery movement in Britain and North America. It horrified planters in the Caribbean and the southern colonies of the British North American mainland, especially when they became aware that their slaves had caught wind of the extraordinary news (carried around the Atlantic by Black sailors). After 1772, Black and white observers—antislavery and proslavery—grappled with the realisation that Britain, suddenly and emphatically, had become free soil.[17]

In the United States, meanwhile, every state north of Delaware agreed to abolish slavery (either immediately or gradually) between 1776 and 1804. But slavery was expanding in the southern states, fuelled by cotton and the expulsion of Indigenous people. Black sailors knew that 'man stealers', who threatened to drag both runaway and freeborn Black people into slavery in the South or the Caribbean, operated as far north as Boston during the first half of the nineteenth century. They also knew that anti-Black prejudice was a mainstay of white sentiment in the northern states, even as the institution of slavery contracted wherever its economic and social footprint was limited. Virtually nowhere was safe from the reach of slavery and prejudice, and the sea enabled Black people to transmit and share knowledge about different communities and regimes among African diasporic peoples everywhere. It was by this means that Black communities—free and enslaved—gained an extraordinary knowledge of the Atlantic world. Sailors were the vital points of connection between nodes of Black resistance and self-rule, enabling runaways, uprisings, and revolutions and providing hope to those trapped within the plantation system. The historian Julius Scott puts it this way: 'Whereas slavery and its regime demanded a fixed status and clear boundaries, ships and the sea came to symbolize, for many people, possibilities for mobility, escape and freedom.'[18]

Black mariners went to sea with an obvious interest in alternatives to white supremacy. They found these in many places: among the Maroon communities of Jamaica, which comprised enslaved people who had run away from plantations and formed free settlements in the island's interior; among Black and Native communities in Florida, which remained outside the United States until 1821; and, particularly, on the island of Saint-Domingue, which became the scene of the Haitian Revolution (1791–1804), the largest Black uprising in the history of the Western Hemisphere. Black enterprise and self-determination were everywhere if you were paying attention: among the free Black women who kept stores and ran boarding houses across the Caribbean's major cities and among the African Americans who stitched sails or unloaded cargoes in the seaports of the United States. But sailing constituted a kind of refuge for Black people, and for many the sea became a destination in itself.[19]

AMERICAN SAILORS, WHITE AND BLACK, CAME TO THEIR PROFESsion from a vast number of places and backgrounds. Did their time at sea bind them together as Americans? One historian has urged us to see sailors as 'individuals invested in their national origins and articulate about their instrumentality in world affairs'. This may have been true in the second half of the nineteenth century, but in the three decades between the Revolution and the War of 1812 neither American power nor the idea of the nation was a fait accompli. Sailors certainly imbibed prejudices from their upbringing and culture, but they also found themselves spending months or years at a time away from the United States. Even those who confined themselves to the coastal trade traversed the very different political and social worlds of Massachusetts, Maryland, South Carolina, and Jamaica. Sailors who visited Europe, the Baltic states, and Russia—let alone the Pacific whaling grounds or China—encountered diverse cultures, languages, customs, and political arrangements. The age of revolutions was thrillingly (and often dangerously) vivid: men at sea would move through wars and upheavals seeking opportunity, while always scouting the exits.[20]

Sailors who began their journeys on American ships didn't always return on the same vessel. A ship might be damaged en route from New England to the Caribbean or laid up in a foreign port for months awaiting cargo. Captains fell sick, cargoes spoiled, business deals collapsed, personal relationships went sour. Sailors' wages were paid in arrears, giving them a strong incentive to see the voyage through. But circumstances and possibilities changed, and a sailor who refused to serve on ships of other nations could end up stranded, destitute, or both. Although it's impossible to give a precise figure, a substantial number of Americans who spent time at sea would have worked on foreign ships under a non-American captain. This makes it harder for us to fix the merchant marine of a particular country or empire within the simple bounds of nationality.[21]

The idea of the sea as a place where national affinity wielded a looser grip than on shore isn't completely alien to our own historical moment. In the twenty-first century, pirates and outlaws exploit the emptiness of the oceans in defiance of national interests and international law. Even for those who do their business in the open, the patchwork of national conventions and standards makes the sea a place of creative exploitation. From industrial fishing vessels to giant cruise liners, the merchant marine snatches up men and women from every nation and places them under flags of convenience—for the most part, the flags of nations with permissive labour and environmental laws. The sea is a space of exception in our world of nation-states, and at the opening of the nineteenth century it was just as unruly.[22]

For a sense of how the sea might shape the experience of a young American sailor, we should re-join George Little as he stepped from his Boston counting house to find a sailing ship in December 1807. It didn't take him long. The *Dromo*, bound for China via South America and Mexico, was in a hurry to leave. The ship's captain nonetheless instructed the sixteen-year-old to think carefully before signing on: 'Young man, you have chosen a life full of toil and hazard,' the captain told him. 'As this voyage will perhaps be one of great period, it would be well for you to reflect maturely on the measure you are about to adopt.' Little was warned that the voyage would bring him little money and that he'd be gone for a very long time. And yet here he was, standing on an actual sailing ship, his eye drawn from the harbour to the sea stretching past the horizon. He had longed for a 'career of dazzling adventure', and now his childhood dreams drowned out the captain's warning.[23]

The *Dromo* and its crew of eighty sailed all the way to Tierra del Fuego at the foot of South America before making their first stop. Technically, Americans were not permitted to trade with the Spanish colonies, but the *Dromo* had work to do along the Pacific coast of Spanish America. The Chinese had very little interest in the cloth and other finished goods which had been loaded into the *Dromo*'s hold at Boston, but if the crew could exchange these for seal skins (or Spanish dollars) from South American traders or Indigenous people, they would have a way to pay for tea and silk at the Chinese port of Canton. This was a risky endeavour: mariners' knowledge of colonial Spanish politics and the Indigenous people of the region was limited at best. A seasoned captain had an idea of where he might put in to trade illicitly, but both he and his crew had constantly to expect the worst. The *Dromo*'s twenty-six guns had initially surprised George Little, but he soon realised why his captain thought them necessary.[24]

Despite the hardships of a green hand's life, Little loved his new profession. He gawped at the 'sublime and magnificent' sight of the sun rising behind the snow-capped Andes, and he revelled in the intrigue of finding obliging Spanish colonists as the *Dromo* tacked up the Pacific coast of South America. By the summer of 1808, the ship had reached Acapulco. Steering clear of the port itself, a rendezvous for Spanish galleons carrying gold and silver to Europe, the American sailors made for a small island to complete another assignment. After a moment of wonder as he took in the sight of a beach packed with seals, Little was ordered to begin 'the dire work of slaying as fast as possible.' He and his crew mates killed more than three thousand, along with some elephant seals for good measure (which produced a valuable oil). After the massacre, Little found it hard to get the sounds out of his head: 'The roaring of the old seals, maddened to desperation, and the yelping of the young pups, together with the shouts of the crew, formed, to my mind, a kind of Pandemonium scene, from which I should have been exceedingly glad to have escaped.'[25]

When the 'work of death' was done, and the skins of the seals were dried and packed, the *Dromo* caught another lucky break:

officials in the nearby Mexican town of Guaymas were happy to trade in the open, which meant that the ship could sell almost all of its remaining finished goods. The crew could also socialize properly with other human beings for the first time since they had left Boston nearly a year earlier. The *Dromo*'s captain organized a party for fifty local notables, and the crew and townspeople drank and danced together for days. The flurry of 'dinner-parties' made the Americans happy to linger, but the captain insisted that they resume their voyage. After another few weeks of trading with Native peoples on the California coast, the *Dromo* had exchanged all of its linen for furs, skins, and Spanish dollars and the ship was finally ready to sail across the Pacific. The Americans reached Canton in May 1809—eighteen months after their departure from Boston.[26]

George Little and his crew mates spent four months in China, waiting for 'teas which had not yet come in' and traversing the cramped area in which foreigners were permitted to circulate. China maintained tight restrictions on foreign trade and sailors, a regime which outraged British and American visitors alike. (Britain's determination to undo Chinese 'arrogance' would inspire its Opium Wars of the mid-nineteenth century.) With little to do but wait, the *Dromo*'s sailors bought fancy goods for sweethearts at home and looked for sex in the floating brothels of the Pearl River delta. A few contracted smallpox, but the *Dromo*'s captain took so long to strike his deals with local merchants that there was plenty of time for them to recover. Eventually, at the start of October 1809, the ship began its long voyage home. After carrying a group of Dutch passengers to the colony of Batavia (in what is now Indonesia), the *Dromo* sailed across the Indian Ocean, round the Cape of Good Hope, and back through the Atlantic towards North America. On 6 March 1810, two years and three months after setting out, George Little stepped back onto American soil. He was nearly twenty, and no longer a green hand.[27]

Little's family, delighted to see him again, was convinced that he 'must have had enough' of the sea, but he was back at the Boston wharves in a matter of weeks. His second voyage was less fortunate than his first. On discovering that his new captain was a drunkard and a tyrant, Little decided to leave the crew at Rio de Janeiro. He spent the next year sailing brigs on the lucrative route between Rio and Buenos Aires. The money was good, but South America was in ferment. Napoleon's invasion of the Iberian Peninsula in 1807 had initiated the slow collapse of the Spanish American empire. Revolutions broke out across the continent, and Little did business in Buenos Aires even as local political elites declared their independence from Spain. Riding these swells as best he could, Little was finally undone by a more local catastrophe: his bosses went bust and disappeared with the $3,000 Little had made in their service. Virtually penniless, Little heard rumours that Britain and the United States might soon go to war. Securing passage on a ship heading for Baltimore, he arrived in the final days of June 1812, two weeks after that war had begun.[28]

During his four and a half years as a sailor, George Little had spent barely a month in the United States and had witnessed things that most Americans would never see. He'd encountered Chilean colonists, Californian Indians, Pacific Islanders, Chinese and Dutch merchants, Brazilian secret police, and howling seals. He'd toured the fringes of Spain's crumbling American empire and glimpsed the heavenly throne of China, the largest non-European empire in the world. Whether this made Little feel more American is a difficult question to answer. We know about his experiences from a book he published in 1843: *A Life on the Ocean; or, Twenty Years at Sea*, a memoir within the hugely popular genre of the sailor's yarn. Mariners who wrote up their experiences were fully aware of the genre's conventions of exoticism and excitement but also of the prejudices against seamen. Little noted sadly that the American public had been inclined to see sailors as 'a class of isolated beings, scarcely worthy to be ranked among the lowest and most degraded of human kind'. He wanted his countrymen to acknowledge their dependence on American mariners: 'Seamen are the great links of the chain which unites nation to nation, ocean to ocean, continent to continent, and island to island.' Insisting on their virtues and emphasizing their patriotism was another genre convention, and the form of Little's narrative tidied sailors' identities and allegiances into a simple commitment to America. The truth was more complicated than that.[29]

THE MULTINATIONAL NATURE OF AMERICAN CREWS WAS MEMO-rably captured in the nineteenth century's most celebrated maritime novel, *Moby-Dick*. In one chapter, Herman Melville lists the men of the whaling ship *Pequod* according to their national origins: Spanish Sailor, China Sailor, English Sailor, Iceland Sailor, French Sailor, Dutch Sailor, Tahitian Sailor, Danish Sailor, Lascar (South Asian) Sailor, and more. The crew is drawn from every part of the world; the harpooners are from India (via China), West Africa, the Pacific Islands, and the Wampanoag nation on Nantucket. *Moby-Dick* romanticizes the ocean as a place of 'open independence' for sailors, albeit one threatened by the terrifying fixedness of Captain Ahab's vengeance. 'In landlessness alone resides the highest truth,' writes Melville's narrator. 'Better is it to perish in that howling infinite, than be ingloriously dashed upon the lee, even if that were safety! For, worm-like, then, oh! Who would craven crawl to land!' The passion of Melville's prose leads us to a stirring conclusion: the sea was a refuge from the fixed and apparently immovable injustices of the shore. But for a couple of reasons we should resist the temptation to embrace Melville's contrast between the sea's 'open independence' and the 'treacherous shore' or to imagine that sailors experienced the ocean only as a place of refuge.[30]

First, there was plenty of injustice and inequality at sea, even before we consider the question of impressment: the skills and mobility of sailors offered them only a measure of protection against exploitation by their employers. Second, the power of states (and especially of the United States) *on land* can easily be overstated in this period. National sovereignties could be contingent and inchoate;

governance and self-determination frequently slipped national bounds, either through revolutions or via self-sustaining communities that eluded the reach of kings and emperors. But we also have to acknowledge that, even if the sea allowed sailors to maintain a more fluid sense of national affinity, wars invariably brought the question of allegiance into sharp relief. When nations fought each other, sailors were forced to choose sides, or would find themselves bundled onto one side or the other. Suddenly, their nationality became the most important thing about them.[31]

Another aspect of maritime culture affected these questions of national allegiance: the sea was a supremely male world. Women weren't impossible to find: thousands travelled as passengers each year aboard oceangoing ships, and a small but significant number appear in the archives on board naval and commercial vessels. In the Napoleonic era, the British Admiralty stated that 'no women be ever permitted to be on board' a Royal Navy vessel 'but such as are really the wives of the men they come to, and the ship not too much pestered even with them.' This referred to the common practice of allowing serving naval sailors to be reunited with their wives on board ships in port. The regulation also hints at the presence of other women: daughters and sisters, hawkers, traders, and sex workers. In some cases, those women might have stayed aboard when a vessel made sail, but because women were not included on ships' muster lists—the register of the sailors aboard each vessel—they appear and disappear abruptly in letters and personal accounts.[32]

In the American merchant marine, women were rarely visible at sea unless travelling as passengers. By the 1820s, it was not uncommon for whaling captains to take their wives with them on long voyages to the Pacific, though crewmembers were denied the same privilege. (They frequently complained about the captain's wife.) But the impact of women on the culture of sailors can also be measured in their absence. Ships incubated all-male cultures in which ideas about women, gender, love, and sex could develop without the rebuke or corrective of sisters, wives, mothers, and lovers. Historians still disagree on the extent and nature of homosexuality at sea; we'll return to these questions when we reach Dartmoor prison itself. But in relation to heterosexual desire and ideas about gender, the caricatures and prejudices of an overwhelmingly male culture shaped the breezy way in which sailors wrote about women in their memoirs and narratives.[33]

However far mariners may have been from female company, the entire business of sailing depended on female labour. Women were a mainstay of port towns across America: they kept boarding houses and shops, they made clothes and candles, they taught children and built ships. They also served as business surrogates during a relative's long absence from home and as crucial sources of support if sailors got into trouble overseas. Living with a sailor brought uncertainty and hardship. Some sailors arranged to have advance payments made to their wives and children from their share of a voyage, which clearly cemented bonds of affiliation between sailors and the people they had left behind. And yet letters from sailors' wives and mothers frequently betrayed an anxiety that a loved one would not return—because of the dangerous nature of sailors' work or the lure of foreign places and ties. Women played a critical role in deterring American mariners from going entirely off the grid, even as they lived their lives with the knowledge that they might already have seen husbands, brothers, and sons for the last time.[34]

According to Nathaniel Ames, who served in the merchant marine and the US Navy in the early nineteenth century, unmarried sailors far outnumbered their married counterparts: 'I do not know that I ever sailed in an American ship with an individual before the mast that was a married man,' he claimed in 1832, 'with the exception of one negro cook, of Boston.' Ames also contrasted British sailors, who preferred to work near their home ports and would 'almost as soon commit suicide as go on a voyage to the West Indies,' with American sailors, who were congenitally intrepid. 'Let any one trace a Cape Cod man, for instance,' he wrote, 'and he will find him performing one voyage from Boston and the next from

New Orleans; to-day carrying plaster from Passamaquoddy to New York and tomorrow in a French whaler off the Falkland Islands.' It would be easier, Ames thought, to predict the movements of 'that most eccentric of all animals, a flea', than to have any sense of where American sailors might go.[35]

For the majority of American sailors who were unmarried, ties to home might be relatively few. Conversely, men who had a wife and children at home, or sailors with property or a stake in a business, had compelling reasons to keep their hometown at the front of their minds. Every sailor had his own story; if older men tended to have stronger ties to the shore, loyalties were rarely simple and consistent. Affinity with home often meant a place before a country: the sailors and residents of America's seaports weren't always happy with the direction of the national government, especially as Thomas Jefferson and James Madison employed high-stakes tactics to settle their quarrel with Britain. By going to sea, Americans had an opportunity to escape at least some of the ties and burdens of nationality. But they left behind a government which had its own views of what the United States owed its sailors and what sailors owed the United States.[36]

WHILE ALL SAILORS HAD THEIR NATIONAL MOORINGS STRETCHED, tested, and sometimes reordered by their profession, slavery and the threat of enslavement produced crucial distinctions between the experiences of Black and white seamen. In the period between 1783 and 1815, Black sailors witnessed profound and abrupt shifts in the geopolitics of slavery throughout the Western Hemisphere. The wars in Europe following the French Revolution spilled quickly into the British and French possessions in the Caribbean. Both Britain and France sought to preserve plantation slavery and to protect their colonies against rival powers. This produced a strange and contradictory set of tactics: military emancipation, whereby European powers promised freedom to enslaved people who would fight for their cause, sat alongside Britain's mass purchase of more than thirteen thousand new enslaved people from Africa specifically to serve in its West India Regiments. (At the end of the eighteenth century, Britain briefly became the world's largest enslaver.) The struggles for personal freedom and for national or imperial advantage were thoroughly entangled.[37]

For white people in the United States, already anxious about Black loyalty and identity, these were fraught questions. During the American Revolution, twenty thousand enslaved people—mostly from Virginia, Georgia, and South Carolina—had crossed the lines to fight for the king rather than for the new republic. To proslavery diehards, these Black Loyalists demonstrated the need to repress enslaved people more thoroughly. But to other observers—including some with antislavery instincts—the Black Loyalists proved that slavery would always present a terrible danger to the United States. Slave uprisings were a constant threat to the nation, tugging painfully at one of the Constitution's many awkward compromises—the promise that, in the case of 'domestic insurrections' (as the Constitution coyly put it), northern states would be compelled to supply troops. Fears of the 'internal enemy', as historian Alan Taylor has described it, haunted the states of the upper South in particular.[38]

Did Black sailors look to particular nations and empires as the means of securing or preserving their freedom? Or did the sea, and the mobility it enabled, give them the motive and means to move between political communities, seeking safety and advantage where they could find them? Historians have written powerfully about 'Atlantic Creoles', Black diasporic figures who used the political instability of the age of revolutions to extract concessions from white settlers and officials and to glide between empires and nations if those concessions were not forthcoming. The slave trade persisted in the Atlantic for much of the nineteenth century, long after Britain and the United States had outlawed the importation of human beings in 1807 and 1808, respectively. The internal slave trade, meanwhile, led to the rampant commodification and disruption of Black lives within the borders of the United States. For all of this, the

Atlantic world remained a place in which political and social possibilities for Black people were expanding; the question, for peoples of the diaspora, was whether those possibilities could best be delivered by fighting for rights within majority-white nations or through other means.[39]

In 1789, just as the new federal government was taking shape in the United States, the sailor and antislavery campaigner Olaudah Equiano published his autobiography in London. Equiano's *Interesting Narrative* created a sensation on both sides of the Atlantic: it offered the first published account of the Middle Passage by an African survivor of the ordeal, and it detailed Equiano's astonishing journey from his childhood in what is now southwestern Nigeria to slavery in the Caribbean and (belated) freedom in Britain. The sea was integral to that journey. Equiano had been purchased in Jamaica by a Royal Navy officer who kept him as a servant throughout his many voyages; even though that officer broke his promise to free Equiano after they had served together during the Seven Years' War, Equiano eventually bought his freedom and continued to sail the world. He joined a Royal Navy expedition to the Arctic in search of the fabled northern passage to Asia, where he served alongside a young Horatio Nelson. During the American Revolution, he was recruited by a wealthy investor to help found a new British colony on the coast of Central America. He was even tapped by London's philanthropic elite to help with the creation of the new Black colony of Sierra Leone in 1787. Equiano styled himself as a British gentleman and aligned himself with British claims to benevolence and enlightenment. But the truths of his own life had fixed Black endeavour and achievement principally outside the British Isles. The sea had always been Equiano's most consistent and reliable guarantor of opportunity.[40]

Olaudah Equiano knew from experience that freedom for Black people in the age of revolutions was never definitive. Slaveholders and slave catchers, 'these infernal invaders of human rights', would use every trick to ensure that Blackness and slavery were permanently joined. Equiano also knew that the sea offered some defence against this and that Black men who knew how to sail represented a powerful threat to slavery's hold on the Atlantic world. 'It was a very dangerous thing to let a negro know navigation,' Equiano wrote. By the same token, Black sailors in American ships between the Revolution and the War of 1812 discovered a power and opportunity which were harder to find on land. Like white sailors, they went to sea for a variety of reasons. Some had stronger ties to family and friends than others. But Black sailors experienced the turbulence and upheaval of this era with a particular excitement. They knew their claims to an equal place in the United States were vigorously contested by most white Americans. For African Americans who took to sea to escape slavery or prejudice, the calculus of belonging was complicated. The United States might yet be the place where Black people grounded their struggle for equality and belonging, but the wars, revolutions, and uprisings of the Atlantic world suggested something else: there were other options for winning and consolidating Black freedom.[41]

2.

GETTING CLEAR

THOMAS JEFFERSON SPENT DECADES WRESTLING WITH THE problem of how to defend American independence in a hostile world. From his tenure as secretary of state under George Washington to his informal role as adviser to James Madison, his successor in the White House, Jefferson was exasperated by Britain's refusal to respect American neutrality. He was particularly enraged by the tendency of Royal Navy captains to stop and search US ships and drag American sailors into the service of the king. One response would be to build a US Navy on a par with its British counterpart, though this would cost a fortune and concentrate power in the hands of the new federal government. Jefferson insisted that there was a better way to manage America's place in the world, that the nation's material and philosophical advantages could produce something more enlightened than the crude and expensive militarism of Europe. His attempts to find that better way led to the War of 1812 and explain why so many American sailors ended up in Dartmoor.[1]

With the benefit of hindsight, it's easy for us to see the first decades of the American republic as a period of impressive consolidation. Between 1783 and 1820, the United States more than doubled its territory and tripled its population. Commerce was vastly expanded, the franchise was extended, and a network of roads and canals began to connect the seaboard to the interior. Presidents came and went, scrupulously following Washington's precedent of serving for two terms (if they could win re-election) before retirement. The Supreme Court emerged as a truly coequal part of government and the ultimate arbiter of the nation's laws. The Fourth of July became a cherished tradition, and orators across the nation used the anniversary of American independence to predict a still brighter future for the republic. While all this was going on, Europe was submerged in an interminable series of wars that killed millions of people, created millions more refugees, and briefly made Napoleon the most powerful ruler the world had ever seen. Given the global empires France and Britain had already fashioned, European war brought fighting to much of the Caribbean and, after 1808, sent Spanish and Portuguese America into a long struggle for independence. Against this backdrop, the advances of the American republic seem serene.

In fact, the United States was a work in progress during its early decades. The Constitution brought more vigour to its central government, but the federal system failed to address basic weaknesses that threatened the stability and perhaps the survival of the republic. The federal government also attracted new criticisms from those Americans who were sceptical of what power it had. Some of the biggest states in the Union—New York, Virginia, and Massachusetts—had ratified the Constitution by the slimmest of margins following procedural chicanery by the boosters of the new federal system. Even after the US victory over Britain in 1783, the British held on to Canada and their lucrative sugar islands in the Caribbean. Spain retained control of the Gulf Coast from the Mississippi River to Florida and what was then called Louisiana, the vast area between the Mississippi and the Pacific. (Spain had acquired this territory from France in 1763, though its settlements were mostly clustered on the Mississippi River.) The rise of Napoleon in the final years of the eighteenth century shifted the balance of power both in Europe and in the American interior: Spain agreed to hand Louisiana back to France in 1801, an ominous development given Napoleon's rampaging conquests on the other side of the Atlantic. The idea that the United States would eventually control the entire continent seemed very distant indeed.[2]

In his Farewell Address of 1796, George Washington urged Americans to take advantage of their 'detached and distant situation' and to remember that 'Europe has a set of primary interests which to us have none, or a very remote relation.' But Washington was no isolationist: Americans should 'extend our commercial relations' with Europe while having 'as little political connection as possible'. Thomas Jefferson took a similar view. The continent had so much land that every American—and an 'infinite number' of future immigrants—could spread across the hemisphere and become a farmer. (For now let's set aside the crucial detail that this land actually belonged to Indigenous people.) 'Cultivators of the earth are the most valuable citizens,' Jefferson insisted. (For now we'll also set aside the fact that Jefferson compelled enslaved people to do this work, though you can see that these exceptions quickly become distracting.) In an ideal world, virtuous farmer-citizens in the vast American interior would live simply and fend for themselves. But Americans had already acquired 'too full a taste of the comforts furnished by the arts and manufactures to be debarred the use of them'. This filled Jefferson with dread: the industry required to make finished goods would concentrate people and wealth, and his agrarian utopia would be blighted by cities, wage labour, and a restless underclass. Far better to 'let our workshops remain in Europe' and follow a simple rule: Europe would send its manufactures across the Atlantic, and America would supply fish, crops, and raw materials in return.[3]

Jefferson's vision found a sharp critic in Alexander Hamilton, treasury secretary in Washington's first cabinet and a man who delighted in mocking philosophical pretensions. Hamilton conceded that the agrarian way of life was appealing but insisted that Americans had to deal with the world as it was. It would be hard to guarantee a perfect equilibrium between the goods America needed and the raw materials it had to offer in return. A dependence on Europe could easily become a vulnerability for the United States. Hamilton thought the deleterious effects of manufacturing had been wildly overstated and that the new republic could easily withstand a few cities. With a balanced economy of manufacturing and agriculture, the republic would make its own technological advances and foster a huge domestic market that would insulate Americans from the uncertainties of foreign trade.[4]

In the long run, Hamilton won the argument: America became an industrial as well as an agricultural powerhouse. But in the years before the War of 1812, Jefferson promoted his own vision of commercial neutrality with unusual zeal. His problem was that foreign powers were capricious in their recognition of American neutrality, especially when they realised that in Jefferson's plan American ships would happily trade with their rivals and enemies. At the end of the American Revolution, Britain sulkily excluded US ships and merchants from its Caribbean trade. More surprising, though, was the challenge to American vessels and sailors from the Barbary powers of North Africa. These independent potentates—roughly aligning with what is now Morocco, Algeria, Libya, and Tunisia—had preyed upon European shipping for centuries, demanding tribute from governments in return for safe passage through the Mediterranean. Even the British had agreed to this rather than committing resources to subdue the Barbary states, and prior to 1776 American ships safely traversed the Mediterranean thanks to Britain's payments. But in 1784, less than a year after British troops completed their evacuation from what was now the United States, Moroccan ships captured an American brig and imprisoned its crew. News of American independence had travelled quickly, and US ships found themselves under assault from Algiers, Tripoli, and Tunis. Independence, it transpired, had costs as well as benefits.[5]

Defusing these tensions with the Barbary powers formed an important part of Jefferson's mission to France in the mid-1780s. The future president's first instinct was to abandon the European practice of paying tributes and ransoms and simply to offer a free trade agreement without any financial sweeteners. This was typical Jefferson: a performance of principle, with a hint of naivete. But 'if they refuse,' Jefferson continued, 'why not go to war with them?' For the next two decades, Jefferson ruminated on the advantages of military force. This was partly driven by condescension towards the Barbary states, whose disruptive conduct Jefferson found bewildering. That European nations suffered the same difficulties and paid protection money was of no consequence. Wouldn't it be better, Jefferson asked, for the United States to lead an alliance of powers and to humble the Barbary powers, ending the problem for good?[6]

Jefferson's proposals made their way to Congress in 1786. At that point the Articles of Confederation were still in force, giving every state a veto on legislation. Unsurprisingly, a plan to expand the navy massively and forge an alliance with European powers struggled to win unanimous approval. As with other issues in the mid-1780s, Congress's failure to take a more assertive stance was not the end of the matter. Frustrated advocates of a stronger central government (including James Madison and Alexander Hamilton) decided that same year that a convention should be held in Philadelphia in the summer of 1787 to 'revise' the Articles of Confederation; the cool reception offered to Jefferson's proposed assault on the Barbary 'pyrates' had become another argument in favour of the new federal Constitution. But even after the formation of the federal government in 1789, the difficulties of asserting American independence frustrated the Founders—and Thomas Jefferson, in particular. His soaring vision for American commerce remained vulnerable to the political calculations of other powers. And if the United States couldn't make Tripoli or Algiers respect its independence, what hope did it have with France or Britain?[7]

THOMAS JEFFERSON WAS STILL IN PARIS FOR THE MOMENTOUS events of 1789. France 'has been awaked by our revolution', Jefferson told President George Washington, a view that many Americans initially shared. The infighting and factionalism that soon enveloped French politics clouded the comparison between the two revolutions, however. When Jefferson returned to the United States in the fall of 1789 to become secretary of state, he found himself at Washington's cabinet table arguing about France with Alexander Hamilton and the new vice president, John Adams, who quickly soured on the excesses of the Revolution and recommended that the United States align itself with its old enemy, Britain. Then, following the execution of the French king in 1793, Britain and its allies went to war with the upstart French republic. Across the next two decades, Britain and France would wage an epic and devastating conflict that upended Europe and brought violence (and opportunity) to the imperial spaces of the rest of the world. Under George Washington's direction, the United States had declared itself a neutral power. But for those twenty years, both Britain and France tried to draw American ships and officials into their conflict, even as the Founders divided among themselves over which European power posed the greater threat to the future of the United States.[8]

Another American booster of the French Revolution, Thomas Paine, eventually conceded its flaws. 'The principles of it were good, they were copied from America, and the men who conducted it were honest,' he wrote in 1802. 'But the fury of faction soon extinguished the one, and sent the other to the scaffold.' For true believers like Jefferson and Paine, the collapse of the French Revolution and the rise of Napoleon Bonaparte offered a painful rebuke to the hope that Europe might emulate American republicanism. Ironically, though, it was the perpetual warfare unleashed by the French Revolution that created the breathing room for the United States to stabilize itself both commercially and territorially. European wheat production was badly affected by the fighting, and American merchants and ship owners gleefully discovered a vibrant market for their goods. While Britain and France threw ships and men into interminable conflict, American captains and crews could fetch and deliver goods on behalf of belligerent nations—an enterprise known as the carrying trade. European war actually benefited the United States, provided that Britain and France were willing to respect American neutrality.[9]

Here the French Revolution's chaotic aftermath collided with an older set of American grievances about British power. The European war forced Britain to expand the Royal Navy, and the search for sailors to crew these ships led British officials back to their oldest recruiting tactic. Impressment had been an indispensable strategy for staffing British ships since the seventeenth century, and before 1776 American sailors—subjects of the king, after all—were fair game. Victory in the Revolutionary War should have given American sailors immunity from British impressment. But the practice continued through the 1780s and intensified in the 1790s as Britain ramped up its war with France. American leaders looked on helplessly as thousands of sailors were seized. It was, as one US official complained to the British, 'utterly incompatible' with the glorious principles of 1776. Impressment would become one of the primary causes of the War of 1812, and sailors who had fallen into the Royal Navy would comprise a fifth of the American population at Dartmoor.[10]

From Britain's perspective, impressment was an unfortunate but necessary mechanism for defending the nation's interests. Wars happened abruptly and required an instant surge of sailors. Although there were incentives to join the Royal Navy—the food was better than in the merchant marine, and the Navy paid both 'prize money' (a share in the sale of captured vessels) and pensions—sailors in His Majesty's Service were very likely to experience the horrors of naval warfare. Then there were the restrictions on shore leave. Captains who had struggled to fill their ranks were not enthused by the prospect of sailors melting away at every port, and so a sailor in the Royal Navy might travel the world but rarely leave his ship. Although it's hard to fix a precise number, historians estimate that, despite the privations, more than half of the men on British warships in the late eighteenth and early nineteenth centuries had volunteered to serve. This still left the Royal Navy to recruit more than fifty thousand sailors through compulsion rather than persuasion.[11]

The image of the press gang in popular culture is indelible: a group of toughs lies in wait for men to drink themselves to a stupor, then carries them to a naval vessel ready to cast off at first light. In reality, the club-in-the-pub approach was rare. Most impressment took place at sea, where a Royal Navy ship would descend on a commercial vessel and take the crew it needed. When captains recruited on land, they sent sharp-eyed scouts to find men with a very particular set of skills. Individual officers could be creative in their recruitment practices. One captain who made use of impressment would pay sailors' wages in advance and give them immediate shore leave. 'They go on shore and tell the rest that the captain is a bloody good fellow,' recalled the commander in question, who would then receive droves of new volunteers 'out of which I pick the best'. While this was an unusually entrepreneurial approach, there was a widespread recognition among Navy captains that coercion was only part of their repertoire for recruiting and retaining men.[12]

Even within Britain impressment was controversial. To fight a war for liberty against France while suppressing the liberties of tens of thousands of sailors was a contradiction that couldn't easily be squared. In 1805, the First Lord of the Admiralty floated the idea of establishing a gigantic national register of sailors from which the Royal Navy would draw recruits via a draft. (France and Spain had developed a similar system, though with mixed success.) Even a nation as bureaucratically excitable as Britain couldn't handle the logistics of the scheme, but the proposal helps us to see what impressment really was: a crude form of conscription. Built into its model was the idea that men would desert the service, perhaps at a high rate. Despite the harsh punishments for doing so—death, in theory—and the loss of pension rights and prize money for those who disappeared, as many as 10 percent of ordinary seamen went

AWOL each year. This required still more impressment, and the cycle continued. Even a sailor who had fled from the Royal Navy might easily fall back into its clutches before long.[13]

To British officials, American protests about impressment were shrill and solipsistic. Britons insisted that they were the last defenders of liberty on the European continent, especially after Napoleon Bonaparte's rise to power and his repeated threats to cross the English Channel. Then there was the fact that the Royal Navy tried to impress everyone. British law allowed navy captains to stop vessels from any nation and search them for British subjects. International law, which was still in its infancy, gave no sanction to Britain's actions. And yet an American commercial captain could hardly invoke the authority of Grotius, Vattel, and other legal theorists while being boarded by a British warship. Besides, British captains knew that there were plenty of 'their' sailors on American vessels. American shipping boomed in the 1790s and the first years of the 1800s, and seamen in the US merchant marine could earn double the wages they might receive on a British warship. Sailors from Britain and Ireland were especially taken with this bargain: many thousands dodged the Royal Navy's entreaties and instead served on American ships. This, in turn, provided British politicians and military officials with a justification for searching those ships and impressing their crews.[14]

After the British resumption of war with France in 1804, when manpower shortages in the Royal Navy were especially acute, Britain even began posting warships just off the American coast, blockading harbours and searching countless American ships on their way into the Atlantic. While these operations returned some British subjects to His Majesty's Service, they also caught up thousands of sailors who had been born in North America or who had become naturalized as US citizens. The international and mobile nature of the maritime workforce was mostly a huge advantage to the captains and owners who drove American commerce, but impressment revealed a fundamental weakness of the system: if there was enough doubt over who counted as an American, it would be hard to stop Britain from impressing virtually anyone.[15]

AMERICAN OFFICIALS REGISTERED THEIR OUTRAGE THROUGH DIPlomatic channels and looked for ways to counter the argument that US ships were swarming with British sailors. Before long, they crafted the first mechanism for authenticating citizenship in American history. The Impressed Seamen Act of 1796 allowed sailors to apply to the customs collector at any major port for a Seamen's Protection Certificate (SPC). This would describe a sailor's appearance and confirm him to be 'a citizen of the United States of America'. It was neither mandatory nor comprehensive: sailors would opt in by bringing to the Custom House proof of their citizenship (a birth certificate or sworn affidavit) along with twenty-five cents. On reviewing the documents, the collector would record the sailor's name in a book and issue a signed certificate that the sailor could carry and produce when needed—say, when a Royal Navy officer boarded that sailor's vessel in search of new recruits. The decentralized nature of the bureaucracy worked to the advantage of Black sailors in particular. Although most white Americans in the early republic would have dismissed the proposition that free Black people were citizens, the collectors in America's major ports issued SPCs to Black and white sailors alike. In the State Department archive, where many of these certificates ended up, you can find numerous descriptions of African Americans—'five feet four inches, complexion hair and eyes black, being a black man, born in New London'—alongside the uncomplicated determination that, of course, they were American citizens. For any historian familiar with the struggles for Black citizenship before the American Civil War, this paperwork seems luminously simple.[16]

Congress also compelled American captains to make a full report of any seamen who had been impressed by the British during their voyage and, from 1803, to supply customs collectors with 'a list containing the names, places of birth and residence, and a description

Seamen's Protection Certificate for Thomas Wilson
National Archives, Washington, DC

of the persons who compose his ship's company'. But even as they experimented with schemes for identifying and cataloguing sailors, federal officials became exasperated by the limits of their gaze. In 1803, James Madison (then serving as Jefferson's secretary of state) complained to customs collectors that they had described the physical appearance of sailors in such a 'loose and imperfect way' that SPCs 'admit of an easy transfer to others, not entitled to protection as citizens'. Madison also grumbled that captains were failing to report crew members who'd been snatched by Britain. Captured sailors and their families were flooding the State Department with pleas for help in impressment cases; the official mechanism for keeping track of impressed men had so many holes that ordinary people were trying to plug the gaps.[17]

Implicit in Madison's correspondence was a realisation that impressment could only be curbed with a watertight system of identification and authentication, and yet the technology and resources required to maintain one proved beyond the capacity of even the most determined bureaucrats. In July 1804, Madison had the 'disagreeable necessity' of having to write to the British requesting the return of nine US citizens who had been impressed on vessels just off the East Coast. The British official replied that the matter had been carefully reviewed: the nine men had been confirmed by the Royal Navy as subjects of the king, and he would 'not trouble' Madison with copies of the paperwork. With no national registry of citizenship beyond the patchy SPC system, even Madison knew that the authentication of nationality was an art rather than a science.[18]

One drastic solution would have been for the federal government simply to ban foreign sailors from American ships. In 1805, Madison mooted this possibility to James Monroe, US minister to Britain, who was about to begin a new round of talks in London over neutrality and impressment. But restrictions of this sort raised practical and moral questions. Thomas Jefferson and his followers had long argued that the United States had a responsibility to offer refuge to the peoples of Europe. Although his Federalist opponents were sceptical of this, Jefferson's Democratic-Republican Party championed 'elective citizenship'—the right of downtrodden Europeans to choose the United States and to naturalize as American citizens. When applied to the maritime sphere, this romantic view of America's purpose and power was probably misplaced: a sailor's working life meant that national affinities could ebb and flow. But the notion of the merchant marine as an open border for aspiring immigrants flattered the Jeffersonians' vision of American liberty.[19]

Beyond these bureaucratic and diplomatic solutions was a doughty confidence that Europe could ultimately be coerced into respecting American independence. Jacob Crowninshield, a prominent merchant in Salem, Massachusetts, told Jefferson in December 1803 that Britain was trying to 'engross the commerce of the whole world, & to bear down the free trade of all other nations'.

The solution was to 'withhold supplies' from Europe and to allow the suspension of American goods and ships to bring Britain and France to their senses. Securing US neutrality through a trade embargo may have seemed far-fetched, but American shipping faced a series of new humiliations during Jefferson's second term in the White House. In 1807, hoping to deter US captains from breaking the Royal Navy's blockade of French ports, British officials ordered all American ships visiting Europe to stop in Britain or to risk capture. Napoleon responded by demanding that American vessels visit France, on pain of the same penalty. In the face of these cascading outrages, and with Jefferson's encouragement, Congress voted by a large majority in December 1807 to approve a sweeping embargo that would prohibit American ships from visiting *any* foreign ports. Against the warnings of his cabinet, Jefferson confidently signed the embargo into law. Then he waited for the powers of Europe to come back to the negotiating table with a renewed respect for American independence.[20]

This was not a happy experience for American sailors, or for President Jefferson. Some captains had the foresight to hasten their departure from the United States, hoping to reach the open ocean on a voyage long enough to ride out the embargo. (This explains why the green hand George Little found the *Dromo* eager to depart Boston in the early days of December 1807, and why the ship's captain refused to put into any ports until he reached the foot of South America.) But virtually all of the hundreds of thousands of Americans who earned their living at sea or in the nation's ports found themselves laid up by the stark new restrictions. Their frustrations were increased by the unfortunate coincidence of the revolutions in Spanish America. For the first time in centuries, independent governments from Mexico to Chile were casting off Spain's commercial monopoly. With American vessels trapped in their home ports, British ships had this lucrative trade to themselves. By the spring of 1808, Jefferson was receiving angry letters from the entire length of the Eastern Seaboard. Fuelled by pride and a sense that there were no better options, Jefferson maintained the policy in the absence of evidence that it was actually working.[21]

Only in March 1809, a few days before he left the White House, could the president admit defeat. The noble goal of the embargo had been undone by 'evasions' (smuggling) and 'domestic opposition to it', Jefferson maintained. Lurking behind this opposition was an uncomfortable truth: 'Losing $50 million of exports annually by it, [the embargo] costs more than war, which might be carried on for a third of that.' Congress passed a more targeted version of the embargo, but this proved unenforceable. As James Madison assumed the presidency in the spring of 1809, the only remaining possibility for bringing Britain (and/or France) to heel would be a declaration of war. But there was no guarantee that this bleak option would prove any more successful than the embargo.[22]

'DEAR FATHER AND MOTHER, BROTHER AND SISTERS,' WROTE DANiel Baker in June 1812. 'I am now held on board HMS Union, of ninety-eight guns, lying at Lisbon, and expecting to set sail soon for the Mediterranean, and no hope of getting clear.' Baker was from Cape Cod and dearly wanted to 'get clear' of the Royal Navy into which he'd been impressed. He would soon get his wish, through a transfer to Dartmoor prison. For most American sailors, the experience of being forced to fight for Britain was a terrible affront to their liberty. White sailors confidently declared it worse than slavery, though the Black sailors impressed alongside them did not reach for that analogy. Getting clear proved formidably difficult. Some sailors expressed an easy confidence that, when their plight was known to their government, release would speedily follow. Others were more sanguine about their fate. 'I thought last fall that my luck had turned,' Baker told his family, 'but now my hopes are gone.'[23]

A Seamen's Protection Certificate was a flimsy defence against impressment: the British might question its authenticity and even tear it up in front of the stunned sailor. Those without a certificate could do even less to avert their fate, though the State Department's impressment files demonstrate that families and friends could ret-rospectively present documentation to help men in this dilemma. Sometimes impressment was a consequence not of British villainy but of arguments between Americans. In 1809, a sailor named John Williamson wrote to the customs collector in his home port of New York to explain how he came to be impressed in Tenerife. While serving on an American ship, Williamson had consumed 'rather too much liquor which made me and the mate quarrel'. His Virginian captain took the mate's side and, 'being acquainted with the master of [HMS] *Leviathan*', told the British commander that 'I was no American' despite Williamson's brandishing of his SPC.[24]

It was possible to get clear of a British warship, though not quickly or easily. You might choose to stay put and hope for a speedy end to the wars in Europe. You could become a deserter, sneaking away when your vessel was in port. You could bribe your way out; at least some sailors thought this might work, though the impressment files are silent on whether they succeeded. You could contact the American consul at a foreign port if you found a way to draw his attention. Or you could ask your family and friends in the United States to intervene directly with the State Department. From the hundreds of impressment files preserved in the US National Ar-chives, it's striking to see how much of this lobbying fell to women. Sailors enlisted mothers, sisters, and wives to gather identifying information and forward it to the federal government. Women across the seaboard took themselves and their relatives to notaries public, justices of the peace, and customs collectors to swear affida-vits in support of their loved ones' Americanness. The family of one Pennsylvanian sailor even recruited the midwife who had delivered him to swear an oath to his American nativity.[25]

Mothers are especially visible in the archive, not only in their ap-peals to Washington officials but also in the letters they wrote to their sons. Many had heard nothing of their children for years; when they finally received a brief note and a return address, they poured excite-ment and anxiety into their replies. 'My dear child write to me every post you go to and I will send it a thousand if it is possible,' wrote Jane Burk to her son in 1812. Sarah Siters of Philadelphia reassured her son John that she had obtained the paperwork he'd requested, but berated him for leaving his 'disconsolate wife' who 'has little satisfaction in the world in her present situation.' On his expected release, Sarah wrote, John should remember 'that I have done everything that was in my power to free you from your slavery' and that he should 'return to me which will compensate fully for all that I have done for you'. In a separate letter, John's cousin reminded him that 'there is no press gangs agoing here but everything that has a tendency to liberty.' If John was tempted to go to sea again after his release, he should 'remember the pains of trouble that your mother has gone to' and 'set down and spend your days near her.'[26]

Not all sailors needed reminding that their absence hurt family members. Thomas Tebbs, who was forced into the Royal Navy from 1806 to 1809, wrote to the State Department after his release to demand compensation from Britain. 'I will leave it to your imagination to describe the distresses of a wife and infants . . . who have been deprived of a father and husband on whose earnings rested their only dependence or subsistence.' Some sailors sheepishly apologised for being away for so long, especially those who had been poor correspondents even before they were captured by the British. Others resolved to turn over a new leaf if they ever made it back to the United States. Writing in 1808, William Blake of Portland begged his family to get him clear of a British warship; his brother Nathaniel informed him that his mother had died since his last letter and that his father was now infirm. Of course Nathaniel would obtain the paperwork William had requested, but he made no effort to conceal his disappointment with his brother's unreliable character: 'I hope it is God's will you may be liberated and return to your own country a much reformed and better man than you was when you left home,' he wrote. 'From your loving brother.'[27]

For sailors who had lost touch with their families altogether, or whose parents and siblings had died, the appeals bureaucracy was especially daunting. In 1813, an impressed sailor named George Barrett asked his former boss Elisha Gordon to write to the State Department and secure his release. To jog Gordon's memory, Barrett mentioned that they'd both been members of the same Democratic-Republican Society in Lancaster, Pennsylvania, back in the day. 'I fear I cannot afford any useful information,' Gordon dutifully reported to Secretary of State James Monroe. He had only a dim recollection of Barrett as an employee, and in the records of the Lancaster Society he could find no traces of the forlorn sailor. 'Where he was born or raised I know nothing,' he concluded. The State Department did its own review of these appeals, deciding whether the paperwork looked strong enough to bring a case to the attention of the British. In this case, the clerk's verdict was straightforward: INSUFFICIENT is written across the top of the documents. George Barrett would be staying in the Royal Navy indefinitely.[28]

FOR BLACK SAILORS, IMPRESSMENT CARRIED ADDITIONAL DANgers. Even African Americans who were born free might struggle to mobilize the same lobbying networks that white sailors used to petition the State Department. Those born into slavery, including men who had taken to the sea to escape from their enslavers, found it hard to locate someone who could vouch for their origins. For Black sailors born outside the United States, including those who had lived in American towns or worked on American ships for years, the challenge of securing recognition from the US government was even greater. The first US naturalization law, passed by Congress in 1790, specified that only white immigrants could become citizens of the United States. If a Black sailor could obtain a Seamen's Protection Certificate he might circumvent these problems, though the tendency of the Royal Navy to disregard SPCs meant that a direct appeal to the State Department was very often a sailor's best chance of release.[29]

These complicated dynamics can be captured in a single moment: the crisis after the British warship HMS *Leopard* attacked the USS

Chesapeake in June 1807. The *Leopard* was lurking in Chesapeake Bay doing what the Royal Navy usually did: searching for 'deserters' aboard American ships. Four sailors had recently deserted from another British vessel, HMS *Melampus*, and the *Leopard* was determined to retrieve them. The British captain ordered the *Chesapeake* to allow a boarding; when the American captain refused, the *Leopard* opened fire. Three Americans were killed, and the *Chesapeake* was too badly damaged to put up a fight. The British found three of the four men they were looking for and left the American vessel to limp back to port.[30]

This attack by a foreign power on an American warship in US waters astonished the American public and tipped Jefferson towards his high-stakes gamble on a complete shipping embargo. The incident also revealed some of the racial complexities of impressment. One of the four sailors who had deserted from HMS *Melampus* was William Ware, 'a remarkably bright mulatto boy' (according to documents in the impressment files) who 'might pass for a very dark swarthy white man'. Ware had been born in Maryland, the son of a Black mother and a local white man. Although Ware had indeed fled from HMS *Melampus* and joined the crew of the *Chesapeake*, nearly a dozen Marylanders now swore affidavits confirming that he was American by birth. There is very little in the impressment files about his fellow deserter Daniel Martin, who was (according to the testimony of a Massachusetts merchant) a 'coloured boy' from 'some Spanish settlement in America'. Was this enough to confirm to the British that Martin was an American? Did Martin himself see the United States as his homeland? We know he spent a portion of his childhood apprenticed to a businessman named William Howland and that he had begun to sail on vessels bound for China by 1802. Beyond this, Martin's affinities and horizons are unknown.[31]

For the Massachusetts lawyer John Lowell, a fierce opponent of Thomas Jefferson, the racial identity of the *Melampus* deserters changed everything. In a pamphlet arguing for conciliation with

Britain, published while the controversy over the *Chesapeake* was still raging, Lowell insisted that three of the four deserters were not really Americans. 'One of them was born at Bonaire [Buenos Aires],' he wrote. 'Two [of] the others were black men, born slaves in Maryland, and strictly therefore not native *citizens*, though *natives*.' Lowell berated Jefferson for claiming that 'the seamen had been previously ascertained to be *native citizens* of the United States.' In fact, because of their race, 'the case of these men forms no part of the real question.' The State Department took a different view, especially in its vigorous attempt to repatriate William Ware. But Lowell's crude polemic highlighted the particular problems facing Black sailors in claiming their rights.[32]

The *Chesapeake* affair offered one further reminder that race and nationality could easily slip their moorings. In response to the attack on the American vessel, local merchants announced that they would no longer sell supplies to visiting Royal Navy vessels. The British were forced to launch landing parties to secure water and food, and before long five British sailors were captured by a local militia. Around the same time, five enslaved runaways made it to the Atlantic coast, seized a rowing boat, and sought refuge with one of the British vessels moored just off the Virginia coast. The British harboured the runaways and upped the ante. The squadron commander sent word to American officials on shore that unless local merchants agreed to resume supplying Royal Navy ships, Britain would encourage a general uprising of enslaved people on the Virginia coast. The commander's local (Black) informants had assured him that 'more than two thousands of the people of Colour would join if I would only land the soldiers.' This astonishing threat focused American minds: the Black runaways and the British sailors were quickly exchanged, and the merchants agreed to trade with the Royal Navy again. While the deal had averted a war and a slave uprising, it had also reminded Black and white Virginians that slavery and emancipation could easily scramble national affinities and belonging.[33]

Conversely, the State Department's files offer examples of impressed Black sailors who secured glowing testimonies from employers and friends at home. Shepard Bourn, a Black sailor from Massachusetts, begged his mother to write to the federal government on his behalf. Soon James Monroe (now returned from London to serve as Madison's secretary of state) was reading of her 'deep sighs, her tears, [and] her despair' for her stricken son. Rebecca Cuffe, whose son Silas had been seized by Britain, enlisted the collector at Sag Harbor on Long Island to write to the State Department on her behalf. He reported that Rebecca and her husband 'though persons of colour are respectable, and have all the feelings of affection for their son as people whose skins are of a lighter shade'. Jacob Israel Potter, another Black sailor, had been impressed in London in 1804. Writing to James Monroe in 1811, Potter reported that his British commanders had wondered why, after so many years away, he retained any interest in the United States. 'The reason,' Potter told the captain, 'was because I was an American and likewise I was a citizen and had a wife and family.' Potter was particularly keen for Monroe to know that 'I have not entered nor taken any bounty'—the payment made to Royal Navy sailors on 'agreeing' to serve His Majesty. Despite Potter's loyalty, the State Department did not secure his release. He, too, would end up in Dartmoor.[34]

DID ANY AMERICAN SAILORS, BLACK OR WHITE, RESIGN THEMselves to British service? Did anyone switch sides? The obvious answer is—of course they did. But the archive works hard to deny this conclusion. Sailors who wrote up their adventures for publication were unlikely to confess that they had accepted the fact of their impressment or (even worse) that they had consented to join the Royal Navy. The impressment files of the State Department comprise correspondence from sailors (or their families) who were seeking repatriation to the United States. The vast majority of impressed sailors do not appear in these files. Many may have wanted Washington's help but lacked the contacts or good fortune to spirit a letter from their British warship to an American relative or friend. Others accepted their fate with resignation or looked for opportunity and advantage even within the confines of the Royal Navy. Those men left traces elsewhere—in the muster books of Royal Navy warships or in the thick registers that tallied a sailor's prize money and pension entitlements. Every archive contains and denies possibilities. Some of the men who ended up at Dartmoor narrated their own stories; most of them are elusive.[35]

But we have many glimpses into a world of uncertain loyalties, especially for sailors who had spent years on British ships. As the historian Sara Caputo has shown, the Royal Navy was careful to offer foreign sailors pathways to British belonging. Navy captains gladly welcomed Swedes, Danes, Spaniards, Dutchmen, and Americans into their ranks even when the countries of their birth were at war with Britain. All sailors who had served two years on a Royal Navy ship became British subjects, providing they swore an oath to the king. It's unlikely that any foreign sailor woke up on the 730th day of his service with an excited determination to claim his new privileges: lower customs duties, the right to buy land in Britain or to own a British ship, and so on. But when set alongside the benefits of prize money and a naval pension—both of which would be lost if a foreign sailor moved away from Britain when he left the Royal Navy—these inducements could complicate an American's determination to get clear.[36]

American sailors were already used to serving in the merchant marine of other nations. From there, the distance to Royal Navy service may not have been great. The State Department files tell many stories of American sailors juggling national affinities. James Brown had been in the West Indies in 1807 but then headed to Europe rather than the United States, perhaps recognizing that work in American ports would be hard to come by after passage of the Embargo Act. He was captured by the British and taken to Portsmouth in England, somehow escaped to Lisbon (he was blurry on the details), and then was impressed again. Enoch Chapman of New Hampshire was captured by the French in 1809, talked himself out of prison after just a few days, then spent seven months touring the country before shipping out on a French merchant vessel bound for the island of Réunion in the Indian Ocean. To his horror, the British seized the island two days after his arrival and impressed him into the Royal Navy. Another American sailor, William Worthington of Baltimore, went to sea in 1805 and learned his trade sailing between the American mainland, the Caribbean, and Europe. He soon became captain of his vessel and kept his post even after the ship was reflagged in 1808—presumably because of the US embargo—at the Swedish island of St Barts. He remained in charge when the ship subsequently flew the French flag for a while, sailing out of Martinique. When Worthington was finally seized by the British off the French coast, he was taken to a prison in Plymouth rather than impressed into the Royal Navy. From there, he begged his family to explain his complicated loyalties to the US government. The Baltimore collector of customs reported to the State Department the visit he had received from Worthington's desperate sibling: 'Deponent believes his said brother was led into the situation by reason of his Youth and Inexperience.'[37]

Occasionally, a request to repatriate an American sailor was met with a British response that the sailor in question had signed up voluntarily. These claims were impossible to verify and, in any case, *voluntary* is a complicated word. Sailors made choices in dangerous and fast-moving environments. This could leave them with some explaining to do. 'How to begin?' wrote Peyton Page to his brother in 1812. Page had been in England in 1808, looking for work as the embargo locked down American shipping. When the press gang came for him, he produced his protection certificate but was seized regardless. Page demanded to see the US consul who—'behold, the rascal!'—refused to believe he was American. Soon he was aboard HMS *Warspite*, cruising off the French coast in Britain's war with Napoleon.[38]

Some of the claims in Page's letter to his brother seem very fishy. The muster books from the *Warspite*, which are still in the UK National Archives, confirm that Page was aboard. But was it really true that the *Warspite*'s captain thought Page a lovable rogue and quickly promoted him through the ranks? 'I was only one week on the forecastle before I was voted quartermaster, then the Captain Coxswain, then a mid[shipman],' Page boasted. 'And so now I am Second Master of a seventy-four gun ship.' Page insisted that his time with the British hadn't dented his loyalties: 'I do not think so much of them as to make me forget that I am an American.' But his seniority had made it hard for him to desert. And then there was the cash: 'Having made between three and four thousand dollars prize money, I thought that too much money to throw away, so I will try and weather this out.'[39]

Page's extraordinary letter was not a cry for help. He was writing to catch up, not to secure his release, but his family forwarded Page's letter to the State Department anyway. This story is an outlier in the impressment files, which are mostly populated by sailors who hadn't become second mate on a British warship and accumulated thousands of dollars in prize money. And yet Peyton Page reminds us that loyalty and opportunity could easily drift apart in this turbulent political moment. On the face of it, the thirteen hundred or so impressed US sailors who ended up in Dartmoor prison had a greater call than anyone on the sympathies of their government. Some had been in the Royal Navy for more than a decade before 1812, when the outbreak of war compelled most (but not all) to beg for a transfer into the British prison system. The impressment files are filled with stories of men who wanted only to go home. But the taint of serving the British and the possibility that their loyalties might have shifted would follow them to Dartmoor, a place where affinity and nationality were never as simple as they seemed.

3.

SPARE THE VANQUISHED

A T SOME POINT IN THE SPRING OF 1805, THOMAS TYRWHITT decided to build the world's biggest prison in the middle of nowhere. Tyrwhitt's father was a clergyman, though a very rich one: Thomas was sent to Eton and then to Oxford. He struggled at school, where the other boys called him 'Clod Tyrwhitt', and wasn't much happier at Oxford. His diminutive stature and romantic disappointments produced another cruel nickname—'the Squab Cupid'—to accompany his modest degree. But at Christ Church, the largest of the Oxford colleges, Tyrwhitt made a connection that would change his life. The dean of the college introduced him to George Augustus Frederick, Prince of Wales, an almost exact contemporary. The two became friends, and Tyrwhitt was soon working for the future George IV. In 1795, he was appointed the prince's private secretary, and for most of the next two decades he filled a variety of roles while the prince waited (and waited) to be king. He also helped George to administer one of his many distractions, the Duchy of Cornwall. A vast tract of land and property concentrated in Devon and Cornwall, the duchy was first given to the Prince of Wales in the fourteenth century and even today brings the heir to the throne an income of more than £20 million every year. George gifted Tyrwhitt two and a half thousand acres on Dartmoor, within the largest tract of duchy land, and encouraged him to think big. Surely, the barren region could be recovered for civilization and industry if only a visionary would champion its cause? Tyrwhitt gratefully built a house, Tor Royal, in the splendid isolation of the moor. If everything went to plan, he would soon have plenty of company.[1]

Working for the Prince of Wales was a challenging job. Great wealth and power—or, at least, the expectation of power—did not instil great responsibility. George's drinking and affairs alienated him from his father, and the king's frustrating longevity alienated him from his son. George III's apparent madness was first diagnosed in 1788, but it would be more than two decades before his son assumed the title and authority of Prince Regent. For much of the intervening time, the younger George drowned his disappointments in alcohol. (He drank so much on his wedding night in 1795 that he fell into a fireplace, to the relief of his already long-suffering wife.) Thomas Tyrwhitt was an unusually loyal servant during those years, perhaps because his upbringing had inured him to abuse. When George and other members of the royal family mocked him for his height—they called him 'the twenty-third of June', the shortest night of the year—he smiled and carried on. In turn, George was happy to support and even indulge Tyrwhitt in their pet project: the transformation of Dartmoor's lifeless expanse into a thriving region of farmers, labourers, and artisans.[2]

George even made Tyrwhitt a member of Parliament, shuffling him through a number of 'rotten boroughs' (where the powerful could win election without opponents or voters) until Tyrwhitt became MP for Plymouth, the Royal Navy's centre of operations on Britain's south coast. Dividing his time between Dartmoor and London, Tyrwhitt built a pub and a mill near his new house, along with a road to bring visitors from beyond the moor. He carefully laid out crops in his grounds, hoping to prove that flax and wheat could thrive on Dartmoor despite the fog and solitude. Then, in 1805, he learned that the government wanted to build a new facility

Thomas Tyrwhitt (1762–1833), by Friedrich Muller
By permission of the Governing Body of Christ Church, Oxford

for the vast number of French prisoners piling up in hulks at Plymouth and at Chatham near London. Tyrwhitt talked to his friends in the Admiralty, and almost certainly to his boss, who had visited him at Tor Royal on a number of occasions (so often, in fact, that the locals insisted that George had taken a mistress there). By the summer of 1805, an architect had been agreed and Tyrwhitt was elated. What better way to advance his dream for Dartmoor than to put a gigantic prison at its centre?[3]

Tyrwhitt's outlandish proposal was rooted in two developments: the codification of the laws of war, and the rise of the modern prison. In the final months of the American Revolution, Benjamin Franklin reminded a British friend that it had been standard practice just a few centuries earlier for states to execute prisoners of war. Victorious armies had later progressed to enslaving rather than murdering their captives. Now, in the enlightened eighteenth century, a new body of international law mandated that prisoners be treated humanely and exchanged as quickly as possible. Franklin's pride in this process of 'humanizing by degrees' was not entirely justified: POWs in the second half of the eighteenth century could still meet with medieval treatment, though in theory warring powers had three attractive options for disposing of prisoners. They could exchange them like-for-like, a system which relied on each side taking an equal number of prisoners. They could ransom them, agreeing on a fee to secure the return of a given number of prisoners. Or they could parole them, a system usually applied to civilians and to officers. Parole originally meant that a prisoner would be freed and sent home after swearing an oath not to take up arms again in the conflict; by the end of the eighteenth century, it meant instead that a prisoner would be placed in private accommodation in a town or village under the equivalent of house arrest rather than in the grim confines of a war prison.[4]

If these systems worked properly, every captive would be speedily released. But during Britain's endless battles with France (and the Revolutionary War with the United States), a number of problems became apparent. Thanks to its naval superiority, Britain quickly amassed a huge surplus of prisoners. Exchanges broke down and, with wars dragging on for years, British officials scrambled to repurpose buildings to accommodate a large and embarrassingly permanent POW population. The perpetual fallback option was to hold prisoners in ships—originally working vessels, though eventually retired 'hulks'—which was both expensive and harmful to the well-being of prisoners. During the American Revolution, British prison ships in New York served as perfect incubators for smallpox: their mortality rate of over 40 percent was roughly ten times that of land-based prisons. The same grim ratio applied to the hulks that dotted the British coastline during the Revolutionary and Napoleonic Wars. With Britain styling itself as enlightened and benevolent in its conduct of war, keeping prisoners out of the hulks became an urgent necessity.[5]

The other development that shaped Tyrwhitt's thinking about Dartmoor was the rise of the modern prison. Given how indelible they seem in our own era, it's surprising to learn that prisons are a relatively recent invention. Before the American Revolution, most convicted criminals in Britain were banished to the North American colonies. Although debtors could be imprisoned indefinitely, criminals were subject to execution, transportation, or some form of public humiliation. The Declaration of Independence cut off the flow of felons to North America, creating a backlog of prisoners in the British justice system. Australia would later provide a new outlet for criminals, but British reformers used the disruptions of the Revolutionary War to advance a radical new idea: instead of simply holding prisoners before their trials, prisons might themselves serve both to punish and rehabilitate wrongdoers.[6]

The greatest prison theorist of the eighteenth century was John Howard, a British reformer who spent the 1770s and 1780s on an endless tour of jails in Britain and overseas. Howard was mostly appalled by what he found: crumbling and unsanitary facilities, hollow-eyed prisoners, avaricious jailers who supplemented their income by allowing taprooms, billiard tables, gambling, and sex work in their jails. 'A prison mends no morals,' Howard sadly observed at the end of his tour. But it didn't have to be this way. With the proper resources and thinking, prisons might turn back the tide of criminality and redeem society as surely as individuals. Howard led a public crusade that insisted on custodial sentences for all but the most terrible crimes, to be served in purpose-built prisons. His vision inspired architects, politicians, philanthropists, urban planners, and a host of others in late-eighteenth-century Britain, and animated a parallel prison reform movement in the new United States.[7]

At first glance Howard's crusade had little to do with Dartmoor. A war prison, after all, was intended to secure combatants rather than rehabilitate criminals. But Thomas Tyrwhitt knew that eventually Britain and France would stop fighting, and that Dartmoor would need an engine of development when peace broke out. Given the sunny thinking of reformers about the societal benefits of a modern prison, he assumed that Dartmoor would welcome criminals in place of sailors at the war's end. The slippage between a war prison and a criminal facility brought dangers as well as opportunities, however. John Howard had originally become interested in prison reform after being captured by the French on a visit to Portugal during the Seven Years' War. 'What I suffered on this occasion,' he wrote in his most famous tract, 'increased my sympathy with the unhappy people whose case is the subject of this book.' Howard's acknowledgement that 'a prison mends no morals' spurred his attempts to create new and more humane forms of incarceration, but it also offered a warning to Thomas Tyrwhitt and the British officials who approved his plans in 1805. If Dartmoor wasn't designed and operated as a modern prison, with humanity and dignity at its core, it might easily turn captives into criminals.[8]

WILLIAM PITT THE YOUNGER BECAME PRIME MINISTER IN THE dark days of December 1783, as Britain was struggling to process its defeat in the Revolutionary War. Pitt spent the next decade rebuilding Britain's economy, armed forces, and mechanisms of government. Instead of waiting for another war to break out, he addressed the mistakes that had hampered the British response to the American Revolution. He insisted on clearer coordination between the different arms of government responsible for feeding soldiers and sailors, transporting materiel to far-flung theatres, manufacturing weapons, and taking care of sick and wounded servicemen. These changes extended to virtually every aspect of Britain's war machine—including arrangements for processing and detaining prisoners of war.[9]

For much of the eighteenth century, enemy POWs had been overseen by the Sick and Hurt Board, a body within the Admiralty headed by six senior officials, including a representative from the navy and several doctors. In 1794, the Pitt administration revived an office that had lain dormant for much of the century: the

Transport Board, an arm of government that would take primary responsibility for wartime logistics. Pitt hoped the Transport Board would resolve squabbles between rival wings of the British military over the procurement of ships to move food, people, and guns around the world. When the board proved successful at this, it was given the additional responsibility of managing prisoners of war.[10]

Even in a government renowned for its efficiency, the Transport Board gained a reputation for bureaucratic ruthlessness. It was headed by an admiral but located away from the main Royal Navy buildings by the Thames, in hard-to-find offices near Downing Street. At the end of the eighteenth century, Britain was a leading example of what historians have termed the 'contractor state'. Although wartime spending was enormous and the machinery of government vast and intricate, the private sector was fundamental to the fight against France (and later the United States). Private contractors built most of Britain's warships, competed with each other to supply food and water to British servicemen, and submitted tenders to construct new dockyards, storehouses, and other facilities. The Transport Board's principal task was to negotiate with private shipowners to bring sections of the British merchant marine into the war effort, carrying guns, soldiers, food and water, and even prisoners across Europe and around the world. By 1815, the board had secured more than twenty thousand vessels—around 10 percent of the entire British merchant fleet. Still more impressively, it had done so while establishing a reputation for thrift and probity.[11]

When the Transport Board assumed responsibility for prisoners of war in 1796, there were more than eleven thousand foreign prisoners in Britain. This number rose beyond thirty thousand by 1801, though the board was able to arrange regular exchanges and ensure that most prisoners were quickly released. Then, in March 1802, Britain and France reached a fragile peace, and the board emptied its prisons and hulks completely. Barely a year later, unnerved by Napoleon's creeping influence over continental Europe, the British government declared war once again. Eleven years of continuous fighting followed the resumption of hostilities in May 1803, and more than a hundred thousand prisoners were captured. British and French representatives met sporadically to discuss a general exchange, but the two sides rarely reached agreement. Commanders and some high-ranking officers were occasionally freed, but for the vast majority of French and British servicemen, capture meant indefinite captivity.[12]

As in previous conflicts, the failure of Britain and France to reach agreement on exchanges was rooted in political calculation. Although the ratio of French to British prisoners varied from year to year, on average there were around four times as many French captives in British hands as vice versa. From Napoleon's perspective, French prisoners were a clear and obvious drain on his enemy's resources: Britain would spend millions of pounds every year clothing, feeding, and housing the prisoners, while deploying thousands of its own men to guard them. In effect, French soldiers and sailors were continuing to advance Napoleon's cause even after they had surrendered. British officials saw things differently. France's population was nearly twice that of Britain, and many of the prisoners who fell into British hands were sailors—men with skills that could not easily be replaced. Alongside Britain's blockade of the French coast, denying France so many of its sailors would consolidate the Royal Navy's advantage at sea. Both sides, then, accommodated themselves to a vast (if unequal) build-up of captives.[13]

In a report for the British government, the Transport Board tallied the financial and human expense of incarcerating so many French prisoners. Seven land prisons and twenty-one prison hulks had been drafted into service for this purpose, but the system was soon past capacity. 'There not being sufficient room in the prisons on shore,' the report admitted, 'it has been found necessary . . . to order several Line of Battle Ships to be fitted for the reception of the overplus.' The Admiralty howled at the repurposing of its proud warhorses for such tawdry work. Even when laid up in harbour, hulks required sailors and officers who might otherwise be fighting the French. They also bled money: the report made the extraordinary claim that prison ships cost the government thirty times more per prisoner than facilities on land. Even if this number was exaggerated, it was clear to British officials that the hulks should be a stopgap rather than a long-term solution.[14]

For most of the eighteenth century, Britain's detention facilities for enemy captives—like its prisons for debtors and criminals—were adaptations of existing buildings. But the scale of the prisoner build-up in the 1790s encouraged the Transport Board to think again about how very large numbers of men could be incarcerated. Norman Cross in eastern England, which opened in April 1797, was the first fruit of this new thinking. The chosen site was more than seventy miles north of London but close to the road which linked the capital and the north. It was well connected by waterways to the sea, but sufficiently distant to deter runaways. The prison's architects kept things simple: the buildings and fence were made from local timber, which hastened construction and kept costs low. Although a breakout in 1807 forced the Transport Board to question the wisdom of a wooden fence—they replaced it with a stone wall—Norman Cross was a cheap and effective solution to a difficult problem. It took barely four months to build, and it housed around six thousand men until it was dismantled and sold at auction in 1816. Some of the timber was reused to make houses in the nearby town of Peterborough; most of it became firewood.[15]

Though Norman Cross had its share of problems with disease, discipline, and morale, it was an efficient and unfussy answer to Britain's growing prisoner problem. Dartmoor prison was an inefficient and baffling answer to the same problem. In fact, given the sound reasoning that had guided the Transport Board in the building of Norman Cross, it seems incredible that the same officials could approve both projects. Dartmoor was both inaccessible and fantastically expensive. The board's reputation for frugality and incorruptibility was well established before it approved the

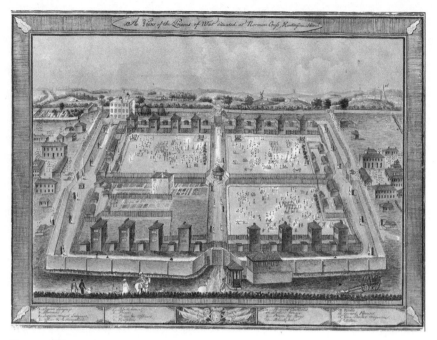

Norman Cross prison
Courtesy of Peterborough Museum and Art Gallery

construction of Dartmoor prison in 1805. Board members met formally to conduct the nation's business on every day of the week save for Sunday, and even the slightest evidence that an official or contractor had succumbed to bribery would result in permanent exclusion from the tendering process. And yet somehow Thomas Tyrwhitt managed to persuade these upstanding men to build a huge and flamboyantly impractical prison right next to his house. The best explanation is the most obvious: not even the Transport Board would pick a fight with the Prince of Wales.[16]

THE MEMBERS OF THE TRANSPORT BOARD WERE ACCUSTOMED TO dealing with powerful men, but Tyrwhitt's patron was hard to ignore. George supported the scheme and offered the board a practical inducement: he would make available nearly four hundred acres of moorland on a ninety-nine-year lease for a modest rent. The site was less than twenty miles from the naval base at Plymouth, where in 1805 around four thousand Frenchmen and Spaniards were held in prison hulks at great expense and considerable risk to their health. Strategic concerns reinforced the humanitarian argument for Dartmoor. Since the war had resumed in 1803, Napoleon had amassed a huge land force on the northern French coast and had loudly telegraphed that an invasion was imminent. Moving French prisoners away from Plymouth would give the port's defenders more breathing room in the event of an attack and would reduce the risk that jailers and prisoners might swap places.[17]

The strained state of Britain's war effort made Dartmoor plausible (or slightly less implausible) in another respect. Supplies of timber had been plentiful in 1796, when Norman Cross was assembled at high speed. In 1805, with the Royal Navy racing to build or repair its ships, a wooden prison would cannibalize a scarce strategic resource. The site chosen on Dartmoor, a mile to the northwest of Tyrwhitt's house at Tor Royal, was surrounded by granite, which Tyrwhitt proposed to mine at low cost. As he walked the site in July 1805, Tyrwhitt made a list of the advantages—local stone, a good water supply, abundant land—and ensured it found its way back to London. The Transport Board approved the proposal and by October had issued a tender 'for the BUILDING of a PRISON, for the confinement of Five Thousand Prisoners of War, on Dartmoor.'[18]

Accompanying Tyrwhitt on that first site visit was Daniel Asher Alexander, the architect he had chosen to design the new prison. Alexander was a few years younger than Tyrwhitt, but the two men had been friends for more than a decade. An obituary in 1846 recorded that Alexander 'always regarded architecture as a reality based upon common sense . . . not as an exotic to be merely transplanted from another clime without reference to circumstances'. Dartmoor prison may not have been the best example of this sensibility, and although Alexander's other designs were distinguished by his engineering skill, he could be precious about his calling in life. Alexander's career spanned an era in which the role of the architect assumed a new level of professional visibility. When asked at one point if he was a builder, he replied that he was 'more than that: I am an architect.' When his sceptical interlocutor inquired in turn if Alexander could name the architect of the Tower of Babel, the reply came quickly: 'There was no architect; hence the confusion.'[19]

Alexander's plans for Dartmoor looked very different from any existing war prison, and nothing like Norman Cross. Where that prison had clustered its captives in low-slung barracks in each of its four quadrants, with the site initially bordered by a plain wooden fence, Alexander gave Dartmoor a vast circular wall made of dark granite stretching nearly a mile in circumference. The circle itself was divided in two: on the north side were several large prison blocks sweeping outwards from a central hub; on the south side were the hospital, barracks, storehouses, and residences for the prison's surgeon and governor—who was known as the agent. Just within the huge outer wall was a 'military walk' for the guardsmen to patrol, then another inner wall studded with guardhouses and lookouts. It was a gigantic and conspicuously permanent design. Confirmation that Tyrwhitt and Alexander planned to convert Dartmoor into a criminal prison at the war's end comes from *Ackermann's Repository*, a popular London journal that ran an effusive article on the prison soon after its completion in 1809. The piece was probably commissioned by Tyrwhitt himself: it carefully acknowledged his 'amenity of manners', 'suavity of disposition', and 'inexhaustible' stock of anecdotes. It also alerted readers to the post-war future of the project: 'It is said to be in contemplation to convert this vast, and then useless building, into a receptacle for convicts.'[20]

When we know that Tyrwhitt and his architect expected Dartmoor to become a criminal prison, it's tempting to compare Alexander's striking circular design with the most famous prison proposal in history: Jeremy Bentham's panopticon, which was introduced to the world in a pamphlet published in 1791. Bentham became one of the leading philosophers and reformers of his age, and he gladly adopted John Howard's crusade for prison reform and prisoner rehabilitation. The panopticon was a circular building in which every inmate could be seen from a central observation point. This design was driven by what Bentham termed 'the inspection principle': the idea that people requiring instruction, correction, guidance, or protection would benefit from being perpetually visible to those charged with their care. (The 'inspector' would remain invisible to the panopticon's residents, however.) Bentham's enthusiasm for the inspection principle was boundless. It could be used for 'punishing the incorrigible, guarding the insane, reforming the vicious, confining the suspected, employing the idle, maintaining the helpless, curing the sick . . . or training the rising race in the path of education.' It was obvious to Bentham that 'the more constantly the persons to be inspected are under the eyes of the persons who should inspect them, the more perfectly will the purpose of the establishment have been attained.' Applied to prisons, this concept seemed revolutionary: rather than the gloomy dungeons that John Howard had spent years traversing, a panopticon would be filled with light and powered by the visibility of its inmates.[21]

Bentham had an underdeveloped sense of how creepy he could be. This was a man who arranged in his will for his own corpse to be mummified, 'clad in one of the suits of black occasionally worn by me', and preserved in a glass cabinet at University College London (where it welcomes stupefied visitors to this day). But his 'inspection principle' has long fascinated scholars eager to understand both the transformation of prisons and the rise of the state in the early nineteenth century. Foremost among them is Michel Foucault, who wrote indelibly about 'Panopticism' in his book *Discipline and Punish* (1975). Foucault was interested in a striking transition: from the public executions of the eighteenth century, in which the state wreaked vengeance on the human body in front of gawping crowds, to the isolation and concealment of the nineteenth-century penitentiary, in which the prisoner's soul might be redeemed through unrelenting surveillance. In a panopticon, the public could no longer see the criminal and yet the criminal was made to feel that the jailer's gaze was perpetual. Foucault found this transition alarming. For the prisoners unlucky enough to end up in Bentham's fiendish prison, Foucault wrote, 'visibility is a trap.'[22]

Bentham's promiscuous enthusiasm for panopticism led Foucault to conclude that the fabric of the modern state had been woven from the inspection principle. This may be an overstatement. The panopticon remained firmly in Bentham's imagination even in an era when prison reformers rushed to break ground on new buildings. Its arresting appearance certainly resonates in the Dartmoor design, but in tracing the line of influence we need to acknowledge that Jeremy Bentham wasn't really the inventor of the panopticon. That distinction belongs to his brother, Samuel Bentham, who came up with the design in 1787 when he was working in Russia. Grigory Potemkin, Catherine the Great's confidant and factotum, had initially hired Samuel in 1780 as a shipbuilder and engineer. But when Russia seized Crimea from the Ottoman Empire in 1784 and Catherine put Potemkin in charge of the region's incorporation, Bentham pursued a raft of improvement schemes which could bring glory to his employer. Ahead of Catherine's tour of south Russia in 1787, Potemkin asked Samuel to train local peasants in a variety of crafts that might impress their distinguished visitor. Samuel hired skilled artisans and teachers from England to deliver this training, but found that it was they, rather than the peasants, who seemed feckless and work-shy. The panopticon was born in this unusual moment: it gave Samuel Bentham a means of monitoring his unreliable compatriots and telegraphing to Catherine that south Russia was a place of enlightenment and instruction. Viewed from this perspective, Samuel's panopticon seems less like Foucault's fearsome instrument of the all-powerful state and more like his boss's other innovation for the empress's tour: the infamous Potemkin village. What mattered about the first panopticon was not whether it worked but whether onlookers *believed* it worked.[23]

When Samuel Bentham returned from Russia in 1791, he worked with Jeremy to refine and promote the panopticon before accepting a post as Inspector General of Naval Works. In 1797, he was

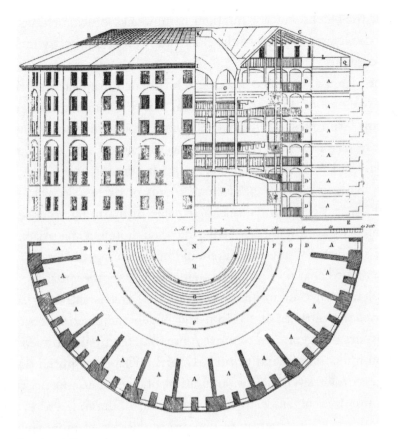

Bentham's Panopticon
Courtesy of Wikimedia Commons

sounded out by the British government about building a huge war prison 'on the principle of the Panopticon'. Thomas Tyrwhitt and Daniel Alexander almost certainly encountered the design through Samuel (and his Admiralty contacts) rather than through Jeremy Bentham. But beyond the immediate similarities between these giant circular prisons, Alexander's blueprint for Dartmoor diverged significantly from a true panopticon. Jeremy Bentham's 1791 plan envisaged a round building of six floors or higher, with individual cells around the circumference of each floor and windows allowing a vantage from a central viewing platform. At Dartmoor, by contrast, the five large accommodation blocks of Alexander's original design were made of solid stone, with just a few windows. Prisoners inside the blocks would hang their hammocks from stanchions running the length of each of the floors and would be mostly invisible to the guards outside.[24]

The idea that prisoners needed to be isolated from each other had been one of John Howard's key insights in his campaign for prison reform. Criminals would inevitably prey upon the poor morals or weak resolve of other criminals, Howard insisted, and so the modern jail had to prevent prisoners from fashioning their own society. 'I wish to have so many small rooms or cabins,' John Howard wrote, 'that each criminal may *sleep alone*.' It might be necessary for prisoners to work together during the day, though some prison theorists suggested that even this should be discouraged. (Jeremy Bentham argued that no prisoner should ever see another prisoner, with complete silence maintained at all times.) But isolating prisoners reduced the capacity of a prison and hugely increased its cost. The Transport Board needed to move more than ten thousand men from prison hulks into inland prisons. Daniel Alexander's initial designs for Dartmoor envisaged a population of five thousand prisoners; soon this was increased to seven and a half thousand, and eventually (after the construction of new prison blocks) to more than ten thousand. A panopticon of Babel-like proportions would struggle to house this many prisoners.[25]

After the war, when Tyrwhitt lobbied the British government to make Dartmoor a criminal prison, members of Parliament summoned Alexander to Westminster to give evidence on the proposal. Alexander was confident that the prison blocks could be refitted to accommodate cells in place of the unbroken, warehouse-like floors of his original design. But he conceded that they would probably have to house multiple prisoners 'because in these buildings the solitary cells would be larger than I have ever seen them executed for civil purposes.' Dartmoor was built to house huge numbers of men, but not to isolate and surveil them in the ways that Jeremy Bentham and John Howard had proposed. Although Alexander was bullish about a criminal prison for around two thousand inmates, the practical problems of adapting his original buildings deterred MPs and ministers from approving Tyrwhitt's conversion plan. Without an easy and economical way of introducing individual cells into Alexander's imposing design, the British government would struggle to find any purpose for Dartmoor beyond the end of its wars with France and the United States in 1815.[26]

JOHN HOWARD'S CRUSADE HAD INSPIRED A WAVE OF PRISON BUILDing in the 1780s, including a number of facilities designed by his friend William Blackburn. Unlike Bentham, whose radical ideas never left the drawing board, Blackburn designed and built more than a dozen prisons across Britain. His plan for Liverpool Borough Gaol, constructed between 1785 and 1789, closely resembles the upper half of Dartmoor's confined circle: six blocks radiate outwards from a central area, an arrangement which Blackburn followed in his other prison designs. All of these facilities were for felons, debtors, or people awaiting trial, however, so they adopted Howard's principle of confining prisoners to cells. Daniel Alexander would certainly have known Blackburn's work, and the Liverpool design probably had a stronger influence on him than any other prison facility that was actually built.[27]

Alexander's biographers mention one further influence which may explain why American prisoners found Dartmoor so unnerving. Clearly, the location did most of that work; a gigantic prison in the middle of a barren and foggy moor was unlikely to lift the soul of anyone. But Alexander was also an admirer of a man who, on the face of it, you wouldn't want to design your prison—at least, not if you were forced to spend time on the wrong side of its walls. Giovanni Battista Piranesi was an Italian engineer and architect who, unlike Daniel Alexander, spent most of his life struggling to find commissions. After moving as a young man to Rome from his native city of Venice, he became one of eighteenth-century Europe's most influential engravers. He was particularly celebrated for his *Vedute di Roma* (*Views of Rome*), first published in 1748, which captured the city's most celebrated architecture in exceptionally vivid scenes. Piranesi became a favourite among the new generation of Romantic writers. Coleridge recommended his etchings to everyone he met; Goethe, who got to know Rome principally through Piranesi's sketches, was a little disappointed when he finally saw the city with his own eyes. Architects admired Piranesi's details and pored over his designs—which, like Jeremy Bentham's, rarely left the page. Foremost among these was a series of extraordinary sketches he called the *Carceri d'invenzione*—his *Imaginary Prisons*.[28]

These sketches (1749–1761) offered glimpses into a vast stone prison, or perhaps many prisons, each more unsettling than the last. Piranesi took the monumental architecture of Rome and turned it inside out. Magnificent exteriors became vast and chilly interiors, simultaneously crowded with detail—huge staircases, colossal statues, the occasional torture instrument—and flooded with emptiness. The spaces were so huge that one could almost ignore the tiny human figures scratched onto the stairs like shadows or cowering beneath the rack and the giant wheel. For Coleridge, Piranesi's work conveyed 'the delirium of architectural genius'. (Coleridge assumed that the images were the product of a near-death experience.) Coleridge's friend Thomas De Quincey, who learned of the *Prisons* solely through a breathless account from Coleridge, was convinced they were visions from a nightmare. The 'vast Gothic halls' that Coleridge described were filled with precipitous drops, terrible machinery, and the overpowering sense of a void from which no escape was possible. Piranesi's vision was 'expressive of enormous power put forth, and resistance overcome'.[29]

Admirers of Piranesi knew he was imagining the impossible. But Daniel Alexander was one of the very few people in history charged with actually building an enormous stone prison. While some of the more baroque details of Piranesi's vision would not make the journey to Dartmoor, Alexander clearly imbibed the monumentalism which supported the Italian's towering stonework and Gothic arches. The alarming details of Piranesi's design and aesthetic ran in

Giovanni Battista Piranesi, 'The Smoking Fire' (1761), from
Carceri d'invenzione
Courtesy of the Metropolitan Museum of Art, New York, Harris
Brisbane Dick Fund, 1937

the opposite direction to the humanitarianism and order demanded
by John Howard. Even the panopticon's twisted benevolence had
a kind of reforming logic, and its disciplined use of space and vantage was far removed from the hopeless grandeur of Piranesi's interiors: his prisoners could see for miles, it seemed, and this only
made their confinement more dreadful. Piranesi's many admirers
toured the *Imaginary Prisons* with a vicarious fascination for suffering: imagine being trapped inside one of these vast dungeons,
confronted by a thousand pathways to nowhere! We can't know
for sure how explicitly Alexander drew on Piranesi as he sketched

his own gigantic prison, but in some of Dartmoor's more imposing elements—especially its towering stone gate—the debt seems both obvious and unfortunate.

THE TRANSPORT BOARD'S DECISION TO APPROVE DARTMOOR prison offered two huge benefits to Thomas Tyrwhitt. First, it brought hundreds of labourers to the new village he had founded between the site and his home, which he named Princetown in gratitude to his patron. Carpenters, masons, and quarrymen rushed to work on the prison, and at last Tyrwhitt had customers for the pub he had expensively constructed. (He called it the Plume of Feathers, yet another Prince of Wales reference.) The second benefit would be even more lucrative. He persuaded the board that inmates should be permitted to leave the prison during the day and undertake improvements within and beyond Princetown: working the fields, quarrying stone, or turning the village into a town. These gruelling tasks could be remunerated at a fraction of the cost of waged labour, another way in which Dartmoor anticipated the prison-industrial complex of our own era. Daniel Alexander later guessed that 40 percent of the market wage would be generous; prisoners might work for even less in return for 'little luxuries' like 'an extra blanket'. With a prison population of ten thousand or more, Tyrwhitt had considerable resources to draw upon as he plotted Dartmoor's transformation.[30]

In the twenty-first century, our privatized prisons seem like a departure from an earlier order in which the state closely held and managed these facilities. In fact, both Tyrwhitt and Jeremy Bentham believed that private industry would flourish from the business of incarceration. Bentham insisted that his panopticons would be privately owned and managed, and that every social institution which could be transformed by the inspection principle—prisons, workhouses, schools—might be run on a for-profit basis. Tyrwhitt, who had greater access than Bentham to the huge purchasing power of the state, was happy for the Transport Board to fund the building and operation of Dartmoor. But he imagined the prison as a turbine that would power mining, agriculture, and even industry in the empty lands around Princetown. There was something distinctly utopian about these plans for social, spiritual, and economic transformation: from the soul of the individual to the economic health of the nation, prisons properly conceived and constructed might benefit everyone. The challenge was to sustain such bright visions against the inconvenient truths of reality.[31]

At Dartmoor, those truths were never far from embarrassing Tyrwhitt's dream. In the last months of 1805, the Transport Board arranged the tendering process around a single set of requirements: bidders were invited to submit estimates for the entire construction job, rather than for specific elements of the project. (This was highly unusual for the time.) Four bids were received: the highest expected the work to cost £115,337; the lowest asked for £66,815. Although that lowest bid fell below even the government's most parsimonious projections, the Transport Board greedily accepted it—and inserted a clause declaring that the contract could be cancelled without notice if the Napoleonic Wars ended before the prison was opened. Tyrwhitt was probably happiest in the winter of 1805–1806, just before the work began. As soon as it did, problems piled up like snow in the unforgiving Dartmoor winter. The craftsmen and labourers who began marking out the site and building the walls struggled with the exposure and the freezing temperatures. Virtually all of the workmen were too poor to board in Princetown and instead became the first residents of the prison. Work was miserable, if not impossible, on the many days of intense rain or deep snow. On the rarer mild days, labourers were urged by their overseers to rush the work and get back on schedule. 'This hath been a hindering week,' wrote one of the contractors during a particularly nasty spell. 'The sun hath scarcely made its appearance, and we may safely say that £120 hath been lost this week in wages!'[32]

Building the prison on such an aggressive fixed contract gave no headroom for contingency. The price of labour increased considerably after 1805, and even though timber was used sparingly, it became so hard to find that the contractor threatened to terminate building work unless the Transport Board could secure a supply. The board raided its ship-breaking yards and sent beams from retired Royal Navy ships; these became the floor and roof of each of the prison blocks. With the work running far behind schedule and the prison hulks bursting, the board became desperate. Daniel Alexander had promised that Dartmoor could open by Christmas 1807, but that estimate proved absurdly optimistic. When the board's chief inspector, Ambrose Serle, descended upon the moor in August 1808, the prison was still a long way from completion. Serle's terse letter to London conveyed his disappointment: 'Upon the whole, I am of the opinion that the Depot will not be complete or fit for use during the present year.' The board had already recruited a contingent of militia from Yorkshire to guard the first cohort of French prisoners awaiting transfer to Dartmoor. Serle recommended that they return home immediately. The board should await solid evidence of the prison's

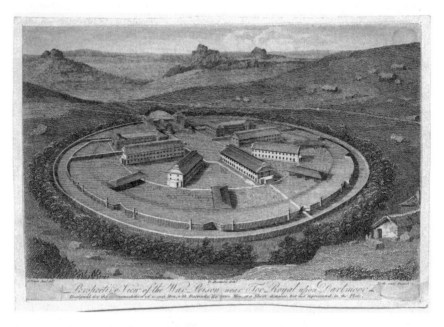

Samuel Prout, 'Dartmoor Prison' (1807)
Courtesy of The Box, Plymouth

completion before 'a single soldier in the first instance, or a single prisoner in the next, should be allowed to reside'.[33]

The winter of 1808–1809 saw more setbacks. The floors had to be re-laid, the pointing on the prison blocks never seemed to keep out the damp, part of the external wall collapsed. But by the spring of 1809, nearly four years after Tyrwhitt had persuaded the Transport Board to embrace his vision, Dartmoor was on the verge of receiving its first inmates. The last weeks before the grand opening were frantic. After so many months when it seemed that the prison would never be finished, the knowledge that thousands of French prisoners would soon march northward from Plymouth prompted a frantic accounting of their needs: uniforms, blankets, food, translators, coffins, and more. Finally, on 22 May 1809, the first consignment of prisoners arrived. The board and the navy were so desperate to relieve the pressure on the hulks at Plymouth that more than two and a half thousand Frenchmen came to Dartmoor in just four days.[34]

The very first to enter was Etienne Pagert. The prison clerks recorded a few facts about him: he was born in the Basque town of Bayonne close to the French border with Spain; he was a little over five feet tall, of a stout build, and with a 'long and swarthy' countenance. He was given a hammock, a blanket, and a few other supplies, though the clerks judged that the prison uniform he had received in Plymouth might still serve him in his new home. Pagert had been captured on the *General Manon*, a French privateer, in the Mediterranean. He was fifty years old—far older than the average prisoner, as things would turn out. He had entered British custody on 14 August 1803, which meant that he had already spent the better part of six years enduring the horrors of the hulks at Plymouth. We don't know what Pagert made of his new surroundings, but he could be forgiven for having abandoned hope long before he made it to Dartmoor. Whereas the prison was new, its prisoners were not.[35]

When Pagert took the final steps of his journey from Plymouth, he must have noticed one of Daniel Alexander's final flourishes: on the imposing stone archway of Dartmoor prison, which could easily have come from Giovanni Piranesi's sketchbook, Alexander had ordered his workmen to inscribe PARCERE SUBJECTIS. The phrase comes from Virgil's *Aeneid*, and specifically the passage in which the hero Aeneas, still reeling from the fall of his home city of Troy, travels to the underworld to meet the ghost of his father, Anchises. Aeneas finds out from Anchises that he is destined to found the mighty empire of Rome and that this empire will be distinguished not by artistic greatness or the eloquence of its leaders but by its ruthlessly enlightened understanding of power:

> Others, I doubt not, shall with softer mold beat out the breathing bronze, coax from the marble features to the life, plead cases with greater

Main Gate, Dartmoor Prison
© *Baz Richardson*

eloquence and with a pointer trace heaven's motions and predict the risings of the stars. But you, Roman, be sure to rule the world (be these your arts), to crown peace with justice, to spare the vanquished and to crush the proud.

'Spare the vanquished': in chiselling that phrase into his prison's monumentally bleak gateway, Daniel Alexander sent a message that was just as scrambled as Anchises's advice to Aeneas. The Roman Empire would subdue the world with justice and mercy; Dartmoor prison would show benevolence to the men it detained indefinitely. Even before the Americans arrived in 1813, the logic of this promise had begun to unravel.[36]

4.

AMONG THE ROMANS

ONE OF THE CLERKS ENTERED THE STOREHOUSE AT THE CENtre of the prison. A mountain of bread confronted him, recently delivered from the bakery on Two Bridges Road. He looked for the best loaf he could find, wrapped it in cloth, then took it through an inner gate and past the heavy stone entrance marked with PARCERE SUBJECTIS. A coach was waiting outside. The clerk handed the bread to the driver, along with the day's correspondence, and the loaf began its journey to London. It was February 1810; the weather was bad, and the days were still short. Nonetheless, when the coach picked up the post route from Plymouth to the capital, one of the better roads in the kingdom, it covered nearly two hundred miles in a day. Another clerk met the coachman outside an inconspicuous building on Whitehall, just down the road from the prime minister's residence on Downing Street. The clerk brought the mail and the loaf up to the offices of the Transport Board. There, a board official unwrapped the cloth, took a bite from the loaf, and thought for a while. He picked up a pen and wrote to Dartmoor's agent, the prison's most senior officer. 'The Loaf of Bread sent by coach has been received,' the official wrote. 'We have only to observe concerning it, that none of a quality <u>in any degree</u> inferior is on any account to be received.'[1]

The recipient of that letter, Captain Isaac Cotgrave, had not expected the Dartmoor job to be glamorous. Since the arrival of the first prisoners in May 1809, things had not gone as smoothly as he had hoped. More than six thousand French POWs had been marched to Dartmoor between May and September; nearly half had arrived in the final days of May, during the prison's chaotic opening week. By the autumn, Dartmoor was so full that Cotgrave had to beg the board to stop sending prisoners. The next major consignment was postponed for more than a year, by which point escapes, deaths in the prison's infirmary, and suicides had created new vacancies. In February 1810, Cotgrave was nine months into the task of running a small town filled with desperate men. The prisoners were far more restive than their counterparts in Plymouth. The prison had numerous building defects, all of them more apparent when it was packed beyond capacity. And basic issues—ensuring that the bread was edible, for example—needed constant attention. Isaac Cotgrave was sixty-six years old, closing in on half a century in the king's service. If Dartmoor was an unhappy place for the prisoners, it seldom raised the spirits of the agent either.[2]

The Transport Board, not to mention the enterprising Thomas Tyrwhitt, continued to promote Dartmoor as a leap forward in prison design. A London magazine lauded the 'humane arrangement and control of the Transport Board', who were pursuing 'an undeviating system of philanthropy' on the bleak moorland. The article's author conceded that 'a more healthy spot might have been selected', but (in line with Tyrwhitt's boasts) he was confident that cultivation and improvement of the surrounding moor would improve the climate. In the meantime, 'every comfort' would be extended 'to alleviate the prisoners' unhappy lot', and the Frenchmen unfortunate enough to be confined in the prison would receive better medicine and food than even the British servicemen fighting Napoleon in Portugal and Spain.[3]

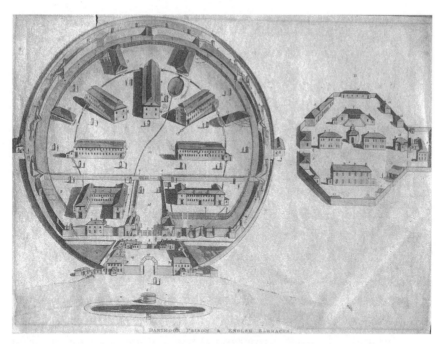

Plan of Dartmoor Prison from *Ackermann's Repository* (1810)
Courtesy of Neil Davie

This puff piece was accompanied by a striking illustration of the prison, the first widely circulated image of Daniel Alexander's masterpiece. On the left of the image was the giant stone circle, with five prison blocks radiating outwards in the upper half and a number of elegant buildings (including the storehouse) in the lower. To the right was the octagonal structure housing the barracks for militiamen who would serve as prison guards. A few guardsmen are pictured, but no prisoners can be seen: the yards seem roomy, even pastoral, in marked contrast to the overcrowded scenes that would greet the American arrivals in April 1813. The image was entirely in keeping with Tyrwhitt's idealized vision of the prison, a space of liberality and order, with none of Piranesi's epic dread. But already, in the prison's first year, a different reality was emerging. Dartmoor would become much harder to govern when the prisoners surrendered to despair. But for Cotgrave and the Transport Board, the real danger was that the British public would lose faith in what they were trying to do.[4]

FOR A MAN WHO HAD SPENT NEARLY HIS ENTIRE LIFE IN THE Royal Navy, Isaac Cotgrave left few footprints before Dartmoor. We know he fought in the Revolutionary War, though principally because an American parish register tells us that he met and married Margaret Blake of New York in 1778. His rise through the ranks was slow: he was still a lieutenant when he turned forty in 1785, and it would be another dozen years before he made commander. During the first phase of the wars with France, he sailed cutters in the English Channel, before serving aboard the aptly named bomb vessel HMS *Volcano*. Bomb vessels were outfitted with mortars rather than cannons and were used to lay siege to coastal towns and cities. (They make a cameo appearance in the 'Star-Spangled Banner' launching those 'bombs bursting in air' at Baltimore in 1814.) Eventually, Cotgrave was given command of HMS *Gannet*, a sixteen-gun naval brig, which became the scene of his most celebrated adventure. In August 1801, Horatio Nelson led a surprise attack on Boulogne, hoping to pre-empt the feared French crossing of the English Channel. Cotgrave commanded a small division of gunboats armed with howitzers, and he slipped through the night towards the largest of the French ships. 'I lost no time in making the attack,' Cotgrave later wrote to Nelson. But the French response was fierce, and Cotgrave 'received so many shots through the boat's bottom, that I soon found her in a sinking state.' He bravely drew the enemy's fire to allow his colleagues to fall back before escaping to Nelson's flagship. Not for the last time in British history, the press celebrated a speedy retreat from France as if it were a victory.[5]

Cotgrave was promoted to captain for his heroics, but as he approached his sixtieth birthday, he traded his new ship for the post of Agent for Prisoners of War at Plymouth. The appointment was made a week or so after the collapse of the Treaty of Amiens in

1803, which triggered the second phase of the Anglo-French wars and an alarming build-up of prisoners. With the two sides failing to reach agreement on exchanges, Cotgrave found it almost impossible to release anyone in his custody. One exception came in 1806, when he was ordered to escort the French admiral Pierre-Charles Villeneuve to a ship in Plymouth harbour that would return him to France. Villeneuve had commanded the French fleet at Trafalgar; after obtaining permission from the Admiralty to attend Nelson's funeral, he had spent his captivity ruefully assembling newspaper accounts of his defeat. He carried these with him as he and Cotgrave took a short boat ride from the shore to the waiting French ship. Villeneuve had 'piercing black eyes', one observer wrote of the scene, but appeared 'dejected' as he bowed slightly to Cotgrave and said farewell. A few days later he would be found dead in a hotel in Rennes, having stabbed himself multiple times rather than face the wrath of Napoleon.[6]

When the Transport Board looked for a Royal Navy man who could run the new prison at Dartmoor, Cotgrave was a natural choice. He had handled the demanding work at Plymouth with calm and rigour, and he could be expected to settle quickly into his new role. But from the moment of his appointment in September 1808, Cotgrave found Dartmoor a tougher assignment. Construction problems dominated his first nine months in the job; then the prisoners arrived, and Cotgrave got no respite from their troubles and complaints. He also discovered that his room for manoeuvre as agent was limited. On the open ocean, a Royal Navy captain enjoyed considerable latitude to interpret and execute his orders. Running a land prison demanded a sharp adjustment. The board outlined its expectations in a closely printed booklet entitled *Instructions for Agents*. Then there was the mail coach to London, which put the agent within easy reach of Transport Board officials in Whitehall. Although Cotgrave's letters to the board have not survived, we have a near complete account of what the board wrote to him during his six years at Dartmoor. A letter made its way from London almost every day, and the voluminous correspondence reveals the board's interest in the tiniest details.[7]

Cotgrave needed the board's permission, for example, to open each individual prison block as Dartmoor began to fill up with Frenchmen. His superiors in London also acted as a brake on Cotgrave's more humane instincts. When it became apparent in November 1809 that the prison was bitterly cold, Cotgrave begged for extra blankets. The response from Whitehall was glacial: 'The Board conceive that in buildings where so many sleep, one blanket ought to be sufficient for one person.' At a distance of more than two hundred miles from the human misery piling up in Dartmoor, the Transport Board found it easy not only to mistreat the prisoners but also to bully and harass their own agent. Cotgrave's house at the front of the prison was spacious, especially compared to the hammocks and cabins in which he had spent most of his career. And yet none of his previous posts would feel as cramped as the years he spent at Dartmoor.[8]

TO MANAGE THE PRISON'S HUGE POPULATION COTGRAVE RELIED on fifty staff and five hundred militiamen. The staff, who mostly lived within the prison, ensured that the buildings were maintained, the prisoners were registered on arrival and mustered every day, the blocks were locked each night, and the prison hospital was ready to receive the sick. Beyond Tyrwhitt's lonely pub in Princetown, there was very little for them to do when they weren't working. For the militiamen in the barracks adjoining the prison, the situation was even more wretched. Virtually every British county had its own militia, and though some men volunteered for service, most were selected via a ballot. (Well-off Britons could dodge service through buying a substitute.) The militia's main task was to defend the home front against a French invasion. The Transport Board knew the men had no training in the delicate work of guarding a prison, and so it kept them on short rotations: two to three months on average, long enough to despair at Dartmoor's weather and isolation, but not to lose the hope of deliverance.[9]

The board's *Instructions to Agents* outlined the basic rules of the prison, including the clothing and blankets provided to prisoners and the daily allowances of food. Despite its remoteness, Dartmoor was far from a closed economy. For one thing, the prisoners had been allowed to keep whatever belongings they had with them when captured, hence the caravan of baggage carts that crawled from Plymouth to the main gate with each consignment of new prisoners. Even though prisoners were not permitted to correspond freely, they could receive mail (including money) from relatives or friends after letters had been inspected by the prison staff. As we'll see, there was a huge amount of money inside the prison, though it tended to aggregate in the hands of relatively few prisoners. Agent Cotgrave was authorized to pay prisoners to work in the kitchens, in the hospital, and around the prison and to inform on the activities of their fellow prisoners. The flow of money to and between the prisoners kept them engaged with the main attraction of the prison economy: the market.[10]

Markets had been a fixture of war prisons since the mid-eighteenth century. The work of feeding the prisoners was mostly outsourced to contractors, but the Transport Board also gave local people an opportunity to sell (and to buy) within what was literally a captive market. Every morning except Sunday, a little before nine o'clock, traders from the towns and villages on the outskirts of the moor formed a line outside the prison. The regulations required that they be searched for prohibited items—'liquors, knives, or weapons of any kind'—then allowed through the main gate. Beyond two further gates was the market square, a walled-in space around twenty meters on each side. Traders would set up their stalls and wait for the turnkeys to allow prisoners to enter from the prison yard. The square could hold only a couple of hundred people at one time, but the stalls remained open for three hours each day. For prisoners with no other contact with the outside world, the market became the centre of the universe.[11]

Local traders did a brisk business. The flow of goods also sustained an out-of-hours trade within the prison blocks, away from the gaze of the guards. This secondary market was both an essential feature of the prison economy and a headache for Agent Cotgrave. It was naive to imagine that local traders would soak up all the commercial activity of the prison, and from one perspective the cultivation of a shadow economy seemed like enlightened prison governance: Frenchmen who reinvented themselves as traders of vegetables or coffee (or coffee made from vegetables, in some cases) were easier to marshal than those who surrendered to despair. But the daily introduction of new items and desires into Dartmoor created an endless stream of jealousies which could easily explode into violence.

The market was also a place where prisoners could sell their own possessions, along with any items they made during their countless hours of captivity. The board prohibited prisoners from selling most items of clothing, fearing that uniforms and blankets issued at government expense might be repurposed for financial gain. They also banned prisoners from selling 'obscene pictures, images or toys'. One thing they were allowed to sell was bone carving, which Dartmoor's inmates refined to an extraordinary level. French prisoners—and later the Americans—scavenged for bones in the scraps left outside the kitchens, then spent their endless free time fashioning intricate models of the ships on which they had been captured. (One French prisoner produced a miniature guillotine.) From Agent Cotgrave's perspective, the detailed and even obsessive nature of this work was to be applauded: it kept his prisoners busy. It might also bring them a decent return from the market traders if they were willing to part with their work on completion.[12]

The archive can make Dartmoor seem an entirely male space, but this wasn't the case. Many of the market traders were women, as were several members of the prison's staff. Mary Brooks, employed by the board as a seamstress, even brought her children to live with her at Dartmoor. Cotgrave himself had thirteen children, and though several had died or grown up before he took over at Dartmoor, around half a dozen lived with him and his American wife Margaret in the house at the front of the prison. Officially, women were only allowed in the prison in a small number of staff roles—mostly working in the hospital and the storehouses. But they popped up frequently in the board's correspondence with Cotgrave. Several lived around the prison in huts that had been left behind by the construction staff, or so the board complained to Cotgrave in December 1810. Earlier that year, the militia commander had tipped off the board that some of Cotgrave's turnkeys were 'harboring women' elsewhere in the prison. We don't know who these women were. The tone of the board's protests implies that they may have been sex workers, but Dartmoor's unusually isolated situation makes this far from certain. More junior staff in the prison may have moved their wives or daughters to be closer to them, concluding that the prison's many crannies could conceal a family member more or less indefinitely. Cotgrave may also have acquiesced in these arrangements, which would explain why the board had to order him to curtail them.[13]

But women and children weren't only to be found within the staff areas of the prison: they were also in the prison blocks themselves. The board's regulations specified that only men could be taken as prisoners of war, but women and children regularly found themselves in combat zones—acting as camp followers to an army, for example, or living aboard a merchant vessel or privateer. The board insisted that any captured women and children should be returned immediately to their country of origin. What if they wanted to stay with a loved one or had nowhere else to go? The convention in debtors' prisons in the early nineteenth century, and even in some criminal facilities, was that family members might live within a prison. Amy Dorrit, the heroine of Charles Dickens's *Little Dorrit*, grows up alongside her debtor father in the Marshalsea Prison in London; she chooses to stay with him, while her siblings live outside the prison and visit as they please. With French prisoners piling up in the Plymouth hulks, the board was unwilling to countenance a similar arrangement at Dartmoor. This put Isaac Cotgrave in the invidious position of having to separate prisoners from the family members who had followed them into the prison. In August 1809, just three months after Dartmoor's opening, the board demanded that Cotgrave supply a list of the women and children in his custody and that he expedite their return to France. Cotgrave stood his ground, and the board wrote a week later that 'the women and children at Dartmoor Prison may be allowed to remain for the present.' Board regulations expressly directed that women and children be excluded from the prison register, so we don't know how many stayed behind (or for how long). But their fleeting appearance in the archive reminds us that the prisoners' world wasn't as overwhelmingly male as it might appear.[14]

Mary Brooks, the seamstress, created a different set of problems for Cotgrave. At the end of 1810, Brooks confessed that she had mislaid a pistol within the prison, which she feared had made its way into the hands of the French prisoners. The board, with admirable sangfroid, ordered Cotgrave to 'make particular enquiry and report to us how Mrs Brooks came into possession of the pistol stated to have been stolen from her'. Cotgrave played for time; a week later, the board acknowledged the receipt of another letter from him but still demanded that Brooks explain how 'one of her pistols got into the possession of the prisoners'. (The board also asked, not unreasonably, 'if she should have any arms whatever in her possession in future'.) The board continued to harass Cotgrave until Brooks herself wrote a letter, forwarded to the board via the agent, that 'satisfied' officials in London. This reprieve was short-lived, however. A few months later, after another murky incident, the board told Cotgrave that 'they cannot possibly allow Mrs Brooks to remain at Dartmoor after what has recently taken place.' Originally, the board sanctioned a transfer to another prison 'in compassion for her children', but after one further intrigue she left the board's service entirely. Only fragments of Brooks's story remain, but they demonstrate that Cotgrave's challenges at Dartmoor went far beyond guarding the prisoners.[15]

IN THEORY, DARTMOOR WAS TO BE GOVERNED WITH THE CONSENT of its captives. The French prisoners were invited to appoint representatives to liaise directly with Cotgrave and were given inducements and concessions to encourage good behaviour. Cotgrave also invited prisoners to inspect supplies of bread and beer as they arrived, with a view to keeping the contractors honest. The contractors hated this. In the summer of 1810, one complained directly to London that 'the acceptance or refusal of the provisions is left entirely to the prisoners'. The Transport Board informed the angry contractor that 'this must be incorrect', though given Cotgrave's approach to managing the prison the charge has a ring of truth. Governing Dartmoor was a constant battle: against militiamen who might be trigger-happy or overfriendly with the prisoners, against staff who were recalcitrant or incompetent, and against prisoners who despaired at the open-ended nature of their confinement. Although it might seem mundane, the quality of bread in the prison became the front line of many of these struggles. It also placed Cotgrave in a complicated position: scrutinized by the board, who continued to ask for loaves to be sent to them in the mail coach; pressed by the prisoners, who were entitled by the board's regulations to a fixed quantity and quality of bread every day; and tormented by the contractors, who protested their innocence while substituting ground rice (or worse) for flour. Dartmoor's location left Cotgrave with so few competitors for his contracts that he never resolved the bread problem. Instead, each day's delivery provided a new battleground for the various interests he was required to manage.[16]

Cotgrave was more successful in his efforts to put the French prisoners to work. Initially, the board was nervous about letting Frenchmen outside. Within the prison yards there were always three walls between a prisoner and the prospect of liberty; by contrast, the moor's emptiness could prove irresistibly tempting to members of a work party in Princetown or beyond. The majority of paid labour continued to take place inside the prison, especially in the construction of two additional blocks to extend capacity in 1811. But Cotgrave soon received permission to put prison gangs to work on the roads, digging peat from the nearby moor, and on new buildings outside the main complex—including a church for Princetown. Prisoners agreed to do this work partly for the diversion, but mostly for the dribble of money it provided. The dreams of Jeremy Bentham or Thomas Tyrwhitt that prisoners could transform the world beyond the prison were not realised. Instead, by building those two new blocks within the main yard, the prisoners' chief contribution was to facilitate the transfer of even more people to Dartmoor.[17]

For Louis Catel, who arrived at the prison during its frenetic opening week, Dartmoor was a 'depot of human misery'. Catel was one of the few Frenchmen to leave behind a detailed account of his experiences. Born in the Normandy port of Granville, he was twenty years old when he was captured on a French privateer in January 1808. He'd spent more than a year in Mill Prison at Plymouth when he was directed on 25 May 1809 to march northward; even though he arrived on the prison's third day of operation, he was already no. 2310 in the register. Like all prison memoirs, his cannot be confidently relied upon: he wrote up his recollections in 1846, and some of the details don't match up with the official records in the UK National Archives. But he was at Dartmoor for virtually the entire period of French captivity, from May 1809 until the mass release of French prisoners exactly five years later. Across hundreds of pages, he offers an eyewitness account of the slow disintegration of morale and discipline among Dartmoor's first residents.[18]

The experience of captivity initially generated camaraderie among an extraordinarily diverse set of people: Catel recalled the 'feeling of sympathy, humanity and brotherhood' which bound together men from a huge number of places and backgrounds. But he also divided the prison population into distinct groups, an arrangement which called into question some of his loftier paeans to *fraternité*. The first of these, the Lords, were prisoners who had gained considerable wealth through their success in the prison's economies or through remittances sent by family and friends. The Workers were men who lacked benefactors on the outside but who made a comfortable living for themselves through trading or providing services within the prison. The *Indifférents* were resigned to their fate and reliant on what the Transport Board provided. The Gamblers were prisoners who would gladly wager their shirt or their food ration in games of chance. The *Kaiserlics*, fanatical devotees of Napoleon, were a more extreme contingent of the Gamblers. None of those terms appears in the board's communications, though the final group on Catel's list became notorious throughout the prison system: the Romans. These were Dartmoor's wildest inhabitants, and they made the other prisoners seem as docile as the residents of Bentham's panopticon.[19]

The Romans emerged in response to rising levels of despair in the prison, which reflected both the harsh conditions and the mental agony of open-ended incarceration. Within days of the prison's opening in May 1809, Cotgrave could see that its new population was thoroughly demoralized even before arriving at Dartmoor. Most of the prisoners had been in Plymouth—either in Mill Prison or in the hulks—for at least a year, and many had already spent five years or more in British custody. For some, escape was their first and only thought. Catel claimed that the first successful breakout took place within days of his arrival. Two sailors named Sevegran and Auvray took advantage of the chaos of the prison's opening week, finding jackets which looked like guardsmen's coats and forging fake bayonets from tin left behind by the builders. In Catel's account, Sevegran and Auvray tagged onto a company of fifty militiamen as they marched out of the prison. When the militia turned left to enter their barracks beyond the prison's walls, the French imposters scampered through the village and took the road back to Plymouth, where they bought tickets for a stagecoach to London. Dartmoor's register makes no mention of this. But it's possible that a prison in such a state of disarray might have been no better at noticing this escape than preventing it.[20]

Further breakout attempts that summer caused Cotgrave and the board more embarrassment. Throughout 1809, the agent was told to send any recovered escapees to Plymouth, with the thought that the prisons there were more secure than the supposedly impregnable fortress on the barren moor. After 1810, unsuccessful runaways would be returned to the prison and consigned to the 'cachot', or black hole, a tiny and dark cell where the gravest miscreants were held on half rations. (In 1812, Cotgrave intercepted a loaf of bread containing an iron file before it could be delivered to the cachot's desperate inhabitants.) But escape was only one way for prisoners to confound their captors. Cotgrave found himself hunting for daggers and knives which had somehow made their way past his guards and turnkeys, along with numerous other items of contraband. Some forms of smuggling may have perturbed the board more than the agent: preventing the circulation of newspapers, for example, was not Cotgrave's priority. With prisoners killing or injuring each other in knife fights—and some cutting their throats or stabbing themselves to death, in the manner of Admiral Villeneuve—he had more pressing things to worry about.[21]

FORGERY AND GAMBLING WERE AGENT COTGRAVE'S MOST PERsistent headaches, and he was particularly exasperated by the ingenuity with which the French procured equipment for both pursuits. Partly, this was a consequence of processing so many new arrivals at breakneck speed in 1809. It was also a reflection of the skewed reality of a war prison. People could and did bring virtually anything into Dartmoor because they had no idea how long they might be there: libraries of books, clothing and fabric of every description, even a diverse selection of theatrical scenery. Some of these items entered by clandestine means. Others were waved through by Cotgrave and his staff because they, like the prisoners, had a stake in the vitality of Dartmoor's worlds. Forgery was an unfortunate by-product of this permissive attitude, and fake notes exchanged in the market were soon confounding traders and customers as far afield as Plymouth and Exeter (thirty miles to the north). The board's solution—to appoint a new clerk in 1810 with a remit to write his and the prisoner's name on every bank note exchanged in the market—did little to stem the problem.[22]

Cotgrave's other headache was gambling. The flow of cash through the prison sustained countless wagers, and the lax regime on searching prisoners' possessions ensured that the inmates had plenty of things to bet on. In 1812, the board ordered Cotgrave to use 'every means in your power for totally suppressing the whole of the Billiard Tables' which had somehow made their way into the prison. (The board noted that these emerged only after dark, and that the lanterns used to illuminate them could produce 'most alarming consequences'.) Confiscation hardly solved the problem; as Cotgrave already knew, prisoners would gamble on *anything*. A local newspaper reported in 1810 on the 'ingenuity' of Dartmoor's gambling culture. 'Among other attempts to frustrate the intentions of the Governor,' the newspaper wrote, 'was the tying of mice by their tails and betting on their comparative speed.' Gambling was diverting, but it accentuated the prison's inequalities and fuelled new addictions. When an unlucky gambler ran out of cash, he would wager his shirt, his rations, even his blanket. Should officials intervene to supply a desperate prisoner with the essentials he had just gambled away? Or would this perpetuate the cycle that British authorities hoped to break?[23]

The Romans were the prisoners at the bottom of gambling's downward slope: having wagered everything and ended up with nothing, they decided to league together. But they had also been corrupted, in Louis Catel's words, by 'moral and physical tortures which no one would have the strength to withstand'. The Romans got their name from their decision to separate from the other prisoners and live in the 'capitol', the name the French prisoners had given to the space beneath the roof of each prison block. (This area had originally been designated for indoor exercise when the weather was bad.) The Romans, in Catel's telling, had three simple rules for membership: they agreed to sell their hammocks and sleep on the floor; they would go naked at all times within the capitol; and they would pierce their blankets and leave them in a pile by the stairs so that any Roman needing to visit the rest of the prison could wear one outside. Was it true, as Catel insisted, that the naked prisoners were packed so tightly on the floor of the capitol that one of their number gave an order in the middle of the night for the entire cohort to switch sides and resume sleeping? Maybe not, though the letters between Cotgrave and the board confirm both the nakedness of the Romans and their feral mien within and beyond their lair.[24]

Catel guessed that more than two hundred of his compatriots had become Romans by the fall of 1809. In 1813, when the board was minded to deal with them once and for all, more than five hundred Frenchmen were among their ranks. To the other prisoners, they were a curiosity and sometimes a menace: they fought over the rubbish thrown out from the kitchens and cast surly looks at anyone who met their gaze. Towards the end of 1812, an interruption in Dartmoor's bread supply led other prisoners to seize the kitchen scraps which usually went to the Romans. Catel could not easily forget what followed. Agent Cotgrave sent a cart drawn by two horses into the yards to collect the remaining rubbish, and the Romans, 'exasperated by anger and hunger, seized these innocent beasts'. They dragged the animals into their prison block and set upon them: those who had knives tore into the horses, and 'those who had no knives bit their bleeding and still throbbing flesh'. The figure of a Roman 'smeared with blood and eating the living flesh' was carved into Catel's memory. He felt no hate for the Romans, but instead 'real pity' for the damage Dartmoor had done to them.[25]

Other British prisons had similar populations of desperate Frenchmen—at Norman Cross, they were known as *Les Misérables*— but stories of naked and desperate prisoners reinforced the narrative that something had gone badly wrong at Dartmoor. So did the high rate of sickness at the prison during the winter of 1809–1810. Confusion arose in London over a renegade report that more than seven hundred of the prisoners had died in the prison hospital. This proved to be an exaggeration, but Dartmoor's remoteness allowed self-styled philanthropists in London to insist that the prison was a charnel house. The first winter brought typhus, smallpox, and measles: in the six months from October 1809 through March 1810, 384 prisoners died—nearly 7 percent of the total French population at Dartmoor. Among the draft of nearly five hundred prisoners who arrived on the prison's opening day—22 May 1809—the mortality rate was even worse: seventy-nine were dead within a year, around 16 percent of the total. The Transport Board and its defenders offered hasty explanations—perhaps a group of prisoners had brought exotic ailments from the West Indies, or prisoners from warmer climes had struggled to adjust to British conditions? A growing band of critics in London entertained a theory of their own: the British government had built its signature prison in the wrong place and was determined to cover up its mistake.[26]

The most colourful exponent of this theory was Thomas Cochrane, one of the most famous men in Georgian Britain. The son of a Scottish nobleman, Cochrane enlisted in the navy against the objection of his father in 1793. He won a series of outrageously unlikely victories, but his candour and impatience with bureaucracy brought him more admirers outside the navy than within it. After briefly enrolling as a student at the University of Edinburgh during the Peace of Amiens, Cochrane returned to the sea in 1803 and became even more popular with the British public. He also acquired a taste for politics. Despite his noble background, Cochrane found that he shared an interest in exposing hypocrisy and corruption with the London radical William Cobbett. In 1807, Cobbett persuaded Cochrane to stand for Parliament in the constituency of Westminster, and Cochrane held on to this very visible seat for nearly a decade. During that time, he juggled his duties in the House of

Commons with active service in the Royal Navy. Given Cochrane's strong and loudly performed interest in abuses of power, he was the ideal MP to bring Dartmoor to the attention of Parliament.[27]

When Cochrane rose in the House of Commons on 14 June 1811, he explained that he'd received 'many letters' urging him to investigate what was happening at Dartmoor. His navy duties regularly brought him to Plymouth, and that spring he had decided to visit the nearby prison to see if the rumours were true. He had assumed, both as an MP and as a war hero who had 'contributed to place many individuals into this depot', that he would be welcomed with open arms by Cotgrave and his staff. Instead, the agent panicked. Cotgrave asked Cochrane for proof that he was on official business. When Cochrane admitted he had come out of curiosity, Cotgrave directed him towards 'a grating into the outer courtyard' which only heightened Cochrane's curiosity about what was really going on. Forced to rely on his imagination, Cochrane claimed the fog was so bad that you couldn't see the walls from the middle of the prison; that the prisoners got soaked every morning when they went outside to get their breakfast; and that this was a place where even 'Scotchmen refused to live'. Worse, Cochrane noted that the prison's sewers appeared to lead directly to 'a neighboring and elevated estate belonging to the secretary of his Royal Highness the Prince Regent'. Thomas Tyrwhitt wasn't only responsible for subjecting seven and a half thousand Frenchmen to 'perpetual rains and eternal fog'. He was stealing their shit to fertilize his crops.[28]

Unfortunately for the French captives at Dartmoor, Cochrane's reputation for impetuosity and exaggeration preceded him. Other MPs insisted that his innuendoes and insinuations were 'injudicious and careless'. The Transport Board hastily presented the House of Commons with 'several papers relative to the prisoners in Dartmoor Prison' refuting Cochrane's claim that thirty or forty prisoners died each week. Tyrwhitt sheepishly admitted that the sewer led to his land, but he insisted it had been built and maintained 'at his own expense'. Cochrane, who was easily distracted, moved on to other crusades. It was left to the London press to scrutinize the allegations, with a print war breaking out in the summer of 1811 between commentators on either side of the question. Cochrane's claims about the weather and the mortality levels were hashed out by 'Humanitas', 'Veritas', and other pseudonymous pundits who claimed to have visited the prison. 'I leave the public to judge,' wrote one of Cochrane's supporters, 'what must be the consequence of placing a multitude of men in such a situation.'[29]

THE BOARD CONTINUED TO REPORT THAT ALL WAS WELL AT Dartmoor, though officials in London knew that conditions were deteriorating. Andrew Baird, the board's own inspector, visited early in 1812: 'Dr Baird reports that he observed a vast number of the prisoners in a dirty, naked and miserable state,' the board complained to Cotgrave. 'We desire you to explain the circumstances.' Cotgrave did his best to account for the strange fraternity of the Romans, who made an indelible impression on Baird during his visit. But in the spring and summer of 1812 familiar problems seemed to recur at a faster tempo. Men who had been confined to the cachot were somehow receiving blankets and provisions from their compatriots in the rest of the prison. A prisoner had supposedly made his escape 'by climbing over the walls', a feat which the board had thought impossible. Forgery remained an acute problem even after Cotgrave began cycling its practitioners into and out of solitary confinement. One prisoner had stabbed a turnkey; another had brazenly approached a guard offering three pounds in return for his help to escape. As always, the prisoners and Cotgrave's staff fought with local contractors over the terrible quality of the daily bread deliveries.[30]

Bread was an index of the misery within Dartmoor. The board heard about it from multiple sources, including the prisoners themselves (who would occasionally find a way to get letters to London without Cotgrave's scrutiny). The agent was asked to draw up a table—the board loved tables—of the days during the previous quarter when the bread had been deemed 'of inferior quality' and of the days when supplies had been so bad that the prisoners had been given 'biscuit' instead. If prisoners thought the bread in Dartmoor was bad, they really hated the biscuit. Made from flour of the very lowest quality, biscuit was hard, tasteless, and likely to contain unwanted surprises: beans, barley, clay, and worse. One prisoner recalled that 'it would move in our hands alive with worms and weevil.' The storehouse contained a daunting supply of biscuit in case bread deliveries were disrupted, especially during Dartmoor's brutal winters. Its purpose was to keep prisoners alive; beyond that, it was as bleak as everything else there.[31]

Agent Cotgrave and the Transport Board recognized that the most mundane dispute over food could easily escalate into a rebellion against Dartmoor's many injustices. This was why the board asked that loaves be sent by the fastest coach to London, and why so much of its back-and-forth with Cotgrave focused on the idiosyncrasies of flour quality and the supply chain. On a Sunday in the middle of September 1812, over three years after the first prisoners had arrived, Dartmoor finally erupted. The bakery that supplied the prison had burned down the previous week. The prisoners were placed on an allowance of biscuit, which had itself been reduced from the specified ration to ensure that the supply would last until the bakery could be rebuilt. Cotgrave and his staff explained the situation to the French prisoners but found them 'absolutely deaf to remonstrances'. Seven thousand men massed in the yards, shouting at the militia overlooking them on the prison walls and demanding the bread they had been promised.[32]

Cotgrave sent word to the garrison commander at Plymouth that an uprising was imminent. The men of the Cheshire militia, the soldiers on duty at Dartmoor that autumn, were ordered to load their weapons in front of the prisoners. This failed to quell the fury of the French: the prisoners 'bared their breasts to the troops, and seemed regardless of danger'. One report suggested that a prisoner had even attacked a soldier who had come down into the yard, though the soldier had the presence of mind not to fire his weapon. The situation remained tense throughout that Sunday, and Cotgrave and his men feared the inmates would set fire to the prison blocks and attempt a mass escape. When the authorities in Plymouth learned of the danger, they acted decisively: three large artillery pieces were dragged up the winding road to Dartmoor by fifteen horses. They were placed in the market square, where they could be seen by the prisoners. 'This had the desired effect,' noted one newspaper, 'and order was restored.'[33]

In the view of the London papers reporting on the abortive uprising, the prisoners had been shockingly ungrateful. 'It is to be noticed,' wrote one, 'that the allowance of bread these men have so indignantly spurned, is precisely the same as that which is served out to our own sailors and marines.' But the troops fighting Britain's wars were, after everything, free men. By contrast, some of the prisoners who tore off their shirts and goaded the sentries at Dartmoor had been in British custody for nearly a decade. They had no idea when they would retrieve their liberty. While newspapers and politicians in London sparred over Dartmoor's mortality rates or annual rainfall, the French prisoners endured the agonizing experience of relentless, endless captivity. Among the Romans, this pushed people from diverse backgrounds into a brotherhood of nihilism and despair. Cotgrave and the Transport Board knew that some portion of that despair was shared by every prisoner. If anyone could become a Roman, and if everyone could see why the Romans had fallen into their terrible state, Dartmoor could never be a humane or liberal undertaking. Nor would it ever be secure.[34]

PART II

KING DICK AT BORDEAUX

EVEN THE CREW OF THE *REQUIN* MAY NOT HAVE BEEN SURE IF their ship was French or American. What they could agree upon was that they were in real trouble. They had run aground in March 1814 where the Dordogne and Garonne Rivers meet, about twenty miles north of Bordeaux and fifty miles upriver from the Atlantic Ocean. Usually this stretch of water was safe: if an American or French ship made it past the Royal Navy blockade on the coast, it had done the hard part and could complete its journey to the wealthy port of Bordeaux without further incident. But as winter turned to spring, the entire region was in chaos: after more than a decade of uninterrupted fighting, Napoleonic France was on the verge of defeat. An allied army of British, Spanish, and Portuguese troops was making its way northward from the Pyrenees, and Napoleon's commanders had concentrated their limited resources more than a hundred miles away in defence of Toulouse. Officials in Bordeaux were left to defend the city with volunteers or capitulate to the allied troops. Either way, it was clear to the crew of the *Requin* that they needed to be somewhere else.[1]

Privateering ships were commercial vessels repurposed in wartime as a kind of outsourced navy: the owner of a ship would obtain a license from his government to engage in privateering activity and would then take to the ocean in search of merchant ships and cargoes belonging to hostile powers. The *Requin* was almost certainly a French privateer, but among its crew of around forty sailors there were at least a dozen Americans. This wasn't especially surprising. Since June 1812, when the US Congress had declared war on Britain, French and American sailors had shared a common enemy. But with Napoleon's forces in retreat, and the alarming possibility that Bordeaux might soon surrender to the British, loyalties and alliances were suddenly under threat. What would happen to the American sailors if Bordeaux fell?[2]

Initially, at least, the captain and crew of the *Requin* stuck together. They had recently seized an English ship as a prize vessel, and they began to offload cargo and fittings to that ship in the hope of making the *Requin* light enough to float off its sandbar. They succeeded just in time to slip away from an approaching French gunboat, which was about to demand that the *Requin* surrender its twenty-two guns to help in the defence of the region from allied troops. By now, the *Requin* had decided it was safer to fly American than French colours: this might buy the crew time and help them avoid the squabbles among French factions over whether to fight on or surrender. The captain steered the ship further into the interior, up the River Garonne towards Bordeaux. An American privateer would almost certainly have gone the other way, dashing for the Atlantic and taking its chances with the Royal Navy blockade just off the coast. But the *Requin* eventually laid up on the riverbank just north of the city, which had by now surrendered to the allies without resistance. The *Requin* was still flying the Stars and Stripes but it was about to lose most of its crew.[3]

What happened next was a matter of dispute for years to follow. A junior British officer named James Ogilvie paid a group of French sailors to accompany him on a sweep of the Garonne River for hostile ships. Ogilvie came upon the *Requin*, noticed its American colours, and sent a messenger to demand that the captain surrender. No response was received. As Ogilvie considered his options, he spotted a man jumping from the side of the *Requin* into a rowing boat. The zealous British officer ordered his French associates to intercept the runaway, and before long Ogilvie was holding the ship's armorer at gunpoint. This man, who was apparently French, confessed that much of the crew had already departed—including the captain, which explained why Ogilvie's ultimatum had gone unanswered. Determined to seize the American prize, Ogilvie waited until nightfall, then stormed the *Requin* himself. He met no resistance. Ogilvie sweated briefly when the ship's mate was slow to come up from belowdecks, but this was because the cornered sailor was determined to finish his dinner. A small detachment of British soldiers had also arrived, and they helped Ogilvie to take the *Requin*'s thirteen remaining crew into custody. One was a Swede, the other twelve were Americans, and five were Black. Nearly a foot taller than the rest was Richard Crafus of Vienna, Maryland.[4]

The American complement on the *Requin* was drawn from half a dozen states, from South Carolina to Massachusetts. One of Dick's crewmates was the extraordinary Scipio Bartlett, a sixty-four-year-old Black man from Boston, who had been born into slavery in Massachusetts but had then become one of the first African Americans to enlist in the cause of the United States during the Revolutionary War. Bartlett was at Valley Forge during the darkest months of the Revolution for the Patriot cause; he also fought in the Battle of Saratoga, which turned the war decisively in favour of the new United States. In his pension application to the federal government, Bartlett declared that he 'was emancipated at the commencement of the Revolutionary War and was a free man during my whole term of service'. His pension application was denied, which might explain why a man of his advanced age was still at sea nearly forty years after taking arms in service of his country. It may also indicate that Bartlett had an elastic conception of allegiance, though in truth American seamen were used to sailing under the flags of other nations. Being aboard a French privateer facing the common enemy of Britain made things relatively straightforward, until the *Requin* ran aground and was drawn into the endgame of the Napoleonic Wars.[5]

The paper trail that eventually enveloped the *Requin* was silent on the fate of the French crew members and offered different estimates for how many had been aboard in the first place. (James Ogilvie claimed it was around fifty.) Ogilvie testified that the missing Frenchmen had 'gone on shore not an hour before the capture'. Another witness claimed that part of the *Requin*'s crew had made away in the smaller prize vessel which had accompanied the ship to the River Garonne. The most likely explanation is that the French crew members simply wandered ashore when they learned that Bordeaux had surrendered. It would be easier for them to take refuge in the city than explain to British officers what they were doing on a ship flying the Stars and Stripes. This would mean abandoning the *Requin* and their American crew mates, but in the middle of a war, self-preservation was the most pressing consideration.[6]

For James Ogilvie, what began as an easy catch would become an enduring obsession. After delivering the Americans into British custody, he attended to his duties while the allied armies consolidated their control over the region. Then, at the news of Napoleon's surrender, he went back to the *Requin* with the intention of sailing it to Britain and claiming his prize money. Ogilvie was adamant that the ship belonged to him, and he polished the narrative of his daring raid on its diminished complement. Having hired forty French crew and a river pilot, he sailed a few miles down the river before a boatload of gendarmes halted his progress. The marine officials at Bordeaux had sent word that the ship did not belong to Ogilvie, and the Briton was ordered to surrender the vessel. Had the ship's French owners surfaced just in time to deny Ogilvie his prize? The young officer reluctantly gave up the *Requin*, but vowed to return.[7]

In 1815, with the Anglo-French wars finally over, Ogilvie spent six fruitless months trying to persuade French officials that the ship belonged to him. His efforts became so aggressive that the French minister in London registered an official complaint. The man who had led the allied campaign in southwestern France, Arthur Wellesley, had now been made Duke of Wellington in recognition of his heroics. As the ultimate authority in the region during the *Requin*'s capture, Wellington was drawn into the dispute. Any vessels in the vicinity of Bordeaux were the property of the British government, he maintained, not of any individual officers. Ogilvie bristled at this: he doubled down on his claim that the *Requin* was an American ship, and he noted that twenty-six other US vessels had successfully slipped away from the Garonne during the surrender of Bordeaux. It was Ogilvie's courage which had prevented the *Requin* from following suit, or so he claimed. That the ship had actually moved closer to Bordeaux after getting free of the sandbank and that the majority of its crew (including its captain) had vanished were inconvenient reminders that the case was more complicated. Throughout the 1820s, Ogilvie made repeated demands for remuneration. He even persuaded MPs to convene a debate on the matter in the House of Commons in 1823. After Ogilvie's supporters regaled the House with a long account of his case, the Chancellor of the Exchequer wearily rose to acknowledge Ogilvie's 'gallantry' but to remind MPs that the twelve thousand allied troops stationed near Bordeaux probably had something to do with the ship's surrender. Ogilvie received a trickle of money paid to Wellington's officers for 'bounty' captured during the campaign, but the *Requin* slipped through his fingers.[8]

For Richard Crafus, Scipio Bartlett, and the other ten Americans—plus the lone Swedish sailor who remained on the *Requin* when the French crew dispersed—these questions of ownership were irrelevant. They had signed up on a French privateer but had found themselves overhauled by events. The legend of King Dick would later insist that Richard Crafus had been forced to serve on a Royal Navy warship until the start of the War of 1812 and that he had bravely offered himself up as a prisoner of conscience by refusing to fight against the United States. In fact, he had been fighting for Napoleon, albeit against the same enemy he would have faced had he sailed out of Boston or New York. Despite his imposing height, there is nothing in the documentary record of the *Requin*'s capture to suggest that Dick stood out in any way, and the capture itself was ignominious. The Americans on the *Requin* realised that the game was up and submitted to Ogilvie without a fight. They were carried away to Britain, where they would all end up in Dartmoor. Only there would Dick assume his full stature.

5.

THE UNHALLOWED PURSUIT

GEORGE LITTLE HAD SAILED THE *DROMO* TO CHINA AS A green hand and had made (and lost) a fortune plying the coastal trade between Rio and Buenos Aires. When he got home to his family in Massachusetts just after the outbreak of the War of 1812, he received a stern talking-to: 'Every persuasion was now used to induce me to change my vocation, backed by the strong reasoning that the war would destroy commerce, and that no alternative would be left for seamen but the unhallowed pursuit of privateering.' Little could see their point, and he went to meet a distant kinsman in Norfolk, Virginia, who had agreed to establish Little as a merchant rather than a sailor. But the start-up funds failed to materialise and Little felt his hopes were 'blasted'. Away from the chiding of his sister and father, he idly watched the Norfolk locals put up bunting to mark the outbreak of the war. Soon the old itch returned. The sea, after all, was his 'favorite element'. There was no work to be found on shore, and plenty of vessels fitting out. But was he ready to become a privateersman?[1]

'I must confess, in my cooler moments, that I had some qualms,' Little wrote. Privateering brought the prospect of 'making a fortune' but also of 'getting my head knocked off'. In the end, his curiosity got the better of him. He signed on to the *George Washington*, a 'beautiful schooner' with three large guns, as first lieutenant. The officers were knowledgeable and energetic, but the rest of the crew 'were a motley set indeed, composed of all nations; they appeared to have been scraped together from the lowest dens of wretchedness and vice'. It wasn't long before the realities of Little's new life were made clear to him. The *Washington* was set upon by a British frigate within hours of leaving Norfolk, though Samuel Sisson, the ship's 'rough, uncouth' captain, expertly sailed them to safety. They were headed for Cartagena, a port on the Caribbean coast of what's now Colombia that had recently declared its independence from Spain. The Spanish knew its strategic importance to their crumbling empire, and in 1815 they would muster enough men and ships to recapture the port. In 1812, though, it was a magnet for merchants and privateers alike.[2]

Captain Sisson knew that the seas between Cartagena and the West Indies would be filled with British merchant ships, which had established a strong presence in the Latin America trade while Jefferson's embargo had kept American vessels in their ports. The *Washington*'s first prize was an English brig out of Jamaica laden with sugar and fruit. Captain Sisson approached from the stern; when he gave the word, his men jumped to the other vessel 'like so many locusts'. The *Washington*'s superior numbers made the outcome certain, but the battle was unexpectedly gruesome. As the Americans jumped aboard, the brig's crew raised 'boarding pikes' which impaled several of the invaders. 'This affair very much disgusted me with privateering,' Little recalled. Once more he doubted his place among 'a band of ruthless desperadoes—for such I must call our crew—robbing and plundering a few defenseless beings'. He resolved to leave the ship as soon as possible. 'No conscientious man could be engaged in privateering,' he concluded, 'and certainly there was no honor to be gained by it.'[3]

THE WAR OF 1812 FORMALIZED A MUCH LONGER STRUGGLE BEtween Britain and the United States, one which had never really ended with the Patriot victory in 1783. One front involved the fight between the United States and Native Americans south of the Great Lakes, where the British had allied with an Indigenous uprising led by the Shawnee brothers Tecumseh and Tenskwatawa. A second front involved the invasion of Canada by US troops; 'a mere matter of marching', according to Thomas Jefferson, though as usual the Canadians were stubbornly resistant to American overtures. The third front was the battle at sea—and in the Great Lakes—pitting the Royal Navy against the scrappy forces of the American republic.

Congress had created a permanent US Navy in 1794, but its size and remit had become yet another source of contention between Federalists such as John Adams and Alexander Hamilton, and Republicans such as Thomas Jefferson and James Madison. Adams had recommended a modest force of, say, twenty ships of the line and forty frigates. Ships of the line were the most feared vessels of the age: the largest in the British fleet carried more than a hundred and twenty guns and a crew of nearly a thousand men. Adams knew that a US Navy featuring twenty of these behemoths would still be no match for the Royal Navy, but it might be enough to break up a blockade or disrupt the supply lines of another British invasion. Jefferson and Madison adamantly opposed the idea, and during their combined sixteen years in the White House, they pointed the nation towards a very different method of waging war at sea.[4]

The 'antinavalists', as John Adams dubbed the Jeffersonians, grounded their aversion to an expanded US Navy on principle and pragmatism. Unlike Alexander Hamilton, who had lobbied aggressively for increasing the army during the Adams presidency, Jefferson and Madison believed that a large military would inevitably corrode American liberties. A small permanent class of soldiers and sailors might be necessary, along with an officer corps to direct them—it was, after all, Thomas Jefferson who founded West Point in 1802. But Jefferson and Madison preferred to draft civilians when circumstances required their service; the US military would comprise citizen soldiers (and sailors) who could return to civilian life as soon as peace returned. On land, this theory could be mapped onto national loyalty with some confidence: ordinary citizens who did militia service had skin in the game in terms of expanding or defending the nation. Around 90 percent of the soldiers who fought in the War of 1812 were drawn from state militias. But at sea, sailors of many nations worked under the Stars and Stripes. Could the United States outsource the maritime fighting of the War of 1812 to private vessels crewed in part by foreigners or itinerants? Absolutely, thought Jefferson. It would be 'folly' to fund a large navy and go head-to-head with the capital ships of Britain. Instead, the United States government should 'leave the war on the ocean to our privateers', which would 'immediately swarm in every sea and do more injury to British commerce than the regular fleets of all Europe would do'. Congress would license private vessels to hunt for British ships; any captured prizes and cargoes could be sold in American ports, with the owners (and the officers and crew) receiving a share of the proceeds. The profit motive meant that neither the morals nor loyalties of these sailors mattered much: privateers and their crews 'will cheat us enormously', Jefferson acknowledged, but 'no matter, they will make [British] merchants feel, and squeal, and cry out for peace.'[5]

During the first six months of the war, the 'antinavalists' were triumphantly vindicated. The tiny US Navy acquitted itself with distinction on the open ocean and the Great Lakes, but the huge privateer fleet seized around 450 British merchant ships—a number so large that the Royal Navy was forced to divert some of its vessels from the blockade of France to escort duty in the Atlantic. This made privateering even more dangerous, as American captains and crews pushed closer to the islands of the British Caribbean and even into the coastal waters of the British Isles in the hopes of catching vessels unaware. Britain and France each had more than a hundred ships of the line and hundreds of other warships; the US Navy comprised just a handful of frigates and a few dozen smaller vessels. Privateering had made the difference: 'In point of real injury and depredation on the enemy,' Jefferson gleefully observed, 'our priva-teers without question have been most effectual.' For all of Jeffer-son's plaudits, privateersmen were held to be mercenaries, willing contractors in the transfer of danger and opportunity from the gov-ernment to the individual. There would be no preferential treat-ment for them if captured. What was missing in this calculus of risk and advantage was any serious consideration of whether America's sailors—becalmed by the commercial disruption of the conflict—had much choice over going to war.[6]

DESPITE HIS PROMISE TO GIVE UP PRIVATEERING, GEORGE LITTLE remained with the *Washington* after it made port at Cartagena. The 'sordid gain' of prize money, as he called it, was just too great. It was only after a disastrous incident in which he was briefly held hostage by Wayúu Indians on the Colombian coast that he informed Cap-tain Sisson he wanted out. He and another officer were paid their prize money—nearly $2,000—and returned to the United States. Although Little thought about quitting the sea, within months he had joined the crew of a letter of marque bound for France. Letters of marque were merchant vessels intending to trade rather than to prey on enemy ships, but they had a license to attack British vessels if the captain thought it desirable or necessary. As Little soon discov-ered, the distinction between privateers and letters of marque didn't count for much. His vessel safely crossed the Atlantic and began its dash past the British blockade into the French port of Bordeaux. Then, with harrowing abruptness, the wind fell away. Before the Royal Navy could intercept Little's ship, a British privateer drifted into view and claimed its prize.[7]

Privateering was a safer line of work for the owners and captains of British merchant vessels, given the ubiquity of the Royal Navy. But sometimes the tables could be turned. As Little and his crew mates were sailed up the French Atlantic coast towards the war pris-ons of southern England, the eighteen-gun American privateer *Paul Jones* raced into view and captured the smaller British ship. Within half an hour, George Little was sailing under the Stars and Stripes again—and on another privateer. In his memoirs, Little claimed that he had spent the next month trying to quit the *Paul Jones* and its colourful crew: 'The English language is too poor adequately to do them justice,' he wrote. 'Imagine to yourself, reader, a company of eighty men, selected from the very elite and respectable portion of the lowest sinks located in the Five Points and other places of like celebrity in New York.' To be cooped up on a ship with this crowd 'could not be an enviable situation to a man of taste', or so Little claimed. In fact, British prison records show that Little spent the next six months on the *Paul Jones*; the ship took most of its prizes after Little had joined its crew. A careful reader of his memoir might detect overcompensation in his description of why he stayed on the *Paul Jones*. There was, he claimed, only 'a short time for reflection' when aboard a vessel at sea. The 'hurry-scurry, uproar and excitement on board of a privateer' was distracting and infectious, and 'although my better judgement taught me to despise this mode of warfare . . . yet I soon became in some degree reconciled to it.'[8]

HMS *Leonidas* captures US privateer *Paul Jones*
Courtesy of the Naval History and Heritage Command/National Archives

The adventures of the *Paul Jones* ended in May 1813, soon after the ship had seized its seventeenth prize. Its captain had appointed a prize crew—a small group of sailors who would steer the captured vessel back to the United States to be sold—but as the two ships parted ways, HMS *Leonidas*, a Royal Navy frigate, appeared on the horizon. The captain of the *Paul Jones* knew the prize would fetch a lot of money and that his own ship had a better chance of outrunning the frigate, so he sailed towards the *Leonidas* hoping to buy time for the prize to escape. It was the wrong choice. The frigate opened 'a most murderous fire', and once again Little watched crew mates die in front of him. The sails of the *Paul Jones* were shot away, along with the mechanism allowing the ship to raise its flags. The Americans couldn't show that they had surrendered, which encouraged the *Leonidas* to empty more and more shot into the crippled privateer. When the battle was done, the *Paul Jones* had been cut in half. To make things worse, the *Leonidas* also caught up with the escaping prize crew—whose master had apparently taken to the bottle—and everything was lost. Little, the seasoned privateersman who hated privateering, was again a British prisoner. Within a few days he was on a hulk in Plymouth; Dartmoor would be his final destination.[9]

ANOTHER PRIVATEERSMAN WHO ENDED UP IN DARTMOOR WAS Benjamin Frederick Browne, who was born to a family of limited means in Salem, Massachusetts, in 1794. Apprenticed to the town's pharmacist, Browne completed his training in 1812 but struggled to find a job on shore. He shipped out instead as a surgeon's assistant aboard the *Alfred*, a privateer of sixteen guns and 130 men. Browne was not a natural sailor. During four months at sea, he dwelt on the prizes that had gotten away and struggled with the stress of the job. Whenever another vessel came into view, Browne carefully laid out the surgeon's instruments—'rolls of bandages and sticking plasters, together with the tourniquet and amputating instruments'—and expected the worst. Miraculously, his shipmates survived their voyage without a single serious injury.[10]

When he found himself back on the wharf at Salem in January 1813, Browne resolved to look again for a job on shore and to make the most of his deliverance. But the New England economy was even worse off in the first months of 1813 than it had been a year earlier. The British had tightened their blockade of the American coast, and Browne's search for alternative work was fruitless. In April, he returned to the wharves and signed up for the *Frolic*, an ugly vessel captained by the charismatic John Odiorne. Like Browne, the captain was an uncommonly short man but smart and casually authoritative. As a schoolboy, Browne's slight stature had brought him protection and even affection from his teachers, whom he'd happily repaid with hard work. He struck the same bargain with his new master, and Odiorne put Browne in charge of the *Frolic*'s small complement of marines. Browne was grateful for the affirmation, though privately doubted he was worthy of the captain's trust.[11]

Unlike George Little, Browne freely confessed to enjoying the company of his fellow privateersmen. The sailing master was calm and meticulous in his stewardship of the rigging, but swore loudly and in all directions. During a still moment, he would grip Browne's arm and profess his belief in 'ghosts and goblins, and in haunted houses and haunted ships'. The surgeon was warm and generous and could deadpan jokes with a face 'as grave as a Methodist parson's'. He was always seasick and in the slightest bad weather could be found curled up 'wishing himself at home again'. Browne marvelled at the way Captain Odiorne led the crew. 'I have seen it said somewhere,' he wrote, 'that every man has two characters: his Sunday character, in which he dresses himself up and appears before the world, and his week-day character, in which he shows himself to those to whose praise or censure he is indifferent.' The captain offered each of these faces to the crew at precisely the right moment: he could be 'prompt to reprove and severe to punish', especially when the ship was in danger; or he could relax with his crew mates over a drink, 'ringing his jocund laugh till the very deck resounded with it'.[12]

The *Frolic* tacked north, to the British fishing grounds of Newfoundland. Odiorne and his men captured more than a dozen British ships, though none was worth much. Taking scores of prisoners but little cargo, Odiorne scuttled the ships and decided to sail the *Frolic* back to New England and to try again in the Caribbean. As the *Frolic* took on supplies in Portsmouth, New Hampshire, Benjamin Browne had another chance to quit the privateering life. But since he had made almost nothing from his first two voyages and the economy of New England was still moribund, he resolved to follow Captain Odiorne on his next adventure. When the *Frolic* reached the Caribbean Sea, a Spanish ship appeared on the horizon and Odiorne set off in pursuit. The captain soon realised he was pursuing HMS *Heron*, a British warship which had been flying false colours to lure American privateers into range of its guns. Speed was not one of the *Frolic*'s virtues, and Browne ordered his crew mates to throw overboard everything that wasn't nailed down: the smaller deck guns, rifles, provisions, water casks, the lunch that the sailors hadn't had time to eat, and then the copper pans in which it had been cooking. (One of the sailors solemnly ditched the cook's bellows, insisting that 'every little helped'.) When it became clear that the *Heron* was still going to catch them—an epiphany sounded by the cannons in the British ship's bow—Browne knew that Captain Odiorne would surrender: it would be 'utter madness for us to think of contending with her'. Instead, the man who had become Browne's idol turned the *Frolic* around and trained everything it had on the *Heron*.[13]

With thirty-two-pound shot and bullets screaming through the air, Browne could finally see the virtue of being short. Odiorne ordered most of the men to take refuge in the hold, but Browne remained on deck viewing his captain's sangfroid at close quarters: 'He himself kept bustling about, watching chances, giving orders, and cracking his jokes, as coolly as if he was on a mere pleasure excursion.' It was only when the British were close enough to fire pistols rather than muskets that Odiorne climbed the rigging to signal surrender. The firing continued; it was now night, and the British couldn't see the flags. Odiorne started shouting across the waves at his British counterpart and the guns eventually stopped. The Americans gathered their possessions and were rowed towards the *Heron* under British guard. In this tiny boat on the dark ocean, Browne assessed his prospects. He was alive and unscathed, but his future had never been more uncertain. Would the British imprison him in the Caribbean? Take him to Canada? Swap him for one of their own in American custody? His reverie was interrupted by the sea moving suddenly upwards and capsizing the rowing boat. The British sailors aboard the *Heron* rushed to rescue him and the other prisoners. Browne survived, as he usually did, but his bag slipped from sight. He was hauled onto the British warship, cold and miserable. 'When I stood upon the *Heron*'s deck,' he later wrote, 'the checked shirt and duck trousers which I stood in constituted my whole earthly possessions.' Benjamin F. Browne's brief career as a privateer was over. For the next eighteen months, he, too, would be a prisoner of war.[14]

AROUND 70 PERCENT OF THE AMERICANS WHO WOULD EVENTU-ally be imprisoned at Dartmoor were captured on privateers or letters of marque. The prospects of their speedy release were not good. As in its wars with France, Britain quickly established a huge surplus of prisoners, which limited the number of exchanges it would agree to with the US government. Regardless of when they had been captured, privateersmen were placed on the release list behind captives from the US Navy and Army and the various state militias. Assuming an exchange could be negotiated, uniformed personnel always went home first. Around 10 percent of Dartmoor's American inmates were from US Navy ships, and privateersmen watched with envy as they were fast-tracked for release. The taint of privateering brought non-naval sailors a more casual and quotidian form of opprobrium from the British authorities, and so American followers of the 'unhallowed pursuit' had to acclimate themselves both to a long captivity and the contempt of their jailers.[15]

As Britain expanded its empire in the eighteenth and early nineteenth centuries, it built a global prison complex which easily swallowed American sailors during the War of 1812. Virtually everyone who ended up at Dartmoor had already travelled through Britain's sprawling network of detention facilities. Frank Palmer of Stonington, Connecticut, got to know the North American wing of the prison complex very well. In December 1813, having just turned twenty, he travelled to Newport, Rhode Island, with a couple of friends to sign up for the privateer *Rolla*. When he saw the ship with his own eyes, he had second thoughts. 'Not much pleased with her,' he wrote in his journal. 'Had I not have gone so far, I believe I should return home, as I dislike the privateer very much.' He set sail on the morning of December 10, expecting to punch through the British blockade and begin his adventures on the open ocean. Instead, he was captured by HMS *Loire*, a British frigate, and thrust into the hold with dozens of other prisoners. 'Negroes and sailors, fiddlers and taylors, three deep in the hole,' he wrote in his journal. 'O god, what reflections this sad night!' Palmer's career as a privateer had lasted less than twenty-four hours; his tenure as a prisoner would last for 545 days, and eventually take him to Dartmoor.[16]

Palmer's account of his captivity was recorded contemporaneously in a journal rather than written up for publication. As a result, it has a rawness and despair which makes it alternately affecting and monotonous. The crew of the *Rolla* were first taken to a prison hulk in Bermuda. Palmer found a quiet corner and wrote furtively about his compatriots' vices. The other American prisoners refused to attend the church service on deck on Sundays because they preferred 'cards, gambling &c.' to prayers. The heat, confinement, and boredom were bad, but the open-endedness of Palmer's captivity was his greatest torment. If the Americans were still in the hulks when summer arrived, Palmer predicted that they would only make it home in a 'cargo of coffins'. But who knew if an exchange might happen within days, months, or even years? Trapped between hope and dread, Palmer transcribed the routines which shaped the prisoners' lives: washing the decks twice a week, gambling, more gambling. Occasionally, his desperation broke through the surface: 'We are out of money, out of coffee, and out of credit, alas!' he wrote in March 1814.[17]

Sickness and death were the prisoners' constant companions. On 21 March, Palmer recorded that 'one of our crew had departed this life after a lingering illness'—an 'honest, faithful old Negro' named James Boone. Though Boone was nearly twice Palmer's age, the men had clearly formed a bond during their four months in captivity. Palmer imagined the epitaph he would carve on Boone's headstone:

> Underneath this holy Stone—
> Lies the Body of Jim Boone—
> Death has now called him home
> To a place where he'll have room.
> For room there was none here for him
> And all I hope he's clear from sin.

Palmer wasn't much of a poet and his racial views were muddled. Elsewhere in his journal he bemoaned the indignity of being crammed into a space with 'half a dozen stinking negroes'. At Dartmoor, he would be fascinated by Black preachers and entertainers but also used his journal to interrogate their hold on his imagination. In Bermuda, though, the death of James Boone offered him another opportunity to indulge his gloom.[18]

In April 1814, Palmer and his crew mates were told to gather their belongings. Their excitement at the prospect of release collapsed, though, when they learned that they were being transferred to the Canadian outpost of the prison complex. In 1803, the Transport Board had established a prison at Melville Island near Halifax to detain sailors captured on French privateers in the western Atlantic. During the War of 1812, Melville Island became the principal destination for US soldiers and sailors captured in the Great Lakes region, as well as privateers like Palmer; by 1815, more than eight thousand Americans had been imprisoned there.[19]

Palmer's Canadian routines quickly became as dreary as the ones he'd chronicled at Bermuda. Each day began with the turnkey unlocking the doors. Everyone would be ordered to roll up their hammocks and take them outside. 'The piss tub being emptied we open the windows and let in some fresh air,' Palmer noted. There was a rush to brew coffee, then 'mostly gambling'. Palmer was by now calloused to the moral failings of his fellow prisoners but remained vulnerable to their worst trick: the circulation of hopeful rumours. Most prisoners, he wrote, 'pass their time in collecting, making, and spreading all the news possible'. In his journal, he found a shorthand for recording this—'//Hoax//'—but he couldn't always resist the lure of optimism: perhaps an exchange was really imminent, and he might finally get back to Connecticut. The letdown was perpetually brutal. 'I almost seem to wish my dissolution to come,' he wrote in June 1814. 'Day after day passes slowly on . . . and nothing like Liberty appears.' Palmer found it especially hard to process the fact that American soldiers captured on the battlefield in Canada— like US Navy personnel captured at sea—jumped to the front of the line for exchange. Hundreds of these men arrived at Melville Island after he did, and he watched all of them leave while he languished in despair. 'For us poor Privateersmen,' he wrote that summer, 'NO EXCHANGE.'[20]

BENJAMIN BROWNE FARED BETTER IN BRITISH CAPTIVITY, AT least to begin with. The *Frolic*'s crew was put ashore at Bridgetown in Barbados, where Browne 'gazed with wonder and delight' at the bay. 'Everything I saw wore an air of novelty,' he later recalled, 'which not even the disastrous situation in which I was placed, and the gloomy anticipations of a long imprisonment, could repress.'

On the march to Bridgetown's jail, Browne was suddenly aware of being—for the first time in his life—in a town that was mostly Black. He had known African Americans growing up in Salem, Massachusetts, but they were a tiny minority in his hometown. Here, even on the walk from the wharf to the jail, he felt the gaze of 'a large number of negroes, of every age, of both sexes, and of every variety of shade.' When they reached Bridgetown's prison, the *Frolic*'s thirty-seven crew members were placed alongside local criminals, Barbadians awaiting trial, hundreds of French prisoners, and a few other Americans. The prison was already crowded, and the new arrivals made things worse for everyone.[21]

But Browne was in luck. Scanning the crew list of the *Frolic*, the local agent of the Transport Board determined (incorrectly) that Browne must be eligible for parole. In the War of 1812, parole functioned as a more privileged form of captivity. Prisoners remained in British custody but were permitted to live among local civilians with milder restrictions—a nighttime curfew, usually, and a pledge not to leave the town or village to which they had been confined. The board was generous in granting parole to even lower-ranking officers on naval vessels but characteristically contemptuous of privateersmen: only a captain and perhaps one or two senior crew members would be spared the horrors of prison. Browne, a very lowly officer on the *Frolic*, couldn't believe his good fortune. He was released from the jail and told to remain in Bridgetown until an exchange could be agreed.[22]

Browne spent the next five months exploring a society that was totally alien to him. The British parole official charged with keeping him in Bridgetown was 'not very rigid in his espionage' and Browne became increasingly bold in his sallies. Soon he was touring the entire island and spending much of his time in the company of free Black people. Browne was quick to consider their role alongside the position of African Americans at home. They enjoyed 'one privilege of citizenship, which the same class of men do not have in the United States': they were recruited into the militia, and in fact formed 'the most effective part of it'. Browne was fascinated that many of these free people of colour held their own slaves but wary of the claims of local whites that free Blacks were the island's most vicious enslavers. 'All the whites talked of the blacks as an inferior race of men,' Browne noted; but 'intellectually, I think, they were very much on an equality.'[23]

Since Browne didn't write up these reflections until the 1840s, it's hard to shake the feeling that he was mapping the politics of the American antislavery debate onto this portion of his memoir—with the island's white planter class standing in for the enslavers of the American South. 'The notion that no others but negroes can labor under a tropical sun . . . I believe to be a false one, propagated to excuse the demoralizing system of slavery,' Browne wrote. His observations of plantation life on Barbados persuaded him that an 'American farmer' (it wasn't clear if he meant a white farmer) could do as much in two hours as an enslaved person could do in a day. White Barbadians were indolent and deluded; 'even their conversation was slow and drawling.' While Browne maintained a casual aversion to romantic contact across the colour line, his verdict on Black ability was conveyed with an anthropological authority: what 'the negro . . . might become under proper culture, with a restoration to his right of freedom, has never been tested'. The 'friends of humanity'—among whose number Browne surely counted himself—would need to 'forward the work of experiment' and prove to the world that all men were created equal. When he finally got to Dartmoor, Browne would find an ideal testing ground for this experiment.[24]

ON THE OTHER SIDE OF THE WORLD, FORT WILLIAM, KOLKATA, formed the eastern fringe of the prison complex. It had been the site of the most famous prison in the world, at least before Dartmoor: the 'Black Hole of Calcutta', a place that became a byword for cruel confinement. In 1756, an Indian ruler named Siraj ud-Daulah led an uprising against the British forces which occupied the city. On securing the fort, Siraj supposedly confined 146 British troops in a tiny cell measuring fourteen by eighteen feet; the morning after they had been crushed into the 'black hole', the door was opened and 123 of them were dead. The story became a totemic example of Indian savagery and a rallying cry for the civilizing decencies of the British Empire. It was, however, a wild exaggeration. Only 40 men had been confined; around 8 had died. The myth lingered because it was useful to the British project in India, and it reached American audiences too. One of the first published accounts of Americans at Dartmoor angrily complained that the 'horrors of the Black Hole of Calcutta' had been remembered only 'because *Englishmen* suffered and perished in it'. There were 'more than a thousand black holes' in the British prison complex, and Dartmoor was the worst.[25]

The Americans held in Fort William during the War of 1812 were not actually in the original Black Hole, since the entire fort had been rebuilt by the British after 1756. This fact was conveniently overlooked by American newspapers when they noted the extraordinary feats of Captain John Trowbridge, a man so dangerous that he simply had to be held in an iconic prison. Trowbridge was born in New Haven in 1780. In 1810, his merchant vessel *Thomas* was captured by a British naval squadron in the Indian Ocean near Mauritius. Although the United States was not yet at war with Britain, the captors of the *Thomas* declared that it was either a French vessel or that it had been trading with France, both of which made it fair game for the Royal Navy. Trowbridge and his men were sent below, and a British prize crew was ordered to sail the prisoners (and the *Thomas*) to the British outpost of Cape Town—site of yet another detention facility which would welcome hundreds of Americans during the War of 1812.[26]

During the long journey to the cape, Trowbridge persuaded the prize crew—some of whom were South Asian sailors, known as Lascars—to join him in taking back his ship. Then, when he'd taken command of the *Thomas* once more, a French frigate appeared. The French captain assumed that Trowbridge's ship was British and forced the *Thomas* to Mauritius. To make things even more chaotic, Trowbridge and his French captors arrived at Mauritius in December 1810 at precisely the moment that the Royal Navy was attempting to seize the island. In the confusion, Trowbridge somehow managed to sell his ship and cargo and take passage on another vessel to the Dutch colony of Batavia. According to a newspaper report of his exploits, he then spent 'a year or two' in Southeast Asia, punctuated by a 'most daring enterprise' to recover $250,000 of coins from a sunken galleon 'by aid of divers'. But as he was sailing his plunder back to the United States in March 1814, he was captured once again by the British, who took him to Java and then to Fort William in Kolkata. He would remain there until the summer of 1814, when he was summoned to Dartmoor, along with the rest of the American prisoner population scattered around the world.[27]

Lewis P. Clover, who was also held at Kolkata, took a more prosaic route to captivity. Born in New Jersey in 1790, Clover developed a love of adventure stories which led him inexorably to the sea. At the start of the War of 1812, he signed up for the *Union*, a privateer bound for the Indian Ocean and its lucrative 'Indiamen'—tall, richly laden merchant ships which brought tea and spices from South Asia to Britain. It was dangerous but exhilarating work: the Royal Navy didn't have sufficient resources to escort every Indiaman, but there were plenty of British warships in the sea lanes. Then there was the challenge of how to cash out your winnings. Sailing an Indiaman back to the United States would swell the profits of the voyage, but it would also deplete the *Union* of a portion of its crew. The more successful the cruise, the greater the number of prizes, the more men were required to sail them back to American waters, and the more short-handed the *Union* would become. This was a delicate balancing act, and the *Union* finally overreached. In January 1814, Clover and the rest of the crew were captured by HMS *Malabar* and taken to Fort William.[28]

When he eventually wrote up his Dartmoor story in 1844, Clover made no mention whatever of his career as a privateersman.

'It was my fortune to be taken prisoner in India during the war of 1812' began his long narrative, serialized in the popular New York *Knickerbocker* magazine. Clover was soon placed on the transport ship *Lord Wellington* bound for Britain, but here his captivity assumed a surreal quality. The *Wellington*'s crew was 'made up of all nations', but like many British support vessels during the Napoleonic Wars, it was chronically understaffed. Clover was therefore offered a modest wage in return for crewing his own prison transfer. The journey took months. The *Wellington* stopped at Ceylon, Madras, Cape Town, and St Helena, until in the dying days of the summer of 1814 Clover sailed up the River Thames to Gravesend, on the edge of London. He felt that he had reached the 'heart's core of the world' and wished he could see the sights.[29]

Suddenly that opportunity materialised. Clover was paid his wages and ordered to await the Transport Board clerk who would arrange his transfer to a new prison facility. As he stood patiently in the appointed spot, Clover realised no one was watching him and nimbly jumped into a ferry heading upriver. When he disembarked an hour later, the 'vast and mighty city' was his to explore. With wages in his pocket, Clover found a boarding house and began to check off his list: the fair at Smithfield, St Paul's Cathedral, the Tower of London. Even in 1814, two weeks in London could be an expensive prospect; with his funds running out, Clover decided it was time to leave. He went back to the wharves in search of a ship that would take him 'to any port out of the jurisdiction of the British government'. The French war was over and he soon joined a crew headed for Marseilles. Then, just as the vessel was readying to leave, he met the gaze of a man looking intently in his direction. Clover knew immediately that the man was from the Transport Board, and wondered if he should run. But the War of 1812 would surely be over soon; what was the worst that could befall him in the meantime? Clover felt calm, even serene, as he was taken into custody. 'Had I imagined half the trouble and sorrow that awaited me,' he later wrote, 'I should have acted with more caution.'[30]

FOR PRIVATEERSMEN WHO WROTE UP THEIR STORIES FOR PUBLICA-
tion, the nature of their work during the War of 1812 presented an
awkward challenge. George Little styled himself as too good for
the trade, even as he persistently failed to quit privateering. Benjamin Browne was kinder about his crew mates than Little, but insisted that he'd had no choice in his wartime occupation. Lewis
Clover failed to mention what he was doing in India, and we only
know about his privateering from other sources. These sailors' reluctance to defend privateering stemmed not only from the widespread
assumption that it was a form of piracy but also from a general prejudice among Americans about the weak loyalties of sailors. In his
1844 magazine narrative, Clover lingered on the joy he felt when
the *Wellington* caught sight of an American privateer on the horizon. 'A thrill shot through my nerves,' he recalled, 'as I beheld the
Flag of my Country for the first time for many months.' Clover's patriotism may have been sincerely felt, but he must have been aware
that Thomas Jefferson's low view of privateersmen was widely held.
'No one can imagine the love he bears his native land,' wrote Clover
in 1844, 'until he tests it as I have done.' During and after the War
of 1812, Clover and other American privateersmen would struggle
to prove that claim to their countrymen.[31]

As American privateers were tearing up the British merchant fleet
in the winter of 1812–1813, congressional representatives began a
fraught debate over the national loyalties of sailors on US ships. The
Federalist Party had been calling for a blanket ban on foreign sailors,
insisting that the tensions with Britain over impressment and neutrality stemmed from the permeability of the maritime workforce:
as Lewis Clover had noted on the *Wellington*, you could find sailors
from many nations on every ship. The Republican majority in Congress gave in to this complaint, and with the war already unpopular
in New England (a Federalist redoubt), the Republicans proposed a
Seaman's Act which made it unlawful to employ 'on board any of the
public or private vessels of the United States any person or persons
except citizens of the United States, or persons of color, natives of

the United States'. Felix Grundy, a Republican from Tennessee, told Congress that foreigners 'form no part of our political community; they form part of a different community'. Banning them from the merchant marine would 'diminish the points of collision' between the American republic and other nations and deny Britain its excuse for impressment. Republicans and many Federalists rose to make the same point: the sea was a place of maddening disloyalty, where sailors were 'Englishmen yesterday, Americans today, Swedes or Danes tomorrow'. The United States should not waste blood and treasure 'for the protection of mere aliens'.[32]

It was left to the renegade Federalist Josiah Quincy of Massachusetts to make the obvious point: Wasn't the United States supposed to offer refuge to people from *all* nations? And hadn't Thomas Jefferson and his supporters spent 'the whole extent of their political lives' arguing for immigration and naturalization, rather than exclusion and criminalization of foreigners? It came down to a simple question: Were Americans 'a simple homogenous race of men'? Of course not: 'The fact is altogether the reverse. The American state is neither composed of flint nor granite, but rather a sort of pudding-stone: of a casual collection of distinct individuals, aggregated together, with no selection in the particulars, and little strength in the cement.' His colleagues weren't sure if Quincy was joking, but he insisted that the exclusion of foreigners at sea would cast a long shadow over naturalization on shore. In the end, his dissent was a lonely one. The Seaman's Act passed into law in March 1813, but it lacked any clear enforcement mechanism. In practice, its principal impact was to reinforce the American public's prejudice that the merchant marine was stuffed with foreigners; that a 'numerous and hardy race of *real* American sailors', as one Federalist put it during the debate, had yet to be recruited to the nation's service.[33]

One telling detail in the 1813 Seaman's Act was its handling of sailors of colour. These were expressly given the right to continue in the merchant marine but were also listed separately from citizens as 'persons of color, natives of the United States'. Black sailors had successfully applied for Seamen's Protection Certificates since their invention in 1796, and each SPC expressly confirmed that its bearer was a *citizen* of the United States. The shabby wording of the 1813 act responded both to a continuing reluctance on the part of white Americans to accept African Americans as citizens and to the suspicions of disloyalty faced by Black sailors (and African Americans more generally) during the War of 1812. Despite its acute manpower shortage, the US government refused to allow even free Black people to enlist in the army. Skilled Black sailors were permitted to join the US Navy and probably comprised over 15 percent of the entire merchant marine. But US officials were paranoid that the British would encourage a slave revolt in the southern states once the war had begun; when more than three thousand enslaved people in those states crossed the lines in 1813 and 1814, white Americans became even more paranoid about Black loyalty.[34]

Black privateersmen left no accounts of their experiences during the war, but one tantalizing source in the State Department's files gives a sense of what Black sailors were up against. In November 1813, the *Rambler*, an American letter of marque, left Boston with a cargo of wheat bound for Bordeaux. Although Britain was blockading the American and French coasts, the *Rambler*'s captain, Nathaniel Snow, was willing to take the risk: James Madison himself had asked the captain to bring him French cologne, almond paste, and 'one dozen long Grenoble gloves' (presumably for Mrs. Madison). Captain Snow and his crew narrowly evaded a British warship on their way into the Atlantic and then encountered a more manageable foe: the *Agnes*, a British schooner carrying fish from Newfoundland to Bermuda. The *Rambler* was bigger and better armed, and the *Agnes* surrendered before anyone was hurt. Snow appointed a prize crew to take the *Agnes* back to the United States but fretted that this would leave him short-handed. He decided to keep back four of the *Agnes*'s crew, all of whom claimed to be American and all of whom were Black. The four men helped Snow to slip past the blockade at Bordeaux, to load his cargo of olives, prunes, silk, and brandy—along with President Madison's shopping list—and to get the ship safely back to Boston. On arrival, however, Captain Snow marched the men ashore and ordered port officials to detain them as British prisoners of war.[35]

Transferred to the jail at Salem, the men were interrogated by US Marshal James Prince. The first, John Williams, told Prince he had been born in New Orleans in 1766, had left 'when that place was ceded to the United States'—in other words, after the Louisiana Purchase of 1803—and had since then crewed ships between the Caribbean and the American mainland. John Brown, the second prisoner, told the marshal that he'd been born in New Jersey in 1764, giving the names of his parents and his first employer to ground his claim. Brown, like John Williams, claimed to have been stuck in Antigua when the War of 1812 broke out. Needing to earn a living but with no prospect of finding an American ship, Brown and Williams eventually joined the crew of the *Agnes* on its voyage to Newfoundland. William Charles, the third man, was from Bristol in Rhode Island. He had been serving on a privateer in 1812 when his ship's magazine exploded. He'd then drifted on the wreckage for a week until he was rescued by the British and brought to Barbuda, then Antigua. Charles insisted to Prince that he'd repeatedly tried to find an American ship and that he'd briefly made it back to the United States (on a Swedish vessel) before being forced by its scheming captain to crew the return leg to the Caribbean. He, too, had boarded the *Agnes* out of desperation. The fourth and final prisoner, John Taylor, had grown up as an enslaved person in the household of a prominent Virginia planter; he had ridden racehorses for his enslaver, but when he grew too big, he had gone to sea. (He didn't clarify whether his enslaver had approved this plan or he'd run away.) He, too, became caught up in the complex dynamics of the Caribbean trade, until the War of 1812 suddenly made his nationality the most important thing about him.[36]

All four men told versions of the same story to James Prince, the marshal: they were 'persons of color, natives of the United States' (as the 1813 Seaman's Act would put it); they had served on ships of other nations, including Britain and Sweden; they had boarded the *Agnes* at Antigua to escape enemy territory. But two of the men confessed that they had already been captured and freed by the British during the conflict—presumably they dissembled about their American origins when questioned—and one admitted that 'he had taken an oath of fidelity to the Swedish government.' Presumably, none had Seamen's Protection Certificates, though only a minority of sailors ever applied for them. (And an SPC might have been a liability to the men if they were captured by another power.) Even for a US marshal accustomed to maritime intrigue, this was a challenging case. Clearly Captain Snow had taken a liberty in treating the men as Americans at sea, while having them imprisoned as British subjects when they made landfall. But without paperwork to corroborate their story, or an easy method of following up the leads they had provided to New Jersey or Virginia, Marshal Prince felt unable to free them.

The State Department archives contain Prince's detailed interview notes, but no further correspondence on what happened to the men. All four appear on the register of British POWs drawn up at the end of the war, but only John Brown—the man who had provided the names of his parents and his first employer—is listed as having been freed. (His release date was around three months after his interview with Prince, so it's possible the marshal contacted Brown's parents to confirm his identity.) For the other three men— including William Charles, our unfortunate privateersman—we can only speculate. The lack of a release date in the register probably means that the men were not evacuated with the rest of the British prisoners. Most likely they took advantage of the war's end to go home, or back to the Caribbean, or wherever else brought the greatest opportunity and the least prospect of harassment. The war had reminded them of something they already knew: the United States was a poor custodian of their nationality.[37]

6.

MISTER BEASTLY

The first American prisoners were wet and miserable when they arrived on the evening of 2 April 1813. The heavy rain that had accompanied their day-long march from Plymouth had become colder as they'd gained elevation. Outside the stone walls there was snow on the ground, and the Americans recalled what they had been told on the hulks: Dartmoor was 'by far the most dreadful prison in all England', a place 'in which it was next to impossible for human beings long to survive'. The new arrivals were met by clerks and turnkeys who issued hammocks and blankets. The prison blocks were heaving with Frenchmen, and 'among these fluttering, ghastly skeletons we were directed to take up our abode', wrote one prisoner. The Americans went to sleep tired and hungry; the next morning they would be initiated in the prison's customs and cruelties.[1]

Dartmoor's agent, Isaac Cotgrave, had to put the Americans somewhere, though housing them with the Romans may not have been his best idea. In the spring of 1813, the US prisoners were vastly outnumbered by the eight thousand Frenchmen now occupying seven prison blocks (including the two additional buildings completed the previous year). Cotgrave initially squeezed the Americans into whichever gaps he could find, but he soon managed to shuffle the inhabitants of the central building—Number Four—to free up more space. The Americans were given one of the three floors, the cockloft, or 'capitol', as the French had called it. But that meant hoping that the Americans and the most desperate Frenchmen in the prison would play nicely together. Despite everything, Cotgrave decided it was worth the gamble.[2]

The winter of 1812–1813 had already produced tensions in Prison Four. Cotgrave acknowledged the Romans' incorrigible behaviour by designating Four as the prison block for other misfits and troublemakers in the French ranks. From 1809 until the end of 1812, prisoners had usually chosen where to sling their hammocks, and Four had been self-selecting in the inhabitants it drew to its three floors. But in the first weeks of 1813, not long after the bread protests and the Romans' gruesome attack on the horses, Cotgrave decided to cauterise the block's unruly occupants. He ordered two walls to be built in a V shape, moving outwards from the point of the market gate (in the centre of the prison) to the inner fence and walls near the prison's circumference. When the London magazines had reprinted early engravings of five undivided blocks, the central area of the prison had seemed airy and even spacious. Now there were three smaller yards—one for Blocks One to Three, a central yard for Four, and a third for Prisons Five to Seven. They were connected by a gated passageway near the market square. It was still possible to move around the prison if this passageway was open, but the purpose of walling off Four from the other blocks was clear: Cotgrave wanted to stop Dartmoor's most alarming captives from spreading their influence.[3]

When the American prisoners were herded into Four a few weeks after their arrival, they must already have heard about the Romans from the turnkeys. But nothing could have prepared them for the horror of meeting their new neighbours. 'They were literally and emphatically naked,' wrote the Rhode Island sailor Charles Andrews. 'The mind cannot figure to itself anything in the shape of men, which so much resembled the fabled ghosts of

Pluto, as these naked and starved French prisoners.' Andrews acknowledged that at least some of the Romans' desperation was their own fault; their 'imprudence and bad conduct' had exacerbated the difficulty of their long confinement. What concerned him most, though, was that American prisoners would now be forced to accept the Romans as their 'associates'. During their brief tenure in the other prison blocks, the Americans had discovered Dartmoor's daily market and moved freely through the yards. Now they were stuck with the prison's outcasts, in an area with restricted access both to the other blocks and to the market. Charles Andrews, for whom even the appearance of the Romans was 'really shocking to human feeling', offered a crisp summary of this latest indignity: 'So the Americans dwell among the damned.'[4]

BETWEEN AGENT COTGRAVE AT DARTMOOR AND THE DISTANT United States government in Washington stood one figure of hope for the American prisoners: a Virginia merchant named Reuben Gaunt Beasley who, in the summer of 1812, became the official US representative for American prisoners of war in Britain. At the outbreak of the war, the US minister in London and most of his staff were recalled to Washington. Beasley, who had been working in the consular office since 1809, was left behind to liaise with the Transport Board on the welfare of POWs and to lobby for their release. The Americans who left accounts of their captivity disagreed on whether Beasley was incompetent, derelict, or actively hostile to their welfare. Every prisoner at Dartmoor knew his name, though: 'Beastly, it should be,' wrote one.[5]

Just as the United States had outsourced much of the fighting in the War of 1812 to ordinary sailors, so it assigned the task of upholding their rights to an amateur. The entire diplomatic service was a work in progress during the early decades of the American republic. Ministers plenipotentiary—the equivalent of modern ambassadors—conducted high-level diplomacy with foreign governments and courts, along with an endless calendar of social engagements. The importance of this work to the early United States is reflected in the calibre of individuals who undertook it: Benjamin Franklin, Thomas Jefferson, John Adams, James Monroe, and John Quincy Adams all served their country overseas. Consuls, by contrast, did the dirty work: they verified the arrival dates of American ships, supported insurance claims for delayed or lost cargoes, and adjudicated disputes between Americans. Later in the nineteenth century, the State Department would appoint dedicated public servants to consular posts. In our period consuls had no training and (in some cases) little aptitude for the work. The salary was low; some postings offered remuneration via commissions on the fees charged for consular services, an arrangement which hardly encouraged honest behaviour. And yet the position of consul was coveted by office seekers in the United States because it enabled its holders to spend a good deal of time attending to their own commercial interests rather than the concerns of their compatriots. This wasn't a dereliction of duty but a feature of the post.[6]

Reuben Beasley was born in 1778 in Fredericksburg, Virginia. Before he turned thirty, he became a partner to two brothers, the tobacco merchants (and enslavers) William and John Bell, who were based in Petersburg. The Bell brothers had emigrated to Virginia from Ireland; by the mid-1800s, they had significant shipping interests in Europe and were sending regular cargoes of tobacco and cotton across the Atlantic. William moved to London to keep a closer eye on business, and Beasley may have won the brothers' trust by serving as their local agent in mainland Europe: he lived in Bordeaux for a while, and then in Hamburg. After a promotion to partner in the firm, in 1809 Beasley relocated to London and became vice consul to William Lyman, a former congressman from Massachusetts. Lyman died in office in 1811 and Beasley was appointed his successor. Most major British ports had a US consul, but London—with its boundless opportunities to advance one's own business interests—was the most coveted posting of all.[7]

Exactly how Beasley secured this job is a mystery, though evidently he had acquired powerful friends in the United States. In a letter to James Madison in 1816, he noted that he'd already been offered a consular post in Sweden in 1810 but that his commercial interests, which were centred upon Britain and Germany, had forced him to decline. Beasley left no papers but plenty of red flags in the archive. When he and the Bell brothers lost lawsuits brought by business partners in Virginia, for example, they simply failed to comply with the court's sanctions. (The absent Beasley continued to appear in Virginia lawsuits relating to the Bell brothers through the 1820s.) In 1812, the partners were also accused of an elaborate insurance fraud, though by this point William Bell—who had helped Beasley direct the firm's business in London—had already died. That unfortunate event had 'thrown our affairs into confusion' Beasley later told James Madison. Since the firm was a partnership rather than a corporation, Beasley and the surviving Bell brother were personally liable for their mounting debts.[8]

One bolthole from creditors in Virginia and London was on the other side of the English Channel: during his time in Bordeaux in 1808 Beasley had befriended Daniel Guestier, a French Huguenot merchant who became a leading exporter of wine to the United States. He had also charmed Guestier's daughter, seventeen-year-old Jenny Adelaide Guestier. Working as American consul in Britain, France's arch enemy, presented a considerable obstacle to Beasley's designs on Jenny, though the Virginian was nothing if not resourceful. In an ideal world, the Napoleonic Wars would be over and Beasley would persuade James Monroe, the US secretary of state, to appoint him consul in Bordeaux. Beasley could walk away from his liabilities in Virginia and Britain and start again as the heir to a claret empire. (The firm of Barton & Guestier is still making wine today.) Unfortunately for Beasley, with the outbreak of the War of 1812 his fate was tied to London. The Napoleonic Wars and their disruption to Atlantic trade had already stretched

Beasley's resources and wits; a war between Britain and the United States would bring him to the edge of ruin.[9]

IN THEORY, BEASLEY'S JOB AS AGENT FOR AMERICAN POWS BUILT upon the work he'd already been doing as consul. During the phony war which preceded the outbreak of hostilities in 1812, Beasley had frequently received communications from desperate American sailors who had been impressed into the Royal Navy. While an impressed sailor or his family might contact the State Department for help, the first port of call was a US consul—and given Beasley's plum posting in London, these requests kept him very busy. In retrospect, so many of the things that went wrong for Reuben Beasley (and the prisoners he was supposed to help) were in embryo during the year or two before the war. Beasley was nowhere near as insouciant as American prisoners would come to believe, but he was always inclined to place too much faith in British decency—again, partly because his own business interests were deeply bound up with Britain.[10]

One vivid example: In May 1812, six weeks before war broke out, Beasley served as one of twelve organizers of the annual dinner of the Society of Friends of Foreigners in Distress, a philanthropic organization which provided financial assistance to foreign nationals who fell on hard times in London. The celebrated antislavery campaigner William Wilberforce was a vice president; the Duke of Gloucester, the king's nephew, was the society's patron. By that point Beasley had spent years fielding requests from a particularly unfortunate group of foreigners in distress: US sailors forced to serve on British warships. But here was Beasley glad-handing London's philanthropic elite, listening to the duke himself making an 'elegant and appropriate speech' on Britain's boundless benevolence. The crowd cheered, 'several excellent songs and glees were sung,' and Beasley encouraged the guests to part with £500 in donations to the 'admirable institution' while his own government debated war over Britain's persistent cruelty to foreigners. Being in the wrong place at the wrong time was Reuben Beasley's superpower, but his scrambled motives were fatally enabled by the limited remuneration of the consular service. When American sailors needed Reuben Beasley to put everything on the line for their interests, the Virginian simply didn't feel able to abandon his own.[11]

For impressed Americans desperate to leave the Royal Navy, Beasley would become a pantomime villain. The circumstances of their ordeal had drained them of patience and fuelled their expectation that the US government should be doing more to secure their release. Consider the experience of Joseph Bates, the young Massachusetts sailor we met briefly in the first chapter. Bates's first Atlantic crossing, when he sailed to London as a green hand, had been charmed: apart from nearly being eaten by a shark after falling from the main mast into the ocean, Bates had taken immediately to the sailor's life. But during his second voyage, on an American vessel bound for Archangel in the Russian Arctic, Bates and his crew mates were captured by Danish privateers who assumed they were British, not American. (Denmark had initially remained neutral in the war between Britain and France, but took Napoleon's side after the Royal Navy pre-emptively bombed Copenhagen in the summer of 1807.) The Danish authorities eventually set Bates and his compatriots free, but they seized his vessel and left him in Copenhagen, 'in company with a strange people who had stripped us of all but our clothing'. Plotting a course back to America through a war-torn Europe was challenging: Bates crewed ships to Prussia and then to Ireland before finally hopping across the Irish Sea to Liverpool. It was now the spring of 1810. Britain and the United States were at peace, Bates was in one of Britain's major ports, and he felt confident he'd find a ship heading back across the Atlantic. Instead, after he had retired for the evening in his boarding house, a knock at the door brought a dozen Royal Navy sailors into his room demanding proof of his nationality.[12]

Bates produced his Seamen's Protection Certificate, signed by the customs collector at New York. The officer at the head of the press gang examined the certificate, handed it back, and ordered his men to take Bates away to a cell. The astonished American kept expecting that, as his pleas for liberty moved up the British chain of command, the mistake would be remedied. Instead, an Irish officer was produced to swear that Bates's parents 'lived in Belfast, Ireland', which settled the matter. Bates was dragged to Plymouth, and then below the decks of HMS *Rodney*, a seventy-four-gun ship of the line. For the next two years, Bates was forced to fight Britain's war with France, mostly in the Mediterranean. When the *Rodney*'s tour of duty ended, the British simply transferred Bates to a similar vessel, HMS *Swiftsure*, and started the clock again. Bates became resigned to his fate: 'I was doomed to drag out a miserable existence in the British Navy.'[13]

In the spring of 1812, with all hope lost, the captain of the *Swiftsure* called Bates to the deck and asked if he was really an American. One of the letters Bates had sent to his family had finally slipped past the British censors, and Bates's father had persuaded the captain of an American merchant ship to pester Royal Navy officials on his next voyage to the Mediterranean. The captain informed Bates that 'the admiral' would soon call for him, and for the first time in two years Bates indulged the hope that his ordeal would soon be over. The two dozen or so Americans who were also serving on the *Swiftsure* kept telling Bates 'what a lucky fellow he was,' but 'the admiral' failed to materialise. Instead, Bates received a letter from his father's friend, the American captain, telling him that his case was now 'hanging in uncertainty'. It was several more weeks before Bates understood what had happened. Just as his case had become conspicuous enough to expedite his release, the War of 1812 had broken out. With hostilities declared between Britain and the United States, the Royal Navy was now digging in. Not only would Joseph Bates be denied his liberty—he would be kept aboard the *Swiftsure* and ordered to fight his compatriots.[14]

For the first ten months of the war, Bates and the other *Swiftsure* Americans stayed put. When Bates wrote about this period more than fifty years later, his conscientious objection assumed an epic quality: he was held prisoner belowdecks and placed on one-third rations, but he embraced the risk of being shot to pieces in his cell over fighting on deck against his countrymen. Like most sailors who produced a memoir, Bates depicted himself as a super-charged patriot who never wavered in his love of country. But he quietly acknowledged that his fellow Americans on the *Swiftsure* were more pragmatic in their allegiances: they brought him news of the ship's heading and engagements while continuing to serve the king. British commanders kept American sailors on board their ships after the declaration of war in June 1812 because they felt confident that they could continue to extract their labour. The *Swiftsure's* captain only gave up this hope—for Bates, at least—in October 1813. At that point, instead of being allowed to go home, Bates was dumped into the British prison system. The Royal Navy finally conceded that he wasn't Irish, and as an American he was rewarded with a new form of captivity.[15]

JUST BEFORE HE RETREATED TO WASHINGTON IN THE SUMMER OF 1812, the US chargé d'affaires in London, Jonathan Russell, left Beasley a note on what the United States should be doing for men like Joseph Bates. Given the assumption that these sailors had been illegally impressed into the Royal Navy, it would be 'very unjust to discharge them from the British service simply to make them prisoners of war'. But Russell had been in Britain long enough to doubt the Admiralty's commitment to justice. It would be much better for them to be placed in 'simple captivity'—a hulk or a prison away from the fighting at sea—than kept aboard Royal Navy ships where they might 'expose their own lives and attack the lives of their fellow citizens'. Behind this calculation was a gnawing anxiety on the part of American officials. Impressed sailors were the greatest victims of British cruelty: they had been denied their liberty for years and were now forced to fight against their own country. But what if some of these Americans had been less than strenuous in their efforts to escape from the service? What if some had prioritized personal survival, or slipped from the moorings of nationality to claim prize money in the king's cause?[16]

This anxiety became a critical fault line among the prisoners in Dartmoor, and in the summer of 1812 it led Jonathan Russell and Reuben Beasley to consider a parallel problem: with thousands of privateersmen and ordinary American sailors falling into the British prison system, might the Royal Navy look for new recruits among US POWs? As Russell generously put it, a filthy and desperate prison experience might be enough 'to persecute them into treason against their country'. In October 1812, Beasley told Secretary of State James Monroe that he had learned of efforts 'to entice some, who were confined as prisoners, to enter into British ships of War & Merchantmen'. The Royal Navy's strategy was coming into focus: it would sweat its warships of American sailors who *really* didn't want to be in the service, while retaining those willing discreetly to remain at their posts. It would then replace the most ardent American patriots with new recruits taken directly from the British prison system.[17]

Jonathan Russell wanted to break this disgraceful cycle. Because Beasley didn't have access to the various registers within the British prison system, he had no way of knowing how many American sailors were leaking out of captivity and into the Royal Navy. All he had to go on was Russell's concern that leakage was likely, along with Russell's direction that he (and only he) had the power to arrest it: mostly through signalling to American sailors, both on Royal Navy ships and in the prison system, that their release was imminent. A gap opened up between a realistic assessment of Britain's intentions and the hope Beasley felt compelled to generate among American prisoners. Russell had been clear: Britain wouldn't free impressed sailors, and a transfer from the Royal Navy to the prison system was probably the best outcome the United States could hope for. But in Beasley's public pronouncements and especially in his letters to individual sailors, he implied that impressed Americans might indeed be released despite the war—if they could supply him with the paperwork to fight their battles with the Transport Board and the Admiralty.

In May 1813, Beasley drafted a circular letter to be sent to the hundreds of impressed sailors who had already been taken from Royal Navy ships into the British prison system. He began by insisting that, contrary to rumours, he and the American government had shown no 'indifference' to the plight of impressed sailors. Then he repeated the line he'd been given by the Lords Commissioners of the Admiralty: that whenever proof of American nationality was produced by an impressed sailor, 'the person will be immediately released from prison . . . freely and without restriction.' It was up to prisoners to 'write immediately to their friends in the United States' to request the paperwork which would confirm their identity. Those 'weak men' who had already agreed to join the Royal Navy in return for their release would 'expose themselves to the punishment due to traitors, for the sake of escaping the inconvenience of a temporary captivity'. Beasley reassured the remaining American prisoners that 'no effort of mine shall be spared to effect your early release.' The circular offered real hope to impressed sailors that their fate was in their own hands. Beasley ended by assuring these sailors that 'the eyes of your country are upon you': the prisoners were not forgotten, but if they traded away their national identity, they would surely be punished by the US government. Like much of the circular, this was an act of bluster: Beasley had no idea what was really happening in the prisons. His calculation was that, through assurance and intimidation, he could prevent a mass defection of American prisoners to the Royal Navy. What he failed to account for was the sense of betrayal that would surely follow if impressed sailors did what he asked but were still denied their liberty.[18]

BEASLEY'S EFFORT TO GAUGE THE INTENTIONS OF THE BRITISH WAS made harder by their constant gaslighting. Officials at the Transport Board and the Admiralty sent outraged replies when he stated the obvious fact that Americans had been forced to serve in the Royal Navy and that their pleas for release had been ignored. 'Neither since the war with America nor before', went one, 'have their lordships declined to release American seamen, admitted or proved to be such.' Beasley's exasperation with these clearly false statements crept into his replies: 'What justification, what excuse, can be set up for this conduct of Great Britain towards the impressed American seamen?' Jonathan Russell had warned him that he might eventually have to shelve the diplomatic approach and call out the Admiralty for its lying, but in the case of impressed sailors there was no obvious way to promise reciprocal outrages on Britons. The US Navy also made use of impressment, but on a far smaller scale (since it was a fraction of the size of the Royal Navy) and with American rather than British sailors in its sights. As the War of 1812 continued, and the US government continued to put privateersmen in harm's way, the British were seizing considerably more American prisoners than vice versa. If Beasley wanted to force British officials to live up to their rhetoric, he had very little leverage to do so.[19]

Beasley may also not have realised that his promises to impressed sailors were making their way into newspapers and magazines at home, as the paperwork he shared with Washington was leaked to the press. This was standard practice: the Madison administration wanted the American public to know that its representatives were doing what they could to uphold the nation's honour. Dozens of Beasley's letters to the British foreign minister, Lord Castlereagh, and to the officials of the Transport Board and the Admiralty were reprinted in American newspapers and pamphlets, which in turn were read by the families of men who languished in British prisons. These reinforced the idea that proper documentation could produce an early release for impressed sailors, and desperate families back in the United States rushed to swear affidavits and procure baptism certificates for submission to the State Department. When the requisite paperwork produced only excuses from the British (or silence), it was Beasley who became the scapegoat.

In the impressment files in Washington, dozens of messages from sailors name Beasley as the person who reassured them that the right documents would secure their freedom. Jacob Israel Potter, the African American sailor we met in Chapter 2, had been impressed since 1804. In 1813, he wrote to James Monroe from a British prison hulk on the outskirts of London with a simple request: 'I am directed by Reuben G. Beazley . . . to solicit [from] you a protection as the British Government are determined to detain us until the arrival of such proofs from the United States.' He politely directed Monroe to the Custom House where his protection had been granted. But even if the secretary of state had taken the time to request a duplicate certificate, it would have made no difference. Potter was transferred to Dartmoor in September 1814 and would not be released until the following April—months after the war had ended. At least half a dozen Americans who appear both in the State Department impressment files and in the prison register at Dartmoor received the same encouragement from Beasley. He had begun sending sailors reassurances about the power of paperwork in 1811, the year in which he became US consul, but he continued to instruct sailors (or their families) to assemble evidence even when it became clear that Britain would not keep its side of the bargain.[20]

Beasley learned quickly that the Transport Board had endless excuses for refusing to authenticate prisoners as American: 'Documents were irregular'; 'were said to be imposters'; 'had voluntarily entered the British service'. Even when he had lost his belief in British fair play, he could succumb to naivety. In the summer of 1813, a Massachusetts sailor named Jonathan Bigelow walked into Beasley's London office to report that he had been illegally impressed on a Royal Navy warship. Unusually, the crew had been given shore leave and he now wanted the United States to arrange his repatriation. Bigelow had proof of his nationality and Beasley wrote to the Admiralty on his behalf. He was told in reply to send Bigelow back to his ship 'in order that the necessary enquiries might be made into his case'. With the war raging, Beasley couldn't send Bigelow back to the United States and was reluctant to harbour him in his own home. So the US agent for POWs told the desperate sailor to return to the king's service and await confirmation of his discharge. The navy promptly transferred Bigelow to a different ship bound for the West Indies. Beasley felt so bad about his part in this fiasco that he told the whole story to James Monroe, along with his belated realisation that the navy's letter to him advising Bigelow's return to his ship was 'merely for the purpose of again obtaining possession of him'. This anguished letter was more than a form of self-exculpation: Beasley wanted Monroe to know that he was fighting an impossible battle against a ruthless foe, alone and behind enemy lines.[21]

By the fall of 1813, Beasley had made 165 applications to the Admiralty for the release of Americans still stuck in the Royal Navy. Not a single request had been honoured. When he eventually received a reply in the case of one sailor in November of that year, the board promised only to transfer the American in question from HMS *Pomone* to a prison hulk—exactly the outcome Jonathan Russell had anticipated a year earlier. Beasley eventually conceded that his task was hopeless. He lamented to James Monroe the fate of 'those unfortunate men' forced 'to linger in prison or to fight against their country'. The British insistence on paperwork was worse than a sham: 'It is insulting to talk any longer of evidence when it is manifest that none that could be produced would be found satisfactory.' And yet we know from the impressment files that Beasley continued to tell Americans that they should procure paperwork from family and friends at home. He did so because he received letters every day from desperate men in British custody. But with the war dragging on, and with little prospect of a prisoner exchange, it seemed ever more likely that Beasley's promises would be found wanting.[22]

IMPRESSED SAILORS MADE UP A MINORITY OF THE AMERICAN PRISoner population during the War of 1812, though their sense of anger and betrayal at the hands of Beasley anchored many conversations in the hulks and the prisons. American sailors were already suspicious of consuls' loyalties. 'I am very sorry to say that a great part of the consuls abroad troubles themselves very little about American seamen,' wrote one sailor in 1811. 'The captains of men of war invites them to dine and drink on board, and that is the most some of them cares for.' In 1812, an impressed sailor in the Mediterranean complained that 'the American consuls in this part of the world are too intimate with the British to take any pains to get a man clear.' What remains of Beasley's correspondence refutes the charge that he sided with Britain or that he disregarded prisoners' appeals, especially in impressment cases. But in failing to make good on his promises, he fed an existing narrative among sailors about the fair-weather nature of consular support.[23]

And Beasley was bad at the basics. He didn't enjoy visiting prisoners and gladly entangled himself in the red tape the Transport Board placed around his activities. Although he was generally free to move around the country, he needed a passport for each prison he meant to visit. In his letters back to Washington, he admitted that the board hadn't ever denied him a passport, though the fact that American prisoners were scattered across four sites—Plymouth, Dartmoor, Stapleton (near Bristol), and Chatham (near London)—would have created logistical challenges for even the most assiduous prisoner advocate (which Beasley was not). He appointed 'sub-agents' to visit prison facilities while he remained in London fielding his substantial correspondence. With his pen, Beasley raised prisoners' grievances loudly and often. He complained about overcrowding, the lack of suitable bedding, and the spread of disease through the prisons and the hulks. The prisoners themselves, however, expected to see their agent—especially as the promises he'd made to impressed sailors were endlessly deferred. 'The American agent has never been to see us,' wrote the imprisoned sailor Henry Fleischman in March 1813. Fleischman was at Chatham, thirty miles from Beasley's house on Harley Street in central London. 'We think the American government authorized him to afford us some relief in our distressed state, but that he neglected to grant it to us or send us home in order to enrich himself.' As the months went by without an appearance from Beasley, prisoners stored up their grievances for his eventual arrival.[24]

Before the fall of 1814, when the French surrender allowed the board to transfer nearly every American prisoner to Dartmoor, the hulks at Chatham were the main prison facility for US POWs in Britain. Nearly four thousand were held in half a dozen retired Royal Navy vessels anchored to the muddy bed of the River Medway, beyond London's eastern edge. (The British government also imprisoned thousands of felons in adjoining hulks, many awaiting transportation to Australia.) This part of England, like Dartmoor, had a magnificent bleakness—at least, to those who weren't held prisoner. It captivated the young Charles Dickens, who moved to Chatham in 1817 when he was five years old. Dickens's father worked as a clerk in the dockyards, and Charles spent his early childhood exploring the marshes and mudflats which stretched for miles along the estuary. The unsettling emptiness of the area stayed with Dickens long after he moved back to London in 1822, and it re-emerged with extraordinary power in the opening of *Great Expectations* (1861). The book's hero, a young orphan named Pip, lives with his older sister and her husband on the marshes close to Chatham. One evening, while visiting the local churchyard where his parents are buried, Pip encounters the convict Magwitch, a strange and terrifying figure who has escaped from a nearby prison hulk. Magwitch—cajoling and pleading—asks Pip to bring him food. Pip returns the following night with a pork pie and brandy and Magwitch professes his eternal gratitude. The convict is recaptured soon afterwards but never forgets his debt to Pip. Magwitch was a convict rather than a prisoner of war, but Dickens staged his meeting with Pip on Christmas Eve, 1812—at which point more than three hundred American prisoners were already in the hulks.[25]

Chatham was not an easy place to escape from. After their first meeting, as Pip watches Magwitch retreat into the marshes, he realises that even the shortest human being has a stark verticality against the landscape's void: 'The marshes were just a long black horizontal line then, as I stopped to look after him; and the river was just another horizontal line, not nearly so broad nor yet so black; and the sky was just a row of long angry red lines and dense black lines intermixed.' The only thing interrupting the 'bleak stillness' of the scene—apart from Magwitch himself—was a prison hulk, squatting against the mud 'like a wicked Noah's ark'. The worn and beaten appearance of the hulks, along with the mass of rusty chain anchoring them to the river bed, made Pip believe that the ships themselves were prisoners. The Americans held at Chatham in 1813 and 1814 learned to appreciate the view; they spent most of their days belowdecks, where the gloom was perpetual.[26]

Joseph Bates was taken to Chatham after he was finally discharged from HMS *Swiftsure* in the fall of 1813. So was Jacob Potter, the impressed African American sailor who finally got clear of the Royal Navy (though not of British captivity) that spring. So too was Lewis Clover, the privateersmen who crewed his own prison transfer ship from Kolkata to London and then briefly escaped his captors to tour St Paul's and the Tower of London. When Clover was recaptured and taken to the hulks, his first impressions were not promising. 'I never beheld a set of more wretched human beings,' he wrote. The 'squalid, cadaverous throng' of six hundred prisoners were 'nearly starved and almost naked'. Following their practice belowdecks at sea, the sailors formed 'messes'—groups of six which prepared and cooked food on the hulk's upper deck—and did everything they could to keep their spirits up. Each night they would sling their hammocks in three tiers, with the men on the top tranche marooned until the next morning. Even when the hammocks were packed up in the morning and aired on the main deck, the feeling of claustrophobia was intense.[27]

Reuben Beasley finally made the short journey from central London to Chatham in March 1813. His visit did not go well. Beasley toured only one of the hulks—the *Nassau*—amid a phalanx of

British troops, then retreated to the shore and vanished as suddenly as he had arrived. In a letter of complaint to President Madison, a group of *Nassau* prisoners accused Beasley of spending barely ten minutes on their ship before leaving, 'like the midnight assassin after perpetrating the deed'. (Prisoners on another Chatham hulk didn't even know about the visit and wrote a separate complaint about the missing agent.) Beasley continued to reassure the Americans that they could be freed with the 'proper documents', despite the fact that men on the *Nassau* who had already supplied those documents remained in captivity. 'It is a well known fact,' the prisoners told President Madison, 'that the grand basis of an American consulate or agent in any country . . . is to protect such citizens of the United States as the fate of war or the dangers of the seas has thrown under his protection. The conduct of Mr Beasley in regard of us has been the reverse.'[28]

The hostile feedback from Chatham reinforced Beasley's aversion to prison visits. He made only a single, disastrous trip to Dartmoor—we'll follow him there in the next chapter—and for the most part directed his 'sub-agents' to absorb the prisoners' frustrations. The most prominent of these was a Mr Jacobs, whose presence at Chatham and Dartmoor revealed a casual anti-Semitism among the Americans. Britain's small Jewish community was formally excluded from service in the Royal Navy until the 1820s, though Jewish traders and suppliers played an important role in outfitting the fleet. Lord Nelson, Britain's legendary naval hero, was friendly with Benjamin and Abraham Goldsmid, his neighbours in the tony London suburb of Merton, and British Jews had established a foothold within elite social and political circles in the early nineteenth century. This was, of course, inflected by class and wealth; poorer Jewish 'peddlers' were routinely subject to derision and harassment, and prejudices about the supposed acquisitiveness of Jews were widespread. American prisoners manifested the same anti-Jewish prejudices as ordinary Britons. One Dartmoor prisoner complained that 'a Jew merchant of London, Mr Jacobs,' had brought new clothing on Beasley's behalf but of 'very coarse blue cloth', inferior to the quality issued by the board itself. Another recalled that 'a London Jew' had come to the prison 'with his boxes of ready made or basted clothing' but that these had been distributed haphazardly: some prisoners who didn't need clothing managed to grab some, while others who were in desperate need went without. Jacobs supposedly failed in his job of assessing the needs of the prisoners, while Beasley—'by letter', of course—'justified his agent, and paid little or no attention to our grievances'.[29]

The sense that Beasley was both derelict in his duties and suspect because of his willingness to work with Jews drove some prisoners to conspiracy theory. One of the most fantastical accounts of Beasley's villainy came from James R. Pynneo, a sailor from New York, who rushed to the offices of his local newspaper soon after his return to the United States in 1815. Reuben G. Beasley, he told the newspaper's staff, had paid no attention to the prisoners' requests for assistance. He was never at the prison, despite the train of letters to London bemoaning the conditions of men with 'scarce a rag to their backs'. Worse, Beasley 'had married, in England, the Daughter of an *Israelite*; and this Israelite frequently attended at the prison, to discharge the duties which it was Mr Beasley's province to perform'. This led some prisoners to suspect that their agent was 'speculating upon their necessities'. The story was a complete fabrication. Beasley actually slipped away to Bordeaux in May 1814, as soon as Britain's war with France had ended, to marry Jenny Adelaide Guestier (who wasn't Jewish). Pynneo's feverish allegations built from prejudices, disappointments, and frustrations which had become rife among American prisoners by the war's end. Beasley was supposed to help them; when they felt abandoned, he was the easiest person to blame.[30]

BEYOND SECURING THE RELEASE OF IMPRESSED SAILORS AND CARing for American POWs in Britain, Beasley's final task was to organize the 'cartels' which would convey exchanged prisoners back to the United States. Given the relatively small number of British prisoners seized by the United States, exchanges were infrequent events. Prisoners had no way of knowing if they were being released in the order in which they had been captured, and the priority given to US Navy personnel sat uneasily with Americans who had been compelled to serve in the Royal Navy even before the outbreak of the war. (For men like Jacob Potter, who had been on a Royal Navy ship since 1804, it must have been especially galling to wait behind US Navy sailors captured a decade later.) The prisoners themselves suspected that Beasley was not applying the rules fairly. At Chatham, the captives who petitioned James Madison in July 1813 claimed that multiple cartel ships had passed over impressed sailors who'd been promised an early release. They also accused Beasley of accepting paying passengers in the cartels, 'taking up the room of people that are lying in prison', and of telling those American sailors 'that has got their wives with them' that their spouses could only be returned to the United States on the payment of £5. (We'll come back to these women.) Many tall tales were told about Beasley, but given the chaotic and outsourced operation he was running anything seems possible.[31]

As usual, the prisoners' contempt was rooted partly in unrealistic expectations. The difficulties of hiring private vessels during a major war had prompted the British government to revive the Transport Board, and Beasley found himself competing against the board itself when trying to hire vessels to serve as cartel ships. When he could finally bring a ship under contract, Beasley had to manage the grievances of those prisoners lucky enough to be selected for exchange. 'Confinement naturally inclines to discontent,' Beasley told James Monroe in March 1813, 'and as it answers the purpose of the enemy to encourage that disposition in our countrymen, I have had more than my share of complaints.' When overseeing the loading of one cartel ship that spring, a group of liberated prisoners 'found fault with everything' and refused to comply with Beasley's instructions. The situation became so tense that Beasley was forced to remove one prisoner—a paroled captain—and relegate him to the next cartel.[32]

The captain of another cartel ship, Benjamin Waine, visited the marshal's office at Boston in July 1813 to explain that the American prisoners he'd been carrying back from Chatham had mutinied during the Atlantic crossing. In May, Beasley had sent 'Jacobs the Jew' to oversee the loading of provisions for the voyage, but the 150 exchanged prisoners were desperate for blankets and clothing the moment they set foot on the ship. Waine distributed the blankets but insisted that clothes should only be given to those in dire need. The prisoners 'came aft and swore they would take them by force if I would not give them up'. Waine managed to squirrel away a small portion of the clothing with the intention of giving it quietly to the prisoners 'I should find naked.' The angry Americans seized the main supplies, then stole everything in Waine's stash as well. The journey itself was miserable, with Waine commanding an unfamiliar and surly crew (who were mostly Spaniards) while being harassed by the mutinous prisoners. The final insult came at Boston: Waine himself was mistaken by the customs officials for a prisoner and arrested on suspicion of having started the mutiny. All of this could have been avoided, Waine felt, if Beasley had provided proper instructions both to the prisoners and to Waine himself. 'As many years as I have commanded a ship,' Waine told the authorities at Boston, 'I never sailed before without orders.'[33]

The sheer number of complaints about Reuben Beasley tells its own story. Mister Beastly earned his soubriquet, but he had been placed in an impossible position. The American government had little leverage with Britain. Thomas Jefferson and James Madison had left the war at sea to ordinary sailors, and they lacked the capacity (and perhaps the will) to construct a robust system of support for the ten thousand or more POWs who passed through the British system. Beasley was a man of modest abilities and limited virtue. He could not fairly be called selfless, though, in his defence, he owed his office to a system that placed no value on that quality.

Among Beasley's biggest mistakes was his decision to keep ped-
dling hope in British decency long after he recognized its absence.
He did so partly from credulousness but also from a fear that Britain might easily retain or even recruit American sailors in the Royal
Navy if these men imagined that all hope of release was lost.

In retrospect, Beasley and the US government overestimated the
danger of POWs flooding into the king's service. American officials
could not have foreseen that the war with France would end in the
spring of 1814, which brought the recruitment of Americans in the
British prison system to a halt. But the anxiety that prisoners could
easily be peeled from the United States led Beasley to make rash
promises. Britain was never going to let impressed sailors walk free
because a war had started, and it was always likely that the American government's dependence on privateers would put more Americans in British custody than vice versa. By filling his letter book
with appeals and reports, while keeping as far away from the prisons as possible, Beasley told himself he was doing the best he could
in difficult circumstances. For the prisoners, he became a powerful
symbol of the system that had failed them.

7.

EXTREME NECESSITY

THE MORNING AFTER THE FIRST CONSIGNMENT OF AMERICANS arrived at Dartmoor, the turnkeys opened the heavy doors of each of the blocks and nine thousand prisoners moved into the yards to be counted. The turnkeys ordered the Americans to step forward and escorted them to the prison clerks, seated at tables in the market yard. At the centre of this ritual was the General Entry Book, the prison's register—an enormous ledger nearly a meter high. The Transport Board required each prison facility to keep separate registers for 'prisoners of different nations in hostility with this country'; this meant that on that morning—3 April 1813—the clerks produced a fresh volume of bright, empty pages headed with 'American Prisoners of War at Dartmoor'. The first in line was Michel Tower, an impressed sailor from Hingham, Massachusetts, who had (according to the register) 'delivered himself up' from the Royal Navy on 8 January 1813. He was thirty-seven years old, five feet seven and a half inches tall, and stout. His face was 'fresh and round'; brown hair, blue eyes, no distinguishing marks or scars. He'd brought a blanket with him on the march from Plymouth, so the clerks only needed to issue him with a hammock. In the American register at Dartmoor, Tower became prisoner no. 1.[1]

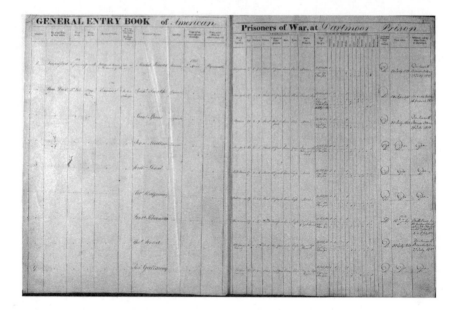

First page of the register of American prisoners of war at Dartmoor
National Archives of the UK

For the next two years, the register would fill up with more than six and a half thousand names. The last to arrive was Francis Gibson, a forty-two-year-old Black sailor from Pennsylvania who was entered into the register on 8 March 1815. Gibson, like Tower, had been serving in the Royal Navy. Whereas Tower had been able to escape from the navy (albeit to the prison system) within the first six months of the war, Gibson served on HMS *Imogene* until June 1814, when the end of the war with France persuaded the navy that his services were no longer required and he was cast into the hulks at Plymouth. Gibson arrived at Dartmoor with a gunshot wound to his left thigh, a dramatic detail which the register recorded without elaboration. He was well enough to walk out of Dartmoor among the final consignments of Americans in July 1815, fully six months after the war was over.[2]

Between Tower and Gibson, the register tells us a little about everyone at Dartmoor, though given the sheer volume of information—and the limited ways of keeping track of it in the early nineteenth century—it may be more useful to the modern historian than it was to the harried officials of the Transport Board. In our own information-saturated age, it's easy for us to miss how unusual the register was in its historical moment. By 1813, Britain and the United States had conducted only a handful of censuses. Citizens might find their way into parish registers, but the gaze of what historians have called the 'identification state' remained very limited. Ships' owners and captains kept lists of sailors in their employ, and customs collectors in American ports kept crew lists for departing vessels. But none of these captured as much detail as the Dartmoor register, which recorded age, stature (height), person (build), visage and complexion (rough markers for facial appearance), hair colour, eye colour, and 'marks or wounds'. This data was set against a prisoner's unique number; periodically the lists would be copied by the clerks and sent off to London to be spliced with records from the rest of the prison system.[3]

For Isaac Cotgrave and other prison officials, the register had many uses. It allowed the turnkeys to conduct roll call in the prison yards. It recorded the supplies that had been issued to each prisoner, from hammocks and bedding to shoes and handkerchiefs. The board offered strict rules on the useful life of these supplies—two years for a hammock, for example; eighteen months for a pair of trousers—and the register allowed the clerks to deny requests for new blankets or shirts from prisoners who had sold or gambled away their initial allocation. It also fixed the order in which the Americans had been captured, which was one of the criteria (but not the only one) for determining which prisoners should be released in any exchanges. As we'll see, inmates found many ways to cheat the register: by pretending to be another prisoner, for example, to get released before their turn. In cases of impersonation, the DESCRIPTION columns came into their own. If the clerks had described prisoners accurately when they booked them in, these fields would (in theory) make it harder to borrow another man's identity. They would also allow the agent to raise the alarm beyond Dartmoor if a prisoner managed to escape. Within a day or two, a description of the fugitive would be with the authorities in Plymouth and London and usually in the newspapers.[4]

This colossal undertaking had two obvious points of weakness. First, it relied on the judgments made by the clerks and the honesty of the prisoners' declarations. Height could be measured precisely, and eye and hair colour were straightforward. The board could confirm a sailor's rank with the authorities in the British port which had received his captured vessel; this was a hedge against any attempt by seamen to claim officer status and parole. The board also circulated details of privateers, letters of marque, and French and US Navy vessels which had been seized by Britain, enabling the clerks to confirm when a particular prisoner had been captured. But the most fundamental information in the register—names, ages, and especially places of birth—could only be established by prisoners themselves. As a rule, American vessels didn't keep muster lists which could allow their captors to identify the sailors aboard. For British and Irish sailors serving on US ships, the 'birthplace' column of a British prison register was particularly unnerving. Samuel Leech, a British-born sailor captured off the African coast on a US Navy ship in 1814, was terrified he would be outed as a traitor and sentenced to death. In fact, when he reached the prison at Cape Town, he was relieved to discover that the authorities were using an older version of the register without a column for birthplace. Sailors arriving at Dartmoor were less fortunate, though in practice there was little to prevent them from dissembling when asked about their origins by the clerks. The same option was also open to African American sailors; those who had fled from slavery were unwilling to leave a paper trail which might eventually facilitate their repatriation to the town or state where they had been enslaved.[5]

The register's second weakness was its sheer size. By 1814, the Transport Board could call upon twenty-seven clerks at its London headquarters to process data from prisons like Dartmoor. But the bureaucracy of the British prison system created what one historian has called 'the fiction of oversight'. With prison agents like Isaac

Cotgrave submitting regular updates from their registers and tens of thousands of data points crossing the cluttered desks in Whitehall, it became ever harder to keep track of the information in ways that realised its potential. There were several efforts to alphabetize the records, though these produced still more lists in the absence of the index cards that might be used a century later. The prison system captured huge amounts of information with unprecedented levels of detail, but it was desperately deficient in technology we take for granted: the ability to sort and retrieve data. The board could never see as far as it hoped to, and this basic futility lay at the heart of its gargantuan efforts to make a disparate population legible. This may have given little consolation to individual prisoners, though their many attempts to cheat the system prospered in the space between the ideal and the reality of the register.[6]

WE HAVE THINGS SO MUCH EASIER. ONCE YOU COMMIT TO INPUT-ting those six and a half thousand entries into a spreadsheet, you can sort and search stories and individuals in a way that the board's most ardent bureaucrats could only have dreamed of. Just a few dozen Dartmoor prisoners left significant traces in the archive. The register lets us know a little about the rest, the vast majority of American inmates who would otherwise be lost to history. It also allows us to corroborate claims made by the few who wrote up their experiences. This is especially useful for the first year of American presence in Dartmoor, for which we have just a handful of written accounts. Barely a thousand Americans were entered into the register between April 1813 and May 1814—about 15 percent of the total number who would pass through Dartmoor's imposing gates. This first phase of the American presence was marked by the overwhelming ascendancy of the French, and by the restrictions and privations this placed upon the Americans. The only substantial account of this period was written by Charles Andrews of Newport, Rhode Island, who was thirty-six years old in 1813. While the Dartmoor register listed him as an ordinary seaman, the Plymouth register gave his rank as second mate—which seems more plausible, given the role Andrews would go on to play. He'd been on the *Virginia Planter*, an American schooner with a cargo of cotton from Charleston, when it was captured by HMS *Pyramus* off the coast of France in March 1813. With the exception of a brief sojourn in Mill Prison at Plymouth in the summer of 1813—possibly for medical treatment—Andrews remained in Dartmoor until the spring of 1815.[7]

When the Dartmoor prisoners streamed back to the United States in the summer of 1815, they rushed to supply newspapers and book publishers with personal testimonies of the terrible 'Dartmoor massacre'. Andrews took a broader view. Across nearly three hundred pages, he situated the massacre in a saga which began with the arrival of those first 250 Americans on 2 April 1813. He had seen it all, he said, and his published account promised 'a complete and impartial history of the entire captivity of the Americans in England'. The register tells a different story: Andrews was captured by the Royal Navy in March 1813 and didn't make landfall in Britain until 22 April. He spent months in the Plymouth hulks before being brought to Dartmoor on 1 July. So how could he offer such a vivid description of those first few months of the American presence at Dartmoor? A clue lies in the title of his 1815 book: *The Prisoners' Memoirs*. Although Andrews was ostensibly the author, the account appears to have been an ensemble piece hastily compiled that fall by Philip R. Hopkins, a young lawyer from Connecticut. Hopkins apologised for publishing the *Memoirs* 'in a more unfinished state than he could have wished', but noted the 'great anxiety of the public' to learn more about the Dartmoor Massacre. To confirm the account's authenticity, Hopkins included a 'certificate' signed by sixty-one prisoners affirming that they had 'carefully perused and examined the following Manuscript Journal' and that they 'solemnly declare, that all matter and occurrences herein contained are just and true'. To ward off potential competitors, they added that 'to the best of our knowledge and belief, this is the only Journal kept at Dartmoor.'[8]

This rickety document—ostensibly the experience of Andrews alone, more likely an edited amalgamation of various prisoners' experiences and claims—supplies the only detailed account of what took place at Dartmoor during the turbulent winter of 1813–1814. This was a period in which the Americans fought with the Romans, with the rest of the French prisoners, with the Dartmoor authorities, and, at last, with each other. It was also the period in which this small group of American pioneers at Dartmoor made a fateful request of Isaac Cotgrave: they demanded to be moved away from the Black men with whom they had sailed before their capture and alongside whom they were neatly logged in the register of American prisoners. *The Prisoners' Memoirs* is our principal source for why Dartmoor became the first segregated prison in American history, but its testimony on this point is particularly partial. Andrews and his sixty-one referees had one thing in common: they were all white.

ONE MIGHT THINK A COMMON ENMITY TOWARDS BRITAIN WOULD bind together the French and American prisoners at Dartmoor. In fact, the new arrivals resented finding themselves confined to a tiny corner of this flamboyantly French prison. Some acknowledged that the French prisoners had spent so long in captivity that they had become inured to, even accepting of their fate. Others indulged the crude prejudice that Americans loved liberty more than the French did. The practical difficulties created by Cotgrave's decision to confine the US prisoners to the top floor of Four worsened everyone's mood. The Americans had no access to the daily market, which left them hostages to illicit trading with the Frenchmen on the other floors of Four. At a pinch, they could trade through the metal gates which divided their yard from the prison's main passageway, which was always thronged by French prisoners going to and from the different blocks. But this incurred a markup that made even the flushest Americans wince.[9]

The confinement of the Americans to Four also prevented them from meeting a group of French prisoners who might have brokered peace between the two sides: the dozens of Americans who had been captured on French vessels and held in Dartmoor long before April 1813. According to the French register, the first American at Dartmoor was not Michel Tower but John Serrick, a thirty-two-year-old sailor from New Orleans, who walked into the prison on opening day in May 1809. Serrick was relatively lucky: his family secured his release later that year. His compatriot Thomas Mumford was considerably less fortunate. In 1809, he was serving as an officer on a French merchant vessel which was captured by the Royal Navy in the Indian Ocean. Mumford was brought to Dartmoor and, despite his pleas to Agent Cotgrave and the State Department, denied release. In 1812, he became so unwell that the Transport Board agreed to free him as an invalid. By now, the United States was at war with Britain, and getting back across the Atlantic would be a challenge. The ailing Mumford returned to France on a cartel ship, then secured passage at Bordeaux on an American letter of marque carrying brandy and wine back to the United States. Soon after putting into the Atlantic, this ship was also captured by the Royal Navy and Mumford was taken back to Dartmoor. He would remain in the prison until the War of 1812 was over, along with dozens of Americans who were quietly transferred from the French to the American register when the rest of the French prisoners went home in the spring of 1814.[10]

Denied the opportunity to learn the prison's secrets and shortcuts from these American pioneers in the other blocks, Charles Andrews and the rump of the American contingent were stuck with the Romans in Four. 'It is difficult for the mind to conceive how human beings could be possessed of fewer virtues or more vices,' Andrews noted. As the initial contingent of 250 Americans was reinforced by the arrival of another 200 from Plymouth in the summer of 1813—including Andrews himself—the yards of Four became ever more fractious. Cotgrave moved the American prisoners to the first floor of Four, which left 900 French 'outcasts'—the Romans and their fellow travellers—crammed into the floors above. A 'quite warm' argument broke out between a few dozen French and American prisoners on the evening of 10 July, and before long 'nearly all the prisoners of both nations' were involved. The guards put an end to the confrontation by 'turning in' the prisoners—locking them in their block for the night—but (as Andrews noted) 'animosities had not subsided.'[11]

The next morning, as the Americans filed out of Four for roll call, the French were waiting for them in the yard with 'knives, clubs, stones, [and] staves'. With most of the US prisoners still inside the block, the French set about the Americans as the turnkeys summoned the militia from the adjoining barracks. Andrews's account insists that 'naked malignants' led the assault. This certainly sounds like the Romans, though their vices didn't usually run to violence. (At least, not towards humans.) Whatever the motive for the attack, it left twenty men on each side badly injured. Agent Cotgrave wrote the Transport Board to propose a wall bisecting the yard of Prison Four. This further restricted the narrow confines in which the Americans lived out their lives at Dartmoor, but it would at least deliver them from the Romans. Charles Andrews was delighted 'to be disencumbered of that outcast tribe'. Barely three months after their arrival, the Americans finally had a space of their own at Dartmoor.[12]

Things got even better the following month when the board decided to send the Romans to the hulks at Plymouth—in fact, to the *Hector*, where the first cohort of Americans at Dartmoor had previously languished. Although it would be expensive to keep them there, the board judged that the maintenance of order at Dartmoor was worth the extra cost. The departure plans were held up by one last detail: Should Cotgrave offer the Romans a new set of clothes on their way out? Onlookers in Plymouth would be horrified by the arrival of hundreds of naked Frenchmen, but the board fretted that the Romans would try to sell any new clothes they were issued before their departure. In the end, Cotgrave was instructed to distribute clothing only as the Romans walked out of the main gate. He was also ordered not to put any new prisoners into Four until the areas occupied by the Romans 'shall have been thoroughly cleansed and purified'. (This was prudent; the Plymouth authorities complained that the Romans had arrived at the hulks with scabies.) When the Romans began their evacuation on 30 August 1813, among their number was Etienne Pagert, the very first prisoner to walk into Dartmoor on 22 May 1809. In his account of the French experience at Dartmoor, fellow prisoner Louis Catel had insisted that desperation was the Romans' chief recruiting tool. Pagert was an easy mark: he had spent exactly ten years in British custody.[13]

THE DEPARTURE OF THE ROMANS DIDN'T RESOLVE THE PROBLEMS in Four. The hardened French prisoners who remained in the block outnumbered the Americans, and in October 1813 Cotgrave asked the board to devise new measures 'to prevent any communications between the Americans and the other prisoners'. With so many Frenchmen in captivity, it was impossible for the Americans to get a block of their own. Glover Broughton, a sailor from Marblehead in Massachusetts, became no. 764 in the American register when he arrived at 'confounded, dreary, doleful, contemptible Dartmoor' in the fall of 1813. When he remembered the experience years later, he felt sure that there were a hundred Frenchmen to every American. To be a US POW in the winter of 1813 was to occupy a prison within a prison, subjected to 'a variety of scenes . . . that would defy all imagination to picture'.[14]

Like every war prison, Dartmoor was a place in which coercion and self-government awkwardly coincided. The agent, turnkeys, and militia guards were responsible for maintaining order, and their insistent and often capricious demands—that the prisoners turn out for roll call every morning regardless of the weather, for example—engendered huge resentment among the prisoners. Dartmoor was not, however, a correctional facility. The agent and the Transport Board occasionally discussed how they might promote religion, but they lacked the determination and resources to sculpt the prisoners' morals. The board's regulations gave inmates a modest influence over their circumstances, not least in the daily inspections of bread and other provisions from the contractors. In everyday matters, they were expected to govern themselves. They did this through the institution of the prisoners' committee, which was one of the most important (and most easily misunderstood) elements of the American experience at Dartmoor.

Prisoners' committees sprang up throughout the global prison complex, and at Dartmoor they emerged in each of the prison blocks. Committees performed two vital roles: they liaised with the prison agent and the local representative of the United States government on issues relating to prisoner welfare, and they enforced discipline and adjudicated disputes between sailors. The first role required that committees work closely with the prison authorities; the second allowed them to operate without the consent (or even the knowledge) of the agent and the turnkeys. Serious misconduct might draw the agent's attention: an offender would be put on 'short allowance'—reduced rations—and thrown into isolation in the prison's black hole, the cachot. But for most offences—stealing, fighting, racketeering, dishonesty—prisoners' committees maintained a shadow system of justice. Although this form of self-government was more democratic than the leadership of a captain or first mate at sea, it borrowed its punishments from maritime practice. Prisoners accused of an offence were far more likely to receive lashes from their compatriots than from the British authorities.[15]

At sea, sailors were subject to brutally clear hierarchies: officers had the power to have miscreants flogged, and a captain could be as tyrannical as his fellow officers allowed him to be. Those leadership structures were thrown into disarray the moment sailors crashed into the prison system. Samuel Leech, the US Navy sailor who ended up in Cape Town prison in 1814, recalled that the entire officer corps from his ship was sent to a parole town far from the prison, leaving the ordinary sailors to organize and police themselves. 'We had lost the natural exactors of discipline

among seamen,' Leech noted. Men accustomed to taking orders
had now to adopt 'a set of regulations in respect to order, cleanliness, &c.' and to elect 'certain of our number to enforce them'. At
Dartmoor, though, the overwhelming majority of prisoners were
from privateers and letters of marque rather than naval vessels.
The board's conventions allowed only the captain (and perhaps the
first mate) from these ships to be spared imprisonment and placed
in the parole towns around the edges of the moor. As a result,
many American crews were tipped into Dartmoor largely intact.
This presented a huge challenge to the usual model of prisoners'
committees, in which ordinary sailors would elect each other to
represent the group. Should sailors naturally promote their former
officers? Or would Dartmoor offer a level playing field in which
talented sailors could wield authority over their erstwhile superiors? Behind these questions was a creeping dread, among the
officers at least, that ordinary sailors might grasp this opportunity
to capsize the shipboard order and settle scores with the men who
had previously been in charge.[16]

George Little didn't arrive at Dartmoor until the summer of
1814, but his memoir offers a tantalizing window on these questions. He was shocked by the disorder among the prisoners and
by the prominence of ordinary seamen who refused to respect the
customary hierarchies of shipboard life. These men 'were a perfect set of outlaws and desperadoes', he wrote, 'selected from the
most miserable haunts of vice in all the seaports within the United
States'. There were some exceptions, but in general 'the loafers and
rough-alleys greatly overbalanced the better-disposed, so that the
law that "might gives right" was forcibly illustrated, and the lev-
elling system was put into effectual practice.' Little was horrified
by the determination of sailors to seek revenge on their former superiors: officers who had 'kept aloof from these miscreants' were
harassed and 'mobbed' in the prison; those who had 'kept a taut
hand and good discipline' on their ships, meanwhile, were 'generally
tied to the whipping-post and flogged'. Although the French had

already left Dartmoor when Little arrived at the prison, he couldn't believe how ready the Americans were to fight each other.[17]

One fascinating aspect of Little's complaint is how much it diverges from Charles Andrews's account of orderly government among the American prisoners. The tensions and rivalries described by Little were almost completely absent from Andrews's narrative, which offered a vision of Dartmoor's inmates as hyper-patriotic. Only one group threatened Andrews's vision of unblemished allegiance: the impressed men coming into Dartmoor, and especially those American sailors who secured early release from the prison by volunteering for the Royal Navy. Reuben Beasley kept telling his superiors in Washington that the United States would 'lose many valuable seamen' to the Royal Navy unless the government agreed to pay American prisoners a daily allowance. 'Respecting the prisoners who have entered into the British service, it is difficult to procure information of them,' he wrote. 'I am informed they are taken from the prison in the night, after the others have retired to rest.' Beasley had no idea how many, though the letters he received from Chatham, Dartmoor, and the rest of the prison system suggested that 'great numbers' were involved.[18]

Around a fifth of the American prisoners brought to Dartmoor from 1813 to 1815 had previously served in the Royal Navy, or had been apprehended in British ports by the navy's Impress Service. Some, like George Little, had demanded a transfer to prison when asked to fight their countrymen. Others had kept their heads down and were finally sent to Dartmoor only when the navy had no further need of their services. Were these men all loyal Americans? What about the prisoners who were spirited away to Plymouth and His Majesty's warships after a hushed conversation with the agent or turnkey in the yard? Charles Andrews approached these awkward questions by emphasizing the horrors facing every American at Dartmoor. 'Their situation was now so abject and wretched,' he wrote of the sailors considering the Royal Navy's offer, 'that they were willing to embrace any opportunity where there was the least prospect of bettering their condition, however repugnant to their feelings or sentiments.' Andrews copied a passage from a law dictionary to establish that enlistment wasn't necessarily treason: 'If a person be under circumstances of actual force and constraint, through a well-grounded apprehension of injury to his life or person, this fear, or compulsion will excuse his even joining with either rebels or enemies in the kingdom, provided he leaves them whenever he hath a safe opportunity.' Andrews's main strategy for defending Dartmoor's defectors, however, was to blame Reuben Beasley. Surely their representative in London must have known that the oppressive conditions were calculated to flip their loyalties. And yet 'to all these petitions, complaints, and remonstrances, Mr Beasley returned no answer.' In fact Beasley had continued to pressure the Transport Board on multiple fronts, but Andrews mistook the agent's powerlessness for apathy.[19]

The register and the Transport Board's letters to Agent Cotgrave allow us to see more clearly than Beasley (or Andrews) the scale of the defection problem. Barely two weeks after the first contingent of Americans arrived at Dartmoor, several quietly asked the turnkeys about joining the Royal Navy. A few more offered to join the British merchant marine, hoping to avoid service on a warship, but the Transport Board firmly declined this compromise: Americans could fight for the king or remain in prison. Cotgrave was to inform his superiors in London of any volunteers, and navy officials from Plymouth came to Dartmoor to follow up on the leads. There's no evidence in the board's correspondence of a deliberate plan to sweat American prisoners into committing treason. If anything, the board and the navy were cautious about who to accept. On 1 July 1813, the board confirmed with Cotgrave that Admiral Sir Robert Calder, commander-in-chief of naval forces at Plymouth, would be sending an officer to the prison to 'select such of the American prisoners' as seemed suited to life on a British warship. By early 1814, with the war against France nearly won, the navy recruiters stopped coming to Dartmoor altogether.[20]

Seven hundred and thirty-two names had been entered into the American register by the start of October 1813. Of that number, the vast majority were sailors from privateers and letters of marque; only fifty-eight had been serving on Royal Navy vessels, around 8 percent of the total. (Impressed sailors would come to Dartmoor in far higher numbers after Britain concluded its war with France in 1814.) As for the sailors who got out of Dartmoor before October 1813 by volunteering for Royal Navy duty, we have a fairly good sense of how to identify them in the register: beside their departure date the clerk wrote 'for HM service' or named a senior navy officer as the prisoner's destination. The number of Americans heading into the Royal Navy was almost exactly the same as those coming from His Majesty's Service—sixty versus fifty-eight. But only one of the sixty sailors who volunteered for early release had come to Dartmoor from a Royal Navy vessel. It seemed that the experience of being in the navy made American prisoners at Dartmoor reluctant to go back.[21]

That conclusion should have been welcomed by Charles Andrews, though after his lavish attempts to exculpate prisoners who felt 'compelled' to volunteer for British service, he dropped a brief hint about what was really going on among the Americans at Dartmoor. 'The majority of the prisoners used every means in their power to prevent our countrymen from entering the enemy's service,' he recalled. Prisoners who betrayed any intention of signing up for the Royal Navy were tied to the prison walls, 'flogged severely', and threatened with death 'if they did not desist'. According to Andrews, Cotgrave offered sanctuary to any prisoners who indicated a willingness to defect. These men were allowed to stay in the guardhouse for weeks until the navy could approve their transfer to Plymouth. Men arriving from Royal Navy ships were the least likely to return to the king's service, but one explanation for their miniscule rate of re-enlistment is that they were watched particularly closely by Andrews and his band of patriotic vigilantes.[22]

Another indication of Andrews's true feelings about Americans who escaped Dartmoor by joining the Royal Navy comes from the appendices to *The Prisoners' Memoirs*. Alongside the lists of those who had died or broken out, Andrews included a list of fifty-nine Americans 'who entered his Majesty's service out of Dartmoor from April 1813 until 1814; to which is annexed their former residence and the ships in which they were captured or impressed'. It can't have been helpful to those men (or their families) to appear in print, with their hometown alongside their name, as traitors to their country. But Andrews and his associates, who had clearly maintained these lists during their captivity, named and shamed their inconstant compatriots regardless. These prisoners may have gotten out of Dartmoor early, but their actions had not been forgotten by those they had left behind.[23]

This is a good moment to re-examine the list of prisoners who signed the 'certificate' in 1815 authenticating Andrews's account as 'the only journal kept at Dartmoor'. Of the sixty-one signatories, we can conclusively identify forty-eight in the register. Nearly half were petty officers, about five times what we'd expect if the testimonials had been sourced at random from the total prisoner cohort. Checking the list against other accounts, we see that Andrews's referees were prominent in the various prisoners' committees, implying that they tried to take the reins of prison governance. However, they were highly unrepresentative not only racially (all were white) but also in terms of their maritime experience: only one of the forty-eight had served in the Royal Navy. Many of the signatories had arrived in 1814, when the proportion of Royal Navy veterans at Dartmoor approached 25 percent rather than the 8 percent of the previous year. The fact that Andrews and his associates recruited so few of these sailors to their ranks tells its own story about loyalty and suspicion among the prisoners.[24]

RACE WAS THE OTHER MAJOR FAULT LINE DURING THE EARLY PHASE of the American ordeal at Dartmoor. In October 1813, approximately 78 of the 556 prisoners in the American register (14 percent) were men of colour. I say 'approximately' because we are reliant on the clerks for our mapping of Dartmoor's racial landscape, and 'complexion' was easily the most tortured field in the register. Eighteen different terms were entered in this column across the six and a half thousand entries in the American register: from 'fresh' to 'sandy' to 'black', with more than a dozen intermediate points. The register was produced at a moment when an older taxonomy of physical appearance based on the balance of humours within every human being (blood, phlegm, black bile, yellow bile) was colliding with a newer taxonomy based on race and skin colour. All racial classification is subjective, but people who might conventionally pass as 'white' in our own historical moment were confidently categorized on the humoral system as 'brown' or 'dark'.[25]

A few clues make our task easier. Clerks tended to use nouns rather than adjectives to describe people of colour ('A Black', 'A Negro'), and in generating estimates of the Dartmoor population, I've mostly used this convention to classify Black and brown sailors. We can also cross-reference the Dartmoor register with other sources. Darius Williams of Saybrook, Connecticut, was taken off HMS *Ruby* in 1812 and placed in the hulks at Portsmouth. The register recorded him as 'Brown', but a clerk had written 'man of colour' in the column set aside for distinguishing marks. He was then transferred to Chatham, where again a clerk wrote 'a man of colour' beside 'brown'. At Dartmoor, however, the clerks simply wrote 'brown'. We might assume that Williams was light-skinned enough to pass as white, though I also found him in the impressment files at the State Department, where a former captain swore an oath that he was 'a colored man aged about twenty seven years . . . and a natural born citizen of the United States'. There are many similar stories of race-making in Dartmoor and the other British prisons, which makes it impossible for us to know precisely how many people of colour were in the prison complex. Whatever the number, Charles Andrews and his associates were determined to be separated from them.[26]

Their request was made to Isaac Cotgrave in October 1813. It came days after Reuben Beasley's only visit to Dartmoor, which had not gone well. This episode would later assume mythical status among the prisoners. Was it really true, as one suggested, that Beasley had been so taken by Daniel Alexander's monumental architecture that he had announced it 'had more the resemblance of a *palace* than a *prison*'? Or, as another claimed, that Beasley callously muttered that he was 'glad that it is not I that is to live here'? Charles Andrews insisted that, instead of using the 'language of consolation and relief' towards the prisoners, Beasley turned to his assistant and said, sotto voce, 'I did not think that the number had been so great!' Inmates were allowed to shout a train of questions in his direction, but his answers only confirmed their initial impression: the agent was not going to save them from whatever Dartmoor had in store.[27]

Soon after Beasley's departure, 'we petitioned to have the black prisoners separated from the white,' Andrews recalled in *The Prisoners' Memoirs*, 'for it was impossible to prevent these fellows from stealing, although they were seized up and flogged almost every day.' Andrews happily reported that 'our petition was granted, and we greatly relieved, and the blacks, ninety in number, occupied the upper stories.' Elsewhere in the *Memoirs*, Andrews conceded that stealing was endemic in the prison: 'Men, otherwise commonly honest, when reduced to extreme necessity, naturally resort to the commission of crimes.' Hunger and despair would 'break through all moral obligation'. Clearly, white prisoners were susceptible to this vice: even 'brothers and the most intimate friends' would steal from each other. So why did he racialize the issue?[28]

The answer lies in his recollection of how the leaders of the early American contingent at Dartmoor had decided to combat prisoner thefts. 'To provide a remedy against this evil, we appointed a legislative body, to form a code of laws for the punishment of all such misdemeanors.' The prisoners also formed a 'tribunal' which would 'try and convict all criminals according to law and evidence'. Those found guilty would receive two dozen lashes, 'as severe as is given at the gangway of a man-of-war ship'. We know that Black and white sailors lived and served alongside each other at sea, and that a maritime career might offer a more level playing field for Black men than many professions on land. But Black sailors were prevented from becoming officers on merchant or naval vessels, except in the very rare circumstances of an all-Black crew. Every single Black person who entered Dartmoor through October 1813 was either an ordinary seaman, a cook, or a cabin boy. Although the memoirs of white sailors occasionally reveal camaraderie and affection across the colour line, the precondition for being a Black sailor on a mixed-race crew was an acceptance that one could never graduate to the top deck.[29]

Charles Andrews's account of the flogging of 'disloyal' white sailors and George Little's descriptions of the battles between petty officers and 'rough-alleys' for control of Dartmoor's prison blocks show that the political worlds at Dartmoor were fiercely contested. The default assumption of American prisoners in captivity was that they would govern themselves when they could, though the process of establishing authority over other sailors was rarely straightforward. Since African Americans comprised close to 15 percent of the American complement in October 1813, they had reason to seek representation on prisoners' committees. This was especially the case because, as Andrews noted, the primary function of the committee was to adjudicate disputes among the American contingent. The request of Charles Andrews and his associates for racial segregation certainly took root in prejudices about Black criminality. But it was also an attempt to ward off a more dangerous prospect than theft: that white sailors would be forced to share political power across the colour line.

There were very few spaces in American life in which this kind of power sharing took place. Even abolition societies in the first years of the nineteenth century restricted membership to white people. Black activists and writers quietly noted that these 'benevolent' whites frequently treated African Americans as beneficiaries rather than equal partners in the work of justice. Black people exercised the franchise in many northern states, though often in the face of resistance (verbal or physical) from their white neighbours. Black politics shuttled between an acknowledgement of the importance of separate institutions—from mutual aid societies to Masonic lodges—and a continuing battle to open up local, state, and national politics to Black participation and representation. The realities of prejudice were everywhere, and they followed Black seamen into the improvised political spaces of the prison system.[30]

Could prisoners of war escape the gravitational pull of prejudice? One answer comes from the hulks at Bermuda, and the journal of Frank Palmer. On 16 February 1814, the American prisoners' committee conducted a trial to test the allegations made by several Black inmates that the 'Cocoa pounders'—a group of white sailors charged with distributing the prison's cocoa allowance—had been 'taking out some of the Cocoa, which was robbing all hands'. At that time, Black people were barred from testifying against whites in every slaveholding state; in the decades before the Civil War they would be prevented from doing so in several northern states, too. But in the Bermuda hulks, the Cocoa pounders were convicted on the basis of Black testimony, and the white sailors found guilty of the deception were 'cobbed one dozen each'. This enraged the men who had been brought to justice. The following day, smarting from their humiliation, they 'passed many threats' against the committee's (white) president, who refused to apologise for his actions. 'Word was then passed to hussle him,' Palmer wrote in his diary. 'He was then hussled pretty quick—and got a clip over the eye.' By the end of the day, the committee that had punished the Cocoa pounders had 'resigned' and a new one was installed. (Palmer noted that this wasn't voted on by the men; instead, the prisoners were 'mustered on deck to know if they had any objections'.) The speed with which the previous committee was usurped lends credence to the view that the sharing of political power across the colour line was too rich for the blood of some white prisoners.[31]

The paperwork on the British side of the Dartmoor segregation decision is maddeningly thin. 'We have received yours of the 21st,' the Board wrote Cotgrave on 23 October, 'and approve of your re-moving the Black [*sic*] and Men of Colour, from among the Amer-icans into the French Prison.' What this meant in practice was that those prisoners deemed to be Black—by Cotgrave or, more likely, by the white American prisoners themselves—were relocated to the top floor of Prison Four, which they would share with the pris-on's most unruly Frenchmen. Cotgrave's motives for approving the request are not evident from the board's side of their correspon-dence, though the agent had spent much of the summer creating physical barriers between the Americans and the French. His will-ingness to erect the same barriers between Black and white Amer-icans strongly suggests that tensions across the colour line—white over-representation on the committees, perhaps, as well as allega-tions of stealing—had spilled out of Four into the yards and the reports of the clerks and turnkeys. If racial segregation made Four less disruptive, Cotgrave was happy to embrace it.[32]

Two other factors are worth noting. First, Black sailors at Dart-moor were almost twice as likely to come from Royal Navy ships as their white counterparts, and given Charles Andrews's attentive-ness to disloyalty, this may have fortified his existing prejudices. One of the many plaintive letters from the prisoners' committees at Chatham in the summer of 1813 warned Reuben Beasley that, although 'the best part of the men would sooner die' than exchange prison for the Royal Navy, 'them that [is] gone is American Blacks that have come from His Britannic Majesty's Ships of War.' The evidence from the Dartmoor register squarely refutes this claim. We know of only one African American who obtained release to serve in the Royal Navy; it's harder to say whether further recruits were deterred by a combination of white American harassment and British prejudice. But the assumption that Black sailors were less loyal to the United States than their white counterparts may well have informed the white sailors' pitch for segregation.[33]

The other factor is more speculative. Andrews and the other white prisoners may have hoped that segregation would secure them a transfer to one of the other prison blocks. Even after the departure of the Romans, Andrews and the American contingent were forced to live amid hundreds of French 'criminals' (as Andrews termed them) with no access to either the market or the other prison blocks. The French prisoners massed in the other blocks 'go anywhere through the several prisons [and] go to market', Andrews complained, while 'the Americans [are] not permitted to.' If the white contingent had hoped that their prejudice might liberate them from Prison Four, they were sorely disappointed: they remained exactly where they were, while the prisoners of colour were moved upstairs. The white Americans continued to bemoan their lot, though Dartmoor's Black prisoners would soon seize the opportunity to govern themselves.[34]

CONFINED TO FOUR AND PREVENTED FROM ENJOYING WHAT passed for amusement in the rest of the prison, the American prisoners experienced one highlight during that first winter at Dartmoor: in November 1813, Isaac Cotgrave retired. His replacement, Thomas Shortland, was forty-two years old—more than twenty years younger than Cotgrave—and had no experience of managing a prison. Shortland had joined the navy at the age of thirteen. Two years later, he had sailed aboard one of the vessels which established the penal colony of Botany Bay in Australia. Like Cotgrave, he served with distinction on a number of smaller vessels during the 1790s, but unlike his predecessor he eventually commanded frigates and ships of the line. When the War of 1812 was declared, Shortland was captain of HMS *Royal Oak*, with seventy-four guns and more than 650 men. Shortland was thoughtful, curious, and cautious. He knew nothing about prisons, but the Americans could rely on him to sweat the details.[35]

Charles Andrews was delighted at the new appointment; unlike Cotgrave, Shortland was 'a man whose feelings had not yet grown callous by being familiarized with human misery'. The new agent discontinued the 'cruel practice' of conducting roll calls on mornings when the snow or rain made the prisoners' teeth chatter. He

Thomas George Shortland (1771–1827)
© *National Maritime Museum, Greenwich, London*

listened sympathetically to the Americans' complaints about Reuben Beasley and promised he would 'do all in his power to procure
us some relief from his government'. He allowed two Americans
to visit the market each day, fulfilling requests for their compatriots, and soon he opened the gates between Four and the other
prisons. Suddenly, the worlds of Dartmoor opened up to Black
and white Americans alike. Even the reviled Beasley delivered on
his promise to secure a government allowance for the prisoners,
putting a little money into the Americans' pockets. The gloom in
the prison lifted a little.[36]

Then, in the spring of 1814, a rumour reached Dartmoor that
Napoleon had surrendered. The French prisoners fell into a strange
despair. Defeat would secure their release, but it also meant that

their leader had been vanquished In this bittersweet mood, the French prisoners offloaded what they couldn't carry onto the Americans. Six thousand Frenchmen passed through the stone archway and down the road to Plymouth, and before long the American residents of Four were the only prisoners at Dartmoor. In May and June of 1814, the board rushed to bring Americans from the hulks at Plymouth, while Thomas Shortland and his staff refurbished the six empty blocks which the French had vacated. Charles Andrews enjoyed having 'the whole prison to ourselves', though he couldn't resist a familiar complaint: 'The blacks being mixed with us were very troublesome.' That summer, as Dartmoor became an exclusively American prison, Andrews and his white compatriots would finally break out of Four, and Americans would begin to populate the rest of the prison. When they did so, Four would be controlled exclusively by Black people. But despite Andrews's complaints and demands for separation, white Americans would be back.[37]

8.

A WORLD IN MINIATURE

A FTER SURVIVING HIS SEA BATTLE WITH THE BRITISH AND blagging parole in Barbados, the privateersman Benjamin Browne must have wondered when his luck would run out. His months of relative freedom in the British Caribbean were abruptly ended in the summer of 1814 by the news that he was to be transferred to Dartmoor. Writing about his ordeal more than thirty years later in an American magazine, Browne remembered the resignation he felt on arrival at the stone prison on the final day of September. After glumly surrendering his details to the register, he decided to explore the place 'where I was destined to spend I knew not how long a portion of my life'. Since the release of the French prisoners in May, a torrent of new arrivals had brought the American contingent to more than three thousand. The prisoners came from every state of the Union, as well as from a host of other countries which had spilled sailors onto American ships. There were men of means and sailors with nothing; men who had been captured under the American flag and sailors who had been serving in the Royal Navy. Browne became fascinated by his fellow prisoners. He quickly realised that behind Dartmoor's grim walls was a 'great world' of commerce, entertainment, friendship, and intrigue. While the British looked on, Browne and the other prisoners built a facsimile of the lives they had enjoyed before the war. For all its strangeness and isolation, Dartmoor became a familiar place.[1]

Immediately after his encounter with the prison register, Browne underwent another initiation ritual. The clerks issued him the prison's distinctive uniform: a jacket made of coarse wool, along with trousers, shoes (made of cloth and wood), and a cap. The uniform bore a mark which would eventually become a cliché of British prison garb: a series of upwards arrows, along with the letters 'T.O.' for Transport Office (as the board was sometimes known). The pattern dated back to the sixteenth century, when the symbol of an arrowhead was first used to denote royal property. You could find it on rifles and casks of gunpowder during the Revolutionary War, and its meaning at Dartmoor was starkly literal: the men wearing the 'King's arrow' belonged to the Crown until their release. The uniform felt heavy and insubstantial at the same time, and prisoners wore out every item long before the board permitted a replacement. It was also bright yellow, making prisoners easier to see if they attempted to escape. 'I regret that I did not procure a suit of this clothing to bring home and deposit in some museum,' recalled Benjamin Browne. His fellow inmate Charles Andrews insisted that the uniform was so hideous that many prisoners declined to wear it. From his distant office in London, the American agent Reuben Beasley eventually dispatched new uniforms in a muted blue. But those prisoners who had brought their own clothes to Dartmoor wore those instead (until they fell apart). Prisoners also received a hammock, mattress, and blanket; the Salem privateersman Joseph Valpey complained to his diary that these were 'as full of lice as the devil is of wickedness'.[2]

Beyond these supplies, the board's only ongoing contribution was food. The stipulated daily allowance for war prisons in the British Isles was a pound and a half of soft bread, half a pound of salted beef, a quarter pint of peas or six ounces of rice, and a third of an ounce of salt. (On Fridays the bread and beef were replaced by potatoes and fish.) Prisoners watched forlornly as the beef was boiled in the cookhouses at the end of each prison block. Before their eyes, the meat would get smaller and smaller and their allowance would seem ever more inadequate. Lewis Clover, who was moved from Chatham to Dartmoor in October 1814, vividly remembered the ritual of meat-watching among the prisoners: 'By the time each person got his beef it was almost too small to be seen.' Glover Broughton of Marblehead remembered the boiled meat 'shrinking like a washerwoman's thumb'. Begging the cooks to let him eat the beef raw was one of his two strategies to 'drive away hunger'. The other was putting a pipe down his throat to make himself sick.[3]

Uniforms and food were supplied on a one-size-fits-all basis. Lewis Clover recalled the absurd sight of 'large stalwart men crammed into trousers that looked like breeches' and 'small men with pantaloons turned up to the knees'. Some prisoners made their ration last from meal to meal, while others became 'almost frantic from starvation' after eating their entire allowance of bread in the morning. Defenders of the board's largesse, especially in Parliament, reminded critics that the rations were similar to those given to British soldiers fighting Napoleon. But the Americans at Dartmoor had plenty of time to think about their hunger and no idea when they would be released. The need to supplement the board's meagre supplies became a major driver of the prison's economies, both official and illicit.[4]

DARTMOOR OPENED UP TO THE AMERICANS GRADUALLY DURING the summer of 1814. The blocks in the South Yard—Five, Six, and Seven—offered the prisoners who moved over from Four much more space outside. The American sailors liked to play a variant of baseball—it may even have *been* baseball, but we probably don't want to get into that argument here. Then the North Yard containing One, Two, and Three was also opened. The board's records and the various prisoner accounts are silent on how, exactly, the prisoners ended up in specific blocks. Lewis Clover later wrote that prisoners were 'assigned' to a particular part of the prison, and the clerks would have required accurate lists of which prisoners were in each block to conduct roll call. (The board insisted that the prisoners be counted every day, though a formal roll call was required only twice each week.) We also know that, for the most part, prisoners were free to move between the different blocks and yards during the day. By the end of 1814, with so many Americans arriving at Dartmoor, the freedom to search for friends or even family members was a rare comfort in a terrible winter. This freedom also meant that scores could be settled from one end of the prison to the other, and that Prison Four—which became known as the 'Black Prison'— would never be truly segregated from the rest of Dartmoor.[5]

Each prison block had three floors, with doors at either end and a few high, unglazed windows which let in enough cold air to chill the prisoners but not enough light for them to read by. According to Benjamin Browne, the blocks were 'very dark, very damp, very

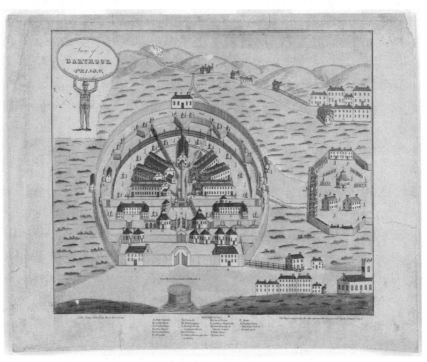

View of Dartmoor Prison by J. I. Taylor
Courtesy of Library of Congress, Prints and Photographs Division

dirty, and altogether about as uncomfortable places of abode as the malicious ingenuity of their contrivers could possibly have hit upon'. Lacking cells or subdivisions, each floor was broken up only by stanchions which ran the length of the block. These left room for hammocks slung in three vertical rows. As at Chatham, this meant that sailors in the top hammock would have to clamber over the lower residents to get in and out. Groups of six or eight sailors lived and cooked together in 'messes', sharing ingredients and utensils and a particularly close bond. Mess members designated someone to take on the cooking permanently or rotated the job among them. The cook would gather each day's allowance for his messmates and use the cookhouse at the end of the block to prepare their meal. Assuming that at least one of the mess had been captured with a chest or trunk, this became the table on which that meal was served.[6]

A good messmate was more than agreeable company. Benjamin Browne fondly remembered the member of his mess who would wander through the blocks each morning helping people with tasks and dispensing advice. On his return to Prison Seven, the gregarious sailor would unbutton his peacoat and reveal 'a nice, luscious, large salt-fish'. In one pocket would be a piece of steak; in the other would be onions or perhaps a potato. Was it really true, as Browne claimed, that his friend would have 'a nice four-pound loaf of white bread modestly shadowing its loveliness under his ample hat'? Perhaps the whole scene betrayed artistic license. ('Best of messmates!' Browne rhapsodised about his friend. 'Prince of good fellows, and paragon of providers!') But every prisoner's account or diary presents the mess as the keystone of prison life. Like most of Dartmoor's daily dynamics, it functioned beyond the gaze of the agent and the guards.[7]

More visible were the prisoners' committees which sprang up in each block. 'The government of the prisons was essentially democratical,' insisted Benjamin Browne, though he was never sure if committee members 'were chosen by ballot, viva voce, or how'. He was also foggy on 'to what extent the right of suffrage was exercised' and fairly sure he didn't participate in an election during his nine months in Dartmoor. Officers dominated the committees and wielded considerable power throughout the prison. They were tasked by Agent Shortland with selecting volunteers to become sweepers, lamplighters, food preparers, and so on. The tasks were not well remunerated, but committee members always had more office seekers than positions to dispense. The committees also appointed judges and juries to hear cases against prisoners accused of wrongdoing. The appointments process was not always enlightened. Frank Palmer, the Connecticut sailor who had languished in Bermuda and Canada before coming to Dartmoor, became friendly with a number of officers during his time in the prison system. Returning to his block after an all-night drinking session elsewhere in the prison, he was amazed to learn that he'd been appointed judge by his friends on the committee. 'I think they made a poor choice among 1500 prisoners,' he told his diary the next morning, still nursing his hangover. Eventually, he declined the appointment.[8]

In his 1846 memoir, Benjamin Browne recalled that the trials in Prison Seven had been 'conducted with a good deal of order and decorum'. The 'sailor-lawyers' who argued the cases would not have seemed out of place in a courtroom on shore, or so he claimed. Frank Palmer had a different perspective. The trial he'd wriggled out of judging involved a number of cooks who had allegedly stolen food from the prison block's allowance—one of the worst crimes one could commit at Dartmoor. Palmer found the whole process stressful. To judge prisoners in these ways was 'a very critical station', and he didn't envy the jury its deliberations. The verdict was hard to fathom: the head cook was acquitted, while the other cooks were found guilty. Each was whipped eighteen times, but then a mob of prisoners went looking for the head cook to insist that he should receive the same punishment. The cook's messmates refused to hand him over and the situation became tense. 'They talked of knives, and it has merely ended in talk,' Palmer wrote. 'However I fear it is not settled yet.' The actions of British officials—and the perceived inaction of Reuben Beasley—gave American prisoners a common cause. But the prison was stratified by rank, wealth, and even precedence: those who had been in Dartmoor the longest dominated the committees and exerted an outsized influence. Prisoners' committees would later be celebrated, both by nostalgic sailors and by historians, as examples of the hardiness of American liberty and democracy. In reality, they were places where desperate men jockeyed for power and advantage.[9]

MONEY FLOWED INTO DARTMOOR FROM A NUMBER OF SOURCES. IN the spring of 1814, the US government increased the prisoners' allowance to $2 per month. By the fall, as prisoner numbers swelled, $9,000 entered Dartmoor each month in allowances alone. Then there were the wages paid by Agent Shortland to prisoners working as nurses, lamplighters, and cleaners, plus the money he quietly directed to the network of informants who kept him apprised of what was happening in each block. Another source of prisoner income became available in the fall when Shortland restarted work parties on the moors surrounding the prison, under Thomas Tyrwhitt's urging. The minority of sailors who came from comfortable backgrounds could circumvent all this by asking family or friends to send money via the agent. These sums could be significant: the Massachusetts prisoner George Dennison successfully obtained £200 from his father in the winter of 1814–1815, insisting that this huge amount was necessary to see him through a captivity which remained desperately indefinite.[10]

The most lucrative, if divisive, source of income at Dartmoor came from prize money due to Americans who had served on Royal Navy ships. In one of the war's many strange ironies, the British government insisted on paying this even to men it had impressed and imprisoned. To Dartmoor's most fervent patriots, prize money was tainted: it represented the liquidation of ships and cargoes (French or even American) which had been captured by British warships. According to Charles Andrews, it had been decided at the Chatham hulks that this money should be distributed equally 'for the good of the whole, as is usual with a generous hearted sailor'. This may not have been true at Chatham, and it certainly wasn't true at Dartmoor. Instead, prize money threatened the prominence and power of the various prisoners' committees. Reuben Beasley had directed that the monthly allowances should be disbursed via the committees, giving 'the most respectable' prisoners the formidable power to withhold the allowances of sailors who broke a committee's rules or questioned its authority. Prize money, by contrast, was paid by the clerks directly to individuals, beyond the control (or even knowledge) of committee members. Benjamin Browne recalled 'one man who had been a boatswain, who was reported to have three thousand pounds'. Lewis Clover wistfully remembered 'a kind of jubilee' as a group of Royal Navy veterans rushed to spend their money. Browne estimated that these additional sums more than doubled the monthly flow into the prison, which he reckoned to be around £20,000 by the end of 1814. Dartmoor was far from a closed system, and the huge sums sluicing through the blocks brought opportunities and dangers to every prisoner.[11]

The principal place to spend money was the daily market, which Thomas Shortland finally opened to Americans in the spring of 1814. Shortland continued Agent Cotgrave's liberal interpretation of the Transport Board's regulations on what could be bought and sold, reasoning that the danger of contraband entering the prison was outweighed by the market's boost to morale. As the French did before them, American prisoners came to see the market as their major source of novelty and comfort. For those with money, it could supply fruit, vegetables, tobacco, soap, thread, sugar, coffee—'anything the country afforded', in Charles Andrews's recollection. For those without, it was a place to dream about how the next allowance payment (or gambling win) might be spent. Whatever a prisoner's means, the market offered a precious opportunity to interact (even briefly) with men—and women—who lived beyond the prison's dreary precincts.[12]

Most Americans who wrote about their experiences at Dartmoor were positive about the locals they met in the market, but prejudices could sometimes warp their experience. The county of Devon had a small but thriving Jewish community, mostly comprising second- and third-generation immigrants from the German states. Jewish traders helped to supply the navy and the shipping business in Plymouth, but most Jews in southwest England ran very small businesses. Charles Andrews became fixated on the 'great numbers of Jews who came here to sell old clothes'. In one of his stories, as nasty as it was redundant, a Jewish trader had supposedly accosted a local farmer on the way to Dartmoor market and accused him of being an American escapee—'thinking to receive the reward, which was three pounds, given by the government for apprehending any prisoner'. When the trader arrived at the prison gates brandishing the farmer, Agent Shortland censured him and demanded he pay five pounds in compensation to avoid a lawsuit. Andrews spread the word about what had happened within the prison 'and every man forbid purchasing anything of the Jew.' The story ended with the trader forced 'to leave the market without disposing of a single article'. There is no trace of this story in the other prisoner journals and narratives, or in the correspondence between Shortland and the board, but it speaks to a casual anti-Semitism which surfaced in a number of prisoners' accounts.[13]

The most concerted efforts to deceive at Dartmoor came from the forgers and the prison contractors. The outflow of fake money and the inflow of adulterated bread formed a constant backdrop to prison life. Jewish traders played no part in these sustained scams—except as victims receiving false notes and coins in the market. The French had been the undisputed masters of forgery at Dartmoor, and when they were released in the spring of 1814, they offloaded their counterfeiting equipment. There were teething troubles in acquiring the requisite skills to make use of this—one American prisoner recalled seeing 'a shower of spurious shillings' tumbling from one of the upper floors after a trainee forger had an accident with his stamping equipment. But before long, the Americans had mastered the art of literally making money, creating yet another panic for the agent and the board. The inability of the British authorities fully to curb the ensuing forgery epidemic was a subset of a larger problem: it was extremely difficult for Thomas Shortland and his officials to police what happened within each prison block.[14]

Taking their lead once more from the French, American prisoners used the market not only to buy and sell goods but also to service the shadow economies which sprang up throughout Dartmoor. Hundreds of Americans ran their own shops, offering staples and contraband items outside of market hours at inflated prices. Before long, outside merchants from Plymouth or the small town of Tavistock (seven miles to the west of the prison) began to invest in this informal economy. Traders would advance goods in the market yard to a prisoner, then receive either payment or unsold merchandise a week or two later. Both Isaac Cotgrave and Thomas Shortland knew that a thriving market furnished them with their most effective instrument of discipline: if a group of prisoners stepped out of line, the agent could announce the closure of the market to everyone. 'It was a great privation to have the market stopped for any length of time,' thought Benjamin Browne. 'In this, as in many other affairs of this life, the innocent and guilty suffer alike.' When the agent closed the market, prisoners with their own retail operations inside the blocks could make even more money than usual, at least until their stock ran out.[15]

AS BENJAMIN BROWNE REMEMBERED IT, EVERY MEMBER OF HIS mess was a trader of some sort. Browne ran a general store from his mess table, with an eclectic if limited stock: a bottle of rum, a wine glass, a few pinches of tobacco and snuff, and a 'little lump of butter, melting and tender as the heart of a young damsel of sweet sixteen'. One of his messmates who had been a tailor before going to sea took up the same trade in the prison. Another, who'd been a brewer, washed clothes in the streams of cold water which ran from the hills behind the prison through each of the yards. Two more messmates formed a 'coffee making business'. The absence of coffee beans was no obstacle to their start-up: they roasted peas and bread crusts, boiled the carbonized residue in their kettles, and relied on marketing to do the rest. The final two members of the mess worked with bones. One followed the example of the French by carving them into models that could be sold to the market traders. The other ground them up, boiled them, then sold the skimmed-off 'grease and marrow' to the prison's many desperate cooks.[16]

Not everyone succeeded. Frank Palmer 'set up shop keeping with the rest' when he arrived at Dartmoor in October 1814. A month later, having struggled to recoup his initial investment, he shuttered the enterprise and tried something new. 'I am now employed in teaching navigation, lunars, writing, &c &c &c, but my scholars bring chiefly writing [which] brings in only 6d per month.' This was 'rather too small', he admitted, but it 'furnishes me in tobacco, which is a monstrous tax in this place'. Palmer had found his way into one of Dartmoor's most popular trades: education. Once again, French prisoners had paved the way. When the Americans were first permitted to visit the French prison blocks in March 1814, Charles Andrews was stunned to find 'schools for teaching the arts and sciences, dancing, fencing, and music, and each of these in great perfection'. The following month, American sailors founded their first school in Four, charging prisoners six pence per month for instruction in reading, writing, and arithmetic. Before long, Dartmoor had become (according to Benjamin Browne) a 'university with seven colleges'.[17]

Browne regarded this as one of the few silver linings to a long and uncertain confinement. While most vices—especially tobacco and alcohol—were exorbitant, 'the means of a very decent education were available at a very cheap rate.' For sailors who had gone to sea as children, or grown up without stepping inside a schoolhouse, prison life offered a second chance. The Americans also took over the dancing schools of the French and added boxing gyms and music lessons to the prison's diversions. Those who preferred to spectate could watch a concert, fight, or play, for a modest fee. Even grizzled old salts found a paying audience for their reminiscences of a life at sea. These 'savored rather too strongly of the marvelous to be readily believed', thought Lewis Clover, but a happy ending or a good scare would bring a few pennies from the grateful crowd.[18]

For those who preferred solitary pursuits, there were many chances to read. The French had brought with them to Dartmoor a huge number of books, though mostly not in English. The Transport Board approved the circulation of Bibles to the Americans in Four, but the prisoners who got hold of the first batch sold them to the shopkeepers within the other blocks—for alcohol, claimed Benjamin Browne—and the shopkeepers sold them on to the 'grocers and market people'. This deterred the board from repeating the effort, and for a while reading in English was hard to come by. On his arrival in October 1814, Frank Palmer lamented that there were 'no books to employ our minds'. But as he got to know the prison's geographies of leisure, he found ways to satisfy his craving. He may have bought books in the market, though the frequency with which he referred to a new novel suggests that he became a patron of Dartmoor's most eccentric entrepreneur: the former Royal Navy sailor in the cockloft of Seven who had invested his considerable prize money in 'several hundred volumes of well-selected books'. These were offered for loan at a modest fee. Before long, Palmer was so consumed that he had to apologise to his diary for not making daily entries: 'I have been reading novels through the day and they have so engrossed my attention that I must defer giving loose to my reflections for the present.' Although Dartmoor contained its share of men who either could not or would not read, the library in Seven did a brisk trade in the fall and winter of 1814.[19]

The most coveted reading in Dartmoor was newspapers, which were banned from sale in the market square. Benjamin Browne thought this prohibition 'foolish and tyrannical', but the board had its reasons. Bad news for British forces might encourage a French or

American uprising; any news could prompt unwelcome speculation about how long prisoners might be stuck within Dartmoor's walls. The value of news was so great that prisoners clubbed together to pay the sky-high fees demanded by the market's smugglers, who knew the agent would expel them permanently from Dartmoor if they were caught. According to Benjamin Browne, prisoners even bribed the bread contractor to have newspapers 'carefully enveloped [and] baked in the middle of a loaf of bread'. Beyond these elaborate ruses, the most effective distribution channel for papers remained the constant stream of American arrivals. Many of these had a newspaper or two packed into their trunks, which proved an easy way to make friends on the inside.[20]

BETWEEN THE BOXING AND THE DANCING, THE BALLGAMES AND the theatrical productions, prisoners tried to replicate the world they had known outside the prison. But the illusion of familiarity could never hold for two obvious reasons: the Americans were not permitted to leave, and almost all of them were men. Despite the women who worked in the prison and the female market traders who interacted with prisoners every morning, Dartmoor was overwhelmingly a male space. Men wrestled and fought; they ate and played together; they slept in close proximity, transferring 'animal heat from one man to another' (as one prisoner put it) against Dartmoor's bitter cold; and they shared their stories and vulnerabilities during the long days and nights of their captivity. At least some must also have had sex, though our sources on this subject are scant. One letter from the board, dated 18 September 1813, orders Agent Cotgrave to send 'the boy stated to have been guilty of unnatural practices' to one of the prison hulks at Plymouth—the usual punishment for prisoners seen as dangerous to Dartmoor's order. Beyond this, the official records make no reference to intimate relations between prisoners.[21]

Benjamin Browne, in describing the prisoners' committees, noted that 'offences against morals were not very strictly inquired into.' He was referring to swearing, failing to keep the Sabbath, and succumbing to drunkenness and lewdness. Did homosexuality fall into the same category? Only two Dartmoor accounts mention sex within the prisons. Josiah Cobb, a Massachusetts sailor who produced a detailed but highly unreliable account of his five months in Dartmoor, reported an allegation of sex between men in June 1815, as the prisons were thinning out during the Americans' belated release. 'There had been but two or three instances of this heinous sin being committed,' Cobb wrote, 'on account of the serious penalty immediately following the conviction of the offender.' His suggestion that homosexuality was an exception to the generally lax treatment of 'offences against morals' is supported by the journals of Nathaniel Pierce and Frank Palmer; Palmer wrote on 4 April 1815 that 'last night three Frenchmen were detected in the act of buggery and this morning they were flogged severely.' The British had freed Dartmoor's French prisoners nearly a year before this incident, but some French-born sailors who had been captured on American ships were still in the prison. The 'three Frenchmen' may have been drawn from this group. It's also possible that the prisoners' committee which prosecuted the offence decided that it was better presented as a French excess than a homegrown practice. Sexual intimacy between male prisoners took place at the prisoners' own risk in the prison's many shadows. Discretion and good fortune may have allowed same-sex relationships to continue throughout the American tenure in the prison. But to be discovered was to expose oneself to harsh physical punishment and excommunication from one's block.[22]

Most prisoners who wrote up their Dartmoor experiences said little about their romantic imagination during their long confinement, but we know from prisoner diaries and journals that 'talking about girls' was a common way to pass the time. Frank Palmer recorded a dream in which his own scrambled yearnings broke the surface. He was back home in Stonington, Connecticut, outside the local tavern. Suddenly, a beautiful woman dressed in black materialised in front of him: 'Her right arm was off and in her left she held an elegant sword.' He couldn't stop himself from racing towards her and enveloping her in his arms. The woman seemed 'startled at first' but then welcomed him home and told him to go into the tavern to meet his parents (!) who were gathered with all his friends around a 'sumptuous table' to celebrate an American victory over Britain. If the one-armed woman dressed in black seemed reassuringly allegorical, Palmer could not help telling his diary that she was in fact 'the amiable Miss Emma York' and that it would be 'no offence to this fair damsel' to mention her name. It's not clear whether Miss York knew that she was Palmer's sweetheart, though at various points in his diary he recorded his dreams of 'future happiness—and my fair Dulcenea, who for modesty's sake I shall not mention'.[23]

Given the board's direction that women and children not be entered into the prison's register, we can't be sure precisely how many prisoners succeeded in bringing family members into Dartmoor's blocks. Lewis Clover told a story from the hulks at Chatham which urges us to look beyond the archive for answers. An American sailor imprisoned in the same hulk as Clover had married an Englishwoman from Liverpool before the outbreak of the War of 1812. When she learned that he had been captured, 'she resolved to partake of all the hardships, privations, and imprisonment with him.' The other prisoners were so moved that they offered the couple the most precious commodity on a prison ship: privacy. They hung a piece of canvas from the ceiling to make a screen for the pair, and in Clover's telling this magnanimous gesture produced an astonishing outcome: 'It was amid these trials and privations that she became a mother, and was covered by the American flag.'[24]

The image of a baby delivered on a prison hulk and wrapped in the Stars and Stripes might stretch credulity. But many sources confirm that the Transport Board was regularly harassed by wives seeking permission to spend time with—or even live alongside—their incarcerated husbands. Henry Fleischman, imprisoned in the hulks at Plymouth in 1813, complained about a British official who had denied one woman the chance to reunite with her husband after an absence of several years. Eventually, she petitioned an admiral on shore who 'gave her permission to come and live with her husband'. Back at Chatham, the wife of another prisoner died in childbirth on one of the hulks. Inconveniently for the board, her baby survived. Although the Chatham agent successfully found a wet nurse for the child—the wife of a marine stationed nearby—the board complained that 'the allowance proposed by him . . . is considerably more, than what is paid for nursing poor infants.' Instead of conveying its relief that a nurse had been recruited, the board grudgingly approved her salary while insisting that 'the woman employed has a sufficiency of milk, and no other child to suckle.'[25]

At Dartmoor, Agent Shortland notified the board in August 1814 that the wives of two American prisoners had requested to live alongside their husbands. The board replied that 'no English women can be suffered to remain in the prison,' but one of the women persisted. Harriet Clark's husband, Elisha, was a thirty-five-year-old sailor from New Bedford in Massachusetts. He had been serving on HMS *Andromache* but had been transferred to the hulks at Chatham in December 1812 before being moved again to Dartmoor. Harriet Clark wrote directly to the board asking to join her husband in the prison; the board granted permission only if she could prove that she had married Elisha 'before he quitted His Majesty's Service'. Clearly, she could not, because in December 1814 she sent another letter to the board asking simply for visitation rights. Other women followed suit: Sarah Paul, Betsy Williams, and Hester Ray all asked to see their husbands 'once or twice a week', and their requests were granted by the board.[26]

Hester (like Harriet Clark) was almost certainly married to an American who had served in the Royal Navy. Sarah Paul was the wife of Jonathan Paul, another impressed sailor who had come from Chatham to Dartmoor on the same transport as Elisha Clark, and who was booked into the register on the same morning. (He'd served on HMS *Hind*, until he was taken into the prison system in March 1813.) Intriguingly, visiting rights were also given to the wife of Caesar Sankey, a thirty-two-year-old sailor from New Hampshire and yet another Royal Navy veteran. Sankey was a 'stout black', according to the register. Assuming his wife was English, as this group of women almost certainly were, she was probably white. In the correspondence between Shortland and the board, race was not mentioned. Instead, Mrs. Sankey was given the same right to visit 'once or twice a week' as the other women.[27]

There is one tantalizing loose end to the fate of women at Dartmoor. In the early 1850s, forty years after the first Americans had been marched to the prison, a group of New York–based veterans led by Lewis Clover founded the Dartmoor Prisoners' Society to remember their time in captivity. In 1853, several members of the society posed for a photograph which is now in the Brooklyn Historical Society. Clover is holding a flag emblazoned with the words FREE TRADE AND SAILORS' RIGHTS. To his right is 'Mrs. George D. Small', whose husband (according to the register) was a privateersman from New York. One figure in the photo is much younger than the rest. The caption declares him to be 'J. Small, son of the above', who was 'born in prison'. Was he born in *Dartmoor* prison? Had Mrs. Small lived there with her husband and given birth to their child under Thomas Shortland's gaze? No other prisoner mentioned this, either in a diary or a published account, and it's possible that Mrs. Small is the woman who gave birth at Chatham. Her husband was held on a hulk there until October 1814, and if the stories line up, Mrs. Small and her son would have accompanied George from the hulk to Dartmoor. But if this took place, it went unnoticed by the many prisoners who recorded their experiences in diaries or elaborated upon them in later years. This, too, may tell us something about the prison's emotional and physical landscape: what happened in the prison's most intimate spaces could be lastingly concealed.[28]

THE MOST THRILLING PURSUIT AT DARTMOOR WAS ALSO THE MOST dangerous: breaking out. With prisoner exchanges mostly on hold

Veterans of Dartmoor (1853)
Courtesy of Center for Brooklyn History, Brooklyn Public Library

from the summer of 1813 and captured men languishing in prison for months or even years, escape attempts became inevitable. Most eighteenth-century detention facilities repurposed buildings that had not been designed to contain prisoners. Dartmoor, by contrast, seemed operatically over-engineered. Its heavy walls were ringed by sentries and a rope ran around the circumference of the prison, linked to a series of bells. If a prisoner didn't trip the wire himself, a sentry could raise the alarm instantly. Hundreds of militiamen were on duty at any time, with hundreds more in the neighbouring barracks to sweep the moors if required. Ten miles of unforgiving countryside lay between Dartmoor and any substantial settlement. Even a prisoner who shed his bright yellow Transport Office uniform could be clearly seen against the empty landscape; assuming, of course, he didn't freeze to death in one of Dartmoor's notorious whiteouts or get lost in the fog and rain. And if a prisoner somehow got off the moor, he still had to cross the Channel (or the Atlantic) at a time when French or American ships were absent from British shores. Most prisoners who attempted to escape didn't make it. The ones who did relied on luck as much as skill.[29]

As in so much else at Dartmoor, the French were the pioneers in breaking out. The correspondence between Isaac Cotgrave and the Transport Board in the summer and fall of 1809 was filled with anxiety and outrage about the number of escape attempts. Some tunnelled under the prison, only to emerge just short of the outer wall. Two men slipped away at night, scurried to the coast, and stole a boat; in a moment of agonizing misfortune, they were intercepted by a Royal Navy ship in the English Channel and taken back into custody. Alarmed by the leakiness of his Gothically terrifying prison, Agent Cotgrave initially wondered if Dartmoor's design could be modified to deter further breakouts. Before long, he came to see escape attempts as the inevitable consequence of keeping desperate people in endless captivity.[30]

The standard punishment for a failed breakout was solitary confinement on reduced rations in the cachot followed by relegation to the very bottom of the release list. The board would also estimate the cost of recapturing a prisoner, then deduct this from his rations (and those of his accomplices). We often think of breakouts as forms of resistance which brought prisoners together. At Dartmoor, they were more likely to reflect or exacerbate existing tensions and inequalities. The most straightforward way to attempt escape was by bribing the turnkeys or the militia. George Dennison, the Massachusetts sailor who requested £200 from his father in the winter of 1814–1815, successfully escaped soon after receiving the money. Isaac Cotgrave, and later Thomas Shortland, repeatedly informed the board that their staff had fallen to the temptation of a prisoner's bribe. It was scant consolation to the authorities that militiamen or turnkeys were sometimes foolish enough to accept payment in 'counterfeit gold coin, and forged Bank of England notes'. Those left behind, meanwhile, suffered collective punishment after a successful escape—including the suspension of the market, which severed the thin thread of goods enlivening Dartmoor's drab economy. Every prisoner faced the temptation of selling out an escape plan to the guards, or nourished the toxic suspicion that someone else had done so.[31]

Plenty of escape attempts inclined towards the theatrical, with the French prisoner Louis Vanhille offering an early example. Captured on a merchant vessel in the spring of 1806, Vanhille was initially paroled (thanks to his officer status) in the tiny town of Launceston on the edge of Dartmoor. He became so friendly with the locals that they turned a blind eye to his many parole violations—which included visiting a racecourse more than twenty miles away—until another French officer impregnated a local woman and the board threw both men into Dartmoor. In August 1812, after spending seven months in the prison, Vanhille vanished. He was only discovered in January 1813 as he arrived in Jamaica on a British vessel. While at Dartmoor, Vanhille had contacted his (British) friends in Launceston, who subsequently arranged for a market trader named Mary Ellis to smuggle a disguise into the market square. In the bustle of the market, Mary handed Vanhille the outfit—which allowed him to impersonate the wagon attendants who drove the carts to the prison. After his costume change, Vanhille casually walked out of Dartmoor with the other traders when the day's business was done. He was so relaxed about this vanishing act that he made three visits to Launceston and a sightseeing trip to London before shipping out to Jamaica en route to his brother's home in New Orleans. The comically nonchalant nature of the escape was confirmed by his retention of the letters and plans which described the scheme in his trunk: Vanhille literally kept the receipts, and they enabled the

Jamaican authorities to send him back to the Chatham hulks for the duration of the war.[32]

Some Americans had attempted escape even before arriving at Dartmoor. David Neal, a childhood friend of Benjamin Browne, tried to commandeer the transport ship which brought him from Halifax to Dartmoor in the summer of 1814. He was convinced that the two hundred Americans aboard the ship would join him, but was left horribly outnumbered when just a handful rose up at the appointed moment. (In the brief shootout which followed, Neal lost three of his fingers.) At Chatham in the spring of 1814, a group of American prisoners spent months scratching a hole into the side of their prison ship—the work was slow because they only had the blunt knives given them to eat with. In an amazing feat of coordination and solidarity, eighteen sailors made their escape before the hole was discovered. A few nights later, the remaining Americans could hear the rattled guards shooting across the river; they learned the next morning that 'a great number of porpoises came up the river last night, and the English supposed them to be Americans running away from the prison ships.'[33]

During the first year of American captivity at Dartmoor, a number of US POWs made unsuccessful attempts to escape. The most spectacular came on a bitterly cold night in January 1814. Richard Philen of Wilmington, Delaware, who was thirty-eight years old and had served as second mate on a privateer, noticed that the sentries on the prison walls thinned out when the temperatures dropped. One evening, with snow lying deep on the moor surrounding the prison, Philen and seven associates fashioned a makeshift ladder and clambered over the first of three walls between their yard and the moor. As they repeated the trick on the second and third walls, one of them snagged the alarm rope. The sentries quickly emerged from their guard posts and rounded up the Americans. Only one prisoner—Philen himself—remained unaccounted for, and the guards assumed he had frozen to death. In fact he was holed up in a shepherd's hut a few miles from the prison, terrified and unsure of his next move. He put up no resistance when a group of farm workers found him, cold and hungry, a few days later. The board congratulated Agent Cotgrave for recapturing the American and awarded the farm workers a guinea for their trouble.[34]

According to the register, the first successful American escape took place on 3 June 1814. James McDadon, a twenty-six-year-old from Baltimore, took advantage of the bustle surrounding the release of the French prisoners and snuck out with them. Across the following year, more than four thousand Americans arrived at the prison, but only twenty-four escaped. John Langford of New Jersey made three attempts, finally succeeding only in February 1815 (fifteen months after his first try). Henry Allen from Salem, Massachusetts, managed to clamber over the walls in October 1814, get off the moor, and even cross the Channel. At the French port of L'Orient, he found an American ship bound for Charleston. But its captain had resolved to try a little privateering before crossing the Atlantic, and to Allen's horror he was captured again by the Royal Navy in the Straits of Gibraltar. Barely two months after his daring escape, Allen was marched back into Dartmoor. Joseph Valpey, who left a diary of his time in the prison, tells us that Allen was still trying to break out in April 1815: he asked Valpey for a loan, intending to bribe the guards. Like many Dartmoor prisoners in the spring of 1815, Valpey was broke, but given Allen's epic story, he 'felt sorry that I could not assist him'.[35]

Not every escape engendered sympathy from those left behind. One morning in November 1814, the Massachusetts sailor Thomas Swaine walked out of the prison in a work party headed for the neighbouring quarry. When the prisoners were counted back that evening, Swaine was no longer among them. He had come to Dartmoor with more baggage than most. As a lieutenant on the Boston privateer *Wiley-Reynard*, he had overseen a raid on a small island off the Canadian coast during the first months of the War of 1812. The laws of war strictly forbade privateers from attacking targets on land, but men from the *Wiley-Reynard* broke into a farm, shot the farmer between the eyes, and behaved 'in a shameful manner' (according to a subsequent newspaper report) towards the farmer's wife and daughters. Swaine was the chief suspect in this atrocity; his entry in the Dartmoor register noted that he had been 'accused of murdering an old man in a most wanton and cruel manner on a small island a little to the westward of Halifax'. This didn't disqualify Swaine from working outside the prison, but his decision to escape had a devastating effect on his fellow prisoners.[36]

'All the workmen were turned into [the] prison and not permitted to go out any more,' wrote Charles Andrews, 'on account of one man we believe to be Capt Swain of New Bedford, Massachusetts.' Absconding from a work party was a special breach of the prisoners' code. The parties brought desperately needed money into Dartmoor, but prison officials paid workers on a quarterly basis in arrears. Swaine's departure—almost certainly secured by bribing a guard—compelled Shortland not only to cancel the work parties but also to withhold the pay due to prisoners who had been labouring for weeks, perhaps even months, to earn enough to get them through Dartmoor's harsh winter. Swaine's actions left 'the whole establishment . . . unprovided with sufficient means to take care of themselves,' Charles Andrews complained. Worst of all, Swaine had done all of this 'without giving notice'. Given the high chance of being sold out by one's fellow prisoners, one can understand why Swaine might keep quiet about his plans. But the episode reminds us that escape was rarely a collective action. The men left behind paid the price for those lucky enough to get out.[37]

WHEN WE TALLY THE DISTRACTIONS AND ENTERTAINMENT ON OFfer at Dartmoor, we can easily miss the boredom which was its default setting. 'I shall omit writing the trifling particulars of each day,' wrote Frank Palmer in October 1814, and 'when anything of note takes place shall make mention of it.' More than a month passed before his next entry: 'From 7th Oct. to this date nothing of note has transpired.' The prisoners travelled the same loops, moving from block to block in pursuit of thrills and diversions with diminishing returns. 'Time rolls heavily on,' Palmer wrote, and 'nothing but cards and backgammon passes the time away.' The weather was usually dreadful—Nathaniel Pierce told his journal that 'we always call it pleasant here when it does not rain'—and the food was monotonous. Cold and hunger were inescapable, and as the nights became shorter, the sense of confinement was hard to bear. Above all else, the indeterminacy of the prisoners' sentence corroded morale. Good news about the course of the war was sporadic and unreliable, and most inmates felt a terrible incapacity. They were completely cut off, their future (and perhaps their lives) reliant on events about which they had little or no knowledge. Despair hemmed the most energetic efforts at entertainment and diversion.[38]

It was Lewis Clover who described Dartmoor as 'a world in miniature', though his observation had a melancholy aspect. It would take 'the pen of Dickens' to capture the 'high-wrought drama' of the American experience there, he wrote. In his old age, the sights and sounds of the prison crowded his dreams and disturbed his sleep; they were scenes 'I should be sorry to survey when awake,' he admitted. But he urged his readers not to see themselves as entirely different from the unfortunate subjects of his story. 'We are all creatures of circumstance,' he observed. If the prisoners at Dartmoor had created a fantasy world to distract from the bleakness of their lot, they were victims of the same delusion that gripped every human being whose life had diverged from the hopes of their youth. 'Half of our existence is imaginary,' Clover thought. 'I believe all mankind indulge in it more or less.'[39]

PART III

KING DICK AT DARTMOOR

AFTER RICHARD CRAFUS WAS IGNOMINIOUSLY CAPTURED aboard the *Requin* at Bordeaux in March 1814, he was taken to the hulks at Chatham. If he made trouble there during his six-month stay, he kept out of the correspondence between the agent and the Transport Board. In fact, he slipped past every one of the prisoners who wrote an account of their time on the hulks. The Chatham register lists Crafus's arrival and departure, along with his capture on the *Requin* at Bordeaux, but nothing else. In the last week of September, he was marched with hundreds of other prisoners to the *Niobe*, a transport ship which would carry them down the River Medway to the Thames and then around southern Britain to Plymouth. On 9 October 1814, he made the long walk north alongside that day's consignment of prisoners and spent his first night at Dartmoor. After an unremarkable tenure in the British prison system, he was about to become King Dick.[1]

Benjamin Waterhouse, who in 1816 published one of the few accounts of Dartmoor to gain traction with American readers, called Dick a 'Black Hercules' who made the residents of Prison Four 'tremble in his presence'. According to Josiah Cobb, the Massachusetts sailor who wrote exhaustively of Dartmoor in his 1841 memoir, Dick was an 'Ethiopian giant' who had Prison Four entirely under his control. Benjamin Browne of Salem, in his New York magazine series of 1846, insisted that Dick had 'deposed' the elected prisoners' committee in Four and awarded himself 'sovereign sway' over the block's inhabitants. Cobb and Browne took their cues from Waterhouse's 1816 book, the *Journal of a Young Man of Massachusetts*. It was a bestseller that year, and the author mailed copies to James Madison, Thomas Jefferson, and a host of other notables. Waterhouse was single-handedly responsible for bringing King Dick to the American public: Dick wasn't even mentioned across the three hundred pages of Charles Andrews's *The Prisoners' Memoirs*. In the dozens of letters and eyewitness accounts which appeared in the months after the massacre of April 1815, Dick was almost entirely absent.[2]

Waterhouse vividly recalled his appearance and manner. Dick wore a bearskin cap and patrolled Prison Four carrying 'a huge club'. He was accompanied by a pair of courtiers—one account suggested they were white teenagers—and kept order through intimidation and violence. 'He is by far the largest, and I suspect the strongest man in the prison,' wrote Waterhouse. 'If any of his men are dirty, drunken, or grossly negligent, he threatens them with a beating, and if they are saucy, they are sure to receive one.' Dick's rounds each morning took him to every hammock, and any resident of Four who failed to keep himself and his berth clean would meet Dick's club. One night, a group of prisoners attempted to take back control of Four by surprising Dick in his sleep and beating him into submission. The irritated Dick simply picked up the smallest of his assailants by the ankle and (Waterhouse, again) 'thumped another with him'.[3]

According to these white writers, Dick ran a protection racket which skimmed a portion of the profits from each of Four's many traders. He also took an interest in the block's most lucrative business: the gaming tables which kept white prisoners in Four even after the turnkeys had locked the doors each night. Benjamin Browne noted that Dick used his boxing skills as a tool of government: challengers to his rule were invited to meet him in the ring and, to the crowd's cheers, coldly dispatched. Benjamin Waterhouse thought Dick's methods were even more direct: anyone who defied the king's authority was punched or clubbed on the spot, 'carried to the hospital sadly bruised, and provokingly laughed at'. Waterhouse couldn't resist the Shakespearian analogue: Dick was 'King Richard the IVth', a man of 'good understanding' but sharp justice.[4]

All three writers felt that Dick's harsh rule was justified. 'Most tightly does he draw the cords of despotism around his good subjects,' Josiah Cobb noted. After all, what was the alternative, in a space inhabited principally by Black people? 'It is thought anarchy would reign where now there is despotism, only for the sway this man of might holds over his sable brethren.' Benjamin Waterhouse offered a similar assessment: 'Negroes are generally reputed to be thieves,' he wrote, echoing the charge that had been levelled against Black prisoners by Charles Andrews when arguing for racial segregation at Dartmoor. 'Their faculties are commonly found to be inadequate to the comprehension of the moral system,' he continued. 'As to the Christian system, their notions of it, generally speaking, are a burlesque to everything serious.' Waterhouse's appreciation of Dick was entirely conditioned by race: the regime in Prison Four would not be appropriate 'where the whites have the control'. But despotism was well suited to the novel phenomenon of Black self-determination. There was a grudging admiration among these white writers for Dick's charisma and ruthlessness, even as Prison Four emerged in their accounts as an exceptional space—the odd man out in Dartmoor's otherwise democratic and liberal prisoner societies.[5]

Browne and Waterhouse patronized Dick from every angle. They spoke of his 'majesty' and claimed that he conferred knighthoods on his courtiers by clubbing them around the ears. They lampooned his friendship with a Black preacher called Simon: 'Here we see the union of church and state in miniature,' wrote Waterhouse. 'Who told [Simon] that to maintain this influence, he must rally round the huge club of the strongest and most powerful man in this black gang of sinners? And who told King Dick that his nervous arm and massy club were insufficient without the aid of the preacher of terror?' The idea that Prison Four contained accidental truths about the human condition appealed to each of its white chroniclers. Dick 'probably had not read the ancient or modern writers on chivalry,' thought Browne. Neither Simon nor Dick 'had read or heard of Machiavel,' wrote Waterhouse. Those observations, freighted with sarcasm, were tethered to a ponderous conclusion: if even Black men could intuit how to govern by force and pacify through religion, perhaps (Waterhouse again) 'the science of government is not so deep and complicated a thing as king-craft and priest-craft would make us believe.' Even 'rude' people might form 'a sort of government', though Dick's tyranny over Four looked nothing like the little republics maintained by white prisoners in the rest of Dartmoor.[6]

These white authors wrote about Dick in a strangely contrapuntal style. They were fascinated by his power, but they sought to package it in ways that fortified their prejudices. Beyond the persistent invocations of despotism, with the attendant claim that only a strongman could bring order to people of colour, Dick's white biographers used one further tactic to peel him from the other men of influence among the American prisoners. 'Big Dick is a great favorite with the authorities of the Depot,' wrote Josiah Cobb, 'and is allowed greater indulgence than any other within the walls.' Cobb claimed that Dick could even leave the prison and spend hours 'roaming about the fields' or visiting Princetown, his reward for being Agent Shortland's loyal informant. Benjamin Browne went further: Dick was not just amenable to the agent's requests, but 'in all cases of conflict between whites and blacks, he invariably took the part of the former.'[7]

Was Dick better disposed to the British than to his American compatriots? Did he more effectively serve the white sailors in the other prisons than the Black men he had subdued with his club? The clear intention of these claims was to negate two potential understandings of Dick's power: that he was a patriotic American, and that he ably represented the interests of men of colour. Most white Americans who wrote about Dartmoor looked to present themselves as good patriots and to depict the prison blocks as microcosms of the United States: though virtue and vice could be found everywhere, they acknowledged, these unfortunate sailors had salvaged republican government from the wreckage of their captivity. But those same white sailors had decided in 1813 to cast out their Black compatriots. In doing so they created a Black-governed space which eventually became the heart of Dartmoor's social and commercial worlds. If Prison Four was as lively and well-run as the other blocks, with at least as many diversions and amusements and virtues, what was the justification for casting out sailors of colour in the first place? The white writers who conveyed Dick's presence and qualities to American readers had the answer to this: Black sailors were not like white sailors, and Dick's despotism confirmed the difference.

To get a better sense of what really happened in Prison Four, we need to go beyond these published accounts to consider the diaries and journals of other white sailors who visited the 'Black Prison' regularly. These have their own hang-ups and blind spots, but were written in the moment and without the filters applied by the passage of time, the shifting of racial attitudes in the United States, and the need to deny that Black people might be as capable of republican government as white people. We also need to consider an odd fact about King Dick's legend. Benjamin Waterhouse, the man who did more than anyone else to craft the myth of Richard Crafus, was unqualified for that role in two crucial respects: he had never set foot in Dartmoor prison, and he had never met King Dick.

9.

PRISON FOUR

ONE EVENING IN NOVEMBER 1814, FRANK PALMER WENT TO the theatre. He left Prison Seven and walked to the passage-way by the market square, then made a right through the central yard and into Prison Four. It was already dark outside, but the prisoners hadn't yet slung up their hammocks and the shopkeepers were still selling their wares from tables running the length of the building. Rumour had it that alcohol was easier to find in Four; gambling was certainly more prevalent than in the other prison blocks, though card tables would pop up everywhere in Dartmoor that winter. In truth, the only major difference between this and the other blocks was that nearly all of the men who lived in Prison Four were Black.[1]

Nearly, but not quite all. And tonight, with a performance in the cockloft at the top of the prison, the crowd was noisy and mixed. Black and white sailors streamed up the staircases to the third floor, where the show was about to begin. Palmer had only been in Dartmoor for six weeks. Older hands would have known that the makeshift theatre was where the Romans had performed their dia-bolical ministries and where Black sailors had taken residence after the Americans were segregated along racial lines in October 1813. Black prisoners kept company with the Romans and Dartmoor's other misfits for seven months afterwards, until the general release of the French in May 1814. With no further need for the costumes, makeup, and theatrical scenery they had painstakingly assembled during their five years in the prison, French prisoners happily sold everything to the Black residents of Four. During the next year, as Dartmoor filled up with Americans, a group of white prisoners regularly staged plays in the cockloft of Prison Five. But everyone knew that the theatre in Four was the place to be.[2]

Tickets were sixpence each. Palmer paid at the top of the stairs but quickly realised that 'a ticket was of very little service.' Every seat was taken, and enthusiastic theatregoers were already standing in the aisles or sitting on the front of the stage. 'Such another crowding you never saw,' Palmer told his journal. When he'd finally found a place to stand, 'a great Negro about seven feet high' stepped right in front of him. Fortunately, someone found the tall man a chair, and 'when he sat down 'twas with difficulty I could see over his head.' None of this mattered when the play began: the 'scenery was very good, and so was the performance.'[3]

The players presented a double bill. First came George Colman's *Heir at Law*, a comedy of manners which premiered in London in 1797. The central character, a pompous and rapacious conman named Doctor Pangloss, preyed on the wealthy by charging outrageous fees to tutor their children. To persuade his credulous employers that he was a man of learning, he would shoehorn endless quotations from literature into his conversation, then immediately identify their provenance: '"Lend me your ears."—Shakespeare, again. Hem!' (Pangloss's catchphrase was 'Hem!') After a short interval, the players moved on to *Raising the Wind*, a popular 1803 farce. The play's antihero, Jeremy Diddler, was another cad-deceiver who used 'bon mots' (*sic*) to ingratiate himself with the rich and part them from their money. Both plays were already fixtures on American stages, and some of the sailors may have known them. The scripts entered Dartmoor through the market or via the formidable lending library in the cockloft of Prison Seven. Palmer didn't say if this was his first visit to the theatre in Four, but he enjoyed himself greatly.[4]

One consequence of seeing a play in Four was that the turnkeys might lock the prison before a performance had concluded. Palmer, along with many other white sailors in the audience, didn't see this as a problem. After the company had taken its applause, the after-party began. 'We had a grand dance,' wrote Palmer, 'and kept it up till daylight.' Four was full of musicians and reputed to have the best beer in Dartmoor. Black and white sailors laughed and sang behind the heavy walls, and the turnkeys and sentries let the prisoners have their fun. When the doors were finally unlocked the next morning, Palmer and the other white theatregoers emerged into the light the worse for wear. 'Each one went to his own prison,' wrote Palmer. They would be back before long.[5]

Frank Palmer wrote casually in his journal about the fun he had in Prison Four. So did the other prisoners who left diaries or journals detailing their captivity. But the white writers who crafted retrospective accounts for publication in the United States—sometimes decades later—performed an anthropological distancing from their Black compatriots. In their stylized and tidied-up narratives, white sailors ventured into the 'Black prison' with caution and scrupulous detachment. Four was, after all, the place where Richard Crafus wielded absolute power. To the memoirists and chroniclers who looked to commodify their Dartmoor experiences for white readers, King Dick was the main attraction—the man feared by everyone in the prison for his despotic rule. But those white sailors who wrote about Dartmoor in real time were more enthusiastic about Four's attractions and strangely oblivious to the cult of King Dick. Frank Palmer saw Richard Crafus that November night—Dick was the huge man who blocked his view—and had no idea who he was.

EIGHT HUNDRED AND TWENTY-NINE SAILORS OF COLOUR HAD been entered into the register by the end of October 1814. Of these, fifteen had already died in the prison and thirty-seven had gotten out: some in the exchanges of 1813, some via service in the Royal Navy, and others in the French release of May 1814. That leaves us with 777 prisoners of colour on 1 November 1814 in a total prison population of nearly five thousand. The youngest was James Johnson, a thirteen-year-old boy from New York captured on a privateer in February 1814. The oldest was Scipio Bartlett, the Revolutionary War veteran who had been seized with Richard Crafus on the *Requin* at Bordeaux in the final weeks of Britain's war with France. Around 30 percent had come from the Royal Navy, a considerably higher proportion than for white prisoners; the rest had served on privateers and letters of marque. Virtually all of the 777 prisoners were living in Prison Four by October 1814. The Black community in Four was by this point self-governing (it probably had been since the board had agreed to segregate the Americans a year earlier). White people weren't excluded from visiting, and some even decided to live in Four. But there was no doubt that Black prisoners were in charge.[6]

Inside the block were African Americans who had already lived rich and full lives: men like Henry Van Meter, who saw George Washington during the American Revolution, escaped from slavery, and witnessed the first major Indian war in the Old Northwest before going to sea in his forties. Most were a lot greener: nearly half of the prisoners of colour were aged twenty-five or younger. The first to have been captured during the War of 1812 was John Newell, a thirty-two-year-old cook who gave his birthplace as Africa. But also in the prison was William Spince, a New Yorker who had been serving on a French merchant vessel seized by a British warship in 1809. When the other French prisoners were released in the spring of 1814, Spince was quietly transferred to the American register. He would spend more time in custody than any other American at Dartmoor.[7]

At least nine of the Black residents of Four appear in the impressment files of the State Department or in the Transport Board's correspondence with Reuben Beasley. Thomas Wilson, a thirty-five-year-old sailor from Delaware, had been impressed on HMS *Edinburgh* when the war began; his family in the United States spent years trying unsuccessfully to secure his release. Charles White of Norfolk, Virginia, was seized by the Royal Navy on a US merchant vessel travelling from Savannah to Liverpool before the war broke out. A family friend wrote to Secretary of State James Monroe in 1814 with affidavits from white Virginians 'stating that he is a citizen of the United States', along with two letters Charles had written to his mother from HMS *Leviathan*. George Jamieson, a fifty-three-year-old sailor from Philadelphia, served on HMS *Hibernia* from 1808 until he was tipped into the prison system in 1813. His former master, Francis Johnston, wrote to Secretary of State James Madison in the final months of the Jefferson administration to secure his release. Jamieson was 'a sailor of the very first grade', Johnston insisted, and had even served briefly in the US Navy under the celebrated Captain John Barry. 'I have heard Commodore Barry say that he was an alert and most powerful sailor,' Johnston reported, 'fit to act on board of any ship of whatever magnitude or to whatever nation she might belong.' That final qualification acknowledged the plastic nature of nationality for sailors: Jamieson could expect to sail under many flags during his career. But Johnston insisted to Madison that it was the federal government's duty to 'bring him back once more to his own country, which he says he will never resent or forsake.'[8]

According to the register, only 6 percent of prisoners of colour were born beyond the North American mainland. Of these, about a quarter gave their birthplace as Africa, another quarter named the Caribbean, and nearly a third, South America. Prisoners could and did dissemble about their birthplace. Black sailors had good reason not to admit to being from Jamaica, Barbados, or other British colonies. (Not a single one of the thousand or so sailors of colour claimed to be from the British West Indies.) A number of sailors were born in France and Portugal, one was from Mauritius, three were from what is now Indonesia, and a man named 'Appene', described as having a 'sallow complexion', was from Canton in China. And then there was the crew of the *President*, a schooner captured by HMS *Pique* in May 1814 off the coast of Puerto Rico. A note in the register acknowledged some confusion about what these men were doing in Dartmoor: 'The *President* is stated to have been captured under the rebel colours of Carthagena,' a clerk had written, 'but there can be little doubt of her being an American privateer.' Cartagena was the independent city on Colombia's Caribbean coast from which George Little had briefly sailed as a privateer in the first months of the war. In addition to being among the first places in South America to break away from the Spanish empire (in 1811), it had also banned the slave trade and conferred citizenship on all free people, Black and white alike.[9]

Forty-six crew members from the *President* were brought to Dartmoor. The ship's captain, James Marthy, was a white man from Paris. Fully half of the complement were from Cartagena or the Caribbean. Twelve crew members were (US) Americans, and twenty-seven were Black (eight from the United States, nineteen from around the Atlantic world). The *President* encapsulated the sea's potential to scramble national affinities: men from four continents, white and Black, had set out from a new republic in the Caribbean under a French captain to prey upon Spain, before being captured by a British frigate which insisted they were American. The confusion about their status may have resulted from an unfortunate coincidence: a month or two before the capture of the schooner, HMS *Pique* had sparred with another vessel named *President*, one of the American republic's tiny fleet of frigates. The British authorities probably mistook the two, aided by the fact that a dozen of the schooner's crew admitted to being from the United States. The sailors on the *President* were sent first to Halifax and then to Dartmoor, arriving in the second week of October 1814. Not all of them would survive the winter.[10]

These are just a few of the stories of the men of colour who found their way to Four. None of these men was named in the prison diaries or memoirs left by white American sailors, and not a single Black sailor left an account of life within the walls of Four. But it was an extraordinary place: by the first weeks of 1815, a self-governing community of nearly a thousand people of colour had formed, offering services, products, and entertainment both to its own residents and to the rest of the prison. It has been hard for historians to appreciate the vitality and achievement of Black life at Dartmoor because the archive is skewed: much of what we know comes from witnesses who viewed Prison Four through the filters of their own prejudice. To make sense of what these witnesses tell us, and what lies beyond their limited vision, we need to consider those filters and prejudices more closely.[11]

WHITE AMERICANS IN THIS PERIOD THOUGHT ABOUT BLACK PEO-ple in three different contexts. The first was slavery. Since the rise of humanitarian sentiments among white reformers in the second half of the eighteenth century, slavery's defenders had developed an increasingly virulent argument about racial hierarchy and Black inferiority. In its most extreme forms, this presented Black people as naturally fitted to subjugation and unlikely to benefit from free-dom. Even many enslavers were embarrassed to make this argu-ment publicly since it seemed at odds with the universalist messages of Christianity and the most up-to-date scientific thinking on racial potential. But, as the Virginia enslaver St George Tucker wrote in 1796, 'if prejudices have taken such deep root in our minds, as to render it impossible to eradicate this opinion, ought not so general an error, if it be one, to be respected?' Regardless of their views on the propriety of slavery, white prisoners at Dartmoor struggled to shed a prejudice about Black ability which had developed over cen-turies in North America.[12]

The second context was the effort of free Black communities throughout the northern states to substantiate not only their liberty but also their claims to citizenship. The obvious riposte to the claim that enslaved people lacked the capacity to enjoy social and political equality was for free Black people to prove their civic potential. But even as African Americans in Boston or Philadelphia founded separate schools and churches and established their own businesses, their white neighbours expressed unease about the trajectory of racial integration. Some white commentators noted with alarm that Philadelphia, in particular, seemed to be drawing free Black migrants from the upper South—especially after the Virginia legislature passed a law in 1806 requiring all newly emancipated people to leave Virginia within twelve months of their manumission. Others fixated on the spectre of racial mixing and its supposedly deleterious effects upon white people. Paranoia about 'amalgamation' was one of the starkest forms of prejudice, and it anchored a set of arguments which sought to limit or deny Black liberties and rights in the North and South alike.[13]

The third context in which white Americans thought about Black people was as prospective citizens of another country, a Black colony which would secure their permanent exile from the United States. Thomas Jefferson had been among the earliest proponents of the view that Black people should be settled outside the United States as a way of encouraging the abolition of slavery, and the idea that African Americans could be relocated beyond America's borders became known as 'colonization'. In 1816, some of Washington's most influential politicians would form the American Colonization Society (ACS) to promote the emigration of free Blacks (and, eventually, freed people). Five years later, with the help of the US Navy, the ACS seized territory in West Africa, named it 'Liberia', and began the work of promoting racial resettlement in earnest.[14]

Beyond these three contexts for thinking about Black political agency and belonging were two concrete political projects which emerged from the age of revolutions: Sierra Leone, the precursor to Liberia, which was founded in West Africa in 1787; and Haiti, which finally won its independence from France in 1804. Both states had a Black majority, but each represented different understandings of Black agency. Sierra Leone had its roots in the British decision to evacuate thousands of African Americans who had crossed the lines to fight for the king during the Revolutionary War. Some had been evacuated by the Royal Navy to Nova Scotia, others to London. In the 1780s and 1790s, both communities were induced to move to a new colony in West Africa by 'benevolent' British reformers with big ideas about race and labour. Sierra Leone, they insisted, would serve as the testing ground for an arresting theory: tropical commodities could be produced more successfully by free Black people in Africa than by enslaved people in the Americas. If their experiment succeeded, these reformers claimed, the rationale for the Atlantic slave trade and for slavery throughout the Americas would dissolve.[15]

From its earliest moments, it was clear that Sierra Leone would not be an experiment in Black self-rule. The white reformers who invented the colony refused to put Black people in positions of authority; the celebrated sailor and abolitionist Olaudah Equiano was initially hired to assist in the enterprise, though when he complained to his bosses about the 'flagrant abuses' of the contractors appointed to outfit the expedition, he was dismissed from his post. This probably saved his life since the first settlers were ravaged by disease and the elements on their arrival in Africa. But even as the colony was rebuilt during the 1790s with an infusion of new Black migrants from Canada, its white managers in London persistently declined to give political power to the colonists. It was governed exclusively by white people, a tiny ruling elite overseeing an enterprise dependent on Black settlers and labour.[16]

Some African Americans continued to hope that Sierra Leone might eventually become a meaningful site of Black self-determination. Paul Cuffe, the Black Native sea captain who sailed to King Dick's hometown in Maryland in 1795, was among them. Cuffe had gotten to know some of Philadelphia's white abolitionists during his visits to the city in the early 1800s, and they wrote excitedly to their friends in Britain—including William Wilberforce and Thomas Clarkson, the leading white campaigners against the slave trade—recommending Cuffe as an ally in the work of consolidating Sierra Leone. Cuffe made several visits, scouting a new triangular relationship between Britain, West Africa, and the Americas which might undo some of the damage caused by the slave trade. (The War of 1812 disrupted Cuffe's plans, and Congress briefly considered exempting him from the law prohibiting trade with an enemy.) Cuffe didn't expect all African Americans to move to Sierra Leone, though in 1816 he gave his blessing to the establishment of the American Colonization Society. He believed that colonization might help some Black Americans, but he continued to support struggles for citizenship and equality within the United States.[17]

Paul Cuffe exemplified an important difference in how Black and white people thought about colonization during this early period. Most white advocates saw racial separation as the means to secure an exclusively white republic. Black Americans saw colonization as an avenue for self-determination, a catalyst for further manumissions in the South, or a recognition of the underlying unity of the peoples of the African diaspora. When it became clear that the white promoters of colonization rooted their arguments in racial supremacy, African Americans began a lengthy debate over whether to fight for equality at home or to pursue self-determination elsewhere. This debate continued until (and even beyond) the Civil War. African Americans changed their minds, clarified their positions, and became increasingly estranged from white colonization enthusiasts who were more interested in exiling Black people than in facilitating Black self-determination. Colonization was interesting to African Americans principally as a means of securing a Black politics which seemed impossible in the United States.[18]

Haiti occupied an even larger place in the white imagination in the early nineteenth century than Sierra Leone. The process by which the sugar colony of Saint-Domingue became the self-proclaimed Black republic of Haiti was long and wrenching: from 1791 until 1804, Black and white Americans watched with fascination as enslaved and free Black people abolished slavery and declared independence from the French. The messiness and violence of the uprising, and its threat to the stability of slaveholding regimes everywhere, led even white reformers in the United States to present Haiti as a cautionary tale rather than an exemplar of Black politics. After 1804, the implosion of the old sugar economy, coupled with internal struggles for control of Haiti's new government, allowed white observers to argue that Black self-rule had produced a failed state. In fact, the disruptions to Haiti's economy and politics owed much to the decision of formerly enslaved people to leave the sugar fields: the nation's society and economy became radically local, with thousands of newly free Haitians seeking alternatives to plantation agriculture. For white observers, Haiti's struggles after 1804 confirmed their prejudices about emancipation and Black political capacity. Black people saw something else: the formidable power of concerted action against enslavers, and the viability of Black self-determination outside of Africa. These very different views of the same events give us further reason to approach white accounts of Prison Four with caution.[19]

ACCORDING TO CHARLES ANDREWS, FOUR HAD BECOME AN EXclusively Black prison by early September. It didn't stay this way for long. As the white prisoners in the rest of Dartmoor became restive during the winter of 1814–1815, Four became an outlet of sorts. A tantalizing note, written (by a prison staff member or a board inspector) on the back of another document in the British National Archives, bemoans the 'turbulent and unruly disposition' of the white American prisoners in the final months of 1814. The conduct of these prisoners 'was so bad that the whole of the petty officers had requested permission to live with the blacks in preference to their own'. Benjamin Browne's account offers support to this extraordinary claim: Browne recalled 'some disturbance between the officers and crew of a privateer, when the officers to escape maltreatment went into Number Four'. Had these officers made a failed attempt to seize control of one of the prisoners' committees? We saw earlier that rivalries between officers and ordinary sailors drove prisoner politics; it's arresting to think that—in opposition to the view of Four as a despotic space—it was actually a safe harbour for those who fell into trouble in the other blocks. The officers were 'civilly received by the blacks', according to Browne, and Four became 'a prison of refuge to many who were uneasy in their positions in the other prisons'.[20]

The accounts of Josiah Cobb, Benjamin Waterhouse, and Benjamin Browne were adamant about King Dick's reign. 'Number Four was an exception to the democratical form of government' which prevailed in the other blocks, according to Browne. 'This was under a regal, or rather despotic form.' We've already seen that the claim that the other blocks were 'democratical' is contradicted by evidence from prisoner diaries and journals; even Benjamin Browne confessed that he could not recall an election during his time in the prison. But this contrast between Four and the other blocks also founders on the question of timing. Dick arrived in Dartmoor in October 1814, a year after Black sailors had been separated from white sailors in the cockloft of Four. During that year, the sailors of colour in Four had organized themselves without Dick's involvement, even as their numbers swelled and they controlled an expanding portion of the block. Were the sailors of colour under the thrall of another despot during this period? Or perhaps the political realities of Four diverged from the caricature sketched by Waterhouse, Cobb, and Browne.[21]

One answer to this is supplied by Benjamin Browne: 'A tall, powerful black man, known among the prisoners as "Big Dick" or "King Dick," from being president of the committee, had contrived to depose his brethren in office and to usurp his sovereign sway, and he ruled the poor blacks with as arbitrary an authority as any other despot could.' So there *had* been a committee in Prison Four, Richard Crafus had been elected to head it, and he had only then morphed into King Dick? No other account mentions these details; Browne himself had arrived at Dartmoor just ten days before Crafus and had no idea of how Four was organized in the year before his election. Was Dick *still* the president of the committee in Four during the winter of 1814–1815? Did the other accounts misread his prominence (inadvertently or wantonly) to fuel their prejudices about Black despotism? The claim that Dick ruled tyrannically was first made in 1816 by Benjamin Waterhouse, who was neither a prisoner nor a sailor but a former professor at Harvard Medical School. A friend and supporter of Thomas Jefferson, Waterhouse rode out the War of 1812 in Massachusetts and got nowhere near a British prison. He became aware of the Dartmoor story in the winter of 1815, when he procured an account of the American ordeal from a returning sailor. He then embellished this, added a political sheen to defend the Madison administration from the charge of abandoning the prisoners, and gave the manuscript to his publisher. We'll return to Waterhouse's role in the myth-making of Dartmoor, but for now we should see the formative account of King Dick's despotism as highly suspect.[22]

The other two accounts of Dick's reign, from Josiah Cobb and Benjamin Browne, were at least written by men imprisoned at Dartmoor. But both wrote in the shadow of Waterhouse's bestseller and cribbed details from his vivid portrait. Cobb and Browne were also writing in the 1840s, a decade in which white views of Black political and social potential had narrowed considerably. The notion that the 'poor blacks' were both the victims of Dick's tyranny and condemned to despotism by their race reflects a hardening of white racism about Black political incapacity. Without even considering the authors' more flamboyant expressions of anti-Black hatred— their lingering emphasis on the disagreeable smell of Four's inhabitants, for example, or their mocking references to Haiti—we have plenty of reasons to doubt what they tell us.

Which returns us to a central problem: in the absence of accounts from Black people themselves, we can only speculate about the true nature of Four's political world. The occasional (if fleeting) appearance of Dick in prisoner journals confirms he was important to the governance of Four: the claims of Waterhouse, Cobb, and Browne that Dick wielded influence at Dartmoor were not completely fabricated. The register tells us that some of the longest-serving Black prisoners at Dartmoor—twenty sailors from the crew of the USS *Argus*—were released at the end of September 1814, just a few weeks before the arrival of Richard Crafus. It's possible that these men had played a prominent role in the management of Four, and their departure created the power vacuum which enabled Dick's ascent. It's also possible that Four was not an island of autocracy in a sea of prison republicanism, as it would later be presented. If the decision of white prisoners to separate themselves from Black prisoners was based partly on a refusal to share political power, we can hardly expect those same white prisoners to credit or even understand the Black politics which flourished in their absence.[23]

IN TRYING TO MAKE SENSE OF WHAT HAPPENED IN FOUR, WE CAN set the overtly racist reportage of Waterhouse, Cobb, and Browne against the accounts of three sailors who actually kept journals during their time in the prison. Frank Palmer of Stonington, who had been captured by the British within a day of becoming a privateersman, was transferred from Halifax to Dartmoor in the summer of 1814. Joseph Valpey of Salem was captured on a privateer off Nantucket that same summer. Nathaniel Pierce of Newburyport, just up the coast from Salem, was another privateersman brought to Dartmoor just after Christmas 1814. These men were young— Pierce was just nineteen—and had their own racial hang-ups: it was Palmer who had howled to his journal about being thrown into the hold of a prison ship in Bermuda with 'half a dozen stinking negroes'. But their real-time reporting captures the ease and frequency with which they crossed the colour line at Dartmoor. 'I went into Number Four prison for to see the fashions and pass the time,' Valpey wrote in December 1814. In his journal he recorded dozens of visits, usually in the company of several white companions. Valpey would spend most days touring the other prison blocks, inspecting the shopkeepers' wares, and scouting new sources of amusement that could blunt the 'dull and tegeous' nature of his captivity. Nathaniel Pierce told his diary that 'in Number Four, the Black's Prison, I have spent considerable of my time.' In the cockloft of Four were teachers of every sort: you could learn to read, write, fence, box, and dance, all things which were 'very diverting to a young person'. The instructors were Black, but this hardly dampened Pierce's enthusiasm for Four. 'Indeed,' he wrote, 'there is more amusement in this prison than in all the rest of them.'[24]

Benjamin Waterhouse insisted that no white sailor could spend time in Four without acknowledging the absurdity of Black pretensions. He snidely observed that 'these blacks have been desirous of having their prison the center of amusement' and poured particular contempt on their theatre and its 'troglodyte dramas'. Waterhouse's tropes were crude: Black actors had no idea what they were saying; they were 'imitative' rather than artistic, better suited to the flailing of pantomime than the nuances of tragedy. Waterhouse ridiculed a performance of *Othello* in Four which featured a male Desdemona in whiteface: 'For a negro man to cover his forehead, neck and hands with chalk, and his cheeks with vermillion, to make him look like an English or American beauty, was too much.' Benjamin Browne conjured a nearly identical scene in which 'a tall strapping negro, over six feet high, painted white, murder[ed] the part of Juliet to the Romeo of another tall dark-skin.' Like Waterhouse, Browne believed that 'the blacks were pretty well in pantomime' but unsuited to emotion and wordplay. Purists could experience drama of an 'altogether higher order' from the white company in Prison Five, who only lacked the props and scenery that had been bequeathed to the Black Prison by the French.[25]

For Waterhouse and Browne, whiteface Desdemona and Juliet were the most wretched of Four's theatrical outrages. Perhaps Four's company really did perform *Othello* and *Romeo and Juliet* that winter, but Browne's account features a curious inversion which again casts doubt on what happened. Browne claimed that while the players of

Four stumbled through crude burlesque, Prison Five would offer 'genteel comedies' to more discerning patrons. He then reproduced a playbill, which he claimed to have copied from a poster on the wall of the prison:

The Dartmoor Thespian Company respectfully announce
that there will be a performance at the Theatre
No 5 this evening, December 29th,
when will be presented the admired comedy of

THE HEIR AT LAW

Together with the favorite afterpiece of

RAISE THE WIND

Browne had transcribed precisely the bill that Frank Palmer had so enjoyed in Four's theatre, performed by Black actors. Perhaps the 'highly respectable' white actors of Five staged their own production, but did so after a Black company had played the same material to a packed and appreciative crowd in Prison Four. Or perhaps Browne was also in the cockloft of Four with Frank Palmer on that happy evening on November 1814 and chose three decades later to remember his happy evening in the company of white people rather than Black.[26]

Waterhouse, Browne, and Cobb described a level of detachment between white and Black prisoners entirely at odds with the casual mixing recorded by the journals of Palmer, Valpey, and Pierce. At sea, many smaller vessels would not have had enough Black sailors to form a mess of six, so acquaintances and even friendships between Black and white prisoners would have predated the arrival of Americans at Dartmoor. Some of these clearly endured despite the segregated nature of the living arrangements. Nathaniel Pierce told his journal of a Black prisoner in Four named Thomas Cutler, 'formerly of Newburyport' (Pierce's hometown), who won a huge jackpot at the gaming tables in Four one night. The next morning, he came looking for Pierce in Prison Seven 'and made all the mess a present of a two penny loaf and a pint of coffee, which was very good in him'. The casual nature of this entry does nothing to suggest that Cutler's arrival was out of the ordinary. What surprised Pierce was Cutler's lucky win, not his visit to Seven.[27]

For Waterhouse, Cobb, and Browne, Prison Four exposed a tension at the heart of their racial thinking. All three were dismissive, even contemptuous of Black culture and politics. They wrote about Four as a place of ersatz entertainment, where white sailors could laugh at Black failure. And yet Four seemed to have become the centre of the prison's society. Waterhouse et al. managed this uncomfortable truth by claiming that some visitors to Four may have lost their bearings. The sense of white people being seduced by the company of Black people was made literal in Benjamin Browne's prurient sketch of King Dick's attendants: 'He kept two white lads continually about his person, whom he took care to select for their comely looks, and to keep them handsomely clad.' No one else wrote about these 'lads'. For Browne, in the (near total) absence of women, they play the role of vulnerable whites who are picked off and corrupted by the Black protagonist.[28]

He applied a similar gloss to white sailors who became addicted to Four's gaming tables. Four was the 'Palais Royale' of Dartmoor, and 'the gamblers were Dick's most strenuous adherents.' The range of equipment left behind by the French had created plenty of opportunity: 'The games were dice and cards,' wrote Browne, and 'in some of the corners might be seen roulette tables continually twirling around.' Gambling was a constant in every prison facility, and the journals of Frank Palmer and Nathaniel Pierce confirm that one could lose a fortune at cards or dice in any of Dartmoor's prison blocks. But Browne presented Four as a place where honest white men lost their fortune, and perhaps also their soul: the nadir of white experience, for Browne, was to end up 'tending a gambling table in No 4, a miserable slave to an ignorant negro'. Browne claimed personally to have 'mourned over the degradation of several youths of my own acquaintance' and even claimed that 'they never recovered from it' when they returned to the United States at the war's end. For a white sailor, to visit the tables of Four was to risk losing money to Black men. Clearly, this prospect did little to dampen the popularity of Four's cockloft among white prisoners at the time. But when Browne wrote up the story in 1846, these experiences became a kind of morality play with a tragic conclusion for the white people who had fallen under Four's spell.[29]

UNLIKE THE OTHER BLOCKS, FOUR SUSTAINED ITS OWN RELIGIOUS community for much of the winter of 1814–1815. A forty-year-old Black sailor named Simon Harris began to preach every Sunday in the cockloft, drawing a congregation of forty or fifty prisoners. In his 1868 memoir, the Massachusetts sailor Joseph Bates remembered seeing Harris emerge from Four on Sunday morning with new converts. These men were 'baptized in a small pool of water in the yard . . . which was generally used by the prisoners in washing their clothes'. The agent and the board had tried to recruit visiting ministers from neighbouring towns to preach within the prison blocks, but with limited success. (One prisoner recalled his disgust at being asked to offer prayers for George III.) Harris's emergence refreshed Thomas Shortland's hopes of a religious revival in the prison. The agent arranged for a white preacher from Plymouth to come to the cockloft of Four every Thursday afternoon, offering an alternative to Harris's Sunday ministry. But it was the Black preacher who continued to win the most converts, both within Four and among the white residents of the other blocks.[30]

Simon Harris was a Baptist, originally from Virginia. These two facts allow us to contextualize his impromptu ministry. Virginia had seen an evangelical revival in the late 1780s and early 1790s, and Black and white Baptists worshipped alongside each other in many of the state's churches. In the years before the War of 1812, some Black preachers addressed majority-white congregations, and a Baptist association in Roanoke even purchased the freedom of one enslaved person they thought 'ordained of God to preach the

Gospel'. Although free Black people in northern towns and cities had begun to respond to white prejudice by creating separate Black churches, Virginia's Baptist community continued to support a lively tradition of interracial worship through the 1820s. Simon Harris grew up in this tradition, though a clear majority of Dartmoor's white prisoners—including every sailor who left an account of their captivity—hailed from northern states in which interracial worship was uncommon. The white sailors must have found it strange to attend a church led by a Black man, but, as with so many other diversions in Four, the extraordinary circumstances of their confinement had created possibilities as well as hardships.[31]

KING DICK AND HIS CHAPLAIN.

W. C. Jackson, 'King Dick & His Chaplain' (1886) *Public domain*

'It being Sunday,' wrote Joseph Valpey in January 1815, 'I went into Number Four prison for to hear the Black preacher, and to my great surprise saw Joseph Pitman on his humble knees offering up his prayers to his Almighty God.' Pitman, a forty-two-year-old (white) privateersman, was nearly twice Valpey's age but had become a good friend in the prison. They often passed an hour or two 'talking about the pleasures of Salem', their hometown. Even though Valpey was a regular at Simon Harris's church, he was taken back by the vehemence of Pitman's conversion. The next day he told his journal that Pitman and another Salem friend 'had moved their bags and hammocks into the Black Prison'. Valpey wasn't sure if the move was occasioned by religious awakening or other motives, but he noted that the two men had been 'taken into the Black Society'. After this, Valpey visited Four even more often, dutifully telling his diary which prisoners had accompanied him on his regular trips to the church.[32]

Frank Palmer was at the same service in which Joseph Pitman fell to his knees. In his subsequent journal entry, he fixated on Simon Harris's appearance and let his prejudices muffle the preacher's message. 'On Sunday last I [went] to [a] meeting in No 4 Prison to hear a Black preacher,' he wrote two days later. 'He is with[out] exception the ugliest Negro that ever I saw: lips as thick as staves, eyes look like a sore kitten and near sighted with all.' And then, after registering his revulsion: 'Had he not those failings he might pass [for a preacher] in the dark.' Palmer didn't tell his journal about Pitman's dramatic conversion, though one wonders what effect it had upon him. Did Palmer feel a frisson of anxiety about a fellow prisoner throwing in his lot with Harris? Unlike Valpey, who continued to frequent the cockloft church, Palmer didn't mention any further visits. But Nathaniel Pierce, an occasional worshipper at Harris's services, guessed that the congregation numbered around forty through the spring of 1815. These were, Pierce judged, 'chiefly blacks'. But among them were white men curious to hear Preacher

Simon's message, along with those who, like Pitman, had embraced Prison Four completely.[33]

As he did when describing the plays held in Four's cockloft, Benjamin Browne approached Simon Harris's preaching with ridicule. 'The Pontifex Maximus of the diocese of Dartmoor was an ugly, thick-lipped, ignorant black man named Simon,' he wrote, 'and I believe, notwithstanding his professions of piety, that he was a consummate rascal.' Crucial to Browne's sketch was the idea of Black people as dupes: Preacher Simon stayed one step ahead of his gullible audience, asking them for money while spouting 'nonsense and blasphemy'. Again, white visitors left Prison Four 'grinning almost audibly at the fun'. Browne acknowledged that there were one or two white people foolish enough to be taken in, but he presented religion as an offshoot of Dick's cruel politics: an unscrupulous Black elite had deceived or browbeaten the ignorant majority.[34]

Browne, Waterhouse, and the other white writers who fixed the myths of Prison Four looked to downplay or stigmatize the block's many racial crossings: Four was a place where white people could have fun, they conceded, but visitors navigated its pleasures and attractions with a robust sense of irony. 'A person entering the cockloft of No. 4,' wrote Waterhouse, 'would be highly amused with the droll scenery which it exhibited and, if his sense of smelling be not too refined, may relish, for a little while, this strange assemblage of antics.' The racist cladding disguised a truth which is clear from the journal accounts: ordinary white Americans at Dartmoor found pleasure, friendship, and even inspiration in Prison Four. It was this simple and shocking reality which Waterhouse and his successors would work diligently to deny.[35]

ONE OF THE SHARPEST CRITICS OF WHITE PREJUDICE IN THE EARLY nineteenth century was Hosea Easton, a free Black preacher and reformer who became a leading abolitionist in Boston. In 1837, a year before his death, he published his *Treatise on the Intellectual Character and Civil and Political Condition of the Colored People of the United States.* Easton was a brilliant analyst both of the Black struggle for citizenship rights and of the deep prejudices among white people which stood in the way of racial equality. 'It is a remarkable fact that the moment the colored people show any sign of life,' he wrote, 'an unrelenting hatred arises in the [white] mind which is inhabited by that foul fiend, prejudice; and the possessor of it will never be satisfied, until those indications are destroyed.' If Black people 'assume the character of capable men'—in business, public speaking, religion, or any other pursuit—'they are immediately made to feel that they are as a carcass destined to be preyed upon by the eagles of persecution.' This wasn't quite true of Dartmoor: we know from the journals of Joseph Valpey, Frank Palmer, and Nathaniel Pierce that even prejudiced white sailors found themselves drawn to Four and that the fragile and transient circumstances of their captivity allowed them to cross the colour line in ways that might not have been possible in the United States. But Easton was surely right about the operation of prejudice on the published accounts which established the story of the 'Black Prison' when the war was over. The effect of those books and essays was to exoticize and lampoon Four's attractions and protagonists and to reassure readers that white prisoners were immune to the Black Prison's appeal.[36]

As for King Dick, who was six feet five inches tall (Waterhouse), or six feet seven (Cobb), or 'nearly seven feet' (Browne), Easton wrote ruefully of the ways in which prejudice warped white perception. If a Black person were found in any station apart from slavery, 'he magnifies to a monster of wonderful dimensions.' White people found it hard to believe that a Black man with agency and self-respect could fit into stagecoaches or steamboats or taverns; 'mechanical shops, stores, and school rooms, are all too small for his entrance as a man.' But if the same individual 'be a slave', Easton noted, 'his corporeality becomes so diminished as to admit him into ladies' parlors, and into small private carriages, and elsewhere, without producing any other discomfiture.' The register had Richard

Crafus as six feet three and a quarter inches, which made him the tallest man in Dartmoor. Every white person who wrote about him thought he was even taller, fixating on his physicality and attributing his influence principally to his size. It was the 'magical power' of prejudice to distort everything, as Easton knew. Beyond this prejudice, in sources we don't have, lies the truth of what happened in Prison Four.[37]

10.

HOPE DEFERRED

N O ONE SAW THE FIRST HANGING OF THE WINTER, AT LEAST not until it was too late. Lewis Clover had noticed Joe Taylor withdrawing from the other prisoners in November 1814, as the snow blew into Dartmoor and the war dragged on. 'Despair seemed to have thrown its pall over him,' Clover thought. On the night of 1 December, the young New Yorker climbed out of his hammock in Prison Five, made a noose from his bedding, then threw it over a bar close to the ceiling. Taking care not to wake up the sailors all around him, he shimmied up a stanchion, put his head through the noose, and let go.[1]

Frank Palmer was shivering in the yard at roll call the following morning when the turnkeys carried Taylor's body from Five. Some men at Dartmoor 'will get inured to the hardships and miseries of this wretched abode,' Palmer wrote in his journal. Others would succumb to the same agonies that had made Joe Taylor end his life. 'I can't say I blame them,' Palmer wrote, 'since it is the easiest method to get exchanged.'[2]

Joe Taylor's death was shocking not only in its circumstances but also in its timing. The prison had been alive with rumours that American negotiators in Belgium were about to reach a peace deal with Britain. For Charles Andrews, who always prescribed patriotism as the antidote to despair, suicide was a form of 'false heroism'. Joe Taylor 'had less courage to live than to die'. In *The Prisoners' Memoirs*, Andrews even claimed to have posted a poem on the doors of each block to warn the other prisoners not to follow Taylor's example:

> Whene'er you view this doleful tomb,
> Remember what you are,
> And put your trust in God alone:
> Suppress that fiend, Despair.
>
> Lo! There's entomb'd a generous youth
> Despair did doom to die;
> By the hard act of suicide,
> Joe Taylor there doth lie.

Suicide was an intensely personal act. It was also a public and political one. Andrews was obsessed with maintaining discipline among the American community at Dartmoor and found Taylor's bleak abdication hard to accept: 'The suicide reverses everything; he does an act which is not natural, not rational, not desirable, and dangerous.' But it was profoundly difficult to maintain one's spirits in the winter of 1814–1815. The cycle of highs and lows, of excitement and despondency, shredded prisoners' emotions and corroded Dartmoor's fragile sense of community. Frank Palmer blamed hope. American prisoners could hardly live without it—'it is thee alone that makes life a blessing'—but its persistent frustration left them exhausted and hollow. 'Hope deferred,' Palmer wrote on Christmas Day of 1814, 'is like a lingering consumption: it wastes away our lives by degrees, and will end only in death.' Plenty of Americans would die that winter: in the prison blocks, the yards, and the hospital. Although news of a peace treaty would reach the prison in the same month as Taylor's suicide, virtually all of the Americans were still there in April 1815. That winter deliverance was always imminent, and never came.[3]

The population of American prisoners increased from around a thousand in June 1814 to more than five and a half thousand in December. Prisoners were reunited with friends and family from their hometowns but also with men they would rather have avoided. Most of the new arrivals were privateersmen, though with the French war over, the Admiralty now discarded more than a thousand Americans who had remained on British warships after 1812. Impressed sailors had always been viewed with detachment, if not suspicion, by some of their compatriots. In the winter of 1814–1815, they poured into Dartmoor to face unbearable scrutiny. Had some decided to remain in the Royal Navy even at the cost of fighting their own countrymen? Agent Shortland and his staff had the unenviable challenge of preventing prisoners from escaping or harming each other. Dartmoor's turnkeys and guards knew just as well as the Americans that the end of the war was approaching, but a fraying of prison discipline tracked the Americans' frustration at their endlessly deferred release. Everyone assumed that they would soon be allowed home, but few realised that their repatriation would depend upon the exertions of Reuben G. Beasley. This too would end badly.

AT THE BEGINNING OF JANUARY 1815, FRANK PALMER, WITH 'nothing new to write and nothing having transpired', described his typical day. He'd wake up in Prison Seven to the sound of gamblers laughing or quarrelling and know it was breakfast time. The messmate responsible for cooking would roll out of his hammock while the other prisoners dozed, draining a few more minutes from the day. A horn would blow in the yard and prisoners would turn out for roll call. In the morning they might read; Palmer loved to write, too, but his paper stocks were limited. Then they would play cards and read some more, and after an eternity it would be time for dinner. A 'scanty meal' was followed by more reading and cards—someone might take up the chequerboard if the mess had one—and then the prison would become noisy, with 'tumult enough for Bedlam', as the gamblers began their evening session. Palmer and his friends would 'pass away day after day, and a mere repetition of the same occurs'. One index of Palmer's intense boredom: two months after this entry he transcribed the routine once more in his journal. Even when his paper supply was nearly depleted, writing the same thing all over again suddenly seemed the most interesting diversion.[4]

It was hard for prisoners not to let their minds wander to the winter's most frightening development: the spread of disease through the crowded blocks. From April 1813 to October 1814, thirty-five Americans died at the prison. In the winter of 1814–1815, more than two hundred would die. The American prisoners knew their health was a fragile commodity even before they were captured by Britain. That winter they faced the possibility that they might die within the walls of the prison just weeks or even days before they were due for release. 'Jail fever' was a common phenomenon in eighteenth-century British prisons, though its science was poorly understood. Dartmoor's design reflected the latest thinking about how to prevent it: each floor of the prison blocks was large and undivided, with windows open to the elements to allow for ventilation (even in winter). Disease had been a problem from Dartmoor's first year, and the Transport Board was prickly at the suggestion that the design of the prison might be to blame.[5]

Dartmoor's original surgeon, William Dyker, pinned the prison's first epidemic—during the winter of 1809–1810—on the Romans. 'They were the chief cause of the sickness,' he told a parliamentary investigation. 'They were a depraved set.' Under questioning, Dyker admitted that the Romans had mostly kept away from other Frenchmen, so their potential to infect the entire prison was limited. But rates of illness after the winter of 1809–1810 dropped considerably, and when the Romans were expelled from Dartmoor in the summer of 1813, Dyker presided over a mostly healthy prison.

Dyker was succeeded in September 1814 by George Magrath, one of the most celebrated surgeons in the Royal Navy. Born in Ireland in 1775, Magrath learned his trade on British warships in the Caribbean in the 1790s. Although a bout of yellow fever cost him the sight in one of his eyes, he attained a reputation for skill and calm as a surgeon. He was rewarded in 1803 with a posting to the navy's flagship, HMS *Victory*, where he served under Horatio Nelson. Magrath would have fought in British history's most famous naval engagement—the Battle of Trafalgar in 1805—if Nelson hadn't appointed him a few months earlier to oversee the British naval hospital at Gibraltar, then in the grip of its own yellow fever epidemic. Magrath was happy to be on land again and subsequently spent nearly a decade as chief surgeon at Mill Prison in Plymouth. When he transferred to Dartmoor in the fall of 1814, Magrath quickly impressed the Americans. He was 'a humane, skillful and attentive man', thought Charles Andrews, 'and a friend to the sick and distressed prisoner'. For Benjamin Browne, Magrath was 'one-eyed but whole-souled.' The surgeon became an increasingly influential figure that winter, even as his hospital became a place of dread for the American prisoners.[6]

'Without the least particle of exaggeration,' announced Benjamin Browne, 'I did not enjoy a single day of good health at Dartmoor.' There was little to shield prisoners from the cold and the damp, and so 'we could not be otherwise than unhealthy.' Measles and smallpox were the major killers in the winter of 1814–1815. 'Our ears had been constantly assailed with the groans of the sick, and the dying,' Charles Andrews wrote. Depending on the extent of their fever, prisoners might be treated to a cold bath on arrival at the hospital; they would almost certainly have their blood drained. 'I knew a man that went into the hospital with a bad cold,' wrote Joseph Valpey in his journal, 'and he at the first bleeding had two hundred and forty ounces of blood taken from him' (an alarming if anatomically improbable claim). Despite his excellent bedside manner, George Magrath's prejudices in this respect were off-putting to the prisoners: 'The doctor here makes a practice of bleeding a person as long as he has breath to draw,' wrote one.[7]

Concerned for its reputation, the Transport Board harassed Thomas Shortland mercilessly when his prisoners fell ill. Andrew Baird, the board's principal inspector, came to Dartmoor in early November 1814 when the first wave of deaths had peaked. He was back again in February during a new outbreak of smallpox. George Magrath had begun smallpox vaccinations in January 1815, but Baird was unhappy with the pace of progress and complained to the board about the surgeon's zealous use of cold baths. When Shortland defended Magrath, the board asked the agent to 'report who are the distinguished writers and judicious practitioners to whom you refer as your authority for practicing cold ablution or sponging in cases of smallpox and measles'. Letters from London often took this withering tone towards Shortland: the board found endless ways to remind him that his authority was entirely circumscribed by their better judgment.[8]

When the board asked its inspector about the deaths at Dartmoor, Baird blamed Shortland's faltering control over the Americans: 'When the usual means of cleanliness, ventilation, and good order was established,' he maintained, 'sickness disappeared.' He also blamed the victims. The Americans fell ill more often (and more severely) than the French had for a simple reason: their government paid them an additional allowance which they used to smuggle alcohol into the prison. In Baird's judgment, this led to 'great excesses' which had 'a very great share in promoting pulmonary diseases'. Surprisingly, given how fondly he was remembered by the American prisoners at Dartmoor, George Magrath took exactly the same line. Illness in the prison, Magrath told a parliamentary enquiry, was driven by 'moral causes' rather than climate or conditions. Americans were 'exceedingly prone to dissipation and undue indulgence in spiritous potations'. As they had done with the Romans, British officials identified Americans as the cause of their own misfortune.[9]

The huge influx of prisoners across the summer and fall of 1814 brought a renewed enthusiasm for escape, including the first (and only) American attempt to tunnel out of Dartmoor. This enterprise would reveal the uncomfortable proximity of solidarity and suspicion among prisoners of war. According to George Little, who arrived at Dartmoor in June, the digging began in Prison Five. The tunnel was 'sufficiently wide to let two men pass abreast,' he claimed, with several ventilation shafts. It would need to stretch at least a hundred feet to get beyond the outer wall: 'an immense undertaking'. Prisoners worked under cover of darkness with enormous effort. Occasionally, the miners would hit solid rock, forcing them to route around the obstacle, making the tunnel even longer. Dartmoor's terrible weather was finally an advantage; rain would send water rushing through the drains in each yard, allowing prisoners to spirit away earth from the excavations. George Little remembered the physical strain but also the mental anguish of concealing the tunnel from the prison authorities. And then there was 'the apprehended treachery of the prisoners'. Even among those who were privy to the secret, 'it could not be supposed that all would prove true.'[10]

Charles Andrews remembered things differently. He claimed that the escape plan was hatched in Prison Four in the summer of 1814, before that block became an exclusively Black space, and that American prisoners dug tunnels simultaneously from Four, Five, and Six. Anyone who blabbed to the agent would receive 'immediate death in a private and secret manner'. For good measure, Andrews and his associates appointed 'a number of confidential persons . . . as spies to watch the conduct of others'. As usual, Andrews's account mixed full-throated patriotism—there was 'not a dissenting voice among the whole'—with an admission that the loyalties of other prisoners were suspect. By the end of August all three tunnels had proceeded more than halfway to the outer wall. Then Shortland swept into Six to close down the operation. His men found the tunnel entrance in that block, though not the entrance in Four or Five.

Shortland moved all of the residents of Six to the other side of the prison and ordered his men to search the blocks of the South Yard again.[11]

Exiled in the North Yard, Andrews and his associates convened a 'court of judicature' to find the informant. A number of people were accused and 'evidence against them was produced.' But the punishment was execution, and the prisoner jury couldn't bring itself to convict anyone. Instead, Andrews and his associates 'gave orders to the blacks in No. 4 to proceed on with their work'. That the white Americans who had demanded to be segregated from their Black compatriots would then direct them to finish an escape tunnel is not impossible: it suggests that Andrews had enough faith in the patriotism or solidarity of Black prisoners to entrust them with a vital secret.[12]

It's harder to see what was in this arrangement for sailors of colour. According to the register, only one Black American escaped from Dartmoor—and that was in a mass breakout in June 1815, when the prison authorities had lost control of the evacuation process. Black runaways faced particular problems blending into the local population: perhaps ten thousand Black people lived in Britain in the 1810s, but half were in London and very few could be found in the Devonshire countryside. A captured Black fugitive might be kidnapped into slavery, especially given his desperation to find any captain willing to offer passage out of Britain. Andrews's account suggests that some measure of solidarity and shared patriotism survived the racist reordering of Dartmoor's human geography. But given the vibrant autonomy of Four's politics, it seems likely that Black prisoners kept digging not because they followed Andrews's orders but because they believed it was in their interest to do so.[13]

By October, the tunnels in Four and Five had reached the outer walls and Andrews and the leaders of the prison committees finalized their getaway. They would wait for a dark and stormy night, crawl through the tunnel, then scatter when they reached the moor. At the coast they would commandeer any craft they could find and head for France—or die trying. They knew Dartmoor would oblige them with terrible weather, but just before they could make their escape Agent Shortland intervened once more. Another informant had emerged—'a man by the name of Bagley,' Andrews wrote, 'who belonged to Portsmouth, N.H.' This time Shortland destroyed both tunnels and slashed the Americans' rations to pay for the demolition work. 'Our hopes were all blown up to the moon,' Andrews wrote, 'and we left to despair.'[14]

Workmen at Dartmoor in 1881 discovered the remains of a tunnel from Prison Five, but it was half as deep as Andrews had claimed and much smaller. Basil Thomson, who wrote a history of Dartmoor prison in the early twentieth century, was 'rather doubtful whether tunnels were ever made from No 4 or No 6 prison' and believed that 'Andrews purposely magnified the enterprise which he himself had devised.' Tunnels may have been started in Four and Six, but Thomas Shortland's correspondence with the Transport Board suggests the discovery of the main tunnel in Five took place in early September and collapsed the prisoners' hopes. The board congratulated Shortland and ordered him to release the informant without delay. Andrews and the other ringleaders were thrown into the cachot and, after months of secrecy, suspicion, and hard labour, the only American who secured his escape was the man who betrayed the scheme. 'Should this work ever reach his infamous hand,' Andrews told his readers, 'it is the sincere wish of every prisoner, that he may fall, and like that other Judas, his bowels may gush out.'[15]

Andrews was sure that 'Bagley' was the culprit. George Little declared that the prisoners had made 'a solemn compact . . . to take his life' should they ever meet the traitor again, but Little didn't identify him. The register supplies the missing evidence. The only Bagley is William Bagley of Portland, Maine (not Portsmouth, New Hampshire), who was another member of that tiny group of Americans who entered Dartmoor twice. His first arrival was on 1 July 1813, when he entered the American register as prisoner no. 369.

He'd been serving in the Royal Navy but spent less than a month in the prison. The register is silent on how Bagley secured his release, but it records his return more than a year later: the clerks noted that he had been serving on HMS *Ajax* until he 'gave himself up' into British custody. The register also dates this second appearance to January 1815—months after the tunnel plan had been discovered even in Andrews's embellished narrative. It was simply impossible for him to have been the mole, so why would Andrews name him with such authority?[16]

Bagley might have gotten out of Dartmoor in one of the rare exchanges in the summer of 1813, but it would have been terrible luck to have fallen back into the Royal Navy so quickly. It's more likely that he was released at the end of July 1813 to serve the king once more. We saw earlier that virtually no Americans at Dartmoor who had been serving in the Royal Navy volunteered to return to the king's service for early release; one reason for this was that men like Charles Andrews put the loyalty of these prisoners under particular scrutiny. If Bagley somehow slipped their grasp and back into the king's service in July 1813, it's no wonder he would have raised the ire of Andrews—especially when he fell back into the prison in January 1815. And then there is the timing of Bagley's first appearance at Dartmoor: he was marched to the prison on 1 July 1813, in exactly the same contingent which brought Charles Andrews north from Plymouth.

Did Andrews speak with Bagley at Plymouth or on their long march? Did they cross paths in the crowded cockloft of Prison Four that July, as Andrews scrutinized his compatriots for signs of disloyalty? One can only imagine Andrews's fury at the news that Bagley had glided back to the Royal Navy just a few weeks after his arrival. Fingering Bagley in print for betraying the tunnel plan would have helped Andrews avoid an inconvenient fact: the board's correspondence with Shortland indicates that the real traitor was Alfred Cooper, a thirty-two-year-old sailor from Newburyport, Massachusetts. There was nothing exceptional about him. He was a privateersman captured by the British in February 1813, and he spent more than a year in the hulks at Chatham before his arrival in Dartmoor in August 1814. On the surface there was no reason to doubt his patriotism, but anyone could put their own interest before solidarity with fellow prisoners or country. Perhaps he wanted to see his family again. Perhaps the thought of another winter in British custody was too much to bear. For Andrews, it was always easier to locate villainy among men like Bagley who had entered the Royal Navy than to accept that loyalty could never be relied upon.[17]

DISPUTES BETWEEN PRISONERS WERE A MAINSTAY OF PRISON LIFE. On the evening of 3 July 1814, James Henry and Thomas Hill had gotten into an argument. They had both been sailors on the *Argus*, one of the US Navy's most successful warships, until their capture by the British in the summer of 1813. They agreed to settle their dispute through a fistfight, which was scheduled incongruously for the following morning: Independence Day. Just before roll call on 4 July, Hill aimed a series of vicious blows at Henry's head, chest, and stomach. Henry, who was just nineteen years old, crashed to the ground. According to Charles Andrews, the prisoners promptly got on with their independence celebrations. They lifted a banner reading ALL CANADA OR DARTMOOR PRISON FOR LIFE—a reference to one of the more extravagant American war aims—and then the 'orator of the day' declaimed on the martial glories of the United States. James Henry saw out the festivities on a slab in the prison mortuary.[18]

Many of Dartmoor's most bitter disputes led back to the *Argus*, whose exploits encouraged both intense patriotism and angry paranoia among the prisoners. The ship had left New York in June 1813 with 153 crewmembers and one VIP: the Georgia politician William Crawford, who had been appointed minister to France. After landing Crawford on the Brittany coast, the *Argus* began hunting for prizes in the busy shipping lanes of the Irish Sea and the English Channel. No American vessel could match the *Argus* that summer in its haul of nineteen British prizes. Its young captain, Henry Allen, chose not to thin his ranks by appointing crew members to sail captured British ships back to the United States; instead, he sank the prizes on the spot. The amazed British prisoners would be sent to the hold of the *Argus*. When their numbers became too great, Allen would load them onto the next captured prize and send the ship to the English coast in an impromptu exchange. The blazing path of the *Argus* caused insurance rates in London to spike, and the ship's brazen adventures within sight of the British coast humiliated the Admiralty. Royal Navy vessels in the area were ordered to find the *Argus* and bring its rampage to an end.[19]

When he sighted HMS *Pelican* at dawn on 14 August 1813, Captain Allen should have sailed away. The British ship outgunned the *Argus*, and Allen's crew was exhausted after capturing yet another prize the day before. But his winning streak had inflated his confidence, and he steered his ship into a bloodbath. Its sleepy gunners fired too high, while the *Pelican* delivered a perfect salvo. Henry Allen's left leg was shattered and he soon fell unconscious from loss of blood. A dozen Americans were maimed or decapitated within a matter of minutes, and the confusion over who was in command of the *Argus* delayed the ship's surrender. Eventually, when the vessels came so close that the Americans could make out the faces of their assailants, the *Argus* struck its colours. Allen held on to life for four days. Then, in the curious theatre that defined the war, he was buried at Plymouth in an elaborate ceremony attended by officers from both sides.[20]

Despite its heroics at sea, even the *Argus* was a place of uncertain affinities. When the captured crew was landed at Plymouth, John Robinson, an ordinary seaman from New York, confessed he had actually been born in Scotland. He persuaded the authorities to set him free by identifying eight of his crew mates as British subjects, prompting a brief and inconclusive investigation into whether they could be tried for treason. The crew (including the alleged Britons) was marched to Dartmoor in September 1813 and saw out that first winter with the other Americans in Prison Four. A year after their arrival, with the prison population now exclusively American and still no sign of an exchange, sailors from the *Argus* volunteered to dig the tunnel that might secure their escape. But then one of their number, Francis Bradt, was accused of betraying the plan to the guards. Charles Andrews maintained that just as Bradt was 'threatened to be put to death by great numbers of prisoners', Shortland rescued him from the yards and let him stay in the guardhouse until a 'cartel'—an exchange of prisoners—could be agreed in November 1814 for Dartmoor's small complement of US Navy personnel. Although Bradt was marched out of the prison with his former crew members, he became so convinced they would harm him that he ran away before they reached the cartel ship at Plymouth. He spent more than three months hiding out in a peaceful Dartmoor village working as a blacksmith until the authorities caught up with him in March 1815. To his horror, they carried him back to the prison, where the Americans were angrier than ever.[21]

And then there was the ship that had vanquished the *Argus*: HMS *Pelican*. The day after Christmas 1814, six of the *Pelican*'s crew quietly arrived at Dartmoor. They were older and wearier than the average American prisoner, but they stood out for another reason: they had taken part in the mauling of their countrymen on the *Argus*. It took less than a week for the *Pelican* Six to be exposed as 'American Englishmen', in Frank Palmer's cutting phrase. Charles Andrews claimed that the Six had played a leading role in the battle and had only given themselves up 'to claim a citizenship and obtain their release'. More likely, they had been thrown out of the Royal Navy when the French war ended in the summer of 1814. One of the prisoners' committees appointed a court to try the men for treason; four were acquitted and two found guilty. One of those, in a recklessly candid boast, told the court that he was 'the first man on board the *Argus* & killed the carpenter with his own sword'. The court ordered the men to be hanged, but before the sentence could be imposed one of the onlookers tipped off Shortland. The agent arrived just in time with a 'large guard' and rescued all six of the *Pelican*'s crew. Five—including Benjamin Jackson, a Black man from Virginia—were spirited out of the prison to HMS *Impregnable* on 9 January. The sixth was evacuated the following week. Shortland found a way to put them back into the Royal Navy despite the fact that the Admiralty no longer needed them. Clearly, the British authorities judged this preferable to the embarrassment of vigilante justice in its flagship prison. Frank Palmer, furious at their deliverance, took to his journal: 'I only pray that they may meet their just reward, which will be the rack.'[22]

These panics over loyalty persisted through the winter. In the middle of January 1815, a rumour began to circulate that two recently arrived Americans had been in the Chatham hulks in 1813 before agreeing to serve in the Royal Navy. Charles Andrews, who narrated their story with frigid precision, insisted that they had 'shifted from ship to ship' after the French surrender in the spring of 1814 in a desperate attempt to avoid being discharged into the prison system. Andrews knew this because his block's committee had seized the men, 'made strict inquiry into the matter', and established their guilt. Keen to deny Agent Shortland another opportunity to rescue the condemned, Andrews and his associates imposed their sentence immediately. They 'fastened them to a table, so that they could not resist, and then with needles and India ink pricked "US" on one cheek and "T" on the other, which is United States Traitor.'[23]

The men were rushed to the hospital, where George Magrath attempted to remove the letters with bleach. This did even more damage, and Andrews reported that the men nearly died from their ordeal. Shortland was furious. He sent four of the tattooists to Exeter, thirty miles to the northeast, to stand trial for 'assaulting, wounding and disfiguring' their compatriots. 'I don't see what right he has to do this,' complained Frank Palmer in his journal, 'but Power, that cursed Power.' The jury in the case considered the charges against the men, but given the size of the mob that had carried out the attack they found it impossible to convict. The assailants were back in Dartmoor by the end of March, though the fate of their victims is harder to determine. Most likely they were harboured by Shortland until the general release of American prisoners in the spring, though it's hard to imagine that their disfigurement would have eased their return to the United States.[24]

OTHER TENSIONS EMERGED THAT WINTER WHICH FURTHER UNdermined solidarity between the prisoners. A day after the tattooing incident in January 1815, a group of Americans from Prison Seven embarked on a heist, or what passed for one at Dartmoor. They had noticed that Prison Six, which had been emptied for repair, had wooden boards nailed to its windows. Reasoning that these might replace their worn-out mess tables, the men broke into Six, stole as many boards as they could carry, and made it back to Seven without being discovered. When a sentry noticed the boards were gone, Shortland demanded that the prisoners give up the wood and the thieves. The committee in Seven declined to part with either, and Shortland closed the prison's market indefinitely. At this point, the Americans in the other blocks intervened. 'The prisoners of No. one three four and five,' according to Joseph Valpey (who was himself in Seven), 'sent a letter into our prison to inform us that if we did not deliver up those men to Captain Shortland that they would come and take [them] by force.' Frank Palmer's journal corroborates the story, adding an arresting detail: when the committee in Seven refused to comply, 'in came a mob headed by Big Dick /a 7 foot Negro/ and by force of arms took out the offenders, and carried them before Shortland.'[25]

The story suggests not only that Dick was a figure of considerable influence in Prison Four but also that white prisoners would ally with Black prisoners *against other white prisoners* when their interests aligned. The calculus of solidarity depended heavily on circumstance. Seven's inhabitants struggled to rally their compatriots around the cause of stealing boards from an empty block. But just a few days later, an American prisoner held in the cachot managed to escape into the yard and was given refuge in Prison Seven. On this occasion, the different blocks made common cause and endured a long week of market closure to defend the fugitive.

It was easier to forge solidarity on this second occasion because the prisoner in question was already a cause célèbre within Dartmoor. In June 1814, Simon Hayes, a twenty-year-old privateersman, had been part of a prize crew taking the captured British brig *Vivid* from the English Channel back to the United States. Before they could reach the Atlantic, the Americans were intercepted by a British warship, HMS *Ceres*, which sent a boarding party to retake the *Vivid*. Rather than give up their prize, Hayes and three other members of the prize crew rushed to the hold and attempted to set fire to the powder store. This was as brave as it was reckless: the men would have been killed by the explosion (or hanged by the British if they had somehow survived). In the event, Hayes and his associates were discovered before they could light the powder. They were sent to Dartmoor with the instruction that they be held indefinitely in the cachot 'for attempting to blow up the *Vivid*'. They were still there six months later, when Simon Hayes made another reckless move. The sailors from the *Vivid* were occasionally allowed exercise just outside the cachot. Taking advantage of a distraction, Hayes jumped over the wall into the North Yard. Before the guards and sentries could stop him, he was enveloped by other prisoners and smuggled into Seven.[26]

The cruel and prolonged nature of Hayes's confinement endeared him to the other prisoners, but he had another reason to count on their loyalty: this was not his first visit to Dartmoor. He had originally been captured on a privateer off Bordeaux in January 1813 and had been marched up from Plymouth in the very first cohort of American prisoners. He had won release in one of the rare prisoner exchanges during the summer of 1813 and had promptly returned to privateering. Given the prominence of old-timers on the various prison committees, Hayes's cause had powerful supporters. Not

every prisoner was happy at the market closure, but a few of the
guards agreed to smuggle beer, bread, meat, and tobacco into Prison
Four to compensate. In another sign of cooperation across the colour line, the prisoners in Four then sold this on to the other blocks.
Shortland, under pressure from local traders to end the standoff,
eventually agreed to resume the market in return for the right to
send soldiers into each block to search for Hayes. That this was even
a matter for negotiation gives a sense of the prison's fractiousness
that winter. Hayes was never found. He slipped away with the rest
of the prisoners during the general release that spring.[27]

The effort to conceal Simon Hayes represented the high water
mark of American solidarity at Dartmoor, but even here one could
see that the structures regulating jailers and prisoners were unrav-
elling. In the middle of the standoff, the turnkeys forgot to unlock
Prison Five one morning and the angry inhabitants simply smashed
down the doors. This enraged the guards and turnkeys, who already believed Shortland to be too liberal towards the Americans.
As the prisoners were being turned into Five a few evenings later,
an overzealous militiaman bayoneted a straggler four times, sending
him to the hospital. Meanwhile, when a storekeeper in one of the
prisons casually suggested that Simon Hayes should be given up, he
was attacked by other prisoners who 'destroyed his shop, one taking
tobacco, another butter, and another rum'. Frank Palmer paid the
storekeeper a visit soon after and found him standing over what
remained of his belongings with tears in his eyes. Palmer felt bad
but offered little consolation: 'Experience is a good schoolmaster,'
he concluded.[28]

The assailants of the storekeeper were the most elusive agents
of disorder in Dartmoor: the Rough Allies. They were, according
to Benjamin Browne, 'as rascally a set of devils as ever escaped
drowning'. Most prisoners who wrote about Dartmoor mentioned
these men, without ever naming one or estimating their numbers. Some called them Rough Alleys, but Benjamin Browne explained the etymology: 'They were rough as untamed bears, and

allied together in the bonds of wickedness.' These were sailors who refused to accept the authority of the prisoners' committees and forged their own community. 'I verily believe that three quarters of all the misery and privations we endured here,' wrote Browne, 'were owing to these human brutes.' Frank Palmer was more circumspect: he admired the Allies for deterring price gouging in the hundreds of prison shops and concluded that their vigilantism benefited everyone. Benjamin Browne presented their leader—'an artful, plausible fellow of very good education'—as a 'demagogue' who had tried to seize control of Prison Seven. This leader was an 'unprincipled scoundrel' who would deceive 'many right-minded but unthinking men of a better character'. For Browne, the leader of the Rough Allies became an analogue of King Dick in Prison Four, though with one crucial difference: when the Allies mounted a coup against the prisoners' committee in Seven, they were unable to consolidate their power. They briefly seized the committee president as a hostage, but it was the Allies' leader who ended up in the cachot.[29]

The parallels between the Rough Allies and the inhabitants of Prison Four are instructive. Benjamin Waterhouse went so far as to claim King Dick sheltered the Allies in Four, though none of the other accounts supports this claim and several pieces of evidence contradict it. Waterhouse also claimed that it was the Rough Allies rather than the regular committees and juries who oversaw the tattooing attacks of January 1815. The various published narratives of Dartmoor carefully drew the line between acceptable forms of justice and solidarity and those moments when the prisoners overstepped the mark. For the self-styled keepers of discipline and community at Dartmoor, the Rough Allies were worse than an irritant. Their rampages through the prison suggested that the committees were only one authority among many.

THE GREATEST SOURCE OF TENSION IN THE WINTER OF 1814–1815 was the collective anxiety over when the war would end. Early in the fall, guards and turnkeys had gleefully informed the prisoners that a British expeditionary force had burned Washington, DC. The slow (and illicit) trickle of newspapers into Dartmoor soon brought better news of the defence of Baltimore and the victories of the US Navy on the Great Lakes. American and British officials continued to negotiate in the Belgian city of Ghent, and the papers predicted that a deal was imminent. In the final weeks of 1814, Frank Palmer overheard Agent Shortland tell his clerks that the treaty was agreed. 'PEACE, PEACE, Huzza for Peace!' he wrote in his journal on December 14. The very next day, he cadged a newspaper from a new arrival and wrote 'WAR! WAR! Rumors of War!' Rumours ricocheted through the blocks. The more judicious prisoners would seek out the newspaper that started the excitement, which usually meant a trawl through several blocks and a fight through a crowd to the sailor reading the original. Even when the papers offered upbeat reports, confirmation of the peace was perpetually in the offing.[30]

Finally, on 29 December 1814, Agent Shortland announced that a treaty had been signed at Ghent. 'We hoisted the American flag on all the prisons and all the prisoners assembled in the yard and greeted the glorious news with nine hearty cheers,' wrote Frank Palmer. On 31 December, the prisoners hoisted their FREE TRADE AND SAILORS RIGHTS banner on Prison Seven, until Thomas Shortland reminded them that prison rules permitted national flags, but not slogans. (When Shortland came into the yard, the band of Prison Four serenaded the agent with 'Yankee Doodle Dandy'.) More than five and a half thousand prisoners were already at Dartmoor, with hundreds still arriving every month. But the prisoners' ordeal was nowhere near over. The board reminded Shortland that the Americans must remain in his custody until news of Congress's ratification reached Britain: a delay of anywhere from six to eight weeks, depending on the weather. This unwelcome news took time to filter through the blocks. Many shopkeepers had given up their businesses on learning of the treaty, keen to avoid holding unsold stock when the gates were thrown open. This made the entire population more dependent on the daily market, which is one reason Shortland's closures in January and February 1815 cut so deep. The militia guards were just as keen to see the war end, and they struggled to maintain their discipline.[31]

For the Americans, news of the peace made their captivity still more unjust. Frank Palmer felt himself falling back into the unhappy cycle he'd lived in November and December, when he had obsessed over news from Ghent. Now he fixated on how long it would take a sailing ship to cross the Atlantic. By the start of March, he was beside himself with anxiety and expectation. Could something have happened to the ship? Could Congress have rejected the treaty text? A loud cheer outside Prison Seven brought him running into the yard. Another prisoner told him that 'the long expected treaty had arrived,' but Palmer had been in Dartmoor long enough to trace every rumour to its source. He rushed through the various prison blocks, looking for the newspaper that would show him it was true. As usual, he was disappointed. 'I followed the labyrinth of this winding fabrication through all its directions until convinced of its falsity,' he told his journal that night. Then he went back to Prison Seven—or, as he put it mournfully in his journal, 'I returned home.'[32]

In London, the man charged with the welfare of American prisoners convinced himself that he was doing everything to get them out. Reuben Beasley couldn't hasten the passage of the ship carrying the Treaty of Ghent to Washington, but in January he asked the Transport Board to 'shorten the sufferings of the American prisoners in this country' by beginning the general release immediately. His letter received a curt reply: 'Their lordships have been pleased to signify that they do not think proper to accede to your proposition.' Beasley had a practical as well as a moral reason to begin the repatriation. The logistical challenge of moving nearly six thousand Americans was enormous. Writing to Washington in early February to report on the board's intransigence, Beasley noted that he would need around twenty-five transport ships when he finally got the green light for the evacuation, and that 'to procure them in a short time will be difficult and expensive.'[33]

The news that Congress had ratified the treaty arrived in London in the third week of March. By then, dozens of prisoners had already written Beasley to ask whether they could arrange their own passage back to the United States. When news of the peace was confirmed, he was initially minded to say yes if prisoners had the means to get home without his help. Among the small number of Americans who walked out of Dartmoor via this avenue was George Little. A friend in London had lobbied Beasley on Little's behalf, and on 25 March he walked through the prison's stone archway to freedom. Two days later he was in London, 'in the midst of the largest metropolis in the world'. After nearly two years in captivity, Little 'thought myself as absolutely green as if I had never seen anything in my life'. Beasley earned the gratitude of men like Little by sanctioning these individual releases, but he sowed discord back at Dartmoor. More letters arrived from individual prisoners, and Beasley began to worry that some of these petitioners lacked the resources to fund their trip home. As he rejected more and more applications, the American prisoners became furious with him for allowing the rich to jump the line.[34]

Then came shocking news from across the Channel: Napoleon had escaped from the Mediterranean island of Elba, where he had been confined after his surrender, and was heading for Paris. Every arm of the British state went onto a war footing. The Admiralty, which had been happily discharging sailors since Napoleon's surrender the previous spring, now announced a 'hot press' which would sweep almost anyone into the Royal Navy. The Transport Board began to tender for commercial ships to carry soldiers and materiel over the Channel for another climactic battle. If Dartmoor's Americans tried to make their own way home, they were now exposed to the press gang in every British port. But if they stayed in the prison, they were reliant on Beasley somehow procuring twenty-five ships from under the noses of the board. Beasley wrote twice to Dartmoor in the final week of March 1815 and, as usual, failed to read the room. The first letter promised that three cartel ships would soon leave London for Plymouth and that the general release and evacuation would begin thereafter. The prisoners would have known that three ships could carry perhaps five or six hundred men, which made the initial repatriation fleet an order of magnitude below what was required. The second letter lamented that the prisoners 'have taken up an idea that any who may have the means of proceeding to the United States would on application receive a free discharge'. It would be better, with the press gang at large, for the American prisoners to stay put.[35]

The evacuation had stalled before it had begun, and Beasley had no reserve of goodwill on which to draw. Instead, his actions confirmed the prisoners' caricature. He had failed to visit Dartmoor since the fall of 1813. His letters to the prisoners were infrequent and usually delegated to his subordinates. (When news of the treaty's ratification reached the prison in the third week of March, the Americans acidly wrote to inform Beasley since 'we don't think it likely that you have heard of it.') They raged at his insistence that they should be inoculated against smallpox before they were allowed to board the cartel ships, and they were amazed to hear that the initial fleet would consist of only three vessels. 'This conduct in our agent certainly is not explicable,' wrote Frank Palmer, 'and deserves reproof.' Many prisoners found it hard to imagine that their government could treat them so badly. In this, at least, Beasley's epic haplessness was helpful. Beasley-bashing became a way of lamenting one's fate without losing faith in the United States.[36]

EVERYONE SAW THE SECOND HANGING OF THE WINTER. ON 26 March, the committee of Prison Seven held a mock trial of Reuben Gaunt Beasley in the South Yard. In *The Prisoners' Memoirs*, Andrews devoted pages to a transcript of proceedings. Beasley, absent as usual, was represented by an effigy made of old uniforms and straw. The charges were solemnly read: Beasley had failed to arrange enough cartels in 1813 before the window for prisoner exchanges had closed; he had failed to secure the release of impressed sailors in the Royal Navy; he had dragged his feet on obtaining an allowance for the prisoners; and he had entered into 'a contract with a *Jew merchant* of London, to supply the prisoners with the very meanest and coarsest clothing that could possibly be procured in all England'. Underlying everything was the old canard that, in discharging his duties as American agent, Beasley had made a 'handsome fortune' from the unnecessary captivity of his compatriots. With such an extensive list of allegations from the prosecution, and not a word in mitigation from the accused, Beasley's proxy was sentenced to death.[37]

A hangman threw a rope around the effigy's neck, and 'Beasley' was lifted high into the air towards the roof of Number Seven. After the cheers subsided, he was cut down and taken to a corner of the yard to be burned 'for his kind attention to the American prisoners of war,' in Joseph Valpey's summary. Thousands of prisoners watched the spectacle, though some were uneasy at finding comfort in the immolation of their countryman. 'I am sorry to say this conduct deserves censure equally as much as Mister Beasley's,' Frank Palmer told his journal. But the rituals and ceremonies of Dartmoor had already taken on a dismal aspect. Death and uncertainty defined prison life even after the Americans had received news of the treaty's ratification. Beasley's messaging had only made things worse. Did the US agent really write the prisoners in March 'that there should not be a man in the prison after a twelve month from this time'—suggesting that the evacuation would drag on until March 1816? Perhaps it didn't matter. With release both imminent and endlessly deferred, Dartmoor was ready to explode.[38]

11.

THE DEAD HOUSE

ALL FRANK PALMER HAD TO DO TO GET OUT OF DARTMOOR was walk from Prison Seven to the main gate. His cousin Bob Palmer had spent the war in the parole town of Ashburton on the edge of Dartmoor; having obtained his own release, he'd persuaded Reuben Beasley to let his kinsman travel home with him. Frank was ecstatic. He thanked the messmate who'd brought him the news, gathered his belongings, and dashed through the South Yard towards the passageway that linked the prison blocks to the market square. Peering through the railings he could see all the way to the main entrance, but he couldn't see Bob. He called to the sentry, who said nothing. Frank raised his voice. *Could the sentry take him to Bob Palmer?* The guard had no idea what he was talking about. *Bob Palmer from Ashburton?* After a few minutes of this, 'the thought popped into my head—that it was the first of April.' Crestfallen, Frank walked back to Seven and the 'laughing audience' that awaited him. He did his best to 'carry off the joke as becomes all April fools', but this seemed an especially cruel trick. Frank Palmer's fate was still in the hands of Mister Beastly.[1]

The weather had improved at the end of March, but the prison was volatile. A lick of sunshine brought the gambling tables into the yards, but it was hard for the prisoners to forget that they should already be free. Nathaniel Pierce thought about the thousands of American sailors who had avoided captivity during the war, and who would now be 'ploughing the ocean and reaping the benefits thereof' while he was still in Dartmoor. He also worried about the sickness surging through the blocks. During the month just gone, thirty-eight Americans had died in the hospital despite the best efforts of the surgeon, George Magrath. Eighteen had died since the news of the treaty's ratification. Even if Reuben Beasley was right about a 'hot press' in Britain's ports, every prisoner believed he would be safer anywhere but here.[2]

Remaining in the prison exposed Americans to another danger: a confrontation with the hundreds of militiamen guarding them. The Somersetshire militia had taken over guard duty in November 1814. Although most of the soldiers were happy to be stationed relatively close to home—their base was in Taunton, sixty miles to the north—their duties required them to live in the barrack house (just across the wall from Prison Seven) or in the larger accommodation buildings to the south of the prison. The militia were led by Major John Twyford Jolliffe, son and heir of a Somerset MP and landowner. Jolliffe's brother was an officer in the British Army; later that spring he would be killed at the Battle of Waterloo. John Jolliffe's posting was a good deal less glamorous but also less dangerous, to him at least: he simply had to keep the Americans in line until Beasley could complete their repatriation.[3]

Jolliffe had watched with disdain as the prison became more unruly: the Americans had seized guards as hostages, refused to allow prison officials to enter their blocks without negotiation, and done unspeakable things to each other. But operational command within the prison belonged to Shortland, and Jolliffe had to swallow his contempt for the agent's excessive liberality. The prisoners, who had time on their hands to study each militia rotation carefully, thought the Somersetshire guards colder and less pliable than their predecessors. The Derbyshire militia had been delighted to smuggle goods into the prison, a vital service during Shortland's frequent market closures. An Irish militia company had seemed to hate the English even more than the Americans did. A few individuals in the Somersetshire contingent could be bribed, either for passwords or contraband. In general, though, relations between the militia and prisoners had reached a nadir by March of 1815.[4]

For Thomas Shortland, the evacuation of prisoners was both an urgent priority and someone else's responsibility. He knew the prisoners were conscious of the twilight state of their captivity. Some kept their heads down, keen not to jeopardize their release by getting caught up in mischief. Others were carefree, even reckless. As the weather improved and the life of the prison blocks spilled into the yards, the younger prisoners roamed Dartmoor's outdoor spaces from morning until turning-in time. Prisoners typically enjoyed access to all three main yards—the North Yard, which contained blocks One, Two, and Three; the separate yard of Four, with the dividing walls still intact; and the South Yard, containing Five, Six, and Seven. The narrow passage just above the market square, where Frank Palmer waited forlornly for Bob, was the highway that linked all of these. Three iron gates separated the passageway from the three yards; another iron gate led to the market square.[5]

Crowds of prisoners thronged through the yards in the first days of April, and the passageway by the market square was always packed. The more unruly prisoners went beyond the bounds that had been set for them. The semicircle which contained the three yards was ringed by a set of iron railings and an inner wall, then the outer wall beyond that. The inner wall had guard posts, where sentries could peer into each yard, though they weren't always occupied; even if a prisoner succeeded in getting over the railings and the inner wall, soldiers regularly patrolled the 'military walk' between the inner and outer walls. At the start of April, prisoners began to hop over the railings onto the narrow patch of grass before the inner wall where, in a nod to their vast boredom, they created the new game of turf throwing. The rules were simple: they grabbed handfuls of turf and slung them at each other while a crowd gathered on the other side of the railings. None of this was allowed, but the prisoners chose their moments and got away with it.[6]

With the inmates finding new ways to stretch the prison's rules, Shortland stumbled into a familiar crisis. After the French uprising over the interruption to the bread supply in the winter of 1812, Dartmoor's officials had kept a reserve of biscuit that could feed the inmates in an emergency. With the war over and the prisoners about to depart, the board and Agent Shortland saw a way to save money on soft bread and to clear their weevil-ridden stockpile. In Joseph Bates's recollection, the prisoners reluctantly agreed to accept the biscuit if their allocation was the same weight as their bread ration. The Transport Board, of course, had a fixed bread-to-biscuit conversion rate of 3:2, which the prisoners would not accept. Frank Palmer's journal presented the standoff more starkly: 'The prisoners refused to take hard biscuit,' he wrote on April 4. Shortland evidently didn't think the impasse over the bread was serious. He left Dartmoor on the morning of the fourth for Plymouth, in the hope of gathering information on the cartel ships which Reuben Beasley was supposed to be sending. In his absence, the chief clerk of the prison told the Americans that they could either take or leave the biscuit ration. The prisoners' committees announced that they would accept only soft bread, which the clerk refused to give them; and so the prisoners were handed their usual beef and the biscuit was wheeled back to the storehouse.[7]

The persistent expectation of imminent release had already upset the prison's internal economies. The storekeepers who had done a roaring trade in September and October had run down their stock, and many prisoners had long since blown their savings. With little money in the prison and few shops still operating, it was hard to satisfy one's appetite even on a normal day. By the late afternoon of 4 April, sentries could see groups of hungry prisoners in urgent conversation. At six o'clock, hundreds of Americans suddenly rushed towards the passageway linking the yards and the market square. Shortland was still in Plymouth and the turnkeys and clerks began to panic. 'It's an old saying,' wrote Frank Palmer in his journal, 'that hunger will go through a stone wall.' The prisoners forced the gate open and crashed into the square. The prison alarm was sounded, and the Americans advanced on the storehouse where the biscuit was kept. The militiamen rushed from the barracks, some of them only partly dressed. Captain Jolliffe told the Americans to return to their prisons without delay; the Americans replied that they would seize the storehouse unless they were given soft bread.[8]

The clerks began an impromptu negotiation. Word was sent to the contractor that a consignment of bread was urgently needed, and the hundreds of prisoners in the market square settled down to wait. For Jolliffe and his men, the experience of being dictated to by the Americans must have been galling. Frank Palmer noticed that the militiamen had 'their hats off, shoes off, coats off, and some with trousers off; they presented a really laughable and ridiculous figure to the lookers on.' Declining the instruction that they wait in their own blocks, the Americans occupied the market square for more than three hours as the prison held its breath. Then, a little after ten p.m., the main gates opened and the bread wagons rolled in. It took until past midnight to feed all five thousand men. Some ate an entire loaf on the spot; others returned to the blocks to savour their food. In the early hours of 5 April, the prison staff made a temporary repair to the lock on the market gate and the militia stood down.[9]

A messenger from Dartmoor had reached Thomas Shortland in Plymouth late in the evening of 4 April with the news that the prisoners had occupied the market square. Unaware that the crisis was already over, the agent requisitioned a company of soldiers to march northwards at first light. When they got to Dartmoor the next morning, the prison was eerily quiet. Save for the damage to the market gate, it seemed as if nothing had happened. The prison's fragile order had been stretched once again, and the officials and soldiers at Dartmoor had avoided disaster. Not a single guard, official, or prisoner had been hurt in the incident, and the clerks were keen to avoid recriminations. The contractor would continue to deliver soft bread daily, and Shortland would need to think again about the biscuit. Frank Palmer, writing in his journal on 5 April, was pleased that the excitement was over. 'I think we have had news enough for one day, and I think more than we shall have again for this week to come.'[10]

THE MORNING OF 6 APRIL BEGAN CLOUDY BUT VERY MILD FOR Dartmoor. By midmorning the gambling tables were outside and the prisoners were playing their primitive version of baseball between Seven and the barrack-yard wall. The prisoners' committees drafted letters to Reuben Beasley and to the board complaining that the current rate of release would keep Americans in Dartmoor until September. 'The prisoners are growing daily more and more discontented,' wrote Frank Palmer in his journal that morning. 'They seem determined to make some bold attempt to escape from this damn prison, and I believe should we remain here much longer they would attempt it.' Benjamin Browne confessed in his Dartmoor memoir that he hadn't seen much of what happened that day, but a sharp-eyed friend of his was out walking in the morning and saw one of the younger prisoners scratching at the stones in the barrack-yard wall. One stone seemed more brittle than the rest, and other prisoners gathered round. Before long, they were taking turns to pick away at the stone, and soon there was a hole the size of a man's hand between the prisoners and the barrack yard.[11]

Whenever the Americans played in the yard, a batter would eventually slice the ball clean over the wall into the barrack yard and shout for it to be returned. After enough badgering, a soldier would usually oblige. On the afternoon of 6 April, the soldiers failed to answer. Before long the hole in the barrack-yard wall seemed full of possibility: Why not send someone through to retrieve the ball? The opening was still too small for even the youngest prisoner to climb through, and a party was dispatched to Prison Five to break loose a few of the window bars. Before long prisoners were attacking the wall with their makeshift crowbars and widening the hole.[12]

If the guards had intervened at this point, the day could have ended very differently. But they were distracted by a more immediate alarm: dozens of prisoners had climbed the railings separating the yards from the inner walls to wage their biggest-ever game of turf throwing. Nathaniel Pierce, one of the combatants, estimated that the 'sham fight' involved three hundred prisoners. The soldiers, 'envying our happiness', ordered Pierce and his friends to clamber back over the railings and return to their yards. The rowdiness allowed the prisoners at the wall to break through entirely into the barrack yard; a militia officer standing on the other side, Samuel White, was alarmed to see prisoners' faces peering through the hole. It was now past six in the evening, and the opening was getting bigger all the time. White later remembered how noisy it was. The prisoners were cheering as they knocked away more of the stones, and they began throwing pieces of turf over the wall. Agent Shortland had already retired for the evening to his house at the front of the prison. Samuel White sent word that something very bad was happening in the barrack yard.[13]

Initially the guards tried to reason with the prisoners: the Americans were so close to freedom that it would be crazy to get yourself killed. When that had no effect, a sentry waved his gun through the hole. This sent the invaders scurrying back into the South Yard, until one of them grabbed the soldier's bayonet and began dragging him through the hole. One prisoner later testified that the Americans were raucous but good-natured. Everyone was enjoying the sight of the lonely guard trapped in the hole: he was raging at the Americans and showing his arse to the militiamen on the other side of the wall. No one meant him any harm. Inside Prison Seven, though, a friend of Lewis Clover rushed to tell him what was happening and predicted that 'there will be trouble soon, caused by that break in the wall.' At least two of the prisoners' committees sent delegates to the South Yard to instruct the hotheads to back down. We can't know for sure if the hole's excavators were Rough Allies, but statements to the ensuing investigation establish two things:

first, that the committees tried to stop the hole from being further enlarged; second, that a number of the witnesses had decided on a story to explain what had taken place. In this version, the hole had only been opened when the British refused to throw back the ball. That story was untrue and disguised the fact that the hole had originally been an end in itself—another form of recreation on that warm spring afternoon, and a novelty in a place where everything was grindingly familiar.[14]

The walk from Shortland's house to the barrack yard took barely a minute. The agent was only half dressed; he hadn't stopped to put his uniform back on as he rushed from the dinner table. Shortland could hear the prisoners before he could see them, and when he got to the hole in the wall, he knew the situation was out of control. The unfortunate sentry had been dragged loose by his colleagues, but the prisoners were still jabbing iron bars and enlarging the hole. Turf and stones rained down onto the barrack yard, and when one heavy clump of earth hit Lieutenant White on the head, he fell forward into the opening—sending up another cheer from the American side. The turnkeys had by now started herding prisoners into the blocks for the night, but Americans in the North Yard could hear the commotion and hurried to see what was going on. So did Black prisoners from Four. Before long, hundreds—perhaps thousands—of prisoners were heading towards the barrack-yard wall.[15]

Rubbernecking Americans converged at the passageway which linked all three yards to the market square. This corridor was around thirty feet long and ten feet wide, and since it connected all of the yards to the market square, it was frequently packed with prisoners. On the evening of 6 April, Americans in the North Yard who had heard about the trouble now streamed into the passageway. They jostled with those coming the other way who were following the turnkeys' order to return to their blocks. A huge crush ensued. This was where the prisoners had broken the gate to the market square exactly forty-eight hours earlier, and at some point in the commotion the makeshift repair on the gate was broken. This may have been accidental; with so many prisoners in the narrow passageway it's not surprising that dozens spilled into the empty market square. Their incursion would normally have posed no threat of escape: there were three more gates between the square and the Plymouth road outside the prison. But at that precise moment all three gates had been opened to admit the bread wagons, which had stepped up their deliveries. The prisoners in the market square were barely 150 feet from freedom.[16]

Much of what went wrong on 6 April can be ascribed to terrible timing. A small group of American prisoners were actually waiting at the foot of the market square to inspect the bread with the clerk who managed the storehouse. They were astonished to see their compatriots tumbling through the broken gate, and the two groups were soon gazing at each other across the yard. Did anyone know what was happening? What should they do next? There had been plenty of warning signs that Dartmoor would erupt, but when the moment arrived, prisoners and officials alike seemed to freeze.

SOLDIERS RUSHED TO THE BARRACK YARD WITH THE NEWS THAT Americans had broken into the market square, and Thomas Shortland ordered the alarm to be sounded. Any prisoners who remained unaware of the drama now realised that something extraordinary was happening. The purpose of the alarm was to tell everyone that an escape was in progress. British soldiers later testified that the Americans had been trying to break out of Dartmoor, but prisoners dismissed this as ridiculous. John Clement, one of the very first Americans to arrive at Dartmoor in 1813, told investigators that the prisoners were 'destitute of money', clothed in rags, and mostly shoeless. How did they expect to get across the moor? And why would they risk being shot or press-ganged for a freedom which had already been promised them? The hole in the wall was 'mere mischief', said one American witness; 'mere play', said another. We know from Frank Palmer's journal entries—including one he'd written that morning—that talk of escape was common in the prison. Shortland told investigators that he'd heard from his informants that the Americans intended to 'liberate themselves on or before 10 April.' This was certainly the kind of thing prisoners were saying, though they said a lot of things that winter out of frustration rather than intent. Shortland might have dismissed the chatter, but with prisoners breaching walls and gates, he assumed the Americans were mad enough to break out. With the alarm bells still ringing, he left a detachment of soldiers to guard the hole and headed for the market square.[17]

British officials later conceded that the alarm had been a mistake. Prisoners rushed into the yards to see what was happening, adding to the crowds who were already massing by the market square. With so many prisoners in the passageway, the number of Americans squeezing through the broken gate was increasing. By the time Shortland arrived at the square, there were hundreds on the wrong side of the gate. In the bottom corner of the yard, the prison's steward John Arnold was standing with John Odiorne—Benjamin Browne's old captain, and one of the American bread inspectors. The three gates between the square and the Plymouth road were still open, waiting for the bread wagons to leave. Odiorne could see hundreds of his compatriots in a state that veered between exuberance and fury, ranged against perhaps fifty militia men. (Major Jolliffe had not yet arrived.) Shortland was joined by the surgeon, George Magrath, who had rushed from his house at the noise of the alarm. The prisoners were still in the upper half of the square, but their ranks continued to swell from the passageway. Odiorne guessed there was about twenty feet between the prisoners and the militiamen.[18]

Shortland and Magrath begged the prisoners to retreat. Magrath told the Americans that 'their detention appeared to be entirely the fault of their own agent, Mr. Beasley.' (Magrath later claimed that a number of prisoners meekly agreed and walked away.) The storehouse clerk testified that Shortland addressed the prisoners with a courtly plaintiveness: 'My good fellows, go to your different prisons, or the military must do their duty!' Given the huge numbers of Americans now watching the scene from the passageway, it's not clear that the prisoners in the square could have retreated through the gate even if they had wanted to. But the memory of their victorious protest two days earlier may also have made them complacent about the danger they were in. A soldier was sent to find Major Jolliffe, and the fifty militiamen inched forward with bayonets raised. The sergeant who directed this manoeuvre testified that his soldiers 'tried to drive them back without committing murder'. Amazingly, given the anger on the American side, they succeeded. Some British witnesses maintained that a crowd remained in the square, but most onlookers agreed that the bayonets had forced nearly all of the Americans back inside the passageway.[19]

This could have been the end of the confrontation, but the Americans—some now bleeding from the nicks they'd received—held their ground in the passageway and raged at the soldiers. Shortland and the militia clearly intended to force them all the way back into the prison blocks; it was, after all, turning-in time. But the entrances to the yards were packed, and it wasn't easy for the Americans at the top of the market square to fall back. Several soldiers later claimed that the prisoners threw stones from the passageway. One of the American prisoners, James Reeves, admitted that he went back and forth between the passageway and the market square to taunt the guards ('I was tipsy, or I suppose I should not have done it,' he confessed to the investigators). Every time Reeves came into the yard, he was 'pricked' once again by a bayonet, which made him and the crowd angrier. Shortland and Magrath were still at the head of the troops, trying to talk down the prisoners who were rattling the gate and jeering at the militiamen.[20]

And then a shot rang out. Then another. Some prisoners heard just a few sounds; others thought an entire volley had been fired. Initially, no one seemed hurt. The prisoners who had dived to the ground got to their feet and jeered that the militia were firing blanks. Then there was another round, and this time no one

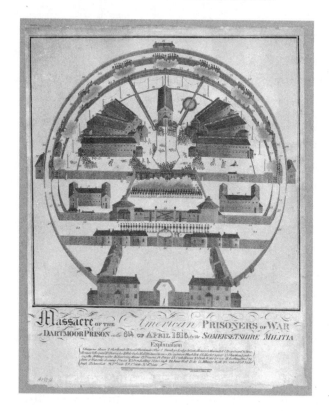

W. Carnes, 'Massacre of the American Prisoners of War'
Courtesy of American Antiquarian Society

doubted the shots were live. Dozens of Americans collapsed; everything else was suddenly in motion.[21]

RICHARD CRAFUS HAD BEEN IN THE YARDS EARLIER IN THE AFTERnoon, but when the turf throwing started he returned to Four to mind his own business. He left the block around six p.m. to visit the privy, and on the way he bumped into his friend John Haywood. Haywood was also a Marylander, from Baltimore rather than the Eastern Shore. He'd been in the Royal Navy before being brought to Chatham, and he'd been in Dartmoor a month longer than Dick. He, too, had been planning to stay in Four, but the noise had drawn him out. Haywood told Dick 'he was going out to see what the firing was about,' and Dick headed for the privy. The next time Dick saw his friend was two days later, when Haywood was laid out on a table in what Dick called the 'dead house'—the morgue next to the hospital. A rifle bullet had entered Haywood's shoulder, torn through his throat, and exited the right side of his neck. There had been a great deal of blood, and Haywood had died quickly. Dick was the only Black inmate interviewed during the subsequent investigation. He was shocked not only by what had happened but also by the suddenness with which his friend's life had been snuffed out.[22]

Dick claimed he'd heard about John Haywood's death just ten minutes after their parting. Assuming Haywood was drawn to the market square by the sound of the first shots being fired, this made him a victim of the massacre's second phase. The first, at the market square gate, was over quickly. The second involved the militia pursuing terrified prisoners into the three yards. Here the Americans faced another terrible misfortune. It was the custom of the turnkeys to lock each of the four doors to the blocks sequentially, gradually reducing the number of entrances as the blocks filled with prisoners. On 6 April, they had already locked several doors when the shouting led hundreds to head outside again. With the militia driving the Americans back through the yards, many tried to take refuge in their blocks without realising that several of the doors were locked. The militiamen, in turn, assumed that any prisoner still outside was asking for trouble. George Magrath's notes confirm that several of the victims were shot by sentries on the walls. Eyewitnesses remembered a hail of bullets—thousands, according to one terrified sailor. Some militiamen even entered the prison buildings, and several Americans testified that the soldiers had deliberately fired through the walls and the doors of the blocks as the massacre unfolded.[23]

Black prisoners had witnessed, and may have participated in, the day's unruly activities. Some had been near Seven when the hole was being dug. The New Hampshire sailor Liberty Carey told a newspaper in the 1820s that he'd seen the hole's creators 'begin to pause and think where this frolic might end'. One white sailor told the investigators that the gate to the market square had been broken by 'a mulatto man who was groggy' carrying a crowbar. One of the turnkeys claimed to have overheard that a Black prisoner had a knife in his pocket and was planning to stab Thomas Shortland. Against these isolated accounts, several white prisoners testified that the residents of Four were unaware of the chaos in the South Yard and the passageway. Their obliviousness made them particularly vulnerable to the brutality that followed. 'The blacks were near the gates of their yard gambling and not mistrusting any harm,' wrote Joseph Valpey in his journal that night, 'when a dreadful fire from the top of the wall killed several and wounded many.' Prisoners found themselves caught between the soldiers on foot who were running from the market square into the yards and the sentries who were aiming down from the inner wall. 'This is real British bravery,' Nathaniel Pierce wrote bitterly in his journal.[24]

The initial volley at the market square gate left a number of prisoners grievously wounded. George Magrath's hospital was next to the North Yard, but as the militia began to chase the prisoners into the blocks the injured in the passageway were trampled or forgotten. John Gatchell, a prizemaster from Massachusetts, noticed a friend who had collapsed in the South Yard. As Gatchell dragged the wounded prisoner back through the passageway towards the hospital, Shortland suddenly appeared and told him to leave his friend to the militia. When Gatchell insisted the man was dying, Shortland lost his patience: 'Kill the damned rascal,' he shouted, and Gatchell was jabbed by the soldiers' bayonets until he dropped his friend and retreated to Prison Seven. James Reeves, the sailor who later confessed to being 'tipsy' during the initial standoff, was carrying another wounded prisoner when Shortland ordered him to return to Prison One. Reeves, his courage fortified by alcohol, tore open his shirt and urged the soldiers to shoot him. In front of dozens of witnesses from both sides, Shortland slapped Reeves so hard that he knocked him over (or, as the loyal turnkey later put it, he 'pushed him . . . but not with violence'). The sight of the agent striking a prisoner only confirmed what American sailors had already supposed: Shortland had been spoiling for a fight all winter and had greedily seized this opportunity.[25]

More sailors were seriously hurt in the yard of Four than any-where else. Men of colour were twice as likely to be killed or wounded as their white counterparts. Writing more than sixty years after the massacre, the Philadelphia sailor Robert Hardie remem-bered 'frequent accounts . . . of the cruelty of the soldiers in the yard where there was more negroes.' Neil McKinnon, a sailor from New York, testified that he had been in the yard of Four and rushed to the passageway just as John Haywood was killed. He tried to re-monstrate with Shortland, who told him to return to Prison One, but then saw the militia rushing through the passageway shoot-ing and jabbing at prisoners. He ran into the yard of Four instead, where he bumped into Major Jolliffe at the head of another group of soldiers. When McKinnon told Jolliffe the militia were killing Americans indiscriminately, the major balled up his fist and 'swore that by God they would not be trifled with any longer by us'. Mc-Kinnon was so sure he'd be shot that he edged backwards towards the door of Four with his eyes fixed on the soldiers in front of him. When he turned to make sure he wouldn't fall over the building's step, a musket sounded and he readied himself for death. Then he heard someone else scream.[26]

All we know of Thomas Jackson comes from the register: 'Slen-der black, broken finger left hand'; born in New York, fourteen years old, barely four and a half feet tall. Jackson had been serving in the Royal Navy until he was abruptly discharged in February 1815. Although the Treaty of Ghent had been signed more than a month earlier, the British sent this child to Dartmoor where, on 6 April, he came between Neil McKinnon and the soldier trying to kill him. The bullet hit Jackson in the side, and on its way out of his body it dragged some of his intestines with it. Jackson lay on the ground, screaming in fear and agony, until he passed out. The door that McKinnon and Jackson had been moving towards was locked. McKinnon owed his life to the African American boy, whose screams had prompted the militiamen to stop firing. The soldiers carried Jackson to the hospital. George Magrath recorded that he 'languished' until eight the following morning, when at last he died.[27]

Thomas Jackson was the sixth prisoner to be killed in the massacre. Three more would die of their injuries in the coming days and weeks; two dozen were seriously wounded, requiring amputations and other dangerous surgeries; another two dozen were shot, stabbed, or maimed during the hour or so from the first bayoneting in the market square to the belated ceasefire in the yards. When the shooting stopped, many wounded prisoners were so scared of the guards that they lay bleeding in their blocks rather than risk the journey to the hospital. Outside, Shortland's staff cleared away the worst of what they had done. It had been more than a decade since George Magrath had served on a warship, but in the dim light of the prison hospital he sliced away legs and arms and hands and removed bullets from prisoners' backs, thighs, and testicles. In Prison Seven, Frank Palmer made his final entry for 6 April 1815. He had ridden out the whole massacre from inside the block. 'Having no hand in the sport' that had started the trouble, he 'did not intend to share in the danger'. But now that he knew what had happened he wanted a part in what followed: 'The blood of the murdered will ever stimulate us to vengeance,' he wrote. 'WE CRY FOR VENGEANCE.'[28]

WHEN NATHANIEL PIERCE WAS TURNED OUT THE FOLLOWING morning, he encountered the 'dismal' sight of 'blood and brains about the yard'. A messenger had already alerted the authorities at Plymouth; two senior British officials, Admiral Josias Rowley and Captain Alexander Schomberg, were en route to investigate. Within the different blocks, the committee leaders began their own inquiries. As they considered the premature sounding of the alarm, the locking of the prison doors, and the killing in the yards, the evidence assumed a brutal clarity: Shortland had planned the massacre all along. Rowley and Schomberg arrived in the afternoon and spoke first to the agent, who attributed the tragedy to the prisoners' unruly behaviour. Then they consulted the prisoners' committees.

Benjamin Browne remembered the investigators as 'cold and supercilious'. Frank Palmer was more optimistic: the admiral and the captain had assured the Americans that a 'proper investigation of this affair' would take place and that 'justice would undoubtedly take its course.' When the British officers left that evening, the committees had already produced a draft of their own report. It concluded that Dartmoor had witnessed a 'premeditated, determined massacre'.[29]

The ten men who signed the report confirm the narrow makeup of the prisoners' committees. All were white. Seven were from New England, and none was born south of Philadelphia. At least seven held rank on the ships on which they'd served, and all ten came from privateers or letters of marque. Nearly a fifth of the prisoner population had served in the Royal Navy and/or had experienced impressment—more than twelve hundred sailors—but not a single one featured among the signatories. Henry Allen, the prisoner who escaped in the winter of 1814 but was then captured again on a privateer in the Mediterranean, was one of the report's authors. So was John Trowbridge, the daring captain who had been accused of murdering a Royal Navy officer in Mauritius and imprisoned in Kolkata. Shortland had kept Trowbridge in the cachot for the first month of his time at Dartmoor, but the American now turned the tables: it was Shortland who had displayed his 'sanguinary disposition', with the evidence visible in the dark stains on the walls and yards of the prison.[30]

The next day, 8 April, the local coroner began his inquest. He spoke to nearly two dozen witnesses, including a handful of prisoners, before reaching a verdict of justifiable homicide. The British government knew that a line could not be drawn so easily under the 'massacre', as the Americans were already calling it, and government officials rushed to contain the situation. The Somersetshire militia were hastily relieved of their duties on 11 April, to the jeers of the prisoners; the Transport Board finally offered to help Reuben Beasley expedite the repatriation; and the Foreign Office agreed to conduct a joint inquiry with representatives from the United States. Fortuitously, two major American political figures were then in London. Albert Gallatin, treasury secretary to Thomas Jefferson and James Madison, had led the US negotiating team in Belgium which produced the Treaty of Ghent. Henry Clay, the Kentucky congressman, was in London helping Gallatin fashion a new commercial treaty between Britain and the United States. A third prominent American, John Quincy Adams, had recently been appointed US minister to Britain by President Madison. Adams had more diplomatic experience than Gallatin and Clay put together, but he was in Paris (after a long journey from his previous posting in St Petersburg) and would not even receive notice of his London appointment until May. It was Gallatin and Clay to whom the British foreign secretary turned in the middle of April. Lord Castlereagh expressed 'much regret' for what had happened at Dartmoor and promised 'that if the British officers had acted improperly they should be punished'. To ensure that the facts were gathered and assessed fairly, would one of the Americans agree to co-direct the investigation?[31]

Neither Gallatin nor Clay wanted the job. A week or more in Dartmoor was, as Clay told a friend, 'inconvenient to both Mr. G and myself, and not falling within our duties'. They briefly discussed whether Reuben Beasley might be drafted for the role, which would have produced an interesting reaction from the prisoners. In the end Clay and Gallatin nominated Charles King, a twenty-six-year-old businessman from New York. King's father, Rufus, had been the US minister to London during the Adams and Jefferson administrations. Rufus King was a Federalist—a political orientation which was fast going out of style back in the United States. More surprisingly, perhaps, so was his son, though Charles King had three qualifications for the Dartmoor job. Given his father's long residence in London, he knew Britain well—in fact, he had gone to school with Lord Byron, for what that was worth. He was in London on business, and therefore available immediately.

And, unlike Gallatin and Clay, he was willing to serve. In retro-spect, the appointment of Charles King as co-commissioner of the Dartmoor inquiry was a terrible decision both for the prisoners and for King. It's tempting to imagine that Clay and Gallatin realised the political hazards of accepting the assignment and deflected the responsibility onto their junior compatriot. More likely, they simply weren't very interested in what had happened at Dartmoor and con-tinued to see the commercial treaty as their priority.[32]

With a callow anglophile now installed as the American commis-sioner, Castlereagh chose Francis Seymour Larpent as his British counterpart. Larpent was a military lawyer who had recently served on the Duke of Wellington's staff during the British campaign in Spain. He was more than a decade older than King, and his day job was conducting military investigations. Lewis Clover, writing sympathetically about Charles King several decades later, explained that he 'was then a very young man, and from want of experience could not reasonably be expected to be as competent as an older per-son for the investigation of so grave and important a transaction'. Larpent and King left London together on 17 April. The two-day journey to Plymouth gave Larpent an opportunity to tell stories of his service under Wellington and to direct the young American on the principles they would adopt in their work. Some of the witnesses had now been released from the prison—including three of the sig-natories to the prisoners' damning report of 7 April. Larpent and King met them in Plymouth, just before they boarded the first cartel ships back to the United States. The commissioners then travelled on to Dartmoor. To Americans who had been entirely dependent on Reuben Beasley for the past two years, King was a welcome sight. The prisoners crowded the commissioner with questions about the evacuation. Eventually, King began taking depositions on the events of April. Frank Palmer hoped in his journal that the prisoners' state-ments 'will not be passed over in silence by our government'.[33]

Agent Shortland had withdrawn to his house after the massa-cre. Extra guards were placed outside his door, and Shortland abandoned his former practice of walking the yards each day. His isolation became more acute as the Americans decided on George Magrath as the massacre's unlikely hero. Even before 6 April, a group of prisoners had written to James Madison to request that he formally recognize Magrath's kindness. The surgeon's best efforts to save lives on the night of the massacre now earned him unanimous praise. When one of the Americans shared with Magrath a new letter they were sending to Madison, the surgeon felt compelled to forward a copy to the board with assurances that he had shown no special favours to the enemy. The board, with a precise cruelty, sent it back to Thomas Shortland and asked him to confirm whether its sentiments reflected the general view of the prisoners. The agent was told to read it aloud to the entire prison.[34]

Nathaniel Pierce's diary confirms that this excruciating scene took place on 25 April, though Shortland deputed the job to an underling: 'The clerk summoned all the prisoners in the yard and then read a letter directed to James Madison of recommendation of Doc Magrath, wishing him to bestow some gift of national gratitude on him for his skillful and unwearied patience to the prisoners.' The clerk then asked if the crowd agreed with the letter's contents. 'The answer was yes unanimous.' What made the experience even worse for Shortland was that the prisoners' praise for Magrath was interspersed with attacks on his own character and behaviour. The Americans charged him with an inveterate hatred of the men he was supposed to be guarding. They claimed that the bread protests of 4 April had triggered Shortland's bloodlust: he 'must then have determined on the diabolical plan of seizing the first slight pretext . . . to butcher the prisoners for the gratification of his malice and revenge'. Shortland had been humiliated in front of five thousand men, and his long career in the navy seemed about to end in disgrace.[35]

The following day, Larpent and King sent their draft report to London. They dismissed all of the prisoners' allegations. The killings had not been premeditated. A series of unfortunate events had led Shortland and the troops to mistake unruly behaviour for a mass breakout. Larpent and King could not determine who issued the order to fire in the market square or if an order had even been given. The first volley of shots was 'to a certain extent justifiable', though the subsequent firing in the yards was 'very difficult' to justify. The report attributed this second phase of shooting to individual soldiers rather than Shortland or Major Jolliffe but, given the confusion on 6 April and the speedy redeployment of the Somersetshire militia, it was impossible to identify anyone who had acted criminally. 'In conclusion,' Larpent and King wrote, 'whilst we lament, as we do most deeply, the unfortunate transaction which has been the subject of this inquiry, we find ourselves totally unable to suggest any steps to be taken as to those parts of it which seem most to call for redress and punishment.'[36]

This tortured summation missed the mark. Even the initial firing in the passageway took place when the American prisoners were on the right side of the railings. What followed was an hour of mayhem in which the Somersetshire militia killed or maimed dozens of Americans who were in panicked retreat. Shortland's defence against the charge that he had ordered the firing in the passageway—that he was standing in front of the troops when the shooting began—is convincing. There were many, many failures in his handling of the crisis, but the darkest crimes that day happened on the watch of Major Jolliffe—who, unlike Shortland, was seen by multiple Americans with the militiamen terrorizing the yards. Jolliffe had even more reason than Shortland to thank the commissioners for giving him the benefit of the doubt.

Charles King sent a copy of the report to John Quincy Adams, who was yet to arrive in London. King's accompanying letter suggests he was already uneasy about its findings. If the prison authorities and troops had been a little more patient, he told Adams, 'this dreadful alternative of firing upon the unarmed prisoners might have been avoided.' On the key question of whether Shortland had ordered the militia to fire at the passageway—the cornerstone of the prisoners' case against the agent, and an allegation dismissed by the report he had just signed—King was suddenly ambivalent: 'I confess myself unable to form any satisfactory opinion, though perhaps the bias of my mind is that he did give such an order.' King may not have realised that this letter would soon find its way back to the State Department and then, almost as quickly, into the pages of American newspapers. For most of the rest of his life, King would be haunted by the charge that he had failed to press his 'bias' more strongly with Francis Larpent. The report effectively whitewashed British officials and soldiers, and Charles King would never truly get clear of the massacre.[37]

In 1811, the Prince of Wales had finally become Prince Regent—the effective monarch, after British officials had at last acknowledged George III's incapacity. Dartmoor prison had been the brainchild of the prince's loyal aide Thomas Tyrwhitt; it had been built on the Prince's land with the hope that it would regenerate the moor and usher a new age of prosperity for the region. In May 1815, exactly ten years after Dartmoor prison had been conceived, the prince spoke with Castlereagh about the latest misfortune to befall Tyrwhitt's vision. Castlereagh knew the King-Larpent report would find few friends in the United States, and he had asked the Prince Regent to issue a pre-emptive statement which might help Americans to move on. In his reply, the prince deeply regretted the 'want of steadiness in the troops, and of exertion in the officers' who had overseen the killings. He promised to convey his 'disapprobation' to the Somersetshire militia. He also offered to pay for pensions to compensate the 'widows and families of the sufferers'. But there was no admission of criminal responsibility; no individuals would be held accountable. Incredibly, the majority of the massacre's survivors were still at Dartmoor. Their complaints against Britain had been dismissed before they could even recover their liberty.[38]

12.

GOING HOME

IVE DAYS AFTER THE MASSACRE, THE LONDON *MORNING Chronicle* finally wrote about the 'serious affray' of 6 April. The paper told its readers that the Somersetshire militia had fired on the Americans only when one of them had brandished a pistol. Brave Thomas Shortland had received a graze to his cheek from a bullet, but the 'insurrection' had been put down. The capital was at that moment preoccupied with Napoleon's sudden re-emergence and the prospect of a new war with France. But one Londoner who paid close attention to the *Chronicle* report was Reuben G. Beasley, horrified to see he had become the villain of the piece. The paper incorrectly claimed that Beasley had been burned in effigy on 6 April—rather than 26 March—and that the prisoners' fury at their representative had fuelled the breakout attempt. Triaging the damage to his own reputation over the harms done to his compatriots, Beasley wrote to the prisoners' committees to protest the 'unfortunate but shameful conduct' of the Americans at Dartmoor. 'It is much to be lamented that, at a moment when every exertion was making to restore them to their country, they should have fallen into excesses which have proved so fatal to some.' And the prisoners had blamed *him*? 'I am at a loss to conceive how.'[1]

In their acrid reply to Beasley, the prisoners reported that they had read his letter 'with astonishment'. Even allowing for his self-absorption, they were appalled that he had taken at face value British propaganda about the massacre. They offered him one final opportunity to manifest basic competence: he could speedily organize the two dozen or so cartel ships required to repatriate the Dartmoor survivors. But even with the Transport Board's belated offer of assistance, this was a considerable logistical challenge for a man with limited experience of organizing successful exchanges. The most recent prisoner cartel—the *Jenny*, which had brought the crew of the USS *Argus* from Plymouth to New York at the end of 1814—had left a trail of complaints and suspicions from prisoners and contractors alike: Beasley hadn't loaded enough provisions, the food which made it aboard was of terrible quality, and Beasley had a financial interest in the cartel. When called upon by his superiors in Washington to answer these allegations, Beasley maintained his innocence: 'I have not, nor ever had, any interest, directly or indirectly, in the Jenny.' Without Beasley's papers we can't know if he tried to turn a buck from the repatriation efforts, but it's telling that the US government had imbibed the prisoners' suspicions. To the very end, Beasley found ways to disappoint the men who depended on him.[2]

BACK AT DARTMOOR, THE PRISONERS' SENSE OF OUTRAGE AT THE various investigations gave way to a familiar obsession: 'Are we never to get home, is the general cry from morning till night,' wrote Frank Palmer. Despite the massacre, he refused to hold the British accountable for the slowness of the general release. 'No, we must blame Beasley, and our government too in some measure.' Beasley had previously functioned as a shield for the Madison administration, but in November 1814 the prisoners had written to their president (the letter was smuggled out on the *Jenny* cartel) without receiving a reply. Had James Madison paid proper attention to this letter, Palmer surmised, he would have 'turned Beasley out of office and placed some more suitable man in his station, and we should certainly have been home ere this'. Palmer began to wonder whether the true villains of the piece might be back in Washington.[3]

It was hard to linger on this given the daily challenges of survival. These had increased with the ratification of the Treaty of Ghent in March, when the US government had stopped its monthly allowances to POWs (on the assumption that their release must be imminent). Most of the prisoners at Dartmoor were broke; the few with money found that even essential goods were in short supply. Frank Palmer's desperation for tobacco filled the pages of his journal that month. Nathaniel Pierce told his diary in early May that he'd been forced to sell his hammock 'to buy a pair of shoes or else go barefoot'. Pierce loved his hammock: 'It was like parting with so much of my blood,' he wrote, 'and it is all owing to Beasley's negligence in not paying our [wages].' The prison's many forms of entertainment had also dwindled. There was nothing to do except 'walking about from one prison to the other'. Pierce spent more of his time in Prison Four, where Simon Harris continued to lead his little church and where some semblance of Dartmoor's former life was preserved.[4]

By the second half of April, Beasley had finally drafted a plan for the evacuation. He would notify the Transport Board and Agent Shortland of each cartel ship he brought under contract. The Dartmoor clerks would determine which sailors to release and notify the lucky prisoners. These men would return their bedding to the clerks and be transferred to Prison Two, which had been kept empty over the winter. This quarantining of released prisoners, intended to stop anyone from sneaking into the cartel, brought one final indignity: prisoners would spend their last night in Dartmoor on a stone floor without even a blanket. The departing men would be roused at dawn and marched through the gates before any of the other blocks were unlocked. In theory this system would prevent prisoners from impersonating one another to obtain an earlier release, though by the third week of April those sailors with money had found ways to buy their way up the release list.

The trading in release slots reflected the commodification of almost everything at Dartmoor. It was also a recognition that, as Lewis Clover put it, 'the system was unjust.' The order of release was determined by the date of one's arrival at Dartmoor rather than the date of capture. Clover, who was seized in the Indian Ocean more than nine months before he got to Dartmoor, complained that 'many who were the first taken were the last to be liberated.' Americans who had spent ten years in the Royal Navy could find themselves behind privateersmen captured in the final weeks of 1814. Given the suspicion that surrounded 'American Englishmen', these wronged sailors were reluctant to draw attention to yet another injustice. But there was a general feeling that the register's order of priority was another engine of inequality in the prison.[5]

It might seem incredible that prisoners would agree to sell their ticket out of Dartmoor, but the sums of money on offer were considerable and the journey back to the United States could be uncomfortable—perhaps even dangerous—for destitute sailors. Joseph Valpey and Frank Palmer, who were both interested in buying slots, were thrilled to hear about this new market. 'I have just been out and find that a great number of the prisoners are buying turns to go home,' Palmer told his journal. Valpey excused his line-jumping by insisting that 'my patience is so much exhausted and my health is declining fast.' Although the prices being offered in the prison yards were steep—some sellers obtained six pounds for their place in the register—both Palmer and Valpey struck a bargain after just a few hours of searching. 'After some length of time,' wrote Palmer, 'I found a black man by the name of Charles Carrol, who sold me his name for £2.'[6]

This was an unlikely pairing. Charles Carrol was a twenty-six-year-old New Yorker who had served in the Royal Navy until February 1814 and had arrived in Dartmoor that May, just as the French were leaving. He was a 'stout negro' of five feet and five inches. Palmer, who arrived in October 1814, was also stout, but he was five seven and a quarter and, inconveniently for once, a white man.

Palmer carried off this unlikely impersonation by bribing prison officials; he arranged to hand his £2 to the turnkey as he left the prison, with the understanding that the sum would be given to Carrol when Palmer had gotten away. (Presumably, the turnkey took a cut from this transaction.) The register demurely obscured the deception. Charles Carrol of New York was released on 27 April 1815, it insists; Benjamin F. Palmer of Stonington left Dartmoor on 9 June 1815. Palmer's journal confirms the reverse. The register's certainties were never reliable.[7]

JOSEPH BATES LEFT IN THE SAME CONSIGNMENT OF PRISONERS AS Frank Palmer, five years to the day that he had been seized by the press gang in Liverpool. His elation was clouded by the 'oppressive bondage' to which he had been subjected. Benjamin Browne left Dartmoor four days later. He was twenty-one years old and felt suddenly unprepared for the rest of his life. 'I was returning, feeble and penniless, and for a while I almost wished myself in Dartmoor again, to stave off for a few months longer that future which I dreaded to encounter.'[8]

At the end of their march down from the moor, Bates and Palmer were met by the newly appointed US consul for Plymouth, Nathaniel Ingraham, who promised they would board a cartel ship the very next day. To Frank Palmer's surprise, Ingraham was accompanied by a crowd of local women seeking news of their 'relations' at Dartmoor. 'A most beautiful young lady came to me and enquired for such a young man as I happened to know,' Palmer told his journal. These were the wives and girlfriends of American sailors who had petitioned the board for visiting rights that winter. Palmer was offered cakes, alcohol, and cash for his answers to the women's questions. He accepted their beer but 'refused taking money' for what he could tell them about their sweethearts.[9]

When Frank Palmer boarded the British cartel vessel *Mary Ann* the next morning, he was finally reunited with his kinsman Bob, the man his messmates had cruelly claimed was waiting to rescue him on 1 April. Bob had become attached during his parole to a local woman, the daughter of a wealthy candlemaker. Romances between imprisoned officers and locals were common in parole towns, but Frank assessed the match coolly: the woman was 'very respectable and quite rich, which is the main point with Bob'. In its own way, Bob's plan anticipated the broader relationship between Britain and the United States across the rest of the nineteenth century. Bob and his girlfriend's brother would cross the Atlantic and establish a textile business, with the candlemaker's family providing the capital. Then Bob would return to Britain to 'get spliced to this fair virgin' and, presumably, bring her back to America. Frank listened only distractedly to this elaborate scheme: he was 'so anxious to see home I can think of nothing else.'[10]

Frank Palmer told the story of another prisoner who had left Dartmoor with him on the morning of 27 April. This man had been conducting an epistolary romance with a local woman and had arranged to meet her in Plymouth the moment he reached the coast. The couple's plan was to find a parson who would marry them immediately, then to travel together on a cartel ship to the United States. The parson they located in Plymouth reminded them that they would need to post notice of their intention to marry fourteen days before the wedding; the sharp-witted American insisted that he'd done this at the tiny church in Princetown, but the parson laughed at his deception. Plan B involved simply smuggling his intended bride aboard the *Mary Ann* and getting married in America. This was going perfectly until the woman's father and brother stormed onto the ship and demanded she be given up. The cornered prisoner apologised, gathered his belongings, and went down the gangway with his future wife. He would have to wait for the right to marry her, and to see the United States again.[11]

We don't know how many American prisoners chose to make their lives in Britain when the war ended. The fragmentary cartel records suggest that between four and five thousand prisoners were evacuated on Beasley's ships between April and July 1815. Men like

George Little, who arranged early release thanks to his benefactor in London, are not counted in this number. Neither are those Americans who joined the crews of British merchant and transport vessels which were then at Plymouth, and who may even have joined (or been pressed into) the Royal Navy—the Admiralty was finally recruiting again, with Napoleon back on the scene. Despite Beasley's promise to keep American prisoners safe from the British 'hot press', the evacuation was anything but orderly. Nathaniel Ingraham, who personally directed the Plymouth operation in the (inevitable) absence of Reuben Beasley, had to contend not only with the chaos at the wharves but also with hundreds of letters from Dartmoor demanding to know when cartel ships would arrive or whether a particular prisoner could expedite his release. Ingraham had worked as one of Beasley's sub-agents before winning the US consul's post at Plymouth, so he would not have been surprised to spend the first few months in his new job covering for his old boss.[12]

One of Ingraham's other challenges involved settling the financial claims of American sailors who had served in the Royal Navy. The Admiralty had initially paid prize money and overdue wages at Dartmoor to the American veterans of its warships, but the mass of new arrivals in the final months of 1814 had overloaded the bureaucracy. Prisoners owed prize money and wages knew that they would never get paid if they stepped onto the cartel ships, but most could not afford to stay and press their claims. Ingraham told the State Department that these prisoners had served the king 'for a long time, and have just claims for wages and prize money for French and other captures'. ('Other' was doing a lot of work in that sentence—some were owed money for American prizes.) Ingraham wanted his bosses to intercede on behalf of these destitute sailors, but his request went nowhere. With this and other crises cascading around him, Nathaniel Ingraham was never far from a loud argument with a desperate man. At any time there might be thirty or forty Dartmoor prisoners in his office, raising complaints or concerns which his small staff struggled to register, let alone satisfy. Ingraham did what he could. He gave the Dartmoor men detailed accounts of the provisions he'd sourced, and he led them on inspection tours of the ships in which he proposed to send them back to America. The cartel captains—mostly Britons, but with a few Russians and Swedes among them—watched Ingraham's mollifying with apprehension. If the Americans were this disruptive on shore, how would they behave when finally put to sea?[13]

NEWS OF THE DARTMOOR MASSACRE REACHED THE UNITED States before the first cartels did. In the last week of May, the *New York Evening Post* ran the report from the *London Chronicle* which had blamed the massacre on Reuben Beasley. An accompanying commentary in the *Post* accepted the *Chronicle*'s claims about Americans wielding pistols and attempting to break out of Dartmoor but insisted that this unfortunate behaviour was the result of 'being kept in prison so long after the ratification of the peace'. Two days later, the *Post* reported on the first Dartmoor prisoner to make it back to the United States: David Neal, the sailor who had lost three fingers during his unsuccessful uprising on a transport ship from Halifax to Dartmoor. Like George Little, Neal had the funds to buy his own ride home and had persuaded Beasley to fast-track his release; Neal had left Dartmoor three days before the massacre, travelled to Liverpool, and paid for passage back to Massachusetts on a Russian merchant ship. He only heard about the killings on his arrival in the United States. The *Post* offered a brief quote in which Neal confirmed that Reuben Beasley had 'maintained the most sullen and contemptuous silence' throughout the war. For the *Post*, this confirmed the initial report that 'disaffection' with Beasley had inspired the train of disaster that followed.[14]

The American public felt differently about the War of 1812 in the spring of 1815 than they had during the conflict. James Madison and his Democratic-Republican Party had been unpopular for much of the war, especially in those parts of New England where the Federalist Party had deep roots. But Andrew Jackson's victory over the British at the Battle of New Orleans in January 1815—waged after the signing of the Treaty of Ghent, but before ratification—offered a timely distraction from the war's disappointments. Madison and his supporters argued that, like the 'Star-Spangled Banner', they had prevailed despite the onslaught of the British Empire. They also used the fact of their 'victory' to attack the Federalist Party, particularly in New England, for being insufficiently loyal to the United States. Madison was focused on rebuilding commercial relations with Britain, hence the dispatch of Henry Clay and Albert Gallatin to London. A full accounting of the Dartmoor Massacre might threaten that aim, but Madison and his allies knew that their Federalist opponents at home were already perceived as being too close to Britain. This gave the president the political headroom to pursue his commercial treaty and finesse the Dartmoor Massacre, despite the howls of its survivors.[15]

It was the homecoming of Charles Andrews that made Dartmoor a national outrage. Andrews arrived on the Swedish cartel ship *Maria Christiana* in early June. Clutching his journal from the prison, which would be expanded into *The Prisoners' Memoirs* later that year, Andrews visited a Brooklyn newspaper office to set the record straight. Although he had plenty of scorn for Reuben Beasley, Andrews was determined to lay the blame for the killings on Britain—and on Thomas Shortland in particular. With other sailors following Andrews's lead, the *National Intelligencer*—the paper of record in Washington, DC—called on the Madison administration to seek recompense, if not retribution, from the British. Based on the testimonies of returning sailors, 'We doubt not but [the administration] will take care that this injury shall not remain unredressed.'[16]

In fact, President Madison was still in the dark. He wrote to his secretary of state on 12 June that 'neither a messenger nor dispatches have been received' on the subject of Dartmoor from the commercial mission of Henry Clay and Albert Gallatin or from John Quincy Adams, the new minister plenipotentiary to Great

'Horrid Massacre at Dartmoor Prison' (1815)
© *History and Art Collection, Alamy Stock Photo*

Britain. All Madison had to go on was a letter sent in haste by Reuben Beasley to another official in Washington. Beasley had reported that the massacre was the fault of 'a cruel & perhaps intoxicated commander', that the British were 'manifesting proper dispositions' in their handling of the enquiry, and that 'a son of Rufus King' had been appointed to co-direct the investigation. Madison had no clue that Francis Seymour Larpent and Charles King had effectively closed the book on the massacre weeks before Beasley's letter had even reached Washington.[17]

The man who should have coordinated the American response was John Quincy Adams, but in the lag between his appointment as US minister in March and his receipt of the appointment letter in May, the massacre and three separate investigations had already taken place. Adams finally reached London on 25 May, and within a few days Reuben Beasley arrived with a stack of paper 'respecting the transactions at Dartmoor Prison'. On 29 May, Adams met Lord Castlereagh, the British foreign secretary, to discuss the commercial treaty. When they eventually moved onto Dartmoor, Adams asked that Thomas Shortland be put on trial. Castlereagh replied that any jury in the land would acquit the agent and that the resulting ill feeling 'would place the whole affair in a more unpleasant situation than it would be without it'. Adams left the meeting with no intention to reopen the matter. That evening he dined at Beasley's house on Harley Street. He met Jenny Guestier Beasley, 'a French lady of Bordeaux', who proved rather too animated during their awkward supper. ('There is no conversation upon any other topic than France,' Adams told his diary, 'and it is scarcely possible to talk in any way upon it without immediately shocking passions and prejudices.') If Reuben Beasley was concerned about the massacre, he didn't let it show to his new boss.[18]

Adams didn't sleep entirely soundly after his meeting with Castlereagh. He complained to his diary at the end of May that 'the affair of the prisoners at Dartmoor' was one of several issues which 'are all assailing me at the same time', even as he struggled to find permanent lodgings and a proper place to work. (Before the opening of the first US embassy in London in the 1890s, diplomats had to find their own accommodation and office space.) His diary confirms, though, that his chief preoccupations were closing on the commercial treaty and establishing his family in their new home. His wife Louisa received an audience with the Queen, while Adams met the Prince Regent. 'He asked me if I was related to Mr Adams who had formerly been minister,' went Adams's laboriously detailed note of the meeting. 'How did I like living at Ghent? . . . Had I ever been before in England?' Amid the small talk, Dartmoor did not come up. Adams had already received the Prince Regent's tortured almost-apology for the actions of the Somersetshire militia, and the willingness of the monarch-in-waiting to descend into the matter in the first place was an olive branch of sorts. Adams knew enough about Britain's ritualistic stuffiness to appreciate the gesture. Whether it would play well at home was another matter.[19]

BEING IN PLYMOUTH AGAIN WAS A STRANGE EXPERIENCE FOR Joseph Bates. He had been briefly held in one of the harbour's prison hulks back in 1810 when he'd been dragged from Liverpool to begin his Royal Navy career. His sense of unease intensified when he noticed HMS *Swiftsure* in the harbour—the first warship on which he'd been forced to fight for the king. He was haunted by the ghosts of these 'past scenes' until his cartel ship, the *Mary Ann*, set sail for America. Frank Palmer was also on the *Mary Ann* and recorded the ship's Atlantic crossing as happily uneventful. The former prisoners played checkers, backgammon, and cards, and their only anxieties concerned the ship's destination. The *Mary Ann*'s British captain, Andrew Carr, had contracted with Reuben Beasley to head for Norfolk, Virginia. The prisoners thought this an odd choice for sailors overwhelmingly from the northern states. Joseph Bates sensed yet another conspiracy: 'Mr Beasley . . . had chartered this ship to land us at City Point (a long distance up the James River) and load with tobacco for London.' City Point was at the junction of the James and Appomattox Rivers, and one of the major lading points for Virginia tobacco. It was an area Beasley knew well from his commercial work with the Bell brothers. But surely even Reuben Beasley wouldn't try to make money from the repatriation of America's most woebegone citizens?[20]

As always, Beasley may have had an excuse: it would be easier for him to charter a cartel ship if he could assure its captain of a commercial rationale for the return leg. To the prisoners, though, this latest surprise confirmed all of their prejudices. 'We considered this a cruel and unwarrantable act of Mr B's,' Bates wrote, 'for only about six of our number would be accommodated while the rest would have to pass hundreds of miles to reach their homes in New York and New England, if they could beg their way.' A group of prisoners approached Captain Carr to request a change of course. The captain insisted that his agreement with Beasley was legally binding and that if the prisoners made trouble he would deposit them instead with the Royal Navy in Nova Scotia. Destitute and with no obvious means of getting from Virginia to New England, the sailors had little to lose in calling Captain Carr's bluff. It was time, thought Joseph Bates, for 'a revolution in our floating castle'. The Dartmoor Americans were about to make another escape attempt.[21]

The mutiny took place on 2 June. Captain Carr later acknowledged that he hadn't put up a fight because 'resistance would be useless.' The *Mary Ann* was placed in the charge of a young prizemaster from Philadelphia, and the prisoners argued the merits of Boston or New York as their new destination. After a period of 'all talkers and no hearers', as Palmer put it, the 'New Yorkers' were ordered to go to one side of the deck and the 'Bostonians' to the other. The New Yorkers were more numerous, and the *Mary Ann* and its cheerful mutineers steered through Long Island Sound to their new destination. During the endless eighteenth-century wars between France and Britain, mutinies aboard transport ships carrying released prisoners were not unusual. Having finally won release, British sailors were petrified by the prospect of being pressed into the Royal Navy the moment they landed on home shores. By seizing their cartel ships and taking them to different ports they hoped to evade any traps their own government might have laid for them. The Americans aboard the *Mary Ann* anticipated a different kind of mistreatment: the officials in Virginia might leave them 'in a state of starvation without money or friends', in Palmer's words. After all that they had suffered, they were desperate to avoid having to beg their way across the country.[22]

The same drama played out on other cartel ships from Dartmoor. The *Maria Christiana*, which eventually landed Charles Andrews in New York, had been heading for Virginia until forcibly redirected by its passengers. Benjamin Browne helped to seize the British cartel ship *Ariel* and point it towards New York rather than Norfolk. Reuben Beasley had appointed a representative from among the prisoners to serve as his 'agent' aboard each of the cartel ships: this man was supposed to liaise with the captain, oversee the fair distribution of provisions, and help maintain order. Some of these agents were drawn from the prisoners' committees and included men like John

Odiorne, whom Benjamin Browne had so admired during their privateering days. But Odiorne had acquired a taste for the company of the cartel ship's captain and stood with him in opposition to the mutineers. Browne was disappointed in his former commander, but the uprising succeeded regardless. The Americans greatly outnumbered the cartel's crew and, as Browne proudly recalled, none of them had forgotten how to sail. Before long the *Ariel* was gliding through the water under its new crew 'as if they possessed the magic of Prospero'. On their arrival in the United States, deposed captains would buttonhole the customs collector and demand compensation for the redirection of their ships. But no returning prisoners were arrested or disciplined for these spontaneous uprisings. The port authorities concluded that the prisoners had suffered more than enough.[23]

THOMAS SHORTLAND HAD NO TIME TO DWELL ON THE MASSACRE or his narrow escape from prosecution. With a new French war expected to produce thousands of prisoners, the Transport Board had shelved its plans to close Dartmoor. Instead, Shortland frantically refurbished each block as soon as he could clear them of Americans. For a variety of reasons, the thinning of the ranks of Americans at Dartmoor created a greater proportion of Black prisoners. Partly, this reflected the purchasing power of white sailors, who bought release slots from those Black sailors willing to sell. It also reflected the greater proportion of Black sailors who had served in the Royal Navy. The surge in prisoners discharged from His Majesty's Service in the fall of 1814 meant that these prisoners clustered at the bottom of the register, last in line for release. But Black sailors also had reason to be nervous about the repatriation process, especially as rumours circulated that the cartel ships were bound for southern states. Being penniless and white brought plenty of challenges, but to be penniless and Black was to risk being imprisoned by southern port officials and even auctioned into slavery. This prospect gave sailors of colour another reason to linger in Dartmoor until they could receive assurances about their destination.[24]

As thousands of Americans were slowly released that spring, the prison reversed its geography: the Americans went from being residents of five blocks to being concentrated in Prison Four, back where they had started out in April 1813. Nathaniel Pierce is our best guide to the tensions this produced in the 'Black Prison'. On 23 April, Pierce went to the cockloft to hear Simon Harris's weekly service and discovered the preacher had been sent to his berth on the first floor of the block. 'The King of No 4,' Pierce told his journal, 'had drove him from the cockloft saying that he was a hypocrite and that he would preach all day and at night would steal his messmates' bread and cheat other people.' The proximity of Harris's church to the gambling tables of the cockloft had always encouraged white cynics to doubt the preacher's sincerity. But at the start of June, Pierce reported, Harris himself 'has left off preaching owing to some of his church going to gambling tables and so he says he is done with the glory'. Thomas Shortland continued to invite white preachers to visit the prison and minister in Four, but even after Harris's retirement none could attract the following he had maintained throughout the winter.[25]

King Dick made one more appearance in Pierce's diary. On 10 June, 'war was declared' between Prison Four and Prison Seven, one of the few other blocks still housing American prisoners. Men from Four and Seven had fought for control of the prison's dwindling supply of luxuries (tobacco, principally), though the following day 'peace was ratified by Big Dick, King of the Negroes in Number 4.' Dick secured this agreement by returning 'a great many prizes'— goods that had been stolen from one prison and hoarded in the other. It was his final act in the prison. On 15 June, Richard Crafus left Dartmoor early in the morning with a hundred other prisoners to meet a cartel ship at Plymouth. The very next day, Shortland ordered that the thousand or so Americans left in the prison should be concentrated in Four. Perhaps this was a coincidence, but the timing suggests that Dick's absence made it easier for Shortland to reorder the prisons to suit his own purposes.

Nathaniel Pierce was happy to move from Seven, and his journal made no reference to how the five hundred or so white prisoners who remained in Dartmoor interacted with the same number of Black sailors in the suddenly reintegrated Prison Four. Josiah Cobb, whose 1841 account of Dartmoor was highly embellished, claimed that the Black sailors 'looked upon the prison as their own' and 'put down every regulation' on how the block should be governed. Cobb also claimed that the white and Black prisoners were segregated within Four—'the blacks occupied the one-half of the building, while the whites had the other'—but this may have been wishful thinking on his part. Cobb smarted at the continuation of Black political power in Four; this was, after all, the spectre that white prisoners had been hoping to avoid when they asked Cotgrave to segregate the prison back in 1813. We know that a number of white Americans had quietly moved into Four to live alongside their Black counterparts in the winter of 1814–1815. Although it's likely that the new white arrivals messed together, the final phase of Four's extraordinary saga brought a new sight to Dartmoor: a world in which Black and white prisoners lived cheek by jowl, but in which Black political power was in the ascendant.[26]

Four's persistence as a space of Black self-determination in the spring and early summer of 1815 coincided with a dismantling of the prison's rhythms and worlds. Dartmoor was never a happy place to be; the general release of Americans brought new anxieties and tensions. The regular calling of prisoners to fill the cartels only heightened the exasperation of those prisoners with the highest numbers in the register. On successive nights at the end of May, dozens of men successfully clambered over the walls and made for Plymouth; so many, in fact, that Thomas Shortland allowed Nathaniel Ingraham to put these prisoners on cartel ships rather than drag them back to Dartmoor's cachot. Ingraham's pragmatism was rooted in a deeper truth: leaving Dartmoor's walls, whether through escape or through the cartels, was only the beginning of a prisoner's journey towards freedom.[27]

PRISONERS ON THE CARTEL SHIPS WHO HAD EXPECTED VERY LIT-
tle from their government were not disappointed. When the *Nep-tunus* disembarked hundreds of Americans at New Haven in June, a group of bedraggled sailors were left to walk the eighty miles to their families in New York. Astonished newspapers reported on their journey: the pitiful men were reduced to begging on the road and were harassed by the keeper of a toll bridge who demanded that they pay to cross a river. (In the end, he 'generously consented to take one of their hats, as a compensation'.) In New York City, members of the public stumbled over an exhausted group of recently landed Dartmoor veterans in a park in Manhattan. A local alderman asked the men to identify themselves, and a crowd assembled to hear their story. The onlookers raised ninety-two dollars which was 'given to these brave seamen on the spot'. Another group of prisoners went to City Hall to demand redress. 'Is it possible that these brave tars, who have been fighting the battles of the country, can be thus ne-glected by the government?' asked one newspaper.[28]

The mayor, Jacob Radcliff, wrote to his friend Alexander Dallas, then serving in Madison's cabinet as acting secretary of war, on the 'truly distressing' condition of the returning sailors. New Yorkers were 'mortified to find that no one here is authorized or willing, on the part of the government, to afford the necessary assistance to men who have already suffered so much in the cause of their country'. Dallas replied immediately that the federal government would offer a helping hand. But when Dallas took the matter to James Madison, the president instructed him to curb his benevolence. Any returning prisoners who had formerly been in the 'public service'—that is, those who had served in the US Navy or Army—could be sent to the naval commander at New York for assistance. Those who had been on privateer and merchant vessels, on the other hand, 'might easily find employment'. Once again, the federal government proved unwilling to accept any obligations to the men who had implemented its policy of privatizing the war at sea.[29]

With no attempt at Plymouth to match prisoners to the intended destination of each cartel ship, most sailors disembarked dozens or even hundreds of miles from home. Lewis Clover needed to get to New York from the wharves at Boston: 'Not one of us had a sixpence in his pocket, and there were few who had decent suits to their backs.' Clover and two hundred of his fellow prisoners were each offered one dollar by the Boston authorities, along with a certificate stating that the City of Boston would appreciate any kindness that strangers might offer them. Clover was furious: 'On reading the document there was but one feeling manifested, and that was deep, burning indignation.' If they had to 'solicit alms' from the public after all they had sacrificed for their country, 'we can do it for ourselves without accepting a begging ticket from them.'[30]

This ostensibly shocking treatment reflected the mores of early-nineteenth-century America. Poverty and hardship were the province of charity rather than government. Contemporaries acknowledged that the Dartmoor veterans had lost a great deal in the service of their country, but there was a logic to the sailors' affliction. A philosophy of limited government had encouraged Jefferson and Madison to put their trust in privateers rather than militias or navies; at the end of the war, privateersmen could be abandoned as easily as they had been engaged. That sailors had always been seen as an itinerant population made it easier for the federal government to disregard their calls for assistance. It also allowed the Madison administration to dismiss their demands for another enquiry into the killings of 6 April. One New York newspaper lambasted Madison for sweeping the affair under the carpet: 'This great protector of *sailors' rights*,' it wrote in January 1816, 'wishes to have the recollection of all their *wrongs* hushed in eternal oblivion.' But by that point, most of the sailors who had shuffled home in rags and broken shoes had already gone to sea again. Though their memories of what had happened at Dartmoor—and on the way home—were unlikely to fade, their threat to James Madison was already receding from view.[31]

Back in London, that pioneer of governmental neglect—Reuben G. Beasley—faced an uncertain future. John Quincy Adams was amazed at the crowds of penniless sailors who called on his residence daily to ask for help in returning to the United States. When Adams asked for an explanation, Beasley dismissively told him that these were 'all imposters', foreign sailors hoping to trick the US government into giving them free passage to the United States. In fact, these supplicants were drawn from the hundreds—perhaps thousands—of American sailors who had served on foreign vessels before and during the War of 1812 and who found themselves stuck in London at the end of the war. The massive demobilization of the Royal Navy after the Battle of Waterloo in June 1815 meant that jobs in the merchant marine were suddenly at a premium, and Britain passed its own law banning foreign sailors which stranded Americans on British soil. These men pestered Beasley in the early summer of 1815, and he was delighted to declare their claims fraudulent when they failed to produce the necessary documents. If he listened to every sailor with a hard-luck story, Beasley told Adams, 'he should have time for nothing else.' These callous sentiments helped Adams to solidify his first impression: for a diplomat, Beasley seemed to have a lot of enemies.[32]

He also had a lot of creditors, and in the summer and fall of 1815 they were nearly upon him. Napoleon's defeat inspired a wave of patriotic rejoicing in Britain and a revival of trade, but Beasley was already underwater. He remained personally liable for the debts contracted by his partnership with the Bell brothers, and in December 1815 admitted to a British court that he was on the verge of bankruptcy. He agreed to surrender his personal effects and asked the court to give him a few months to pay the eight hundred pounds outstanding on the partnership's account. By March 1816, his creditors were meeting in London to discuss their options. They had seized 'household furniture, plate, linen, books, wine and other effects' from the Harley Street house. Having heard that Beasley had fled to France to take refuge with his wife's wealthy family, the creditors discussed whether his 'dotal property'—assets he might have improperly transferred to his wife—could be wrested away by hiring 'some person or persons at Bordeaux'. Beasley later insisted that the War of 1812 had ruined his business prospects, but his finances had been chaotic for many years. His good fortune in romance was his final bulwark against personal and professional ruin.[33]

Undaunted, Beasley returned to the United States for the first time in nearly a decade and lobbied James Madison for his dream job. 'I am now before you,' he wrote in July 1816, 'an applicant for the consulate at Bordeaux.' He passed over the Dartmoor affair with artful understatement—'I exerted myself the more, but had not the good fortune to give satisfaction to all'—and focused on his selflessness as a public servant. 'I was plunged from affluence to the most dependent situation,' he wrote of his years in London. His wife was 'a native of Bordeaux', and her health would be greatly improved by a return to her home city. The Bordeaux post went to another applicant, but Madison didn't abandon his fellow Virginian. In the last days of February 1817, just before James Monroe replaced Madison in the White House, the outgoing and incoming presidents of the United States agreed to make Reuben Gaunt Beasley the new US consul at the French port of Le Havre. Beasley faced arrest if he returned to Britain, he had earned the enmity of thousands of his compatriots, and basic questions remained about his probity and competence; and yet Beasley would retain this new office for more than three decades until his death in 1848. He had made only one visit to the prison on the moor during his long stewardship of its miserable occupants, but it was Reuben Beasley who proved to be Dartmoor's most accomplished escape artist.[34]

FOR AMERICANS RETURNING FROM CAPTIVITY, THE JOY OF COMING home was tempered by a sense of what had been lost. 'Though young, I felt old,' remembered Lewis Clover. 'Like Rip Van Winkle, I had, after a long and troubled sleep, awoke several years older.' Clover was twenty-four but claimed that his hair had turned 'quite gray' after his ordeal in Dartmoor. It took him months to recover his health, though like most prisoners he had gone back to sea before the fall. Joseph Bates shipped for Bremen in Germany in July. David Bunnell spent only days with his family before heading to Canton. Benjamin Morrell joined a merchant vessel for France. These men resumed the lives they had known before the war. They took their grievances about the massacre with them, along with their dissatisfaction towards their government. For most, Dartmoor became a chapter in a longer story of a life lived far from the United States.[35]

For all their suffering, these men were the lucky ones. Several sailors died of smallpox during the Atlantic crossings; disease had followed them from Dartmoor. For the Black sailors who had been in Prison Four, the evacuation brought a new set of dangers. White prisoners had boarded cartel ships with the knowledge that, if they disapproved of the ship's destination, they might seize control and sail for a port of their choosing. Black prisoners knew that a similar mutiny could cost them their lives. Acutely aware of the dangers of enslavement if they found themselves in a southern port, many African American prisoners waited patiently for assurances that their ride home would bring them to Philadelphia or New York rather than Norfolk or New Orleans. Around a thousand Black men were entered into the Dartmoor prison register across the war; a quarter were still in the prison until the very last weeks of the evacuation in July 1815. By then, four months had elapsed since the news of Congress's ratification of the peace had reached Britain. Along with those men who had been seriously wounded in the massacre, it was Black prisoners who would wait longest for their homecoming.[36]

In February 1819, a Georgia judge conducted an examination of an enslaved man from a local plantation. The man told the judge that he had been born in Bristol, Rhode Island, that he'd served aboard a privateer during the War of 1812, and that he'd been 'conveyed to Dartmoor, and there incarcerated within its bloodstained walls'. At the end of the war he had been placed by Beasley and Ingraham on a cartel bound for South Carolina. Penniless and a thousand miles from home, the former prisoner was seized on the streets of Charleston, taken to Georgia, and 'sold to perpetual slavery'. The Dartmoor register lists one man who matched these particulars: Daniel Ballace, a twenty-two-year-old privateersman who had been captured off the coast of Ireland in November 1814. Ballace had left Dartmoor in one of the final consignments in July 1815. He might even have spotted Napoleon Bonaparte in Plymouth harbour on the deck of HMS *Bellerophon*, where the fallen French leader awaited his final exile to the South Atlantic. When he stood in a Georgia court nearly four years later, Ballace presented 'the most positive and unequivocal testimony' of his terrible experience. The judge had not 'the least scintilla of doubt' that he was telling the truth. The man who had purchased Ballace demanded the judge convene a jury trial, brandishing his bill of sale to prove the legality of what had taken place. But the judge disagreed, and Dartmoor's final captive was at last restored to freedom.[37]

PART IV

KING DICK AT BOSTON

R ICHARD CRAFUS LEFT PLYMOUTH ON ONE OF BEASLEY'S CAR-
tel ships in the last week of June. He'd been in British custody
for barely a year, and then he disappeared again. He resurfaced in a
Boston newspaper article in 1821, and for the next decade he seems
to have stayed put: he settled in 'Negro Hill', just to the north of
Beacon Hill, one of Boston's richest neighbourhoods. Negro Hill
was considerably less upscale; a newspaper profile from later in the
century described it as 'the very sink and plague-spot of all the low
vice, villainy, and licentiousness of the old town of Boston'. King
Dick—or Big Dick, as he was better known in the 1820s—became
almost as influential on Negro Hill as he had been at Dartmoor.
But as usual, our view of his activities is obscured by the racism of
our sources: prejudice clings like ivy to every description of Dick,
making it harder to see our subject and constraining his movements.
Superficially, at least, Negro Hill had a lot in common with Prison
Four. But over the decade and more that Dick lived in Boston, the
city would change in ways that would leave no place for him.[1]

Benjamin Waterhouse, who lived just across the Charles River in
Cambridge, had created the myth of King Dick in his 1816 *Journal
of a Young Man of Massachusetts*. Boston's newspapers raved about
the book, but they didn't notice that Dick had relocated until 1821.

The *New England Galaxy* ran a condescending piece on Dick's attempt to revive one of his Dartmoor pursuits: a school to teach boxing to Boston's residents. 'Richard, sir, is the magnum stag amongst the bucks of the ring,' the paper crowed. 'He is no mongrel, no half bred sneezer, he is true blue, game to the finger's end, sound wind and limb, grand cock of the walk.' Newspapers like the *Galaxy* were unsettled to learn that young men were leaving the fancier parts of town to take lessons from this 'celebrity' teacher. In pouring fake flattery on Dick, the paper sought to ridicule his enterprise and bring white Bostonians to their senses.[2]

In the 1810s, wrestling was the sport for American gentlemen—especially for military officers—while boxing remained a brutal and unwelcome import from Britain. Prizefights were mostly unheard of, except via newspaper coverage of huge bouts in Britain (which sometimes involved Americans who had crossed the Atlantic to take part). American reports of these were both disdainful and wildly voyeuristic: readers could learn the gory details of contests which had gone fifty or even sixty rounds, and which had landed one or both antagonists in hospital or the morgue. Britain's obsession with boxing offered a rare opportunity to emphasize American refinement. One 1819 newspaper article offered a long inventory of British cruelty which included Britons' 'shocking amusement of crowding to see men beat each other almost to death in boxing matches' alongside the Dartmoor Massacre.[3]

Boxing, though, was creeping into American gymnasiums by the 1820s, and newspaper adverts for dancing or fencing schools were juxtaposed with offers of boxing lessons or imported gloves. Dick's contribution was to insist that 'pugilism' was a science rather than a rush of blood. Newspapers that loathed the public fascination with boxing complained that Dick's skills in sparring had served to legitimize the sport—among some sections of the public, at least. When a group of 'highly respectable men' began a street brawl in 1825, the *Galaxy* attributed their disorder to Dick's popularising of 'the glorious science of pugilism' in Boston. 'Ever since the renowned

Big Dick sat himself down on the western heights' of the city, the paper claimed, 'the thing has been growing exceedingly popular.' To the paper's disdain, 'many of our most respectable young men have availed themselves of his professorial skill to such purpose as to have already been able to pommel themselves into notoriety.' The idea that sparring and street violence were effectively the same activity frames much of the contemporary newspaper coverage of Dick's time in Boston; and yet despite the moral outrage, young men kept coming to find him in Negro Hill.[4]

Boston's population grew by nearly 50 percent across the 1820s. In 1822, Bostonians adopted a new city charter which created an elected mayor with strong executive authority. For the *New England Galaxy*, always looking askance at the nearly one thousand strong Black community in Boston, this was another opportunity to invoke King Dick. 'When the act of city incorporation goes into effect . . . we shall probably have an intelligent mayor, chosen by the people; and why cannot we at the same time elect a permanent *King* for the negroes?' The paper's suggestion: Richard Crafus, of course. 'We shall then be sure of an efficient town government: the most important part of which, the executive, being fully provided for.' White people would get democracy, and Black people would get authoritarianism—precisely the arrangement which Benjamin Waterhouse had trumpeted in his formative account of King Dick and Dartmoor.[5]

The *Galaxy*'s insistence that Dick essentially ran Negro Hill was no more accurate than Benjamin Waterhouse's caricature of Prison Four. In the first place, Negro Hill was not an exclusively Black area. The residents were 'so various in different degrees of age, color, and depravity, among both sexes, as to be beyond description'—at least according to an extensive historical sketch of the neighbourhood in a Boston newspaper from 1873. This was the part of town in which the 'lower orders' congregated, and in which poorer people offered and pursued entertainment and vice just a few streets from Boston's most distinguished residences. According to the city's annual register, Dick lived on Southac Street, at the heart of everything. Negro Hill drew curious visitors from across Boston (and beyond), but also from the ships in the harbour. It was the final destination on every sailor's bar crawl: the place where (in the words of that 1873 sketch) 'the brothels, the grog-shops, and the dance-houses were all open and ready for them.' Both the men and the women of Negro Hill 'always expected to reap a rich harvest out of the man-of-war boys'. Dick was probably one of those visitors himself when he first landed in Boston, before deciding this was a place where he could settle down.[6]

The attempt of the *Galaxy* to promote Dick as 'King for the negroes' acknowledged the venerable custom of 'negro election'. New England enslavers during the colonial period had allowed slaves to enjoy their own festivities on the annual day of white elections, a forbearance which was (as usual) caked in prejudice: slaveholders accentuated the apparent absurdity of Black suffrage by encouraging slaves to dress up gaudily and engage in elaborate rituals as they chose a 'king' to lead their parades. For white onlookers this was pantomime: they encouraged its staging precisely because it indulged their views of Black people as imitative and limited in their political capacity. But when slavery was abolished in most of New England in the 1780s, enslavers lost some of their control over Black people. African Americans moved out of the houses in which they had previously served their masters and into neighbourhoods like Negro Hill. Black Bostonians no longer needed the permission of a white person to congregate and celebrate, and the Massachusetts constitution of 1780 conferred voting rights without reference to race. Black men could and did vote in Boston, though the *Galaxy*'s suggestion that the city's reorganization in 1822 was essentially a matter for white people—with Black people relying on a figure like Dick to keep them in line—speaks to the ubiquity of prejudice and segregation even in a free state like Massachusetts.[7]

So does the merciless lampooning of Black parades by white Bostonians. The biggest annual event among Black residents of the city

in the 1810s and 1820s was the 14 July celebration of the British abolition of the slave trade in 1807. This became, in the hands of racist
white propagandists, the ceremony of 'Bobalition'. Newspaper articles and broadsides would circulate crude caricatures of Black men
in formal or military dress, emphasizing the absurdity of civic pride
among a community held to be inferior by much of white Boston.
According to a white historian writing in the 1880s, Dick presided
over this parade in the 1820s: 'On that day bright and early Dick
would appear in full dress, a short red vest over which was spread
a goodly-sized collar, his white shirt being fully displayed between
pants and vest.' The echoes of Dartmoor, again, are clear: 'His
round woolly head [was] surmounted with an old-style police cap,
swinging an immense cane.' No contemporary newspaper article
recorded Dick in this role, but the reportage of the 1820s was even
more racist towards the 'Bobalition' ceremonies than the historical
writing of the other end of the century. Moreover, Waterhouse's
portrait of Dick at Dartmoor colours almost every later account.
Whatever Dick may actually have done, his role had been firmly
fixed by a man he had never met.[8]

The grog shops, brothels, and dancehalls of Negro Hill were under threat in the 1820s from two directions. The neighbourhood
had been, in the words of a later profile, 'the acknowledged and
semi-licensed field of social licentiousness' before 1822. Bostonians
from the better-off parts of town continued to frequent the area
throughout the 1820s, but the city's various reforming organiza-
tions had Negro Hill firmly in their sights as they pressured the
new mayor, Josiah Quincy, to stamp out vice. Quincy was initially
hesitant to use the full range of his powers, and in 1825 and 1826
white Bostonians themselves took their moral crusade to Negro
Hill. Like many American cities in this period, Boston saw a good
deal of urban unrest. In the 1830s, Boston's most notorious riots
targeted Catholics and Black people, and the disturbances in 1825
and 1826 have often been presented in a similar register. But they
are better understood as an attack on 'licentiousness'. White rioters

came to Negro Hill in the summer of 1825 and 1826 to attack bars, brothels, and other businesses which undermined public morality. Mayor Quincy denounced the lawlessness of these pious vigilantes but allowed the mob to complete its work.[9]

Many of the businesses targeted by the rioters were owned or staffed by African Americans. But the more 'respectable' Black Bostonians—who lived close to but not at the centre of the Negro Hill district—kept away from the trouble. The 1873 portrait of the neighbourhood notes that 'respectable negro families . . . kept themselves and their families as far as possible from social contact with the denizens of the Hill.' 'Respectable' Black Bostonians living in the area included the preacher Hosea Easton, the merchant and radical writer David Walker, and the activist and author Maria Stewart. This new generation of middle-class politicians and polemicists would powerfully reject racist caricatures of African Americans as vice-ridden and depraved. In doing so, they fashioned a Black politics which prized education, discipline, and respectability. While the 'lower orders' in Negro Hill provided a vivid example of interaction across the colour line, this new Black politics looked to extend racial equality across the social spectrum. In doing so, it required its leaders and followers to turn away from the values and conduct of Negro Hill's insalubrious establishments, even at the price of disowning a world in which Black and white Bostonians had eaten, drunk, played, sparred, and slept together.[10]

A couple of accounts of Dick's Boston days from later in the nineteenth century claimed that he helped white Bostonians to keep order in Negro Hill. The novelist Justin Jones, who in 1846 wrote an entire novella about Dick's Boston adventures, insisted that he had actually led the (white) mob in its attack on Negro Hill in the summer of 1826. Another writer in 1865 said that Dick operated as a kind of special policeman on the Hill for at least part of the decade. The idea that Dick could be relied upon to keep order for white people among a naturally lawless Black population was yet another Dartmoor export, and seems no more reliable than

Benjamin Waterhouse's claims about Prison Four. After all, Dick's career as a 'professor of pugilism' relied on the same dynamic which sustained sex work, the alcohol trade and the other vices of Negro Hill: he was trying to sell something illicit to Bostonians who would visit the neighbourhood to satisfy their curiosity and desire. He had little to gain, and much to lose, by selling out his enterprising neighbours.

But if he retained an investment in the Negro Hill community, Dick was at odds with the new creed of Black respectability preached by Boston's emerging African American leadership. From the 1820s to the Civil War, Boston became famous throughout the United States as a hotbed of antislavery radicalism. Its reputation in this regard was forged partly by the activism and discipline of 'respectable' Black reformers who steered well clear of Negro Hill and its denizens. The incorporation of Boston as a city in 1822 was mirrored by a conscious reorganization of Black political struggle around demands for equal citizenship. Black people would demonstrate their entitlement to political and civil rights by showing their white neighbours that they were already model citizens. Dick's extraordinary life—and the fantastical myths which had enveloped it—began to seem an anachronism.[11]

Dick appears on three more occasions in the official record. In 1824, the newspapers reported that he had been assaulted by a man named George B. Howard, who had only been released from the state prison a couple of days earlier. Howard had been sent straight back to prison, though not before he tried to cut his own throat as he was conducted from the court. Four years later, Dick found himself on the other side of the courtroom. He was accused of assaulting John Spencer, a man 'too familiar with the bottle', who had gotten into a dispute with him at 'the gaming table'. Dick beat Spencer so surely that 'for several days his recovery was considered doubtful.' Dick had also robbed the unconscious Spencer of '$9.94, and a note of $30'. The court accepted that Spencer might have deserved the beating, but concluded that there was 'no palliation' for the robbery.

Nearly fifteen years after he'd been captured on the *Requin*, Dick found himself back in custody.[12]

He was out before long. A newspaper claimed he was attacked again in the summer of 1829, and again it was his assailant who 'got the worst of it'. Dick disappeared once more, and by now his fame was sufficiently robust to prompt another newspaper to wonder where he had gone. Then, in March 1831, he made his final appearance in the archive: the Boston register of deaths recorded simply that 'Richard Seaver (colored)' had died. Dick's previous appearances in the archives had recorded his surname as Crafus, Cephas, and Seavers; the register of deaths offered this final elaboration.

If the information in the Dartmoor register was accurate, Dick would have been forty years old in 1831. But his decade or more in Boston had been hard; the clerk in the mortuary guessed he was fifty-two. No cause of death was given, though the newspapers reported that Dick died of consumption. He lived just long enough to overlap with the first issue of the *Liberator*, the pioneering abolitionist newspaper edited by the white activist William Lloyd Garrison. The newspaper owed its existence to Black subscribers and writers, including the 'respectable' Black Bostonians who were now in the vanguard of the movement for civil and political rights. Dick, the *Liberator* reported, had become ill thanks to 'exposure'—which meant he was likely homeless during the depths of Boston's winter. He had been one of the most famous Black Bostonians of his day, a celebrity during an era in which racism and white voyeurism had jockeyed with Black self-determination and persistence. He died alone, without friends or supporters, and probably without a roof over his head. Under the 'FAMILY' column in the register of deaths, the clerk wrote: 'City Poor'.[13]

13.

REMEMBERING AND FORGETTING

Frank Palmer wanted to tell his journal how it felt to see his hometown again, but he knew this was impossible: 'The Pen of Shakespeare himself would not be adequate to such a task,' he wrote in June 1815. It was the first time in his life 'that ever I shed a tear for joy'. The massacre was all over the newspapers, and Palmer decided to share with the public the three little notebooks he'd filled since his capture. 'The memoir of Mr Benjamin F. Palmer, during his captivity at Dartmoor and other places, is before us,' wrote the *New York Columbian* on June 17. Palmer's journal was 'replete with interesting incident and abounds with sentiment and patriotism'. The paper's readers were promised 'copious extracts' the following week. From Monday to Wednesday, the *Columbian* detailed Palmer's time in the hulks at Bermuda and on Melville Island in Canada. Then, just as Palmer was transferred to Britain, the pieces stopped. No explanation was given by the editor, and because the three published excerpts weren't about Dartmoor other newspapers didn't pick them up. Palmer hadn't embellished or enlivened his detailed account of monotony and despair, and beyond those brief selections his notebooks remained entirely unknown. Palmer may have made a little money from his journal, but it brought him no fame whatever.[1]

Newspapers remained hungry for eyewitness accounts. The *Co-lumbian* claimed that Charles Andrews had sold his journals for the astonishing sum of $900. During the summer of 1815, as dozens of Dartmoor testimonies and documents were printed in the papers, Andrews's manuscript remained out of sight. At the end of September, the *Columbian* announced that it was still being prepared for publication, after being checked and certified by 'every officer of distinction who was confined in the prison'. An advertisement for the published version revived the idea that Andrews had been offered $900, but now insisted that he had refused to profit from the suffering of his compatriots. Then another ad announced that *The Prisoners' Memoirs* was on sale. It escaped the attention of reviewers in newspapers and magazines, and it seems to have provoked little debate. Despite promising the inside story of one of the most scandalous episodes of the War of 1812—and despite the work done by Andrews and his editor to craft a story of unabashed patriotism among the prisoners—Andrews's account had little more impact than Frank Palmer's.[2]

The *Memoirs* disappeared so suddenly that when the Boston publishers Rowe and Hooper announced their own Dartmoor narrative in 1816—Benjamin Waterhouse's *Journal of a Young Man of Massachusetts*—they made the lurid claim that 'a manuscript journal every way inferior to this, was purchased at New York for $900' and then 'suppressed'. This plainly false assertion was in keeping with their marketing strategy for the *Journal*, which was offered to the public as an authentic account of 'a surgeon on board an American privateer . . . who was confined at Dartmoor Prison'. Benjamin Waterhouse was neither a surgeon nor a privateersman, and he had never been a prisoner of war in Dartmoor or anywhere else. Despite these inconvenient facts, it was his book that became the bestseller: it went through its first run of four thousand copies and sold briskly in subsequent editions. Charles Andrews and Frank Palmer, who had witnessed the massacre and the strange worlds of Dartmoor at firsthand, had tried in the summer of 1815 to sell their accounts to their curious compatriots. It was Benjamin Waterhouse who shaped the narrative for the American public.[3]

WATERHOUSE WAS BORN IN RHODE ISLAND IN 1754, THE SON OF A wealthy judge and politician. He spent the American Revolution in Europe, studying medicine in Leiden and forging connections with some of London's most distinguished physicians. When he returned to the United States in 1782, he was excited to learn that Harvard was hiring its first ever professor of medicine. Waterhouse was supremely talented, but not a Harvard graduate; he wasn't even from Massachusetts, which made him a distant outsider for the post. His subsequent appointment was a huge achievement—Harvard Medical School would not appoint another non-Harvard graduate until 1864. But Waterhouse was already bad at disguising his self-regard, which turned out to be a lifelong problem. His success earned him a host of enemies and his arrogance ensured that he kept them.[4]

The scientific feat for which he became best known was the introduction of the smallpox vaccine to the United States, at the suggestion of his medical friends in London. Waterhouse's spectacular (if alarming) public vaccination of his own son in 1800 brought him to the attention of Thomas Jefferson. The incoming president promoted the practice and even brought Waterhouse to Monticello to vaccinate the people he had enslaved. Since New England's elites tended to be Federalists, who viewed Thomas Jefferson with condescension and contempt, Waterhouse's growing friendship with the president of the United States further soured his relationship with his Harvard colleagues. When the medical community of Boston accused him of profiting from the vaccine and restricting its supply to boost his income, Waterhouse wondered whether his friend in the White House might offer him an escape route from academia.[5]

During the last years of the Jefferson administration, and throughout both of James Madison's terms in the White House, Benjamin Waterhouse was an energetic partisan and a serial holder of Democratic-Republican patronage appointments. When

Waterhouse's colleagues finally succeeded in removing him from Harvard in 1812, Madison made him overseer of the army's medical facilities in New Hampshire and Massachusetts. Always looking for additional income and distinction, Waterhouse sent a stream of lachrymose letters to Monticello. His financial embarrassments were the fault of the 'high federalists' who ran New England. It was only his commitment to defending the policies of Jefferson and Madison that kept him in Massachusetts. He knew that he 'must not quit my post, but stand at the avenue of public opinion, resting upon the printing press'. But he desperately needed money and urged Jefferson to 'address a line to Mr Madison' on his behalf.[6]

After seeing out the War of 1812 on the government payroll, Waterhouse lost his job during the demobilization. Just as he began to worry again about his finances, a sailor who had recently returned from Dartmoor—perhaps a shipmate of one of his nephews—gave Waterhouse the diary he had kept during his captivity. Sensing commercial potential in the material, Waterhouse used the source to fashion his own manuscript which he sold to the publishers Rowe and Hooper. He hadn't *exactly* made things up, Waterhouse later told James Madison. The young sailor 'brought me all the stones and bricks, while I designed and built up the structure, finding the mortar, or connecting material'. He had followed a famous precedent: 'Alexander Selkirk, who resided several years on a desert island, put his manuscript into the hands of the famous Daniel Defoe, who out of it made the renowned history of Robinson Crusoe.'[7]

Comparing himself to Defoe was a very Waterhouse thing to do, and the book's reception on its arrival in 1816 did nothing to dent his vanity. It was reviewed everywhere, and although Waterhouse was an incontinent braggart, the secret of his authorship was mostly preserved. The identity of the sailor who had produced the original journal never emerged. Neither that original source nor Waterhouse's manuscript can be found in the extensive Waterhouse Papers at Harvard. Newspapers and magazines which had overlooked Charles Andrews's *Memoirs*, with its sixty-one 'certificates' from respectable Dartmoor veterans, now embraced Waterhouse's central claims. Historians who have written about Dartmoor have usually treated the book interchangeably with the firsthand accounts of the men who were actually imprisoned there.

It was Waterhouse who introduced King Dick to American audiences and who first insisted that Prison Four was a place of despotism. In his correspondence and public life, Waterhouse was friendly with enslavers and contemptuous of Black ability. This didn't make him an outlier among white American intellectuals, though Waterhouse may have seen the antislavery sentiments of many of his Boston colleagues as another opportunity to perform his iconoclasm. In his *Journal of a Young Man of Massachusetts*, Waterhouse had anchored his condescension and sarcasm towards King Dick and Prison Four in a bedrock of confident racism: Black people were thieves; they were unable to understand the 'moral system'; their ideas and expressions were poor imitations of white culture and politics—'a burlesque to everything serious'. Since his original source is lost, we have no idea how much of Four's life Waterhouse invented as he 'found the mortar' to hold his story together. What we can say, though, is that his account of what happened in the prison was profoundly shaped by prejudice.[8]

Waterhouse also brought a sharp sense of partisanship to the Dartmoor story. During the War of 1812, he sent urgent dispatches to Monticello on the disloyalty of New England elites to the Madison administration. In the final months of 1814, as the British occupied parts of Maine, the region's leading politicians wondered if New England might fare better outside the United States. This speculation produced a series of resolutions—passed at a meeting in Hartford, Connecticut, in early January 1815—calling for constitutional amendments limiting the power of the South and restricting presidents to a single term. Commissioners were sent to Washington to present the findings of the Hartford Convention, but they were beaten to the capital by news of the Treaty of Ghent and Andrew Jackson's victory at New Orleans. At a moment of national rejoicing, the Federalists seemed like selfish regionalists, even secessionists. Instead of delivering an ultimatum, the New England commissioners had written their political obituary.[9]

Benjamin Waterhouse, who had been shilling for Jefferson and Madison for the better part of a decade, was perfectly positioned to insert domestic politics into the Dartmoor story. 'The efforts of the Federal party in Massachusetts to embarrass and tie the hands of our government, and disgrace its brave officers, created in us *all* a hatred of the very name of *Federalism*,' the 'Young Man' wrote of the prisoners at Dartmoor. The Federalists in New England had opposed a war for sailors' rights; they were more interested in British raids on sparsely populated Maine than in 'the massacre of our unfortunate countrymen'. The appointment of notorious Federalist Charles King to the Dartmoor investigation was the coup de grace: either King was incompetent or 'predetermined to fritter down the abuses' of the British. Ventriloquizing his brave young sailor throughout, Waterhouse insisted that the political enemies of Jefferson and Madison be held accountable. Suddenly, the villains of the story were not the Democratic-Republicans who had been in office while Americans languished in Dartmoor but the Federalists who had opposed the War of 1812 in the first place.[10]

Thomas Jefferson found this very amusing. Waterhouse mailed him the book, and Jefferson rushed to tell the proud author how much he'd enjoyed it. Jefferson particularly appreciated the attacks on his political enemies in New England, though he urged his friend to treat the humiliated Federalists with magnanimity: 'If they repent, let us give them quarter, let us forget all, and henceforward become a cordial and incorporated nation.' James Madison congratulated Waterhouse on the 'extensive impression' made by the book. By now the peace forged in 1815 was secure, and Waterhouse's political sponsors could enjoy his harsh portrayal of Britain without much anxiety. Better still, they could revel in its gymnastic efforts to pin the Dartmoor Massacre on the Federalists.[11]

The Hartford Convention and the surprise US victory at New Orleans had already dealt a fatal blow to the Federalist Party, and so the association of Dartmoor with its leading lights had a limited shelf life. For Charles King, however, the massacre became a shadow he could never throw off. The King family played an important role in New York politics in the years after the War of 1812. Charles King decided not to seek political office, but in 1823 he bought the *New York American*, a leading newspaper in New York City, and used it to champion his preferred candidates. In response, opposition newspapers in the city relentlessly reminded readers that 'Mr King was not only the apologist for the British' after the Dartmoor Massacre but that he had 'justified the horrid act'. Whenever King backed a candidate, opposition newspapers gleefully denounced the 'Dartmoor party' or the 'Dartmoor ticket'. In these relentless lampoons, King's own newspaper became the *Dartmoor American*. It was only in 1849, when King accepted the presidency of Columbia University and retreated into the obscurity of academia, that his opponents decided he wasn't worth beating up anymore. Until that point, his two-week trip to southwest England had defined his public image for three decades.[12]

ACCORDING TO LOUIS CATEL, WHO LEFT THE FULLEST ACCOUNT of the French presence at Dartmoor, most of his fellow prisoners had been Bonaparte supporters. Some would have stayed in the prison rather than return home in defeat, or so he claimed. Despite his five years inside, Catel managed to put Dartmoor behind him and became a successful businessman in his homeland. Very occasionally, on his travels around France, he would bump into a fellow prisoner. Generally people didn't want to talk about their experience, a reflection of the complicated and still dangerous worlds of French politics. Catel himself only published his memoir in 1847, nearly forty years after he'd first walked through the prison's massive archway.[13]

During this mostly happy afterlife, one encounter stayed with him. In 1829, he was travelling in Picardy, sixty or seventy miles north of Paris, when he decided to go to mass. The priest delivered an excellent sermon, but Catel couldn't focus: he knew he'd seen the man before, but where? The truth hit him with a horrible abruptness: the priest had been one of the Romans. When mass ended, Catel waited with the other worshippers and offered a warm greeting. The priest was polite but clearly had no idea who this overfamiliar visitor was. 'Weren't you a prisoner at Dartmoor?' Catel eventually asked. The priest's face bloomed and he steered Catel away from the other churchgoers. 'Let's not talk about it,' he whispered; Dartmoor had been 'an incurable plague in my life'. Despite the priest's skittishness, Catel talked him into dinner that evening. The conversation was strained, and the priest declined every offer to reminisce about what had happened in Prison Four. But as Catel watched his old acquaintance carefully push at his food, he had a vivid flashback to Dartmoor and what had happened to the horses. 'We left each other good friends,' Catel remembered, 'but he pleaded with me to be discreet about his time in Dartmoor, and especially his membership of the Romans.'[14]

On the coast of northern France, where the River Seine meets the English Channel, Reuben Beasley was no keener to remember Dartmoor than Catel's priest. Fortunately, an American consular post in a moderately busy French port was a good place to keep a low profile. Le Havre wasn't Bordeaux, which meant poorer weather and a longer journey to visit his wife's affluent family, but it was better than being dragged before a bankruptcy court in London or pursued by angry Dartmoor veterans in the United States. Soon after taking office, Beasley did what all successful diplomats in France did—he arranged for the shipment of a huge consignment of books to Thomas Jefferson. 'I am afraid I shall once in every year be obliged to ask your intermediary office between myself and my booksellers,' wrote the former president in 1818. In return, Jefferson promised 'to be useful to you in any way in which my retired situation could render me so'. In truth, the Founder to whom Beasley would always be indebted was James Madison, who had given his fellow Virginian yet another last chance by sending him to Le Havre in 1816.[15]

For the next three decades, until his death in 1847, Beasley clung tightly to his job. He became friendly with a number of visiting Americans, including the writer Washington Irving, who spent nearly fifteen years in Europe after the War of 1812. Irving became a major investor in one of Beasley's more fantastical schemes, a steamboat company which ran services up the Seine to Paris. Even when that investment went bad, Irving could not quite free himself from the 'hospitable oppression of friend Beasley'. Visiting American merchants and captains regularly accused the consul of being deficient in his duties, but Beasley's impressive estate—on a cliff overlooking the English Channel—gave him a venue to charm and defuse potential detractors. One accusation that he had skimmed consular fees for his own advantage seemed especially perilous, but Beasley steered around it. Drawing on his wife's fortune, he lived happily and didn't look back.[16]

Incredibly, in the final years of his life Beasley managed to reprise the drama of Dartmoor, this time casting himself in the Charles King role. On a freezing North Atlantic night in April 1841, the *William Brown*, a British ship carrying sixty-five Scottish and Irish emigrants to the United States, hit an iceberg and sank. (The tragedy took place around a hundred miles from where the *Titanic* would meet the same fate in 1912.) Thirty-one passengers went down with the ship; the other thirty-four found their way into two lifeboats, along with seventeen crew members. The boats were just big enough to accommodate the survivors, but in the rush to escape the sinking most of the passengers jumped into the same one. In the rough seas the two drifted apart before the survivors could rearrange themselves, and forty-one souls were left in a boat which could safely hold only two dozen people. After two terrifying nights on the open ocean, with the sea threatening to consume them, the nine crew members on the boat agreed on a desperate solution: they pushed sixteen passengers—fourteen men and two women—into the ocean. Having drowned nearly half of their lifeboat's complement, the crew (and the remaining passengers) were rescued the following day.[17]

This remarkable episode became Reuben Beasley's problem when the survivors were picked up by an American ship en route to Le Havre. Beasley and his British counterpart met the survivors at the wharf and, after interviewing the passengers and crew of the *William Brown*, produced a report which uncannily echoed the King-Larpent collaboration of 1815. The 'terrible sacrifice of lives' was a tragedy, the British and American consuls conceded, but the alternative would have been the loss of everyone on the lifeboat. And then, in mitigation: 'It appears that scarcely any of the passengers who were thrown into the sea made any great resistance.' (This was the kind of Beasley-ism that Dartmoor's prisoners might have recognized.) The consuls' report concluded that, despite all their concern and scrutiny, 'we have not discovered any fact capable of drawing down blame upon any one whatever.'[18]

Newspapers in Britain and the United States found this bewildering. The two consuls had effectively heard an admission of murder from the *William Brown*'s crew but judged that 'there is more to regret than to blame in the proceedings.' One newspaper insisted that it would have been better for the entire complement to have drowned than for sailors to choose who lived and died; another expressed 'profound amazement' that the actions of the crew, in sacrificing passengers' lives before their own, could be 'endorsed and sanctioned by an American consul'. Feelings in the United States ran so high that in 1842 one of the *William Brown*'s crew members, Alexander Holmes, was arrested in Philadelphia and put on trial for manslaughter. (He was Finnish, of course.) The jury agreed with the prosecution and Holmes was sentenced to six months of hard labour in solitary confinement. Beasley reaped terrible notices in the American papers, but not a single person made the connection with

Dartmoor. Despite the pieties and the scorn of his distant compatriots, Beasley kept his job, as he always did.[19]

THE PRISONERS WHO LEFT THE MOST DETAILED JOURNALS OF their time at Dartmoor went back to sea in the summer of 1815, and none lived anywhere near as long as Reuben Beasley. Joseph Valpey decided not to take a place on the cartel ships at Plymouth, shipping out instead on a merchant vessel heading for the Caribbean. He had planned to take the long way home, but in March 1816 he died in Cuba. His trunk was sent to his family in Massachusetts with his Dartmoor journal still inside. Nathaniel Pierce went back to sea in the summer of 1815 and died in New Orleans in 1823 at the age of twenty-eight. Frank Palmer died the following year, aged thirty-one. The journals of all three men ended up in the hands of collectors and were published in tiny editions in the first decades of the twentieth century. After 1815 Charles Andrews disappears completely from the archive. Andrews's *Prisoners' Memoirs* were reprinted in 1852, at a moment when Dartmoor survivors were pressuring the government to offer financial compensation for their imprisonment, but the book's short, unsigned preface gives no indication of Andrews's fate.[20]

Joseph Bates went back to sea in 1815 before marrying the daughter of a Massachusetts captain and shipowner. After that, family life kept threatening to upend Bates's career: he recorded his guilt at returning home after a voyage of over two years' duration to meet his new daughter, 'a little blue-eyed girl of sixteen months who I had never seen'. But it was only after his wife placed a Bible amid the more profane reading material in his trunk that he experienced his life's epiphany. He became an evangelical Christian, giving up the sea and pledging allegiance to William Miller, one of the most colourful religious figures of the nineteenth century. Miller founded the Adventist movement and promised his followers that Jesus Christ would soon return to earth. When Miller predicted that the Second Coming would take place in 1843—and then in

1844—Bates stood alongside his mentor at the appointed hour and shared in what became known as the Great Disappointment. His memoir began in the harshly material world of the sailor but ended with ecstatic spiritual expectation. For a man convinced that the world was about to end, Dartmoor was a minor detail.[21]

More generally, the interest of the American public in Dartmoor tracked the health of the Anglo-US relationship. In the quarter century after 1815, Americans continued to trumpet their independence from Britain but consumed British culture and news with the avidity of a family member or an old friend. The United States pursued various forms of economic nationalism, especially in public works and infrastructure, and British investors put up much of the money. There was little appetite on the part of journalists or politicians for revisiting the massacre. But in the 1840s, when the United States and Britain very nearly went to war over US expansion into Texas and the Pacific Northwest, Dartmoor suddenly surfaced again. Lewis Clover's memoir was serialized in 1844, and Benjamin Browne's followed in 1846. Both appeared in the most popular magazines of the day, bringing the Dartmoor story to a new generation suddenly hungry for tales of British calumny.[22]

Clover and Browne both abandoned the ocean after 1815. Clover became a shopkeeper in New York; Browne completed his apprenticeship and became an apothecary in Salem. Clover made enough money to send his son to Columbia and acquire a decent collection of American art. Browne dabbled in real estate, married well, and went into local politics. Clover lost most of his fortune in the crash of 1837, but his loyal support of Andrew Jackson and Martin Van Buren secured him a job in the New York Custom House. In 1844, he wrote up his recollections of Dartmoor and offered them to the *Knickerbocker* magazine. They won him plaudits from many newspapers, and the favourable reaction made Clover think he should do even more to keep the memory of Dartmoor alive.[23]

In 1839, Benjamin Browne looked over the journal he'd kept in Dartmoor and decided at last to write up his experiences. He handed the draft to his tenant, a young writer of promise but modest achievement, who had been grumbling to Browne for months about how hard it was to conjure stories from the 'thin air' of his garret. The writer was Nathaniel Hawthorne. It took him seven years to find Browne a publisher—he had to make his own name first—but in 1846 Hawthorne delivered the manuscript to John L. O'Sullivan, the editor of the celebrated *United States Magazine and Democratic Review*. The first number of Browne's seven-part series was published that spring as "PAPERS OF AN OLD DARTMOUTH PRISONER, EDITED BY NATHANIEL HAWTHORNE." Dartmouth was silently corrected to Dartmoor in the next issue, and Browne was happy to remain in the wings as Hawthorne took the applause.[24]

Since we no longer have Browne's prison journals, it's hard to know how much he added or changed when he wrote up his 'Papers' in 1839. The decades after his imprisonment had seen James Fenimore Cooper and Frederick Marryat invent the sea novel, and the 'Papers' followed many of that new genre's conventions. We do have a draft of Browne's 1839 text and can at least track some of Nathaniel Hawthorne's edits. His most significant intervention was to remove the entire section in which Browne recounted his adventures in Barbados during his parole in 1814. Browne's many interactions with people of colour—including dances and socializing—failed to appear in the published version. Hawthorne may have recoiled from Browne's breezy description of mixing across the colour line in Barbados, which formed such a contrast with his cramped portrait of King Dick and Prison Four. Hawthorne was no abolitionist: he believed that Black people (free and enslaved) should be 'colonized' beyond the United States. While his editing of Browne's 1839 text was, for the most part, remarkably light, he took a firm view of Browne's racial crossings in Barbados: readers of the 'Papers' would never get to see them.[25]

IN DECEMBER 1815, JAMES MONROE TOLD THE BRITISH AMBASSADOR in Washington that the United States could not accept the

Prince Regent's offer of compensation for the Dartmoor victims; the hostile reaction of American newspapers (and several congressmen) to the King-Larpent report had put paid to that option. The following spring Congress placed the victims of the massacre on the navy's pension list. This gave relief to nearly fifty sailors and their families but left more than six thousand who had spent months or years in Dartmoor (and other British prisons) without any compensation. During the war, Congress had established a Privateers Pension Fund using money diverted from the sale of British prizes in American ports, but would-be claimants needed to lobby Congress or the secretary of the navy to be added to the list—a process that could take years. Sailors who had served in the Royal Navy were not eligible for any form of assistance. Most Dartmoor veterans were young enough to keep working, but hundreds had died in the prison and hundreds more suffered permanent damage to their health. After the war, these men and their families became mostly invisible to their government.[26]

Occasionally, the newspapers give us a glimpse of what happened to the most unfortunate Dartmoor survivors. In the summer of 1820, Samuel B. Parsons, a thirty-six-year-old sailor from Massachusetts, keeled over on the corner of Washington and Canal Streets in New York City. He had served alongside George Little on the celebrated privateer *Paul Jones*, and he was shot in the leg during the massacre. Although he was entitled to a pension, he had been living on the streets of New York in ignorance of Congress's provision. His leg had never properly healed; one night the wound opened and he bled to death in the middle of the city. 'Sons of American freedom,' wrote one local paper, 'drop the sympathetic tear over his lacerated limbs!' Even war widows struggled to get consideration from the government. Hannah Stone's husband was captured on a privateer in November 1814; he died of pneumonia in January 1815 a few days after arriving at Dartmoor. Since her husband hadn't been killed in the massacre, Stone's wife had no recourse to the funds allocated by Congress in the spring of 1816.

Working with local officials and a sympathetic congressman, it took Hannah Stone nearly twenty years to persuade the House Committee on Naval Affairs to add her to the privateersmen's pension list. But the fund's managers had allowed it to run down, and three years after Stone began receiving her pension, the payments were stopped. Congress was eventually shamed into restarting the fund in 1844, but during the intervening seven years, the US government abandoned even the small number of individuals and families it had deemed worthy of assistance.[27]

By the end of the 1830s, most Dartmoor veterans were fifty or older and had given up the sea. Struggling to make a living in older age, many formed associations to keep alive the memory of Dartmoor—and, more pressingly, to continue their campaign for compensation. Dartmoor prisoners' associations emerged in New England, New York, and Philadelphia. The Philadelphia group hosted a dinner for President John Tyler when he visited the city in 1843 and marched in Philadelphia's funeral ceremonies for Andrew Jackson in 1845. When President Zachary Taylor died in office in 1850, veterans travelled to Washington to join the cortege and were placed on a huge barge with DARTMOOR emblazoned on the front. After writing his memoir in the *Knickerbocker* magazine in 1844, Lewis Clover directed the New York prisoners' association for more than two decades. Privateering and impressment were obsolete by the middle of the nineteenth century, but the prisoners' associations reminded the public that it was ordinary sailors who had carried the United States through the War of 1812.[28]

One of the most vocal and persistent participants in this campaign was Glover Broughton of Marblehead in Massachusetts, the town which saw nearly 10 percent of its adult population imprisoned in Dartmoor by the war's end. Broughton was from one of the town's seafaring dynasties, and when he gave up the sea he became a merchant and a local politician who was well placed to represent the many Dartmoor survivors in his hometown. Broughton's papers document half a dozen sustained lobbying assaults on

Washington. In 1854, he persuaded the House Committee on Invalid Pensions to consider both privateersmen and impressed sailors for pensions or for 'bounty land'—western territory wrested from Native Americans. This plan got through the House but, as an apologetic congressman told Broughton, 'in the Senate there is such a strong prejudice against privateering that it was impossible to do anything for them.' Broughton reminded Washington politicians that the revenue generated from the government's share of British prizes—around $40 million, he reckoned—had kept the nation solvent during the War of 1812. Now privateersmen simply wanted a dignified retirement and an acknowledgement of the sacrifices they had made in the nation's service.[29]

The money proved elusive. Congressional prejudices against privateersmen reflected and amplified an older scepticism towards sailors themselves. Unlike militia volunteers, who took up arms in war then returned to their farms and families, sailors mostly resumed their itinerant lifestyle on the other side of the peace. Privateersmen were dismissed as mercenaries whose suffering was a part of their business model. Impressed sailors, meanwhile, brought claims that were difficult to authenticate. We will never know exactly how many American sailors were serving in the Royal Navy at the outbreak of the War of 1812, though a rough estimate would suggest that fewer than 10 percent left any traces in the State Department's impressment files. Although the cost of a generous and inclusive pension scheme for Dartmoor veterans in 1850 was far smaller than it would have been in 1830, politicians continued to rebuff Broughton's overtures. 'It is true we have the Union to protect, Rebels to silence, and the whole Union to renovate,' Broughton wrote to the House of Representatives in 1861; but surely giving 160 acres to some of the republic's most loyal and brave veterans could only advance this aim? Moreover, 'our ages vary from 65 to 81 years, consequently the pension will soon run out and the land will be just what we want for our heirs and loyal citizens.' Even as the ranks of

Dartmoor prisoners dwindled to hundreds, then dozens, Congress refused to budge.[30]

In 1871, Marblehead's Dartmoor veterans made their final stand. Broughton had died two years earlier at the age of seventy-five. Perhaps he had played a moderating influence on his fellow Marblehead men because the address they composed in his absence was caustic. They excoriated the US government for 'pensioning Rebel sympathizers' rather than Dartmoor veterans, and they finally said the quiet part out loud: 'Had our government been more prompt and beneficent in getting home their prisoners of war, the massacre at Dartmoor Prison would have never happened.' It was bad enough for patriotic Americans to end up in British captivity; 'but to be imprisoned when there was no necessity for it, against your will and consent, without any compensation whatever, for the mere purpose to suit the convenience of your government, is unjust.'[31]

Since the resurgence of public interest in Dartmoor in the 1840s, former prisoners had mostly preferred lavish performances of patriotism over confrontational rhetoric. While this brought John Tyler to their annual dinner and secured them an invitation to Zachary Taylor's funeral, it didn't persuade Congress to open the public purse even when Dartmoor's survivors had thinned to a handful. For the veterans, who had become careful students of the government's willingness to offer money or forgiveness to other nations and even to Confederates, this abandonment defied easy explanation. 'Why is it,' asked the 1871 memorial, 'that our government with its free institutions . . . should turn out to be so tyrannical and partial in her acts to her own sons, and so liberal and prompt to settle foreign claims?' The memorial offered a stark answer: American lawmakers were 'more unjust, dishonest, and hypocritical in their dealings' even than the 'tyrants' who still presided over most of the rest of the world. The real explanation for the government's obduracy was simple: the veterans had little power or influence. The 1871 memorial was steeped in betrayal, but little had changed since 1815.

Sailors had made a valuable contribution to the war effort, but they had always been easy to ignore.[32]

IN THE WEEKS AFTER THE BRITISH VICTORY AT THE BATTLE OF Waterloo in June 1815, six and a half thousand new French prisoners were marched beneath the stone archway; the first group overlapped with the departing Americans, and so the prison maintained its record of being occupied continuously since 1809. Then a peace agreement was signed in November by Louis XVIII, the Bourbon monarch restored to his throne after Napoleon's recapture, and the French were allowed to go home. By February 1816 Dartmoor was finally empty. The Transport Board gave Shortland orders for 'discontinuing your own situation'. The stores were packaged up and sold, the staff were laid off, and Shortland and Magrath were offered passage back to Plymouth. (In a final reminder of its boundless parsimony, the board declined to pay their travel expenses to London, where each had found new work.) Magrath became a medical inspector for the navy pursued his own scientific research. The surgeon's charm and skill brought him election to the Royal Society in 1819 and a knighthood in 1831. Shortland's final act was more modest. He served in a number of administrative posts before agreeing to command the Royal Navy base in Kingston, Jamaica. This wasn't a knighthood, but for a man who might have been cashiered in 1815 it represented vindication of a sort. Shortland died of a fever in November 1827. He was buried in a Kingston cemetery beside his daughter, who succumbed to the same illness two days later.[33]

Long before the end of Britain's wars with France and the United States, Thomas Tyrwhitt, tireless dreamer of spectacular futures for Dartmoor, knew that his prison would require drastic repurposing. In 1814, he sold the Prince Regent on the idea of 'a Royal Asylum for the widows and orphans who may have been left unprovided for, by the 300,000 of our brave countrymen who have fallen during the present war'. When that proposal failed to inspire support in Westminster, Tyrwhitt tracked back to his original idea that Dartmoor should hold criminals rather than prisoners of war. The Transport Board put a typically macabre twist on his proposal. Observing that convicts transported to Australia seemed more susceptible to illness (or even death) when they left Britain during the winter, and guessing this was connected to the sudden change of climate on the journey through the tropics to New South Wales, the board recommended populating Dartmoor with prisoners convicted during the autumn and early winter months. Tyrwhitt promised that nine thousand convicts could be held after the necessary conversion work, though as the board looked more closely at the cost, its enthusiasm drained away.[34]

Tyrwhitt's next scheme was for 'the permanent employment of the pauper poor of the metropolis'. Indigent children aged from seven to twenty-one would be swept from the streets of London—where they drained the patience of the wealthy and the resources of parish welfare schemes—and put to work 'upon tracts of uncultivated land' on Dartmoor. It might even be possible to move entire families to the moor, Tyrwhitt beamed. Whatever his faults, you have to admire Tyrwhitt's ability to persuade powerful people that Dartmoor was the future of anything. (In January 1820, the same month in which Tyrwhitt loudly announced his 'Metropolitan School of Industry', a newspaper reported that the snow on Dartmoor was so deep that 'the rabbits, in very large bodies, visit the neighboring farmers' in search of food.) The Archbishop of Canterbury and the Lord Mayor of London agreed to support the school, and the Prince Regent offered £1,000 of seed money. Tyrwhitt talked up the scheme to secure investors for another: a railway between Plymouth and Dartmoor. Given that the moor was still empty and the route would require a six-hundred-yard tunnel to be blasted through solid rock, only the thought of transporting all those industrious paupers made the railway seem a viable concern. But the school plans had been long discarded by the time Tyrwhitt conducted the railway's grand opening in October 1823. The

South Devon Band assembled at the tunnel to serenade local dig-
nitaries, 'but unhappily the weather was unfavourable, which drove
many away.' Thereafter, the trains would carry granite rather than
people.[35]

One local admirer of Tyrwhitt's endlessly fizzling schemes was
Nicholas Carrington, a Plymouth schoolteacher who wrote earnest
poetry in his spare time. Like most amateur poets in the 1820s,
Carrington had read too much Wordsworth for his own good. Sur-
veying the failure of Tyrwhitt's plans, he produced his own epic
poem—loosely modelled after Wordsworth's 'Tintern Abbey'—
eulogizing the vast expanse of Dartmoor. Carrington traversed the
moor's 'central wastes', stopped to observe the 'half-savage peasants'
who obligingly emerged from the landscape, and acknowledged the
efforts of the region's most persistent booster:

> The civic wreath,
> Tyrwhitt, is thine, distinguish'd 'mid the band
> Of British patriots, glowing with the love
> Of country and of man. The noble thought
> Was thine, to rescue from the withering hand
> Of Desolation, the vast waste.

Impressively, Carrington parlayed Dartmoor's emptiness into
more than fifteen hundred lines of blank verse. The prison was at
the heart of his vision: it became the 'proud pile where England
held / Within her victor-grip the vanquish'd foe'. But for all his
praise of Tyrwhitt, Carrington took inspiration from the failure of
his schemes. The prisoners' lot was to suffer the denial of liberty in a
landscape that was unconquerable and majestically barren:

> O ! who that drags
> A captive's chain, would feel his soul refresh'd,
> Though scenes, like those of Eden, should arise
> Around his hated cage! But here green youth

Lost all its freshness, manhood all its prime,
And age sank to the tomb, ere peace her trump
Exulting blew; and still upon the eye,
In dread monotony, at morn, noon, eve,
Arose the Moor—the Moor!

Posterity has not favoured Carrington, but 'Dartmoor: A Descriptive Poem' drew polite reviews at the time. The poet also secured a prize of fifty guineas from Tyrwhitt's indefatigable patron, who had finally become George IV. Tyrwhitt appreciated the positive press for Dartmoor, though Carrington's focus on 'the vast waste' cut a little close to the bone.[36]

Tyrwhitt died in 1833 with his plans in ruins. More than a decade later, a local writer explored the empty blocks and reported that the prison was falling to pieces. The bullet holes in the wall by the market yard were still visible; cattle on the moor had unearthed the bones of the prisoners who had been buried outside the walls; the wooden floors of the seven blocks had been eaten away. In a dread inversion of Tyrwhitt's crowning ambition, the moor seemed about to reclaim the prison. But then a political movement on the other side of the world brought Dartmoor back to life. The emerging political class in Australia had been arguing for years that Britain should stop the practice of transporting its prisoners there, and British politicians had begun to wonder whether New South Wales—now a thriving settler society—was more of a reward than a punishment for wrongdoers. Lawmakers agreed to end transportation and house Britain's felons at home, at which point the cost of converting Dartmoor into a convict prison finally seemed unavoidable. Several of the blocks were levelled; others were extensively adapted to support a new system of cells. Dartmoor received its first convicts in 1850. It has been a part of the British prison system ever since.[37]

For most of the 170 years after its reopening Dartmoor traded on its grim remoteness. It was a place where hardened criminals and political prisoners could be safely and theatrically marooned. The prison's notoriety derived from the same dynamic Nicholas Carrington captured in 1826: the British public was thrilled by the thought that nothing could live on Dartmoor beyond the narrow and terrible confines of the prison buildings, and that life even there must be pretty miserable. It was only in 2001 that the prison's status was downgraded to a lower security level, a recognition that the buildings were nearing the end of their useful life. Many of Britain's prisons date to the Victorian era, though Dartmoor is even older—a relic even within a system starved of resources and modern facilities. The British government announced in 2015 that Dartmoor would close permanently in 2023. With that date fast approaching, a Plymouth newspaper offered four suggestions for how the prison might survive without inmates: it could become a boutique hotel, a backpackers' hostel, a paintballing experience, or a venue for raves and parties. Thomas Tyrwhitt would have applauded the creativity behind these suggestions, perhaps. But his dreams had been so much bigger.[38]

14.

THE TWO MASSACRES

AS DARTMOOR SURVIVORS LOBBIED THE FEDERAL GOVERNMENT for compensation, a thousand or so of their fellow prisoners disappeared from view. African Americans don't appear among the petitioners to Congress or in the striking 1853 photograph of Lewis Clover and the New York branch of the Dartmoor Prisoners' Association. Clover had barely noticed King Dick and Prison Four in his five-part series on Dartmoor in the *Knickerbocker* magazine. Although Benjamin Browne had more to say, he followed Benjamin Waterhouse in presenting Black-white interaction in Four as a moral failing or a sign of desperation on the part of white prisoners. As we saw earlier, a significant minority of the 'Black' prisoners may not have been African American. Some of the inhabitants of Four will have chosen to stay in Britain or to return to the various outposts of the Black Atlantic diaspora. Sailors from South Asia, South America, or East Asia doubtless tried to find their own way home or resumed the lifestyle of global itinerancy which had brought them into the British prison complex in the first place. Prison Four, like the other blocks at Dartmoor, was an international space as well as an American one. The prolonged and at times chaotic nature of the general release means that we can only speculate on the next move of Black sailors who chose not to board the cartel ships at Plymouth.

For those who returned to the American republic, the battle over Black belonging and citizenship was just getting started. The War of 1812 had provided a platform for Black volunteers to serve the US cause in the merchant marine and, occasionally, as militiamen; it had also given thousands of enslaved people in the coastal regions of the southern states an opportunity to cross the lines to fight for Britain. As Andrew Jackson prepared to wage the Battle of New Orleans at the war's end—a victory which depended on the service of Indigenous and Black troops—the slaveholding general praised his African American volunteers for their commitment to 'the land of your nativity'. But the flight of enslaved people to British lines reinforced many American enslavers in their view that Black people were an 'internal enemy' who would always threaten the United States.[1]

Free Black activists frequently saw themselves as the advance guard of a broader claim to liberty and citizenship: if African Americans in the northern states could convince white people of their respectability and potential, they would strengthen the case for emancipation throughout the nation. White antislavery reformers in the 1800s and 1810s had promoted the same vision, though by 1815 many had tired of the challenges of integration and had begun to advocate for the 'colonization' of Black people beyond the United States. In December 1816, white luminaries in the fields of politics, business, law, and culture founded the American Colonization Society to promote the removal of free Black people to a new African colony. (Enslaved people might go, too, perhaps as a condition of their emancipation, but free Black settlers were to be the vanguard.) Thomas Jefferson and James Madison were energetic supporters of colonization; Madison eventually agreed to become the Colonization Society's president. The Black writer David Walker—who lived on the edge of Negro Hill in Boston—marvelled at their crooked logic. The white boosters of colonization declared free Black people incapable of citizenship at home but judged them superbly qualified for it in an overseas colony. This was the 'colonizing trick', in Walker's memorable phrase, and it was the duty of Black people to resist.[2]

The Colonization Society succeeded in founding Liberia in 1821, but it attracted only ten thousand migrants in the following four decades. Free Blacks, and even enslaved people, refused to leave the land of their birth for a continent most had never seen. They noted with disdain that Liberia's first governors were white agents of the Colonization Society, and wondered if a Colonization Society replete with enslavers was a conspiracy to strengthen slavery's grip on the United States. And yet the idea of self-rule retained a powerful hold over many free Black people throughout the antebellum period and even into the late nineteenth and twentieth centuries. As early as the 1780s, free Black communities in New England passed resolutions acknowledging that white prejudice was an immovable force in American life. For more than a hundred years thereafter, Black individuals and communal societies debated the benefits of leaving the United States, but never wavered on a simple prerequisite: any Black colony would have to be governed exclusively by its Black inhabitants. Self-determination was the key to everything.[3]

The same thinking guided Paul Cuffe, the celebrated sea captain who had sailed into King Dick's hometown of Vienna, Maryland, back in 1795. The conflict between Britain and the United States had disrupted his efforts to build links between African Americans and the British colony of Sierra Leone, but as soon as the peace was ratified in January 1815, Cuffe began to organize a return voyage. He also continued to petition his white and Black antislavery friends in the hope that they would support his colonization initiatives. In December 1815, Cuffe set sail for Sierra Leone with forty African American emigrants from New England. The ship endured a terrible crossing, but in February 1816 Cuffe delivered his precious cargo of colonists.[4]

To the white leaders who would found the American Colonization Society in Washington just a few months later, Paul Cuffe seemed providentially useful: a free Black businessman would give credibility to their attempts to relocate free Black people to West Africa. But although Cuffe knew virtually all of the white celebrities of the Atlantic antislavery movement—including its legendary British architects, Thomas Clarkson and William Wilberforce—he was always his own person. He didn't think that every Black American would want to leave the United States, and his insistence that paying taxes to Massachusetts gave him the right to vote had already confirmed his commitment to equal citizenship at home. For Cuffe, separation from white people was one of several instruments that Black people might use to advance their rights. What united his various initiatives was the conviction that Black people had a basic entitlement to political power, whether exercised alongside white Americans or in separate communities.[5]

Prison Four was an accidental experiment in Black self-determination: it was the product not simply of white prejudice but of the chain of events which followed the initial request of Charles Andrews and his associates in October 1813 to remove themselves from both French and Black prisoners. The 'Black Prison' endured until June 1815, and its residents forged their own community. The published white accounts of Four disparage Dick for his tyranny but acknowledge what the contemporary journals tell us about the block's dynamism and variety. Given both the regular traffic of white people into the block and the fact that some white sailors were permitted to live there, Prison Four was less like a Black colony than a multiracial space in which Black people were in charge. To Benjamin Waterhouse, this was a paradox which could only be resolved by making Dick an authoritarian. Subsequent accounts of Dartmoor took a similar line. In reality, Four was nothing like Sierra Leone, Haiti, or any city or town in the United States. It was a place in which Cuffe's insistence on Black power was respected but to which white people continued to come. This was an exceptional dynamic in the history of the American republic and, since it defied easy categorization or co-optation in the subsequent debates over slavery, it remained almost entirely unremembered.

THE TENSION BETWEEN SELF-DETERMINATION AND INTEGRATION shaped the lives of Black prisoners who returned to the United States. Henry Van Meter had led many lives before coming to Dartmoor: he'd been enslaved by the governor of Virginia during the American Revolution, he'd escaped another enslaver by fleeing across the Ohio River, and he'd worked for the US Army during its war with Indigenous people in Ohio and Indiana in the early 1790s. He was thirty-nine years old when he was captured on a privateer. After six months in Dartmoor, during which (as he later told a reporter) he had 'witnessed the massacre of several of his fellows', he returned to the United States with very little. In the prison he'd put up his prize money as collateral for a loan from another prisoner, who had died on the way home and left Van Meter with no way to recover his entitlement. (Van Meter guessed this would be close to a thousand dollars.) Undeterred, he married a Black woman named Maria Wise and moved to Bangor, which in 1817 was still in Massachusetts (three years later, it would become part of the new state of Maine, created during the congressional compromise which brought Missouri into the Union as a slave state). The Van Meters bought land in the tiny town of Orono, eight miles up the Penobscot River from Bangor, and settled down to life in one of the whitest places in the United States.[6]

A city like Boston or Providence would have given the Van Meters access to Black churches, mutual aid societies, and everyday fraternity with other people of colour. It would also have placed them on the front line of a growing battle with racist whites who targeted the symbols and infrastructure of Black civic life. Orono was more unpredictable: the white inhabitants might find a tiny number of Black neighbours relatively unthreatening, or their racism could be even more devastating and destructive—especially if it kept Black children from schools or excluded Black families from businesses. Despite the fact that African Americans comprised under half a percent of Maine's total population, racism could be just as virulent in rural New England as in New York, Philadelphia, or Baltimore.[7]

Henry and Maria Van Meter spent sixteen years in Orono. Maria gave birth to five children, and the boys all grew up to be mariners. The family farm did well enough to cover the mortgage, but not all of the Van Meters' neighbours welcomed their success. At some point in the 1820s, Henry Van Meter came into contact with a local shopkeeper and businessman named Levi Cram. Cram sold everything: butter, flour, seeds, brass fireplaces, Dr Relfe's Botanical Drops, and 'a variety of other articles too numerous to mention', according to his frequent newspaper ads. Cram was also a promoter of the American Colonization Society. That the ACS's crusade to remove Black people from the United States should draw support from a shopkeeper in rural Maine gives some indication of the breadth of white supremacy in the early United States. Cram, like many northern boosters of colonization, could soothe himself with the thought that the removal of the Van Meter family (and free Black people more generally) might inspire southern slaveholders to manumit and expatriate enslaved people.[8]

Henry Van Meter hadn't known much about colonization until Cram came to his door: 'Levi Cram, the agent of the ACS, stated to me that Liberia was the only place in which I could enjoy happiness and freedom.' Cram lingered on the 'opportunities to educate my children', a sales pitch which suggests the Van Meters had struggled to find a school in Orono or Bangor. A move to Liberia would transform the family's prospects: 'In the space of a few years my children would be promoted to the offices of lawyers, judges, princes and kings.' The idea that African Americans who were 'degraded' in the United States might instantly become model citizens in Liberia was at the heart of the ACS's alchemical offering to Black people. There were plenty of reasons to reject their siren call: scepticism about the society's true motives, anxiety about the healthfulness and political situation of Liberia, and a determination to defend one's presence in the land of one's birth. But it would be wrong to see those African Americans who were curious about colonization as simple dupes of deceivers like Cram.[9]

In 1833, the Van Meters reached a decision. They sold their farm—at a considerable discount on its market value—and made for Boston, from where they planned to sail to Norfolk, Virginia, and the ACS ship that would carry them to Africa. At the Boston office of the Colonization Society, Henry Van Meter found two unpleasant surprises. First, Levi Cram was not an ACS agent. He was a member and a fundraiser, but he'd recruited the Van Meters without any formal sanction from the society. Second, the ACS agents strongly advised Henry Van Meter not to make the trip to Liberia given his advanced age. The mortality rate among new settlers throughout the 1820s had been high, and ACS agents were as worried for their own reputation as for Van Meter when they told him that, at the age of sixty, he might not survive the journey.[10]

Henry Van Meter was mortified. He had sold his house at a loss and been humiliated in front of his family. With nowhere to go, he left his wife and children with friends in New Bedford and travelled on to New York City for an audience with the ACS secretary, Ralph Gurley. James Madison had recently become president of the Colonization Society, but it was Gurley—a prominent Washington clergyman who was also chaplain to the House of Representatives—who had been the driving force of the ACS for more than a decade. Van Meter asked Gurley to help him buy back his farm in Orono. Gurley promised to 'meliorate' the situation and consult with the ACS directors in Washington. When nothing happened for more than a year, an exasperated Van Meter wrote to the *Liberator* to name and shame Reverend Gurley. Van Meter blamed the ACS for his misfortunes and confessed that his family would be headed for the almshouse if they couldn't find a way to recover their farm. The ACS had its own financial problems in 1835, and Ralph Gurley went on the attack: he demanded an apology from Van Meter for circulating the false claim that Levi Cram was an ACS representative. Van Meter signed his name to a pro forma apology but again accused the society of defrauding him. Eventually, he and Maria earned enough money from multiple jobs to get back to Maine, though they had to make do with a much smaller scrap of land in a poor neighbourhood of Bangor.[11]

In the years that followed, Henry Van Meter gave occasional public lectures impugning the ACS and demanding to be made whole for his losses. He never got his farm back. He grew what he could on a small patch of land but worked mostly as a labourer. In one Bangor newspaper ad from 1844, he advertised his services as a 'scientific Vault Cleansor'—in other words, someone who would clean the toilets of Bangor's better-heeled residents. At that point he was about to turn seventy. Maria gave birth to another two children and somehow the family survived. It was only in the 1860s that the Van Meters came to the attention of a wider public. The writer Benson Lossing was working on a history of the War of 1812, and when he heard of a Black veteran in Maine who had also lived through the American Revolution, he rushed to Bangor. Lossing's account of their conversation, accompanied by a handsome engraving of Van Meter, appeared in *Harper's Magazine* in 1864.[12]

HENRY VAN METER.

Henry Van Meter (1864)
Courtesy of Archive.org

After such a long life, Van Meter became a minor celebrity. Newspapers printed profiles which juggled admiration with familiar racist tropes: Van Meter was naive and childlike; he'd been in a court case but didn't really understand the proceedings; he was only distinguished by his longevity. When he died in 1871, at the age of a hundred and one, Henry Van Meter received a respectful obituary in the local newspaper and a dignified notice from the Washington newspaper the *New National Era*—edited by Frederick Douglass: 'Henry was an intelligent and industrious old man, and was fond of relating the stories of his eventful life.' Van Meter didn't receive a pension, of course, and if he talked about Dartmoor, his account never reached a newspaper or writer who could bring it to a wider audience. He would have left the United States altogether in 1833 if he hadn't been turned away by the alarmed ACS agents at Boston. In the event, he lived long enough to see the Fourteenth and Fifteenth Amendments, which embedded Black belonging and suffrage in the Constitution, and to glimpse the new forms of white supremacy which would wage war on Black citizenship long after the death of slavery.[13]

IN PHILADELPHIA, WHERE HENRY VAN METER HAD LIVED BEFORE becoming a sailor, the 1820s and 1830s saw a concerted struggle by free Black people for citizenship, along with a vicious backlash from their white opponents. The city's wealthy elites mostly aligned with the colonization movement, and in 1838 white politicians revised the state constitution to deny suffrage to African Americans. On the streets of Philadelphia, white rioters attacked Black businesses, churches, and people in a series of vicious race riots. It was in this bleak context that another Dartmoor veteran made the news.

Charles Black was born in the city in 1796, in the final year of George Washington's presidency. Black volunteered for military service in the War of 1812 and was assigned to the US Navy's fleet of gunboats on Lake Erie in August 1814. Although American

347

forces triumphed at the Battle of Plattsburgh in September 1814, Charles Black had already been captured in a sneak British attack. He was imprisoned for two months in Montreal and then, despite the advanced progress of the peace talks in Belgium, shipped across the Atlantic to Dartmoor. It was January 1815 before he arrived at the prison; this made him one of the last Americans to get out, in July.[14]

Charles Black re-emerges in the archive on 1 August 1842. He was living on Lombard Street with his young son, close to the heart of Philadelphia's largest Black neighbourhood. That day African Americans were marching through the streets to commemorate the eighth anniversary of emancipation in the British West Indies, an event which Black and white abolitionists cherished as a precursor to the overthrow of slavery on the American mainland. Tensions between Black and white Philadelphians had been running high that summer, and as the parade set off, local whites began to hurl abuse. Before long they were throwing stones. The marchers kept their composure until the white mob tried to snatch the American flag at the head of the procession, at which point a fight began and the situation deteriorated quickly. Outnumbered, the Black participants scattered and the white mob ransacked Black businesses and homes on South Street and Lombard Street. The police were called, but they stood by as the altercation turned into yet another race riot.[15]

Charles Black hadn't attended the march. He had been in his house, up a flight of stairs from the street, when a group of white rioters smashed through his door, dragged him from his apartment, and began to beat him viciously in the street. He was fifty-four years old, and his young son was forced to watch the attack. Some passers-by managed to wrest Black from his assailants before the rioters could beat him to death, and he spent nearly three weeks in hospital. The white abolitionist Henry Wright went to see him to learn more about what had happened, and from his hospital bed Black narrated his service in the War of 1812. He told Wright that he had been impressed into the Royal Navy and had then 'refused to fight against his country, although he had 900 dollars of prize money coming to him from the ship'. Black described his passage to Dartmoor, his release on exchange, another capture, another release, then *another* capture after the Battle of Plattsburgh, and a second stint in Dartmoor. According to the records in the British National Archives, Black had slightly embellished the story: he had only done one stretch at Dartmoor, from January to July 1815. But the moral Wright drew from the tale remained true: 'Thus the man who fought and bled for his country . . . is first *disfranchised*, by the government which he fought and bled to defend, and then, by the churches, ministers and magistrates of Philadelphia, handed over to the tender mercies of a ruffian mob.'[16]

As he studied Black's wounds in his hospital bed, Henry Wright thought it pointless to blame the mob who had actually beaten him. The street toughs, after all, were mere 'tools' of the city's elites. As long as churchmen, business leaders, and politicians were unwilling to defend the civil and political rights of Black people, intimidation and violence were inevitable. White 'moderates' were the 'apologists of slavery', Wright insisted, and the most intractable opponents of Black citizenship. Charles Black hadn't even taken to the streets on the day of the parade, but it made no difference. No one was safe from white supremacy in Philadelphia, and the mob—along with their elite enablers—would target any African American, regardless of their service to their country.[17]

EVEN FOR BLACK DARTMOOR VETERANS WHO WENT BACK TO SEA after the War of 1812, the assault on citizenship rights at home was hard to ignore. In 1822, South Carolina introduced the first of what became known as the Negro Seamen Acts. In response to an abortive Black uprising that summer in Charleston led by the free Black carpenter (and former sailor) Denmark Vesey, South Carolina's legislators mandated that all Black sailors entering the state's ports should be imprisoned until their vessels departed. The sailors (or their captains) would have to pay for their incarceration; non-payment, or any infraction whatever, would send the Black sailor to the auction block to be sold into slavery. Seven other legislatures across the South introduced similar measures, which were a threat not only to sailors but also to the principle of equal citizenship within the United States. This wasn't an exclusively southern problem: Northern states, especially in the West, found their own ways to restrict free Black mobility. But the Negro Seamen Acts were a particularly vicious constraint on the possibility of race-blind citizenship, and on the livelihoods of Black sailors.[18]

The acts provided an urgent pretext for Black political organizing, including among Dartmoor veterans. George Wilson had been captured on an American merchant vessel off the Eastern Seaboard in 1814. He got to Dartmoor on Christmas Eve 1814, witnessed the massacre of 6 April, and was finally released in July 1815. On his return to the United States, he began a new career as a steward on passenger ships. He mostly sailed up and down the Atlantic coast, though occasionally his work took him to Cuba. Wilson was arrested on numerous occasions under the Negro Seamen Acts, a version of which was implemented by the Cuban authorities in 1837 without any objection from the US State Department. He became exasperated by the moral weakness of his white captains, who on one occasion in Havana delivered both Wilson and his wife to the Cuban authorities. In 1841, he decided to organize a meeting in his hometown of New York to protest discrimination against Black sailors. He invited another alumnus of Prison Four, David Roberts, to share the stage with him.[19]

Roberts was born in Virginia in 1790. He'd been impressed into the Royal Navy, and in December 1812 had 'delivered himself up' from HMS *Impetueux*. He spent more than a year in the hulks at Chatham before arriving at Dartmoor in the summer of 1814, just as the American contingent was ramping up. He was in Prison Four for nearly ten months and won his release in a cartel which left Plymouth in early May. Like George Wilson, he spent the quarter century after Dartmoor at sea and had frequently felt the sting of the Seamen Acts in southern ports. The two men stood together in a New York meeting hall in 1841 before an audience of Black sailors and Black and white abolitionists to challenge this grim reality of their professional life. Both were in their fifties, and they spoke 'more in sorrow than in anger' about the grinding prejudices of the nation they had fought to defend. In the War of 1812, Wilson reminded the crowd, the United States 'looked not to white men only, but to Black, and I volunteered in her service'. Briefly recounting his privateering service and the horrors of being held at Dartmoor, Wilson concluded that 'after suffering for my country in this way, it is too hard to be arrested, denied all the rights of citizens, and thrown into a common jail, merely because my skin is black.'[20]

David Roberts told the crowd that he had also been captured on a privateer; given Wilson's pitch about the service of Black men to the US cause, he may have decided that it was too complicated to explain that he'd ended up in Dartmoor via a British warship. But he confirmed Wilson's reminiscences about the prison, and the two men recalled the characters they had known in Four. The white abolitionist who wrote up the event for a newspaper pulled away from their discussion to consider the scene more broadly: 'It was an interesting spectacle to see these two weather-beaten victims of their country's treachery, standing there, and calling up to each other, reminiscences of their old companionship in Dartmoor prison.' The meeting ended in cheers, the adoption of a petition against the Negro Seamen Acts, and the establishment of a committee to strategize on legislative initiatives in Washington and the southern states.[21]

George Wilson didn't have the luxury of being a full-time organizer. His attempts to set aside racially restrictive laws and practices in the following years were interspersed with his work as a ship's steward and his quotidian fights against white prejudice. His name would occasionally appear in the newspapers as he attempted to bring suits against unruly white passengers who assaulted him at sea. In 1842, he complained to the *Emancipator*, a prominent antislavery newspaper, that his activism was limited by 'the want of a little pecuniary aid'. The paper observed that, with tensions rising between the United States and Britain over Texas and Oregon, it was folly for white Americans to alienate a group of fellow citizens who had already shed blood in defence of the republic. African Americans 'may well feel attached . . . to the general principles of our government,' the paper observed, 'and yet they may not feel under obligations to take a voluntary and active part in favor of a government, as now administered, which openly tramples on their rights, and delights to heap obloquy on their persons.' In short, Wilson and other Black men could not be expected to defend their country if it needed their help again.[22]

The use of Wilson's experiences at Dartmoor to craft this theory of Black neutrality elicited a furious response from one of the nation's leading colonization newspapers, which fulminated at the notion that Black people might have leverage in a time of national crisis. Reprinting the *Emancipator* article in full, the *Maryland Colonization Journal* pronounced it 'the most seditious and mischievous of any thing we have lately seen.' The *Journal* thanked the *Emancipator* for bringing into the light a plain fact which the colonization movement had always known: 'It will serve to open the eyes of the good people of this Union to the fact that a body of people among us, numbering some four hundred thousands, are already speculating and determining upon the course to pursue in case of war and invasion.'[23]

The *Journal* deftly demonstrated that even Wilson's forlorn reflection on his service in the War of 1812 could be placed in the service of othering Black people. The notion that African Americans might envisage a reciprocal relationship with the state, especially as the state invited them to put their lives in jeopardy, confirmed the old prejudice that Black people were an internal enemy. That African Americans in New York—with the connivance of white abolitionists—were openly debating a policy of 'organized neutrality' made it clear to the *Journal* that the colonization of free Black people was an urgent necessity. George Wilson had been making a simple point. His military service had demonstrated unwavering loyalty to the United States, but the US government had proved unfaithful to him and other African Americans in the years that followed. The *Journal* seized on his exhaustion to make the opposite point: that Black people were 'truly alarming' because their loyalty to the nation was conditional.[24]

Any Black activist who invoked his suffering at Dartmoor faced the same dilemma. To suggest that military service was transactional was to invite a new round of attacks on Black patriotism. The War of 1812, like the Revolutionary War before it, had empowered Black people partly by commodifying national loyalty: during the years in which the two nations fought each other, Britain and the United States competed for the service of African Americans and other men of colour in the Atlantic world. The same dynamic explained the phenomenon of 'military emancipation' throughout the Americas in the eighteenth and early nineteenth centuries, during which Britain, France, and other powers were forced to offer freedom to enslaved people as a means of preventing them from siding with the enemy. Geopolitics, rather than morality, was the most immediate threat to slavery; battlefield necessity loosened the grip of enslavers and gave Black people options they did not enjoy during peacetime. When these conflicts were over, states swiftly closed down those options and pretended they had never existed. When George Wilson remembered in 1841 that he'd chosen to fight in 1812—and that he might easily have chosen not to—he was sharing an insight which was both true and heretical.

THE CLAIM THAT BLACK PATRIOTISM WAS INEXTINGUISHABLE rather than transactional anchored the work of William Cooper Nell, the pioneering African American historian and abolitionist. Nell was born in Boston in 1816, just as Benjamin Waterhouse's *Journal of a Young Man of Massachusetts* was flying off the shelves of the town's bookstores. The son of a prominent Black activist, Nell excelled at school and became a model for Black potential. White abolitionists and the emerging Black middle class in Boston placed great emphasis on respectability: their arguments for equality and integration rested on the ability of young African Americans like Nell to prove themselves a match for any white man both morally and intellectually. Nell amply justified their hopes. In the 1830s and 1840s, he worked for William Lloyd Garrison as a writer and editor on the *Liberator* and became an important organizer for the American Anti-Slavery Society.[25]

Working for Garrison brought Nell into contact with some of New England's wealthiest individuals, a relationship punctuated by quiet indignities. As the historian Steven Kantrowitz puts it, 'Nell wrestled with the gap between his dreams of joining their world of accomplishment and acclaim, and the reality of his poverty and subordination.' Some Black figures who worked with New England's white antislavery elite grew tired of the roles they were asked to play. Nell, on the other hand, remained fiercely loyal to William Lloyd Garrison and the other grandees of abolitionism. This eventually brought him into conflict with Frederick Douglass, who had himself worked with Garrison in the early 1840s but who eventually quarrelled with him over the tactics of Black liberation. In 1853, Douglass proposed a school for young African Americans to learn mechanical trades; Garrison and Nell were uncomfortable with a racially exclusive institution and quietly accused Douglass of reinforcing the logic of racial separation. Douglass raged that this was an 'absurd' accusation. Equal citizenship and integration were always his ambitions, Douglass insisted, but 'we are simply doing for ourselves, what no others have proposed to do for us.' Black empowerment came in many forms.[26]

William Nell was convinced that Black equality could only be realised by demonstrating that African Americans were and always had been an inseparable part of the American story. To this end, he began work in the early 1840s on Black history—or, more precisely, on the centrality of Black experience to the triumphant course of *American* history. He gathered documents from the American Revolution and the War of 1812 to prove not only that African Americans were loyal but that, as Harriet Beecher Stowe wrote in her preface to the published book, their loyalty was the more extraordinary 'because rendered to a nation which did not acknowledge them as citizens and equals'. Black people had been written out of the nation's founding struggles; Nell was determined to show that they had been hiding in plain sight all along.[27]

Nell's work initially appeared as a pamphlet in 1851 and was then published four years later (in a greatly expanded version) as *The Colored Patriots of the American Revolution*. Nell wrote about James Forten, the young Black sailor from Philadelphia who had served on a Patriot privateer during the American Revolution and had been imprisoned by the British in one of its most notorious hulks; about the Black Boston poet Phillis Wheatley, whose work had helped to demolish arguments about Black inferiority; and about the Black troops at the Battle of New Orleans to whom Andrew Jackson had paid tribute in 1815. Paul Cuffe received a warm notice, and Nell was especially taken with his visit to Vienna, Maryland, in 1795: 'A vessel owned and commanded by a black man, and manned with a crew of the same complexion, was unprecedented and surprising.' Nell briefly noted Cuffe's interest in colonization but said much more about his struggle to implement 'no taxation without representation' for African Americans in Massachusetts.[28]

Nell's most radical act of remembrance involved the Black Wampanoag sailor Crispus Attucks. Attucks was one of five Americans killed by British troops in the Boston Massacre on 5 March 1770. During the subsequent trial of the troops before a Boston jury, only one of the thirty witnesses—an enslaved man named Andrew—placed Attucks at the head of the unruly crowd which had harassed the soldiers before they opened fire. The defence counsel for those soldiers was John Adams, future president of the United States. Andrew's testimony about Attucks was exactly what

Adams had been looking for: evidence that the crowd at the Custom House on 5 March had not been made up of respectable patriots but (as Adams told the jury) a 'motley rabble of saucy boys, negroes and mulattoes, Irish teagues, and outlandish jack tars'. Suddenly the protesters had morphed into sailors, foreigners, and people of colour: in effect, one group of outsiders had attacked another, with true Bostonians looking on in horror. Adams had found a line of argument that would secure the soldiers' acquittal.[29]

In the immediate aftermath of the massacre, as patriot propagandists appropriated the killings to inflame anti-British sentiment throughout the colonies, Adams's narrative was speedily discarded—along with the idea that the protesters had been a 'motley rabble'. The Boston engraver Paul Revere famously captured the moment of the firing, depicting the protesters as respectable-looking white men with neat clothes and shiny shoe buckles—indistinguishable from the crowd behind them. Any (white) Bostonian might have been killed in the massacre, or so Revere's image suggested. The men who had given their lives became martyrs to the cause of the emerging American nation. While the massacre's place in American memory ebbed and flowed in the following decades, Paul Revere's view of the victims as American everymen held sway. Crispus Attucks was consigned to the margins of an event which became pivotal to the story of independence.[30]

It was William Nell's genius to bring Attucks back to the centre of the scene, while retaining the view that the Boston Massacre was the first battleground in the war for American independence. Borrowing from the Italian historian Carlo Botta, who had published a three-volume study of the American Revolution in 1809, Nell positioned Attucks as the organizer of the entire protest. He became the man who had mustered the crowd and directed it towards the Custom House, and then the first person to die for the cause of the United States. 'The colored man, ATTUCKS, was *of* and *with* the people,' Nell wrote, 'and was never regarded otherwise.' In 1851, Nell organized a group of Black Bostonians to petition the Massachusetts state legislature for a permanent memorial to Crispus Attucks. Although this effort was initially unsuccessful, Black activists in Boston and throughout the United States embraced Nell's inventive realignment of Attucks's role. The Paul Revere engraving was supplanted by a new image in which an heroic Attucks—his hand forlornly grasping the bayonet of an implacable British soldier—prepared to give his life for his country. After a long struggle among Massachusetts's political and cultural elite over whether to accept Nell's framing, in 1888 the state commissioned a monument giving Crispus Attucks the leading role. William Cooper Nell didn't live long enough to see the unveiling, but everyone knew that it had been his achievement to make Americans recognize that the pioneer of Revolutionary resistance had been Black.[31]

When Nell turned his attention to the War of 1812, could he do something similar with the Dartmoor Massacre? More Americans had been killed in Dartmoor than in Boston—nine versus five. Three of those fatalities were men of colour, and both the innocence of the prisoners and the villainy of the British had been carefully established by dozens of eyewitnesses. In *Colored Patriots* Nell wrote about two Black men who had witnessed the shootings of 6 April 1815. The first was Charles Black, who had nearly died during the race riot on Lombard Street in Philadelphia in 1842. Nell chose not to recount Black's time in Dartmoor but to paste the newspaper story of the 1842 riot alongside the fact of Black's imprisonment in the War of 1812. Nell noted that Black's father and grandfather had fought in the Revolution and in the Seven Years' War but made no reference to the massacre.[32]

The second Dartmoor prisoner included in *Colored Patriots* was King Dick. Nell reworked an obituary from a Boston newspaper and repeated its many errors: Dick was 'born in Salem, or vicinity'. At the age of sixteen, he enlisted in the Royal Navy, but 'when the war of 1812 broke out he would not fight against his country' and 'gave himself up as an American citizen, and was made a prisoner of war'. Nell applied the same gloss to Dick that he had used on

Crispus Attucks: an itinerant sailor was transformed into a loyal and determined citizen, with each man braving terrible consequences to serve his embattled nation. Nell's main source for Dick's character, though, was Benjamin Waterhouse. He copied nearly a page from Waterhouse's sketch of the 'Black Hercules', focusing on Dick's disciplinarian streak and his determination to bully the 'dirty, drunken and grossly negligent' within Prison Four. Nell decorously ended his borrowing just before the sentence in which Waterhouse claimed that 'Negroes are genuinely reputed to be thieves' and that 'their faculties are commonly found to be inadequate to the comprehension of the moral system.' Nell took from Waterhouse what was useful—the image of a Black authority figure who kept order in Prison Four—and discarded the rest.[33]

But Nell knew more than he was letting on. 'When a boy, living in West Boston, I was familiar with the person of Big Dick,' he admitted. Nell grew up on the edges of Negro Hill, even as his family wanted no part of its seaminess. Did Nell meet Richard Crafus during King Dick's final act? What would he have made of him? Dick represented a very different form of Black agency from the one Nell championed. For advocates of Black respectability and uplift, Dick was hard to assimilate into a story of racial or national advancement. The one fact about Dick which made him a 'colored patriot'—that his love for America had compelled him to exchange a Royal Navy warship for a British prison—was false. He was plucked from a French privateer in Bordeaux in April 1814 without romance or struggle. When Nell was growing up, Dick was a notorious figure in a part of town that Nell hoped to escape. For the advocates of Black uplift, the road to citizenship didn't pass through the exercise of power and influence in these neighbourhoods. It was hard for Nell to see any achievement in Prison Four beyond Dick's willingness to keep more dissolute Black sailors in line with his club—hence his unlikely appropriation of Benjamin Waterhouse, whose presentation of Black life at Dartmoor just beyond the sections quoted by Nell had been luridly racist.

The Dartmoor Massacre was entirely absent from Nell's book. He may have realised that the event had none of the potential of its Boston counterpart; that while the perfidy of the British in 1770 could ground the entire Revolutionary story, the shootings of 1815 were an embarrassment to both sides. If he'd had access to the published accounts of the prisoners' testimony, which were widely reprinted in American newspapers in the months after the massacre, he would also have known that King Dick lingered in the privy while his friend John Haywood went to investigate the shouting from the market square. The contrast with Crispus Attucks is stark. For all his pugilism and influence over the thousand or so inhabitants of Prison Four, Dick chose to sit out this fight.

Did this make him less heroic than Attucks? Was it his duty to stand with his compatriots and rush the gates while the Somersetshire militia pushed forward with their bayonets? The story of the massacre vanished from American history because it didn't serve anyone's purpose: it happened because the British and American governments placed a low value on the lives of ordinary sailors, and it was hushed up for the same reason. The resilience and resourcefulness of the prisoners sometimes pushed them towards patriotic appeals, but most Americans in Dartmoor came to realise that their imprisonment was a form of abandonment by their government. For some, this realisation happened while they were still at Dartmoor. Others reached the same conclusion only years later, as Washington stubbornly refused to grant privateersmen and impressed sailors the pensions their sacrifice demanded.

As for King Dick and the inhabitants of Prison Four, Dartmoor provided an extraordinary opportunity to create a world of their own and set the conditions on which white people could enter it. In this respect, Prison Four was closer to the project of Paul Cuffe than William Cooper Nell. It was a place that privileged Black agency without reference to national allegiance, which may explain why so few African American veterans of Dartmoor found opportunities to reflect on their experiences after their release. Arguments for integration and citizenship in the decades after Dartmoor repeated the unconquerable determination of Black people to prize the United States above all else. William Nell rounded on Black Americans who 'are themselves active in upholding colored institutions', accusing them of undermining the struggle against 'colorphobia' by endorsing Black schools, churches, and political conventions. But Black self-determination was not a denial of American belonging; it was a recognition that collective struggle for African Americans would always depend on the exercise of Black power. 'We have a right to associate with each other to promote our interest,' Frederick Douglass had told his critics. King Dick and the inhabitants of Prison Four lived by the same principle.[34]

ACKNOWLEDGEMENTS

My friends will tell you that I am a taker not a giver; this book is not my best defence against that charge. First I need to thank Alan Taylor, who wrote about Dartmoor in *The Civil War of 1812* and patiently listened to my pitch for this book as I drove him around a dangerously foggy moor in North Yorkshire. (It was Alan who put me on to Reuben G. Beasley, the antihero of *The Hated Cage*.) After finishing my last book I'd originally planned to write something about nineteenth-century ideas of empire, and I'm indebted to the director and fellows of the Centre for Research in the Arts, Social Sciences and Humanities (CRASSH) here in Cambridge for awarding me a fellowship in 2017 on that other topic, then listening politely as I told them about naked Frenchmen and forgotten prison massacres.

In the fall of 2018, I was lucky enough to visit the Vanderbilt History Seminar: many thanks to everyone who attended my talk, and especially to Richard Blackett, Jeff Cowie, Brandon Byrd, and Jane Landers. The following spring I presented at Boston University's History Seminar and got a ton of great questions and advice. Thanks in particular to Nina Silber, Bruce Schulman, and my old pal Brooke Blower. The book's arguments got three more outings: at the University of Newcastle, where I was indebted to the participants and especially to Vanessa Mongey; at Georgetown-Qatar in Doha, where I was looked after by Hagar Rakha and Reina Rosales; and at the Cambridge American History Seminar. I'll thank some of my local friends in a minute, but here I should acknowledge the help of Jonathan Godwin and Lewis Defrates in making the seminar happen.

I completed much of the research for this book before Covid, and I'm especially indebted to the UK National Archives, the US National Archives (I & II!), the American Antiquarian Society, the Massachusetts Historical Society, the Pennsylvania Historical Society, and the Marblehead Museum. After Covid hit, when things were going to hell, Meaghan Wright of the Phillips Library at the Peabody Essex Museum and Mark Bowden of the Detroit Public Library arranged to scan materials and send them to me in the UK. Librarians and archivists absolutely rock.

I wrote the first draft between January and May 2020, and during those months it became increasingly weird to write about a group of people indefinitely confined and largely abandoned by their government. The privilege of being able to keep working on the book, in the office and then at home, contrasted sharply with the fate of those who were losing their jobs or rushing to the front line to risk their lives. This book has certainly been shaped by the pandemic, and I'm hugely grateful to everyone who worked so hard to keep us safe.

One consequence of spending so much time at home (actually, in my garden shed) was that I lost perspective on what might be interesting to other people. With this in view, I'm particularly indebted to the brave souls who read my bloated first draft. Karine Walther was the first to make an intervention. ('Have you thought about whether you need that section on the Korean War?') I'm so grateful to Karine, and it's a real privilege to be her pal. I barely knew Frank Cogliano when I started this book, but he was another wonderfully generous reader of the first draft. Heather Ann Thompson, my colleague at Cambridge in 2019–2020, sent encouragement to add to the inspiration I'd already taken from her work. Matthew Kelly, author of a brilliant environmental history of the Dartmoor region, pushed through the endless pages and let me know what worked and what didn't.

This is a good place for me to acknowledge that Ari Kelman told me NOT to send him my bloated draft, for God's sake don't send it, but to be fair he had been forced to read the bloated draft of my last book and it caused considerable hair loss. I am so happy he still takes my calls and occasionally moonlights as my business manager.

Three other scholars deserve a special thank-you. In her work on foreign sailors in the Royal Navy, Sara Caputo offered me a model of how to write about nationalism and allegiance in the vast emptiness of the ocean. Sara was literally the only reader of my first draft who insisted that it was all pretty interesting; either this is a facet of her kindness or a sign of her super-nerdery on matters nautical. Either way, I have learned a huge amount from her and will always be grateful for her willingness to help a green hand on his first voyage.

Jake Richards has been reinventing the field of Atlantic history with his pathfinding work on the fate of Liberated Africans across the nineteenth century. Jake's focus on the interplay between imperial law and politics and Black agency has been hugely helpful to me. He helped me to think about what really happened in Prison Four and encouraged me to highlight the problems of knowing which previous sketches of Dartmoor have tidied away. I've been very fortunate to have Jake's counsel as I've shaped the stories in this book.

Christa Dierksheide gave me all the proper warnings before I fully committed to the book ('Are you sure you want to write something that requires actual historical knowledge?') and has been a firm friend to the project. Her supremely perceptive read on the draft was a massive help; along with Karine, it was Christa who made me realise that a shorter book was in everyone's best interest. I'm so grateful, and I'm looking forward to collaborating with her on a new book very soon.

Other debts: Charlie Foy, keeper of one of the most amazing databases in eighteenth-century maritime history, was incredibly kind during our meeting at the National Archives in Kew. John

Ellis kindly shared his work on Black sailors. Craig Hammond shared transcriptions of letters about Black sailors who were unlucky enough to sail into southern ports after the War of 1812. Abigail Coppins shared her work on Black prisoners at Portchester Castle. Anna-Lisa Cox got me thinking about Hosea Easton. Alan Lipke offered advice and encouragement on the subject of King Dick. Denver Brunsman, a fellow survivor of the Princeton grad programme, shared his thoughts about impressment and the War of 1812. Nancy Shoemaker allowed me to use her database of whaling voyages and offered some extremely helpful pointers on racial identification on land and at sea. Martha Jones and Annette Gordon-Reed have supported me in so many ways, and I'm forever grateful for their work and inspiration.

In Cambridge, Gary Gerstle has been a wonderful friend over the past few years. He was also unfailingly supportive in 2018–2019 when things blew up at my old college. The full story of that episode is best left for my memoir, but here I want to acknowledge the enormous help I received from Gary, and also from Christopher Padfield, Jeremy Caddick, Lawrence Klein, Peter Mandler, Mary Laven, and many other colleagues. I also want to pay tribute to the students who bravely stood up to the institution that had failed them.

Among my fellow historians, I'm especially grateful to my comrades in the American history group—Julia Guarneri, Ruth Lawlor, Bobby Lee, Sarah Pearsall, Andrew Preston, and Emma Teitelman—as well as to John Arnold, Arthur Asseraf, Julie Barrau, Duncan Bell, Chris Clark, Lucy Delap, Jane Dinwoodie, Michael Edwards, Bronwen Everill, Hank Gonzalez, Rachel Leow, Helen Pfeifer, Sujit Sivasundaram, and Hillary Taylor. For their support as faculty chairs, I want to acknowledge Tim Harper and Alex Walsham in particular.

Geoff Parks, James Clackson, and Sonita Alleyne eased my move to Jesus College in 2019 and made me feel welcome. I've had extremely helpful conversations about the book with many Jesus fellows, but I want to thank two in particular. Nick Ray kindly read my chapter on Bentham, which was the first piece of this book to make it into the wild. Renaud Morieux was just finishing his extraordinary book *The Society of Prisoners* when I got the Dartmoor bug. He's been incredibly generous and supportive, and I've learned so much from him and his work.

In the final straight, Andy Graybill was kind enough to read the revised draft and send comments which I have chosen to read as supportive. ('OMG you have gone FULL TRADE!') I was also fortunate to receive advice and support from Paul Finegan, the curator of the Dartmoor Prison Museum, who read the revised draft and set me straight on a number of important points. Just before the book went into production, I discovered that Neil Davie of the Université Lyon was *also* writing a book about Dartmoor. We had a lovely chat about our respective approaches and I can't wait to see what he's turned up. If we can find enough Dartmoor enthusiasts, we are definitely making a joint appearance at a bookstore somewhere.

Huge thanks to Lara Heimert of Basic Books for letting me sneak under the red rope once more. Claire Potter did an amazing job of cajoling and encouraging me as I tried to shed sixty thousand words from the first draft. Her vision, skill, and patience have made this a much better book. Roger Labrie's line edit was a revelation: if my account of events holds together, it's because Roger spotted the continuity errors and so much more. The Basic production team are second to none: I want to thank Abby Mohr, Brynn Warriner, Jenny Lee and the formidable publicity team, and the various other heroes who materialise in the final stages of a project. A particular word of thanks to Christina Palaia for her Stakhanovite work on the copyedit; copyeditors are the very best people around.

On the other side of the Atlantic, the team at Oneworld have saved my skin and lifted my spirits on numerous occasions. Sam Carter is the nicest man in publishing; I'm extremely grateful for his championing of the book and sharp read of the draft. Rida Vaquas and Holly Knox also made the book stronger with their comments on the draft, and Holly spared me a nervous breakdown by helping to coordinate image permissions. Holly, I really owe you one.

I'm also indebted to my agents: the supremely unflappable David Halpern in the United States, and the brilliant Lesley Thorne in London. I have known Lesley forever and have always been lucky to have her in my corner.

The pandemic has placed strains on academics everywhere, but particularly in the UK where successive governments had already told universities to do way more with far less. I'm sure I'm not alone in feeling that our families often get short shrift as we try to manage impossible workloads. When my dad died suddenly at the end of 2020, I hadn't seen him for nearly a year; I'm grateful for his memory and in awe of my mum's strength and courage. I owe everything to my parents, and I'm so sad I couldn't share this book with both of them.

My own kids are, at this stage, entirely unimpressed by my shtick. But now that the book is done I'm planning to be around the house a whole lot more to annoy them with dad jokes and my ignorance of anime. When I came up with the idea for this book, I promised my wife it would *definitely* be a movie and that we could afford to go on holiday again. Then when I'd finished the draft, I proudly handed her the pages and she made a face like Shelley Duvall when she reads Jack Nicholson's manuscript in *The Shining*. If I embarrass her by getting mushy it will be yet another indignity in our marriage, so I'll just say that I'm grateful to her always, for everything.

NOTES

ABBREVIATIONS

BFB   [Benjamin Frederick Browne], 'Papers of an Old Dartmoor Prisoner, edited by Nathaniel Hawthorne', *United States Magazine and Democratic Review*, nos. 1–5, January to May 1846; nos. 6 and 7, August and September 1846.

BW   [Benjamin Waterhouse], *Journal of a Young Man of Massachusetts, Late a Surgeon On Board an American Privateer* (Boston: Rowe and Hooper, 1816).

DBFP   *The Diary of Benjamin F. Palmer, Privateersman* (New York: Acorn Club, 1914).

FO   *Founders Online*, National Archives, founders.archives.gov.

GBP   Glover Broughton Papers, Series Five, Broughton Family Papers, Marblehead Museum, Marblehead, MA.

GEBA   General Entry Book of American Prisoners of War at Dartmoor, ADM 103/87–103/91, National Archives of the UK.

GEBF   General Entry Book of French Prisoners of War at Dartmoor, ADM 103/92–103/101, National Archives of the UK.

GL   George Little, *Life on the Ocean; or, Twenty Years at Sea*, 2nd ed. (Boston: Waite, Peirce and Company, 1844).

JB   Joseph Bates, *The Autobiography of Elder Joseph Bates* (Battle Creek, MI: Seventh Day Adventist Publishing Association, 1868).

JC   [Josiah Cobb], *A Green Hand's First Cruise, Roughed Out from the Log-Book of Memory*, 2 vols. (Boston: Otis, Broaders, and Company, 1841).

JNP   'Journal of Nathaniel Pierce of Newburyport, Kept at Dartmoor Prison, 1814–1815', *Essex Institute Historical Collections* 77, no. 1 (January 1837): 24–59.

JV   *Journal of Joseph Valpey, Jr., of Salem, November 1813–April 1815* (Detroit: Michigan Society of Colonial Wars, 1922).

LPC   [Lewis P. Clover], 'Reminiscences of a Dartmoor Prisoner', *Knickerbocker*, no. 1 (February), no. 2 (April), no. 3 (June), no. 4 (November), no. 5 (December 1844).

MDP   'Great Britain—Massacre at Dartmoor Prison', 14th Cong., 1st sess., no. 281, *American State Papers, Foreign Relations*, 6 vols. (Washington, DC: Gales and Seaton, 1834), 4:19–95.

RAG   Records of the Adjutant General's Office, War of 1812 Prisoners, Records Group 94, Series 127, National Archives, Washington, DC.

RIS   Records on Impressed Seamen 1794–1815, Records Group 59, Entry 928, National Archives II, College Park, MD.

TBOL   Transport Board Out-Letters to Agents Relating to Prisoners of War, Dartmoor, ADM 98/225–98/228, National Archives of the UK.

TNA   The National Archives of the UK.

TPM   [Charles Andrews], *The Prisoners' Memoirs, or, Dartmoor Prison* (New York: Printed for the Author, 1815).

UJN   Unattributed journal from a sailor aboard the *Nancy*, prize to the *Portsmouth* privateer, War of 1812 Collection, box 1, folder 7, Phillips Library, Peabody Essex Museum, Rowley, MA.

USNA   National Archives of the United States.

INTRODUCTION

1. DBFP, 179, 180.

2. DBFP, 181.

3. JNP, 40–41.

4. JNP, 42; DBFP, 182.

5. DBFP, 180.

6. I'm indebted to Paul Finegan of the Dartmoor Prison Museum for clarifying that, although Dartmoor was a high-security prison before 2001, its habit of allowing prisoners to work beyond its walls meant that it was never a *maximum* security prison.

7. GL, 197.

8. Marc Ferris, *Star-Spangled Banner: The Unlikely Story of America's National Anthem* (Baltimore: Johns Hopkins University Press, 2014), 15–19.

9. BW, 164.

10. Dozens of American prisoners were entered twice (or even three times) in the register. Some had been transferred to other facilities; most had been exchanged (or had escaped) before being recaptured. Dozens more were captured on French or Spanish ships and entered into the French register, and so the exact number of US prisoners of war at Dartmoor between 1809 and 1815 is very hard to establish.

PART I. KING DICK AT VIENNA

1. GEBA, Admiralty Records (ADM) 103/90, no. 4603.

2. The 1790 federal census recorded 5,337 enslaved people and 528 free Black residents of Dorchester County: *Return of the Whole Number of Persons Within the Several Districts of the United States* (London: J. Phillips, 1793), 47; Jennifer Hull Dorsey, *Hirelings: African American Workers and Free Labor in Early Maryland* (Ithaca, NY: Cornell University Press, 2011); Kate Clifford Larson, *Bound for the Promised Land: Harriet Tubman—Portrait of an American Hero* (New York: Ballantine Books, 2003); Erica Armstrong Dunbar, *She Came to Slay: The Life and Times of Harriet Tubman* (New York: Simon & Schuster, 2019); David W. Blight, *Frederick Douglass: Prophet of Freedom* (New York: Simon & Schuster, 2018).

3. 'Frederick Douglass at his Old Home', *Baltimore Sun*, 19 June 1877, 1.

4. Frederick Douglass, *Narrative of the Life of Frederick Douglass, an American Slave* (Boston: Anti-Slavery Office, 1845), 27.

5. Paul Cuffe, *Memoir of Paul Cuffee, a Man of Color* (Liverpool, UK: Egerton Smith and Co., 1811), 8–9.

6. Lamont D. Thomas, *Rise to Be a People: A Biography of Paul Cuffe* (Urbana: University of Illinois Press, 1970); Rosalind Cobb Wiggins, 'Introducing Captain Paul Cuffe', in *Captain Paul Cuffe's Logs and Letters, 1808–1817: A Black Quaker's 'Voice from Within the Veil'*, ed. Rosalind Cobb Wiggins (Washington, DC: Howard University Press, 1986), 45–70.

7. Cuffe, *Memoir of Paul Cuffee*, 4–5.

8. Ashli White, *Encountering Revolution: Haiti and the Making of the Early Republic* (Baltimore: Johns Hopkins University Press, 2010); James Alexander Dun, *Dangerous Neighbors: Making the Haitian Revolution in Early America* (Philadelphia: University of Pennsylvania Press, 2016).

9. Cuffe, *Memoir of Paul Cuffee*, 9.

CHAPTER 1. A SEAFARING LIFE

1. TPM, 11–15; General Entry Book of American Prisoners of War, *Hector* prison ship, 1813–1814, Admiralty Records (ADM) 103/177, TNA; GEBA, ADM 103/87.

2. TPM, 17–18; BW, 112.

3. GEBA, ADM 103/87.

4. TPM, 18.

5. Glover Broughton, 'A Key to the View of Dartmoor Prison, England' (c. 1859?), in GBP; A. Conan Doyle, *The Hound of the Baskervilles* (London: George Newnes Limited, 1902), 108–109; TPM, 18–19.

6. Lisa Norling, *Captain Ahab Had a Wife: New England Women and the Whalefishery, 1720–1870* (Chapel Hill: University of North Carolina Press, 2000), 2; Elmer Plischke, *U.S. Department of State: A Reference History* (Westport, CT: Greenwood Press, 1999), 73; Nancy Shoemaker, 'The Extraterritorial United States to 1860', *Diplomatic History* 42, no. 1 (2018): 36–54.

7. GL, 22–23.

8. Benjamin Morrell Jr., *A Narrative of Four Voyages* (New York: J. & J. Harper, 1832), x, xi.

9. JB, 18, 23.

10. 'Henry Van Meter: Death of a Black Hero of the Revolution', *New National Era*, 23 February 1871, 3.

11. 'Obsequies of a Centenarian', *Bangor Daily Whig*, 15 February 1871; *The Journals of John Edwards Godfrey, Bangor, Maine: 1863–1869* (Rocklane, ME: Courier-Gazette, Inc., 1979), 293; Colin G. Calloway, *The Victory with No Name: The Native American Defeat of the First American Army* (Oxford: Oxford University Press, 2015), 129–164.

12. 'Henry Van Meter', 3. On Philadelphia's Black community in the early nineteenth century, see Erica Armstrong Dunbar, *A Fragile Freedom: African American Women and Emancipation in the Antebellum City* (New Haven, CT: Yale University Press, 2008), 8–69; and Julie Winch, *A Gentleman of Color: The Life of James Forten* (New York: Oxford University Press, 2002), 125–176.

13. Andrew Lipman, *The Saltwater Frontier: Indians and the Contest for the American Coast* (New Haven, CT: Yale University Press, 2015).

14. Nancy Shoemaker, *Native American Whalemen and the World: Indigenous Encounters and the Contingency of Race* (Chapel Hill: University of North Carolina Press, 2015), 1–18, 40–57; Mitch Kachun, *First Martyr of Liberty: Crispus Attucks in American Memory* (Oxford: Oxford University Press, 2017), 21.

15. W. Jeffrey Bolster, *Black Jacks: African American Seamen in the Age of Sail* (Cambridge, MA: Harvard University Press, 1997), 68–101; Philip D. Morgan, 'Black Experiences in Britain's Maritime World', in *Empire, the Sea, and Global History: Britain's Maritime World, c. 1760–c. 1840*, ed. David Cannadine (Houndmills, UK: Palgrave, 2007), 105–133.

16. W. Jeffrey Bolster, '"To Feel Like a Man": Black Seamen in the Northern States, 1800–1860', *Journal of American History* 76, no. 4 (1990): 1173–1199; Charles R. Foy, 'Britain's Black Tars', in *Britain's Black Past*, ed. Gretchen Gerzina (Liverpool, UK: Liverpool University Press, 2020), 63–79; Bolster, *Black Jacks*, 30–31.

17. Gerald Horne, *The Counter-Revolution of 1776: Slave Resistance and the Origins of the United States of America* (New York: New York University Press, 2014), 209–215; Trevor Burnard, *Jamaica in the Age of Revolution* (Philadelphia: University of Pennsylvania Press, 2020), 151–173.

18. Julius Scott, 'Afro-American Sailors and the International Communication Network: The Case of Newport Bowers', in *African Americans and the Haitian Revolution: Selected Essays and Historical Documents*, ed. Maurice Jackson and Jacqueline Bacon (New York: Routledge, 2009), 25–38, 26; Charles R. Foy, 'Seeking Freedom in the Atlantic World, 1713–1783', *Early American Studies* 4, no. 1 (2006): 46–77; Bolster, *Black Jacks*, 131–157.

19. Julius S. Scott, *The Common Wind: Afro-American Currents in the Age of the Haitian Revolution* (London: Verso, 2018); Jane G. Landers, *Atlantic Creoles in the Age of Revolutions* (Cambridge, MA: Harvard University Press, 2010); Sylviane A. Diouf, *Slavery's Exiles: The Story of the American Maroons* (New York: New York University Press, 2014).

20. Brian Rouleau, *With Sails Whitening Every Sea: Mariners and the Making of an American Maritime Empire* (Ithaca, NY: Cornell University Press, 2014), 11; Nicholas Frykman, *The Bloody Flag: Mutiny in the Age of Atlantic Revolution* (Oakland: University of California Press, 2020).

21. Daniel Vickers with Vince Walsh, *Young Men and the Sea: Yankee Seafarers in the Age of Sail* (New Haven, CT: Yale University Press, 2005), 163–198.

22. Ian Urbina, *The Outlaw Ocean: Crime and Survival in the Last Untamed Frontier* (London: Bodley Head, 2019).

23. GL, 27–28; James R. Gibson, *Otter Skins, Boston Ships, and China Goods: The Maritime Fur Trade of the Northwest Coast, 1785–1841* (Seattle: University of Washington Press, 1992), 94–104.

24. GL, 31–50.

25. GL, 61, 106.

26. GL, 109–115, 147.

27. GL, 148–150, 180–181; Paul A. Van Dyke, 'Floating Brothels and the Canton Flower Boats, 1750–1930', *Revista de Cultura* 37 (2011): 112–142.

28. GL, 182–194.

29. GL, 264, 369.

30. Herman Melville, *Moby-Dick* (New York: Norton, 1967), 149–154, 97; Michel Foucault, 'Of Other Spaces', *Diacritics* 16, no. 1 (1986): 22–27.

31. Leon Fink, *Sweatshops at Sea: Merchant Seamen in the World's First Globalized Industry, from 1812 to the Present* (Chapel Hill: University of North Carolina Press, 2011).

32. N. A. M. Rodger, *The Command of the Ocean: A Naval History of Britain, 1649–1815* (London: Allen Lane, 2004), 505–506, 526–527; Suzanne J. Stark, *Female Tars: Women Aboard Ship in the Age of Sail* (London: Pimlico, 2008); David Cordingly, *Women Sailors and Sailors' Women: An Untold Maritime History* (New York: Random House, 2001).

33. Shoemaker, *Native American Whalemen*, 51–56; Amy Parsons, 'Keeping Up with the Morrells: Sailors and the Construction of American Identity in Antebellum Sea Narratives', in *The Sea and Nineteenth-Century Anglophone Literary Culture*, ed. Steve Mentz and Martha Elena Rojas (London: Routledge, 2017), 66–82.

34. Elaine Forman Crane, *Ebb Tide in New England: Women, Seaports, and Social Change, 1630–1800* (Boston: Northeastern University Press, 1998), 102–104; Vickers, *Young Men and the Sea*, 146–156; Norling, *Captain Ahab*, 131–140.

35. Nathaniel Ames, *Nautical Reminiscences* (Providence, RI: William Marshall, 1832), 38.

36. Paul A. Gilje, *Liberty on the Waterfront: American Maritime Culture in the Age of Revolution* (Philadelphia: University of Pennsylvania Press, 2004), 110.

37. Roger N. Buckley, *Slaves in Red Coats: The British West India Regiments, 1795–1815* (New Haven, CT: Yale University Press, 1979).

38. Horne, *Counter-Revolution*, 219–233; Cassandra Pybus, *Epic Journeys of Freedom: Runaway Slaves of the American Revolution and Their Global Quest for Liberty* (Boston: Beacon Press, 2006), 3–55; Robert G. Parkinson, *The Common Cause: Creating Race and Nation in the American Revolution* (Chapel Hill: University of North Carolina Press, 2016), 171–176; Alan Taylor, *The Internal Enemy: Slavery and War in Virginia, 1772–1832* (New York: Norton, 2013).

39. Landers, *Atlantic Creoles*, 233–235; Paul Gilroy, *The Black Atlantic: Modernity and Double Consciousness* (Cambridge, MA: Harvard University Press, 1993), 1–40.

40. Olaudah Equiano, *The Interesting Narrative and Other Writings* (London: Penguin, 2003); Matthew D. Brown, 'Olaudah Equiano and the Sailor's Telegraph: The Interesting Narrative and the Source of Black Abolitionism', *Callaloo* 36, no. 1 (2013): 191–201.

41. Equiano, *Interesting Narrative*, 123.

CHAPTER 2. GETTING CLEAR

1. Francis D. Cogliano, *Emperor of Liberty: Thomas Jefferson's Foreign Policy* (New Haven, CT: Yale University Press, 2014), 204–242.

2. Nicholas Guyatt, 'The United States Between Nation and Empire, 1776–1820', in *The Cambridge History of America and World, Volume 2: 1820–1900*, ed. Kristin Hoganson and Jay Sexton (Cambridge: Cambridge University Press, 2021), 35–59.

3. George Washington, 'Farewell Address', 19 September 1796, FO; Thomas Jefferson to John Jay, 23 August 1785, FO; Jefferson to Washington, 15 March 1784, FO; Thomas Jefferson, 'First Annual Message to Congress', 8 December 1801, FO; Wilson Jeremiah Moses, *Thomas Jefferson: A Modern Prometheus* (Cambridge: Cambridge University Press, 2019), 55–59.

4. 'Alexander Hamilton's Final Version of the Report on the Subject of Manufactures', 5 December 1791, FO.

5. Frank Lambert, *The Barbary Wars: American Independence in the Atlantic World* (New York: Farrar, Straus and Giroux, 2007).

6. Thomas Jefferson to James Monroe, 11 November 1784, FO; Cogliano, *Emperor of Liberty*, 42–75.

7. Lambert, *Barbary Wars*, 71–72.

8. Thomas Jefferson to George Washington, 4 December 1788, FO.

9. Thomas Paine, 'Letters to the Citizens of the United States', in *The Complete Writings of Thomas Paine*, 2 vols., ed. Philip S. Foner (New York: Citadel Press, 1945), 2:909; Brooke Hunter, 'Wheat, War, and the American Economy During the Age of Revolution', *William and Mary Quarterly* 62, no. 3 (2005): 505–526.

10. James Monroe to George Canning, 7 September 1807, in *The Papers of James Monroe, Volume 5*, ed. Daniel Preston (Santa Barbara, CA: ABC-Clio, 2014), 641; Denver Brunsman, *The Evil Necessity: British Naval Impressment in the Eighteenth-Century Atlantic World* (Charlottesville: University of Virginia Press, 2013).

11. N. A. M. Rodger, *The Command of the Ocean: A Naval History of Britain, 1649–1815* (London: Allen Lane, 2004), 396; James Davey, *In Nelson's Wake: How the Royal Navy Ruled the Waves after Trafalgar* (New Haven, CT: Yale University Press, 2015), 20–24; Sara Caputo, 'Alien Seamen in the British Navy, British Law, and the British State, c. 1793–c. 1815', *Historical Journal* 62, no. 3 (2019): 685–707.

12. Rodger, *Command of the Ocean*, 396–398, 497–500; J. Ross Dancy, *The Myth of the Press Gang: Volunteers, Impressment and the Naval Manpower Problem in the Late Eighteenth Century* (Woodbridge, UK: Boydell Press, 2015), 120–156.

13. Rodger, *Command of the Ocean*, 398–399, 497; Davey, *In Nelson's Wake*, 26. (Davey claims that desertion rates were so high that naval service was a 'voluntary profession'.) Brunsman, *Evil Necessity*, 171–209; Dancy, *Myth of the Press Gang*, 128–131.

14. Sara Caputo, 'Foreign Seamen and the British Navy' (PhD diss., University of Cambridge, 2019), 55–56, 103–104; Daniel Vickers with Vince Walsh, *Young Men and the Sea: Yankee Seafarers in the Age of Sail* (New Haven, CT: Yale University Press, 2005), 178–179; Alan Taylor, *The Internal Enemy: Slavery and War in Virginia, 1772–1832* (New York: Norton, 2013), 122–123.

15. Taylor, *Internal Enemy*, 124.

16. 'John Backus', box 1, RIS; Nathan Perl-Rosenthal, *Citizen Sailors: Becoming American in the Age of Revolution* (Cambridge, MA: Harvard University Press, 2015), 172–190; James Monroe, secretary of state, told Congress in 1813 that 106,757 SPCs had been issued by Custom Houses between 1796 and 1812: Monroe to Congress, 18 February 1813, in *Annals of Congress*, 12th Cong., 2 sess., 93.

17. 'James Madison to Customs Collectors', 1 October 1803, FO.

18. James Madison to Anthony Merry, 7 July 1805, FO; Merry to Madison, 6 September 1804, FO.

19. James Madison to James Monroe, 6 March 1805, FO; Perl-Rosenthal, *Citizen Sailors*, 183, 186–187; Paul A. Gilje, *Free Trade and Sailors' Rights in the War of 1812* (Cambridge: Cambridge University Press, 2013), 110–112.

20. 'Remarks on American Commerce', enclosure to Jacob Crowninshield to Thomas Jefferson, 30 December 1803, FO.

21. Cogliano, *Emperor of Liberty*, 236–242.

22. Samuel Harrison to Thomas Jefferson, 28 May 1808; Thomas Jefferson to John Armstrong, 6 March 1809, FO.

23. Daniel Baker to his family, 20 June 1812, 'Daniel Baker', box 1, RIS; Cogliano, *Emperor of Liberty*, 213–214.

24. John Williamson to David Gilson, 22 May 1809, 'John Williamson', box 11, RIS; Perl-Rosenthal, *Citizen Sailors*, 234; Henry Conway to Thomas Jefferson, 10 October 1808, FO.

25. Affidavit of Gertrude Hupert, 22 May 1812, 'Jacob Baird', box 1, RIS; Brunsman, *Evil Necessity*, 192–193.

26. Jane Burk to Thomas Burk, 22 February 1812, 'Thomas Burk', box 2, RIS; Sarah Siters to John Siters, 27 April 1812, 'John Siters', box 9, RIS; E. Siters to John Siters, 27 April 1812, 'John Siters', box 9, RIS.

27. Thomas Tebbs to Robert Smith, 2 May 1809, 'Thomas Tebbs', box 10, RIS; Nathaniel Blake to William Blake, 11 September 1808, 'Thomas Tebbs', box 2, RIS.

28. Elisha Gordon to James Monroe, 20 December 1813, 'George Barrett', box 1, RIS.

29. Perl-Rosenthal, *Citizen Sailors*, 195–197.

30. Cogliano, *Emperor of Liberty*, 227–230; Taylor, *Internal Enemy*, 121–122.

31. Cogliano, *Emperor of Liberty*, 204–207; Max Grivno, *Gleanings of Freedom: Free and Slave Labour Along the Mason-Dixon Line, 1790–1860* (Urbana: University of Illinois Press, 2011), 60–61; Affidavit of Benjamin Davis, 13 July 1807, 'Romulus Ware/Daniel Martin', box 10, RIS; Affidavit of William Bruce, 18 July 1807, 'Romulus Ware/Daniel Martin', box 10, RIS.

32. [John Lowell], *Peace Without Dishonour: Being a Calm and Dispassionate Enquiry into the Question of the Chesapeake* (Boston: Greenough and Stebbins, 1807), 16, 17.

33. Taylor, *Internal Enemy*, 125–128.

34. Stephen Shacken to James Monroe, 8 May 1812, 'Shepard Bourn', box 2, RIS; Henry Dering to James Monroe, 25 May 1812, 'Silas Cuffee', box 3, RIS; Jacob Israel Potter to [James Monroe], 25 November 1811, 'Jacob Israel Potter', box 2, RIS.

35. For the assumption that US patriotism was a default for American sailors, see Elizabeth Jones-Minsinger, '"Our Rights Are Getting More & More Infringed Upon": American Nationalism, Identity, and Sailors' Justice in British Prisons During the War of 1812', *Journal of the Early Republic* 37, no. 3 (Fall 2017): 471–505. On the tendency of printed sailors' narratives to tidy up questions of patriotism, see Myra C. Glenn, *Jack Tar's Story: The Autobiographies and Memoirs of Sailors in Antebellum America* (Cambridge: Cambridge University Press, 2010), 56–60, 73, 80.

36. Caputo, 'Alien Seamen', 691.

37. James Brown to Joseph Thompson, n.d. [late 1811?], 'James Brown', box 2, RIS; Enoch Chapman to Samuel Chapman, 15 May 1811, 'Enoch Chapman', box 3, RIS; Affidavit of John Worthington, 25 April 1809, 'William Worthington', box 11, RIS.

38. Peyton Page to his brother 'or brothers or niece or any of his relations', 'Peyton R. Page', box 8, RIS.

39. Peyton Page to his brother 'or brothers or niece or any of his relations', 'Peyton R. Page', box 8, RIS; Muster Book of HMS *Warspite*, March–November 1811, Admiralty Records (ADM) 37/2883, TNA. The muster book confirms that Page had become 'second master' as of 18 October 1811.

CHAPTER 3. SPARE THE VANQUISHED

1. David R. Fisher, 'Thomas Tyrwhitt', in *History of Parliament: The House of Commons, 1790–1820*, 5 vols., ed. R. G. Thorne (London: Secker and Warburg, 1986), 5:422–423; 'Sir Thomas Tyrwhitt', *Gentleman's Magazine*, March 1833, 275–276.

2. E. A. Smith, *George IV* (New Haven, CT: Yale University Press, 1999), 73; J. Brooking-Rowe, 'Sir Thomas Tyrwhitt and Princetown', *Report and Transactions of the Devonshire Association* 7, second series (1905): 465–481; Fisher, 'Tyrwhitt'.

3. 'His Royal Highness', *Exeter Flying Post*, 4 July 1805, 4; Matthew Kelly, *Quartz and Feldspar: Dartmoor, a British Landscape in Modern Times* (London: Jonathan Cape, 2015), 115–120.

4. Benjamin Franklin to Benjamin Vaughan, 10 July 1782, FO. On the development of European and American thinking about war captivity, see Philippe Contamine, 'The Growth of State Control: Practices of War, 1300–1800: Ransom and Booty', in *War and Competition Between States*, ed. Philippe Contamine (Oxford: Oxford University Press, 2000), 163–194; T. Cole Jones, *Captives of Liberty: Prisoners of War and the Politics of Vengeance in the American Revolution* (Philadelphia: University of Pennsylvania Press, 2020), 12–44; and Renaud Morieux, *The Society of Prisoners: Anglo-French Wars and Incarceration in the Eighteenth Century* (Oxford: Oxford University Press, 2019).

5. Francis D. Cogliano, *American Maritime Prisoners in the Revolutionary War: The Captivity of William Russell* (Annapolis, MD: Naval Institute Press, 2001), 120–132; Judith I. Madera, 'Floating Prisons: Dispossession, Ordering, and Colonial Atlantic "States," 1776–1783', in *Buried Lives: Incarcerated in Early America*, ed. Michele Lise Tarter and Richard Bell (Athens: University of Georgia Press, 2012), 175–202; Roger Knight, *Britain Against Napoleon: The Organisation of Victory, 1793–1815* (London: Allen Lane, 2013), 155; Morieux, *Society of Prisoners*, 200–205.

6. Randall McGowen, 'The Well-Ordered Prison: England, 1780–1865', in *The Oxford History of the Prison: The Practice of Punishment in Western Society*, ed. Norval Morris and David J. Rothman (New York: Oxford University Press, 1995), 111–129; A. Roger Ekirch, *Bound for America: The Transportation of British Convicts to the Colonies, 1718–1775* (Oxford: Clarendon Press, 1987).

7. John Howard, *The State of the Prisons in England and Wales*, 4th ed. (London: J. Johnson, C. Dilly, and T. Cadell, 1792), 10, 218–219, 238, 363; Tessa West, *The Curious Mr Howard: Legendary Prison Reformer* (Sherfield on Loddon, UK: Waterside Press, 2011); Kevin Siena, *Rotten Bodies: Class & Contagion in 18th Century Britain* (New Haven, CT: Yale University Press, 2019), 145, 154–165; Michael Meranze, *Laboratories of*

Virtue: Punishment, Revolution, and Authority in Philadelphia, 1760–1835 (Chapel Hill: University of North Carolina Press, 1996), 139–142.

8. Howard, *State of the Prisons*, 11; Morieux, *Society of Prisoners*, 20–21, 92–93.

9. Knight, *Britain Against Napoleon*, 21–56.

10. Knight, *Britain Against Napoleon*, 109–111, 176–179; Roger Morriss, *The Foundations of British Maritime Ascendancy: Resources, Logistics and the State, 1755–1815* (Cambridge: Cambridge University Press, 2010), 335–337; *Ninth Report of the Commissioners for Revising and Digesting the Civil Affairs of His Majesty's Navy* (London: House of Commons, 1809), 6.

11. Knight, *Britain Against Napoleon*, 177, 180; Roger Knight and Martin Wilcox, *Sustaining the Fleet: War, the British Navy, and the Contractor State* (Woodbridge, UK: Boydell Press, 2010), 1–18.

12. *Ninth Report*, 24; Knight, *Britain Against Napoleon*, 155.

13. Morieux, *Society of Prisoners*, 12–13; James Davey, *In Nelson's Wake: How the Royal Navy Ruled the Waves after Trafalgar* (New Haven, CT: Yale University Press, 2015), 170–171.

14. *Ninth Report*, 22–25.

15. Morieux, *Society of Prisoners*, 185, 206; Harold Mytum and Naomi Hall, 'Norman Cross: Designing and Operating an Eighteenth-Century British Prisoner of War Camp', in *Prisoners of War: Archaeology, Memory, and Heritage of 19th- and 20th-Century Mass Internment*, ed. Harold Mytum and Gilly Carr (New York: Springer, 2013), 75–91.

16. Morriss, *Foundations*, 340.

17. 'Lease of Land Parcel of the Duchy of Cornwall to Be Used as the Site for a War Prison', 10 March 1806, TS 21/285, TNA; Kelly, *Quartz and Feldspar*, 114.

18. 'To Builders, etc.: Prison of War, Dartmoor', *London Morning Chronicle*, 21 October 1805, 1; Paul Chamberlain, *Hell Upon Water: Prisoners of War in Britain, 1793–1815* (Stroud, UK: History Press, 2008), 94–95; Basil Thomson, *The Story of Dartmoor Prison* (London: William Heinemann, 1907), 3–4; Brooking-Rowe, 'Sir Thomas Tyrwhitt', 471–472; Roland Ennos, *The Age of Wood: Our Most Useful Material and the Construction of Civilization* (New York: Scribner, 2020), 199–200.

19. 'D.A. Alexander, Esq.', *Gentleman's Magazine*, 26 (August 1846): 210–213; *Oxford Dictionary of National Biography*, s.v. 'Daniel Asher Alexander', by Annette Peach, 23 September 2004, accessed 18 May 2021; Dana Arnold, *Reading Architectural History* (London: Routledge, 2002), 61.

20. 'Description of the New Prison of War, Dartmoor, Devon', *Repository of Arts, Literature and Commerce*, 21 (September 1810): 161–163.

21. Jeremy Bentham, *Panopticon; or, The Inspection House* (Dublin: T. Payne, 1791), 1–12; Janet Semple, *Bentham's Prison: A Study of the Panopticon Penitentiary* (Oxford: Oxford University Press, 1993).

22. Will of Jeremy Bentham, 21 June 1832, PROB 11/1801/468, TNA; Michel Foucault, *Discipline and Punish: The Birth of the Prison*, trans. Alan Sheridan (London: Penguin, 1991), 200.

23. Semple, *Bentham's Prison*, 99–100; Roger Morriss, *Science, Utility and Maritime Power: Samuel Bentham in Russia, 1779–91* (Abingdon, UK: Routledge, 2016), 177–178; Simon Werrett, 'Potemkin and the Panopticon: Samuel Bentham and the Architecture

of Absolutism in Eighteenth Century Russia', *Journal of Bentham Studies*, UCL Bentham Project, vol. 2 (1999); Morieux, *Society of Prisoners*, 227–229.

24. Bentham, *Panopticon*, 14, 17; Morieux, *Society of Prisoners*, 227.

25. Howard, *State of the Prisons*, 22; Bentham, *Panopticon*, 35; Allan Brodie, Jane Croom, and James O. Davies, *English Prisons: An Architectural History* (Swindon, UK: English Heritage, 2002), 33–35; Robin Evans, *The Fabrication of Virtue: English Prison Architecture, 1750–1840* (Cambridge: Cambridge University Press, 1982), 195–235.

26. 'Testimony of Daniel Alexander to the Committee on the Prisons', 15 April 1818, *Report from the Committee on the Prisons Within the City of London and Borough of Southwark*, 8 May 1818, *Parliamentary Papers*, 392 (1818): 178–181, 180.

27. Evans, *Fabrication of Virtue*, 118–131; Philip Steadman, *Building Types and Built Forms* (Kibworth Beachamp, UK: Matador, 2014), 306–311; Brodie, Croom, and Davies, *English Prisons*, 41–49, 56.

28. Luigi Ficacci, ed., *Giovanni Battista Piranesi: The Complete Etchings* (Köln, Germany: Taschen, 2016), 148–173; Susan Stewart, *The Ruins Lesson: Meaning and Material in Western Culture* (Chicago: Chicago University Press, 2020), 192–193.

29. Morton D. Paley, *Samuel Taylor Coleridge and the Fine Arts* (Oxford: Oxford University Press, 2008), 169–170; Susan Stewart, *Crimes of Writing: Problems in the Containment of Representation* (Oxford: Oxford University Press, 1991), 155–167.

30. 'Testimony of Daniel Alexander', 184; Thomson, *Story of Dartmoor Prison*, 4–9.

31. Semple, *Bentham's Prison*, 282–308; Kelly, *Quartz and Feldspar*, 115–120.

32. Thomson, *Story of Dartmoor Prison*, 7–8.

33. 'The First West York Militia', *Yorkshire Herald*, 7 May 1808, 2; Ambrose Serle to Transport Office, 22 August 1808, Reports of Visitations of Prisoner-of-War Depots and Hospitals by Members of the Transport Board, Admiralty Records (ADM) 105/44, TNA; Thomson, *Story of Dartmoor Prison*, 8–9.

34. Board to Isaac Cotgrave, 20 September 1808, 13 April 1809, 14 April 1809, 18 April 1809, 25 April 1809, 8 May 1809, TBOL, ADM 98/225, TNA; 'Upwards of Seven Hundred French Prisoners', *Edinburgh Advertiser*, 2 June 1809, 4; Thomson, *Story of Dartmoor Prison*, 10.

35. GEBF, ADM 103/92, no. 1.

36. *Virgil: Eclogues, Georgics, Aeneid, Books 1–6*, trans. H. Rushton Fairclough, revised by G. P. Goold, Loeb Classical Library 63 (Cambridge, MA: Harvard University Press, 1916), 593.

CHAPTER 4. AMONG THE ROMANS

1. Transport Board to Isaac Cotgrave, 2 February 1810, TBOL, Admiralty Records (ADM) 98/225, TNA.

2. GEBF, ADM 103/93–103/95.

3. 'Description of the New Prison of War, Dartmoor, Devon', *Repository of Arts, Literature, Commerce*, 21 (September 1810): 161–163.

4. 'Description of the New Prison of War', 161–163.

5. *The Commissioned Sea Officers of the Royal Navy, 1660–1815*, ed. David B. Smith et al., 3 vols. (London: National Maritime Museum, 1954), 1:201; 'Margaret Cotgrave',

Certificates Submitted by Applicants to the Charity, ADM 6/352/27, TNA; *Morning Post* (London), 19 August 1801, 1–2.

6. *Cork Mercantile Chronicle*, 3 June 1803, 3; 'Plymouth', *Exeter Post*, 15 April 1806, 4; 'Villeneuve, Pierre Charles Jean Baptiste Silvestre, Comte de', in *The Oxford Companion to Ships and the Sea*, online edition, ed. I. C. B. Dear and Peter Kemp (Oxford: Oxford University Press, 2006).

7. 'Ship News', *London Morning Chronicle*, 7 September 1808, 3; 'Instructions for Agents for Prisoners of War at Home', *Thirteenth Report of the Commissioners for Revising and Digesting the Civil Affairs of His Majesty's Navy*, 22 December 1807, *19th Century House of Commons Sessional Papers*, 128 (1809): 103–113.

8. Transport Board to Cotgrave, 21 June 1809, 28 November 1809, TBOL, ADM 98/225.

9. *Transport Office: Estimate of the Money That Will Be Wanted for the Several Services of This Office for the Year 1814*, 6 April 1814, *Nineteenth Century House of Commons Sessional Papers*, 110 (1814): 13–14; Renaud Morieux, *The Society of Prisoners: Anglo-French Wars and Incarceration in the Eighteenth Century* (Oxford: Oxford University Press, 2019), 286–287.

10. 'Instructions for Agents', 105. "Plymouth," *Edinburgh Advertiser*, 2 June 1809, 4.

11. 'Instructions for Agents', 107; *Instructions to Agents for Prisoners of War at Home* (London: Philanthropic Society, 1809), 20–21; Morieux, *Society of Prisoners*, 338–349.

12. 'Rules to Be Observed at the Market', *Instructions for Dispensers* (London: Philanthropic Society, 1809), no. 37 [n.p.]; Basil Thomson, *The Story of Dartmoor Prison* (London: William Heinemann, 1907), 66–67. The guillotine model is in the Harmsworth Collection, Port of Plymouth gallery, The Box, Plymouth, England.

13. Board to Cotgrave, 29 October 1808, 3 May 1810, TBOL, ADM 98/225, 21 December 1810, TBOL, ADM 98/226, TNA. Margaret Cotgrave gave birth to thirteen children between 1781 and 1806, nine of whom survived to adulthood. I'm grateful to Paul Finegan of the Dartmoor Prison Museum for sharing his biographical research on the Cotgrave family.

14. *Instructions to Agents*, 5; Board to Cotgrave, 31 August 1809, 5 September 1809, ADM 98/225; Randall McGowen, 'The Well-Ordered Prison: England, 1780–1865', in *The Oxford History of the Prison: The Practice of Punishment in Western Society*, ed. Norval Morris and David J. Rothman (New York: Oxford University Press, 1995), 81–82.

15. Board to Cotgrave, 31 December 1810, 7 January 1811, 15 January 1811, 18 January 1811, 18 May 1811, 21 August 1811, TBOL, ADM 98/226.

16. Board to Cotgrave, 22 August 1810, 6 December 1810, 11 December 1810, 27 December 1811, TBOL, ADM 98/226; 'Account of the New Prison of War at Dartmoor', *Hull Packet*, 9 October 1810, 4.

17. Board to Cotgrave, 5 July 1811, 10 July 1811, 8 August 1811, 14 November 1811, TBOL, ADM 98/226; Board to Cotgrave, 10 January 1812, TBOL, ADM 98/227, TNA; Thomson, *Story of Dartmoor Prison*, 26–27.

18. GEBF, ADM 103/93; Louis Catel, *La Prison de Dartmoor*, 2 vols. (Paris: Chez Les Principaux Libraires, 1847).

19. Catel, *La Prison*, 2:122–123; Thomson, *Story of Dartmoor Prison*, 45–58; Morieux, *Society of Prisoners*, 323.

20. Catel, *La Prison*, 1:21–24. The first mention of escape in the board's correspondence with the agent is from June, when the board approved 'the means suggested by you for preventing the escape of prisoners'. Board to Cotgrave, 30 June 1809, TBOL, ADM 98/225.

21. Board to Cotgrave, 30 June 1809, 22 July 1809, 8 August 1809, 11 August 1809, 18 September 1809, 22 September 1809, TBOL, ADM 98/225; Board to Cotgrave, 3 October 1810, 27 October 1810, ADM 98/226; Board to Cotgrave, 11 April 1812, TBOL, ADM 98/227.

22. Board to Cotgrave, 3 October 1809, 21 November 1809, 7 December 1809, 9 January 1810, 15 January 1810, 25 January 1810, 24 February 1810, 15 March 1810, TBOL, ADM 98/225; Catel, *La Prison*, 1:263–264; 'A Considerable Number of Counterfeit Pieces', *Times of London*, 28 October 1809, 2.

23. Board to Cotgrave, 20 October 1812, TBOL, ADM 98/227; 'The Governor of Dartmoor Prison', *Jackson's Oxford Journal*, 15 December 1810, 4; Morieux, *Society of Prisoners*, 323–325.

24. Catel, *La Prison*, 2:127–132; 'Testimony of William Dyker to the Committee on the Prisons', 22 April 1818, *Report from the Committee on the Prisons Within the City of London and Borough of Southwark*, 8 May 1818, *Parliamentary Papers*, 392 (1818): 194–195.

25. Catel, *La Prison*, 2:137–138; Thomson, *Story of Dartmoor Prison*, 89.

26. Register of French Prisoners of War Who Have Died at Dartmoor, ADM 103/623, TNA; Harold Mytum and Naomi Hall, 'Norman Cross: Designing and Operating an Eighteenth-Century British Prisoner of War Camp', in *Prisoners of War: Archaeology, Memory, and Heritage of 19th- and 20th-Century Mass Internment*, ed. Harold Mytum and Gilly Carr (New York: Springer, 2013), 90.

27. David Cordingly, *Cochrane the Dauntless: The Life and Adventures of Admiral Thomas Cochrane, 1775–1860* (London: Bloomsbury, 2007).

28. Thomas Cochrane, Speech to the House of Commons, 14 June 1811, *Hansard Parliamentary Debates*, first series, vol. 20 (1811): 634–638; Cordingly, *Cochrane the Dauntless*, 229.

29. James Stephen, Remarks in the House of Commons, 14 June 1811, *Hansard Parliamentary Debates*, first series, vol. 20 (1811): 639. Thomas Tyrwhitt, Speech to the House of Commons, 18 June 1811, *Hansard Parliamentary Debates*, first series, vol. 20 (1811): 697; 'Dartmoor Prison', *Examiner*, 11 August 1811, 520–521; 'Dartmoor Depot', *Examiner*, 25 August 1811, 553–554; 'Dartmoor Depot', *Examiner*, 1 September 1811, 568–569; 'Dartmoor', *Examiner*, 29 September 1811, 629–630; 'Dartmoor', *Examiner*, 6 October 1811, 644–645.

30. Board to Cotgrave, 4 April 1812, 15 April 1812, 1 May 1812, 28 May 1812, 25 August 1812, 31 August 1812, TBOL, ADM 98/227.

31. Board to Cotgrave, 17 August 1810, TBOL, ADM 98/226; Board to Cotgrave, 25 July 1812, TBOL, ADM 98/227; C. W. Pasley, *An Inquiry into the System of General or Commissariat Contracts* (Chatham, UK: William Wildash, 1825), 51; Oliver C. Pope to Lewis P. Clover, 3 June 1876, Oliver C. Pope Papers, Burton Historical Collection Manuscripts, 1 LMS, Detroit Public Library.

32. 'Insurrection of the French Prisoners at Dartmoor Depot', *London Morning Chronicle*, 17 September 1812, 2.

33. 'Insurrection of the French Prisoners at Dartmoor Depot', *London Morning Chronicle*, 17 September 1812, 2; 'Provincial Intelligence', *Examiner*, 20 September 1812, 596–597; 'A Disturbance at Dartmoor', *Exeter Flying Post*, 17 September 1812, 4; Thomson, *Story of Dartmoor Prison*, 89–90.

34. 'Provincial Intelligence', *Examiner*, 20 September 1812, 597.

PART II. KING DICK AT BORDEAUX

1. Rory Muir, *Wellington: The Path to Victory, 1769–1814* (New Haven, CT: Yale University Press, 2014), 573–575.

2. Faye M. Kert, *Privateering: Patriots and Profits in the War of 1812* (Baltimore: Johns Hopkins University Press, 2015). The *Requin* does not appear in the list of more than six hundred US privateers in Kert's online appendix: https://jhupbooks.press.jhu.edu /public/books_pdfs/kert_privateering_appendix_2_-table.pdf.

3. *Papers Relating to the Capture of the Ship 'Requin' in the River Garonne*, March 1814, *Nineteenth Century House of Commons Sessional Papers*, 469 (1823).

4. *Papers Relating to the Capture*, 9–10, 12–14; William Francis Patrick Napier, *History of the War in the Peninsula and in the South of France, from the Year 1807 to the Year 1814*, 5 vols. (New York: A.C. Armstrong & Son, 1882), 5:167–168.

5. The crew members of the *Requin* were entered into the Dartmoor register in October 1814 as prisoners 4148–4150, 4242–4249, 4604–4605: GEBA, Admiralty Records (ADM) 103/90. (Richard Crafus was Dartmoor prisoner no. 4603.) On Scipio Bartlett, see Jack Darrell Crowder, *African Americans and American Indians in the Revolutionary War* (Jefferson, NC: McFarland, 2019), 20–21; and Mary Walton Ferris, *Dawes-Gates Ancestral Lines*, 2 vols. (n.p., privately printed, 1931), 2:79, 89, 91.

6. *Papers Relating to the Capture*, 9–10, 12.

7. *Papers Relating to the Capture*, 23–26.

8. Arthur, Duke of Wellington, to Charles Stuart, 6 December 1815, in Arthur Richard Wellesley Wellington, ed., *Supplementary Despatches, Correspondence, and Memoranda of Field Marshal Arthur, Duke of Wellington, Volume the Fourteenth* (London: John Murray, 1872), 605–606; Thomas Fowell Buxton, Henry King, and F. J. Robinson, speeches to the House of Commons, 2 July 1823, *Hansard Parliamentary Debates*, second series, vol. 9 (1823): 1406–1412.

CHAPTER 5. THE UNHALLOWED PURSUIT

1. GL, 195–196.

2. GL, 196–198; Edgardo Pérez Morales, *No Limits to Their Sway: Cartagena's Privateers and the Masterless Caribbean in the Age of Revolutions* (Nashville, TN: Vanderbilt University Press, 2018).

3. GL, 198–199.

4. Thomas Jefferson to William Duane, 4 August 1812, FO; William P. Leeman, *The Long Road to Annapolis: The Founding of the Naval Academy and the Emerging American Republic* (Chapel Hill: University of North Carolina Press, 2010), 11–48.

5. Thomas Jefferson to Tadeusz Kosciuszko, 28 June 1812, Thomas Jefferson to James Monroe, 1 January 1815, FO; Leeman, *Long Road*, 40–48; Donald R. Hickey, *The War*

of 1812: A Forgotten Conflict, Bicentennial Edition (Urbana: University of Illinois Press, 2012), 305.

6. Jefferson to Theodorus Bailey, 6 February 1813, FO; Leeman, *Long Road*, 70; Faye M. Kert, *Privateering: Patriots and Profits in the War of 1812* (Baltimore: Johns Hopkins University Press, 2015), 9–15; Alan Taylor, *The Civil War of 1812: American Citizens, British Subjects, Irish Rebels, & Indian Allies* (New York: Knopf, 2010), 363–364.

7. GL, 200–216.

8. GL, 216–220.

9. GL, 224–227. Little's memoir confidently claimed the *Paul Jones* had been seized on 14 December 1812. The Dartmoor register confirms that Little and his crew mates were actually captured on 23 May 1813. GEBA, no. 1367, Admiralty Records (ADM) 103/88, TNA.

10. BFB, 1:31–39, 1:31–32; Daniel Vickers with Vince Walsh, *Young Men and the Sea: Yankee Seafarers in the Age of Sail* (New Haven, CT: Yale University Press, 2005), 172.

11. BFB, 1:35; 'Memoir of Capt. William Nichols, of Newburyport', *Historical Collections of the Essex Institute* 6 (December 1864): 229–236, 236; Benjamin F. Browne, 'Some Notes upon Mr Rantoul's Reminiscences', *Historical Collections of the Essex Institute* 5 (October 1863): 197–202, 198.

12. BFB, 2:97–111, 2:98–100.

13. BFB, 2:105–106.

14. BFB, 2:106–107.

15. Taylor, *Civil War of 1812*, 362–365; Kert, *Privateering*, 101–102; Ira Dye, 'American Maritime Prisoners of War, 1812–1815', in *Ships, Seafaring and Society: Essays in Maritime History*, ed. Timothy J. Runyan (Detroit: Wayne State University Press, 1987), 293–320. The estimate of naval personnel at Dartmoor is based on my transcription of the five volumes of GEBA.

16. DBFP, 2–4.

17. DBFP, 6, 12, 31.

18. DBFP, 36–37, 44; Register of Deaths of American Prisoners of War at Bermuda, ADM 103/619, TNA.

19. Taylor, *Civil War of 1812*, 364; Brian Cuthbertson, *Melville Prison & Deadman's Island: American and French Prisoners of War in Halifax, 1794–1816* (Halifax, NS: Formac Publishing Company, 2009), 13–17.

20. DBFP, 56, 77, 67.

21. BFB, 2:108–109.

22. BFB, 111; Renaud Morieux, *The Society of Prisoners: Anglo-French Wars and Incarceration in the Eighteenth Century* (Oxford: Oxford University Press, 2019), 240–253.

23. [Benjamin F. Browne], *The Yarn of a Yankee Privateer, edited by Nathaniel Hawthorne* (New York: Funk and Wagnalls Company, 1926), 93, 102–104, 112.

24. [Browne], *Yarn of a Yankee Privateer*, 107–111, 113.

25. Partha Chatterjee, *The Black Hole of Empire: History of a Global Practice of Power* (Princeton, NJ: Princeton University Press, 2012), 1–32; BW, 30.

26. 'Another Veteran Seaman Gone', *Newark (OH) Advocate*, 26 May 1858; 'Obituary of Capt. John T. Trowbridge', *Cleveland Herald*, 8 May 1858; Alexander Mikaberidze, *The Napoleonic Wars: A Global History* (Oxford: Oxford University Press, 2020), 497–498.

27. 'Another Veteran Seaman Gone'; 'New York, April 3', *Norwich (CT) Courier*, 17 April 1811.

28. 'Memoir of Lewis P. Clover', *United States Magazine and Democratic Review*, March 1850, 260–265, 261–262; 'Lewis P. Clover', *Frank Leslie's Illustrated Newspaper*, 13 April 1861, 324–325; GEBA, ADM 103/90, no. 5392.

29. LPC, 1:146–151; LPC, 2:356–360, 2:356.

30. LPC, 2:356–358.

31. LPC, 1:150.

32. Speeches of Felix Grundy, Charles Goldsborough, and Israel Pickens, 3 February, 12 February, 5 February 1813, *Annals of Congress*, 12th Cong., 2nd sess. (House), 962–963, 1052, 1007; Leon Fink, *Sweatshops at Sea: Merchant Seamen in the World's First Globalized Industry, from 1812 to the Present* (Chapel Hill: University of North Carolina Press, 2011), 18–23.

33. Speeches of Josiah Quincy and Charles Goldsborough, 12 February 1813, in *Annals of Congress*, 12th Cong., 2nd sess. (House), 1042, 1047.

34. Taylor, *Civil War of 1812*, 327; Alan Taylor, *The Internal Enemy: Slavery and War in Virginia, 1772–1832* (New York: Norton, 2013), 271–273; Gene Allen Smith, *The Slaves' Gamble: Choosing Sides in the War of 1812* (New York: Palgrave Macmillan, 2013), 38–39, 43–44, 94–95.

35. William Lee to James Madison, 28 January 1814, FO. My account of the imprisoned men is taken from their testimony accompanying James Prince to John Mason, 19 April 1814, box 3, folder 5, RAG.

36. James Prince to John Mason, 19 April 1814, box 3, folder 5, RAG.

37. List of British Prisoners of War Captured by the United States During the War of 1812, ADM 103/466, TNA, no. 518.

CHAPTER 6. MISTER BEASTLY

1. TPM, 17, 22.

2. TPM, 25; Basil Thomson, *The Story of Dartmoor Prison* (London: William Heinemann, 1907), 99.

3. Board to Cotgrave, 16 February 1813, TBOL, Admiralty Records (ADM) 98/227; Thomson, *Story of Dartmoor Prison*, 99, 73.

4. TPM, 25–26, 54.

5. LPC, 3:521; Jonathan Russell to James Monroe, 3 September 1812, *American State Papers, Foreign Relations*, 6 vols. (Washington, DC: Gale & Seaton, 1832), 3:590.

6. Charles Stuart Kennedy, *The American Consul: A History of the United States Consular Service, 1776–1914* (New York: Greenwood Press, 1990), 19–28, 41–49; Matthew Taylor Rafferty, *The Republic Afloat: Law, Honor, and Citizenship in Maritime America* (Chicago: University of Chicago Press, 2013), 151–173; Nicole M. Phelps, 'One Service, Three Systems, Many Empires: The U.S. Consular Service and the Growth of U.S. Global Power, 1789–1924', in *Crossing Empires: Taking U.S. History into Transimperial*

Terrain, ed. Kristin L. Hoganson and Jay Sexton (Durham, NC: Duke University Press, 2020), 135–158.

7. Philip Slaughter, *A History of Bristol Parish, Va.* (Richmond, VA: J. W. Randolph & English, 1879), 233; David L. Holmes, 'Devereux Jarratt: A Letter and a Reevaluation', *Historical Magazine of the Protestant Episcopal Church* 47, no. 1 (1978): 37–49, 48; Editor's note, Reuben Beasley to Thomas Jefferson, 29 September 1817, in *The Papers of Thomas Jefferson, Retirement Series, Vol 12*, ed. J. Jefferson Looney (Princeton, NJ: Princeton University Press, 2015), 43–44.

8. Reuben Beasley to James Madison, undated [July 1816?], FO; 'Virginia: At a Superior Court of Chancery', *Richmond Enquirer*, 29 July 1823, 4; 'Virginia', *Virginia Argus*, 18 March 1815, 4; 'Bell & Others vs. Reed', *Richmond Enquirer*, 5 June 1812, 3.

9. Silvia Marzagalli, 'Was Warfare Necessary for the Functioning of Eighteenth-Century Colonial Systems? Some Reflections on the Necessity of Cross-Imperial and Foreign Trade in the French Case', in *Beyond Empires: Global, Self-Organizing, Cross-Imperial Networks, 1500–1800*, ed. Cátia A. P. Antunes and Amelia Polónia (Leiden, the Netherlands: Brill, 2016), 253–277, 271.

10. Nathan Perl-Rosenthal, *Citizen Sailors: Becoming American in the Age of Revolution* (Cambridge, MA: Harvard University Press, 2015), 213–216.

11. 'Society of Friends of Foreigners in Distress', *Observer*, 19 April 1812, 1.

12. JB, 32–35.

13. JB, 35–38, 49.

14. JB, 51–53.

15. JB, 53–56.

16. Jonathan Russell to Reuben G. Beasley, 14 September 1812, box 2, folder 2, RAG.

17. Jonathan Russell to Reuben G. Beasley, 14 September 1812, Beasley to James Monroe, 28 October 1812, box 2, folder 2, RAG.

18. Beasley, 'Circular', 31 May 1813, box 7, folder 2, RAG.

19. John Barrow to the Transport Board, 5 March 1812, in *Barbarities of the Enemy* (Worcester: Isaac Sturtevant for Remark Dunnell, 1814), 57; Beasley to Alexander McLeay, 9 March 1813, box 7, folder 2, RAG. See also the board's letters to Beasley from November 1812 to February 1813 in Letters from the Office of the Commissioners of Sick and Wounded Seamen to the U.S. Agent in Britain (Reuben Beasley), ADM 98/291, TNA.

20. Potter to James Monroe, 2 July 1813, 'Jacob Israel Potter', box 2, RIS. Other Dartmoor prisoners in the RIS who named Beasley in their pleas for paperwork to obtain their release include John Douglas, Elijah Fargo, Prince Freeman (box 4), Daniel Davis (box 5, in 'Robert Godman' folder), John Wempole Peak (box 8), and David Wingate (box 11).

21. Report of the Secretary of State, 14 April 1814, *American State Papers, Foreign Affairs*, 3:630–632; Beasley to James Monroe, 1 September 1813, box 9, folder 3, RAG.

22. Beasley to James Monroe, 1 September 1813, Alexander McLeay to Beasley, 24 November 1813, box 2, folder 2, RAG. (We can identify HMS *Pomone* from the prisoner's entry in the Dartmoor register: William Dews was no. 2050 in GEBA, ADM 130/88.) Beasley to James Monroe, 10 June 1813, box 7, folder 2, RAG. By March 1814,

Beasley had received only twenty-one replies to his 230 applications for the release of impressed sailors: Beasley to John Mason, 24 March 1814, box 9, folder 4, RAG.

23. James Brown to Captain Joseph Thompson, n.d. [late 1811/early 1812], RIS, box 2; John Howell to his parents, 29 October 1811, RIS, box 5.

24. Beasley to Mason, 24 March 1814, Transport Board to Beasley, 15 and 24 February 1813, 20 September 1813, 16 November 1813, ADM 98/291; Journal of Henry P. Fleischman, 1812–1813, 8 March 1813, mssHM 66770, Huntington Library, San Marino, CA.

25. American Register of Prisoners of War at Chatham, 1813–1815, ADM 103/56–103/59; Michael Allen, *Charles Dickens' Childhood* (Houndmills, UK; Macmillan, 1988), 38–70; Charles F. Campbell, *The Intolerable Hulks: British Shipboard Confinement, 1776–1857*, 3rd ed. (Tucson, AZ: Fenestra Books, 2001).

26. Charles Dickens, *Great Expectations* (Oxford: Oxford University Press, 2008), 7, 32, 37.

27. LPC, 2:358–359.

28. Journal of Henry P. Fleischman, 19 March 1813; American Prisoners at Chatham to James Madison, 20 July 1813, RIS, box 1, folder 1; Nassau (Chatham) Prisoners to James Madison, 24 July 1813, RIS, box 1, folder 1.

29. TPM, 83; JB, 71; Geoffrey L. Green, *The Royal Navy and Anglo-Jewry, 1740–1820* (London: Naval and Maritime Bookshop, 1989); Todd M. Endelman, *The Jews of Georgian England, 1714–1840* (Ann Arbor: University of Michigan Press, 1999), 118–165.

30. [James R. Pynneo], 'The Dartmoor Massacre', *Lancaster Intelligencer*, 15 July 1815, 1.

31. Paul Chamberlain, *Hell Upon Water: Prisoners of War in Britain, 1793–1815* (Stroud, UK: History Press, 2008), 231–232; American Prisoners at Chatham to Madison, 20 July 1813, RIS, box 1, folder 1.

32. Roger Knight, *Britain Against Napoleon: The Organisation of Victory, 1793–1815* (London: Allen Lane, 2013), 181–186; Beasley to James Monroe, 25 March 1813, box 7, folder 2, RAG.

33. 'Statement of the Sailing Master of the Roderigo', n.d. (July 1813?), box 1, folder 2, RAG.

CHAPTER 7. EXTREME NECESSITY

1. 'Instructions for Agents for Prisoners of War at Home', *Thirteenth Report of the Commissioners for Revising and Digesting the Civil Affairs of His Majesty's Navy*, 22 December 1807, *19th Century House of Commons Sessional Papers*, 128 (1809): 103–110, 105; GEBA, Admiralty Records (ADM) 103/87, no. 1.

2. GEBA, ADM 103/91, no. 6549.

3. Edward Higgs, *Identifying the English: A History of Personal Identification, 1500 to the Present* (London: Continuum, 2011), 108–109; Andrew Whitby, *The Sum of the People: How the Census Has Shaped Nations from the Ancient World to the Modern Age* (New York: Basic Books, 2020), 67–94; Vincent Denis, 'Individual Identity and Identification in Eighteenth-Century France', in *Identification and Registration Practices in Transnational Perspective: People, Papers, and Practices*, ed. J. Brown, I. About, and G. Lonergan (Houndmills, UK: Palgrave Macmillan, 2013), 17–30; Nancy Shoemaker, *Native*

American Whalemen and the World: Indigenous Encounters and the Contingency of Race (Chapel Hill: University of North Carolina Press, 2015), 41–42.

4. 'Instructions for Agents', 106.

5. Samuel Leech, *Thirty Years from Home, or, A Voice from the Main Deck* (Boston: Tappan, Whittemore & Mason, 1843), 193–194, 216–217, 220. On crew lists, see Shoemaker, *Native American Whalemen*, 41–42.

6. Renaud Morieux, *The Society of Prisoners: Anglo-French Wars and Incarceration in the Eighteenth Century* (Oxford: Oxford University Press, 2019), 182; Markus Krajewski, *Paper Machines: About Cards and Catalogs, 1548–1929*, trans. Peter Krapp (Cambridge, MA: MIT Press, 2011), 87–106. On the relationship between technology and the materiality of information, especially in the context of databases and the state, see Josef Teboho Ansorge, *Identify and Sort: How Digital Power Changed World Politics* (Oxford: Oxford University Press, 2016), 93–116. (I'm grateful to Duncan Bell for this reference.)

7. GEBA, ADM 103/87, no. 378 and no. 671; Register of American Prisoners of War at Plymouth, ADM 103/268, TNA, no. 1057; James Stanier Clarke and John McArthur, eds., *The Naval Chronicle*, 40 vols. (Cambridge: Cambridge University Press, 2010), 29:339.

8. TPM, ii–vii.

9. TPM, 24–25; Glover Broughton to Timothy Davis, 20 March 1856, GBP.

10. GEBF, ADM 103/92, no. 486; Transport Board to Cotgrave, 4 August 1809, TBOL, ADM 98/225; GEBF, ADM 103/94, no. 4683 ('Thomas Monford'); GEBA, ADM 103/87, no. 390; Stanier Clarke and McArthur, *Naval Chronicle*, 30:3.

11. TPM, 52, 35.

12. TPM, 36–37; Board to Cotgrave, 7 and 22 July 1813, TBOL, ADM 98/227.

13. Board to Cotgrave, 21 and 25 August 1813, 3 September 1813, ADM 98/227. Sure enough, the board was soon made aware that 'the prisoners called Romans on board the Hector [are] in the habit of disposing of their clothing.' Captain Pellowe to the Board, 20 October 1813, Minutes: Prisoners of War at Dartmoor, ADM 99/245, TNA; GEBF, ADM 103/92, no. 1.

14. Board to Cotgrave, 11 October 1813, TBOL, ADM 98/228, TNA; Glover Broughton to George R. Williams, 17 January 1857, Broughton to Timothy Davis, 20 March 1856, GBP.

15. Robin F. A. Fabel, 'Self-Help in Dartmoor: Black and White Prisoners in the War of 1812', *Journal of the Early Republic* 9, no. 2 (1989): 165–190, 177–179; UJN, 24 May 1815, 42–43.

16. Leech, *Thirty Years from Home*, 202.

17. GEBA, ADM 103/88, no. 1367; GL, 232–233.

18. Beasley to John Mason, 28 October 1813, box 2, folder 2, RAG; TPM, 27–28.

19. TPM, 15, 47, 28, 57. Establishing a precise number of 'impressed' Americans at Dartmoor is impossible. The Dartmoor clerks who compiled the register used a number of (inconsistent) formats for recording prisoners who had either been serving on Royal Navy ships or had been 'impressed' by the authorities in a British or Irish port. Of the 6,552 entries in the Dartmoor register, 77 (1.1 percent) were apprehended or 'given up' from non-American (mostly British) merchant vessels; 184 (2.8 percent) were 'impressed' at a named British or Irish port, most likely by the land-based Impress Service;

and 1,032 (15.7 percent) were 'given up' from a named Royal Navy vessel. Although the second group may have included men who recently served on a Royal Navy vessel, it's likely that most sailors in this category had been swept up by the Impress Service and were pending transfer to a Royal Navy ship when they were redirected to a war prison. (Weeks or even months could elapse between the Impress Service seizing a sailor and the sailor shipping out.) The register is silent on whether the largest group, Americans serving on a named British warship, were impressed into the king's service or had volunteered to serve; since the vast majority of this group do not appear in the State Department's impressment files, we have no way of knowing just how many of these sailors ardently sought to leave the Royal Navy. We also don't know how many sailors who came to Dartmoor via privateers and letters of marque may previously have served in the Royal Navy, but from the State Department files we can say that this number was not insignificant. I'm extremely grateful to Sara Caputo for her advice on how best to read the register's signals here. On the Impress Service and its activities, see Nicholas Rogers, *The Press Gang: Naval Impressment and Its Opponents in Georgian Britain* (London: Bloomsbury, 2008), 7.

20. Board to Cotgrave, 21 and 30 April 1813, 25 May 1813, 8 June 1813, 1 July 1813, TBOL, ADM 98/227.

21. Note that two names appeared twice—including Andrews's—since the prisoners concerned had gone to Plymouth and had then been returned to Dartmoor. GEBA, ADM 103/87.

22. TPM, 56–57.

23. TPM, 252–254. Only forty-one of the fifty-nine names in Andrews's appendix actually appear in the Dartmoor register, suggesting that some of these men successfully concealed their real identity either from the British or from Andrews and his associates.

24. TPM, v–vii.

25. GEBA, ADM 103/87; Sharon Block, *Colonial Complexions: Race and Bodies in Eighteenth-Century America* (Philadelphia: University of Pennsylvania Press, 2018), 10–34; Shoemaker, *Native American Whalemen*, 40–57; Honor Sachs, "'Freedom by a Judgment': The Legal History of an Afro-Indian Family', *Law and History Review* 30, no. 1 (2012): 173–203, 177.

26. General Entry Book of American Prisoners of War at Portsmouth, ADM 103/342, no. 128, TNA; General Entry Book of American Prisoners of War at Chatham, ADM 103/56, no. 500; GEBA, ADM 103/88, no. 2152; 'Urius or Darius Williams', RIS, box 11.

27. [James R. Pynneo], 'The Dartmoor Massacre', *Lancaster Intelligencer*, 15 July 1815, 1; TPM, 48–49; Beasley to Mason, 28 October 1813, box 2, folder 2, RAG.

28. TPM 69–70, 44. Andrews dated the segregation request to 22 February 1814, but the only reference in the board's correspondence to a request to 'remov[e] the Black and Men of Colour [*sic*] from among the Americans into the French Prison' was made the previous October. It is possible that the Black residents of Prison Four were moved to a different prison block, then silently moved back to Four, then moved once again on 22 February without leaving a trace in the official record. On balance, I'm inclined to believe that Andrews mis-dated the segregation request (as he did many other events at Dartmoor) and that the board's acknowledgement of a separation of the Black and white

Americans in October 1813 is the more persuasive signal. Board to Cotgrave, 23 October 1813, ADM 98/228.

29. TPM, 44–45; W. Jeffrey Bolster, *Black Jacks: African American Seamen in the Age of Sail* (Cambridge, MA: Harvard University Press, 1997), 68–101; Charles R. Foy, 'Britain's Black Tars', in *Britain's Black Past*, ed. Gretchen Gerzina (Liverpool, UK: Liverpool University Press, 2020), 72–74.

30. Martha S. Jones, *Birthright Citizens: A History of Race and Rights in Antebellum America* (Cambridge: Cambridge University Press, 2018), 1–34; Erica Armstrong Dunbar, *A Fragile Freedom: African American Women and Emancipation in the Antebellum City* (New Haven, CT: Yale University Press, 2011), 26–47; Patrick Rael, *Black Identity and Black Protest in the Antebellum North* (Chapel Hill: University of North Carolina Press, 2002), 12–53; Leslie M. Alexander, *African or American? Black Identity and Political Activism in New York City, 1784–1861* (Urbana: University of Illinois Press, 2008), 1–23.

31. DBFP, 16 and 17 February 1814, 20–21; Douglas Bradburn, *The Citizenship Revolution: Politics and the Creation of the American Union, 1774–1804* (Charlottesville: University of Virginia Press, 2009), 263.

32. Board to Cotgrave, 23 October 1813, ADM 98/228.

33. American Prisoners at Chatham to James Madison, 20 July 1813, box 1, folder 1, RAG. The Black sailor was George Williams; GEBA, ADM 103/87, no. 239. The board eventually told Cotgrave in the fall of 1813 that the 'Lords of the Admiralty do not think it to receive Black men . . . into H.M. Service.' This was in response to five more American volunteers for the Royal Navy, four of whom were Black. Board to Cotgrave, 23 September 1813, ADM 98/227.

34. TPM, 59.

35. Stanier Clarke and McArthur, *Naval Chronicle*, 30:59; John Marshall, *Royal Navy Biography*, 4 vols. (London: Longman, Hurst, Rees, Orme, Brown, and Green, 1823–1825), 2:482–488; *The Commissioned Sea Officers of the Royal Navy, 1660–1815*, ed. David B. Smith et al., 3 vols. (London: National Maritime Museum, 1954), 3:835.

36. TPM, 61–63.

37. TPM, 78–82, 88.

CHAPTER 8. A WORLD IN MINIATURE

1. BFB, 3:200–212, 207; BFB, 4:360–368, 367.

2. BFB, 5:457–465, 459; TPM, 41–43, 83–84; JV, 12; Transport Board to Thomas Shortland, 25 March 1814, Admiralty Records (ADM) 98/228, TNA.

3. 'Table of the Daily Ration of Provisions', Appendix 13, *Instructions to Agents for Prisoners of War at Home*, n.p.; LPC, 3:517–522, 518; Broughton to George R. Williams, 17 January 1857, GBP.

4. LPC, 3:520.

5. TPM, 92; Lewis P. Clover to Oliver Pope, 9 July 1876, Oliver C. Pope Papers, Burton Historical Collection Manuscripts, 1 LMS, Detroit Public Library; *Instructions to Agents*, 5–6; David Block, *Baseball Before We Knew It: A Search for the Roots of the Game* (Lincoln: University of Nebraska Press, 2005), 247–249. Robert Hardie of Philadelphia, who came to Dartmoor in July 1814, later recalled that he was 'placed in Number Four'.

Hardie to Colonel Wilson, n.d. [1878?], Robert Hardie Papers, box 1, folder 2, Historical Society of Pennsylvania.

6. BFB, 3:207; W. Jeffrey Bolster, *Black Jacks: African American Seamen in the Age of Sail* (Cambridge, MA: Harvard University Press, 1997).

7. BFB, 4:363.

8. BFB, 3:209; *Instructions to Agents*, 9; Robin F. A. Fabel, 'Self-Help in Dartmoor: Black and White Prisoners in the War of 1812', *Journal of the Early Republic* 9, no. 2 (1989): 177–180; DBFP, 109.

9. BFB, 3:209; DBFP, 116–117.

10. Beasley to John Mason, 28 October 1813, 22 March 1814, box 2, folder 2, RAG; TPM, 68, 77; Board to Shortland, 8 September 1814, ADM 98/228; George Dennison to his father, 4 October 1814, Coll. S-1966, Maine Historical Society.

11. TPM, 71; Beasley to Mason, 22 March 1814, box 2, folder 2, RAG; BFB, 3:365–366; LPC, 3:521; Fabel, 'Self-Help', 177.

12. TPM, 73.

13. TPM, 154–155; DBFP, 168; BW, 174, 180; Bernard Susser, 'Social Acclimatization of Jews in Eighteenth and Nineteenth Century Devon', in *Industry and Society in the South-West*, ed. Roger Burt (Exeter: University of Exeter, 1970), 51–69; Geoffrey L. Green, *The Royal Navy and Anglo-Jewry, 1740–1820* (London: Naval and Maritime Bookshop, 1989), 147–150.

14. TPM, 54; Board to Cotgrave, 26 August 1813, TBOL, ADM 98/227; LPC, 4:457–463, 458. An accounting of the scandal surrounding adulterated bread at Dartmoor (implicating contractors Twyman and Hagerman) is in 'Supply of Bad Bread at Dartmoor Prison', Prisoners of War, Miscellaneous Papers, ADM 105/60, TNA.

15. TPM, 165–166; BFB, 5:459; Renaud Morieux, *The Society of Prisoners: Anglo-French Wars and Incarceration in the Eighteenth Century* (Oxford: Oxford University Press, 2019), 335–346.

16. BFB, 4:367–368.

17. DBFP, 104, 118; TPM, 74, 81; BFB, 4:363.

18. BFB, 4:362; TPM, 133; Benjamin Morrell Jr., *A Narrative of Four Voyages* (New York: J. & J. Harper, 1832), xvii; LPC, 3:519.

19. BFB, 4:360, 362; DBFP, 106, 107.

20. *Instructions to Agents*, 21; BFB, 4:363; TPM, 104.

21. TPM, 64; Board to Cotgrave, 18 September 1813, TBOL, ADM 98/227.

22. BFB, 3:209; JC, 2:246; DBFP, 176; JNP, 39.

23. JV, 15; DBFP, 110.

24. LPC 2:359; *Instructions to Agents*, 5, specified that 'women, girls and boys under 12 years of age . . . are not meant to be prisoners of war'; the agent was required to make a separate list of anyone in these categories and await 'our directions respecting them'.

25. Journal of Henry P. Fleischman, 1812–1813, 31 January and 2 February 1813, mssHM 66770, Huntington Library, San Marino, CA; Transport Board to Captain Hutchinson, 20 July and 5 August 1813, Transport Board Out-Letters to Agents Respecting Prisoners of War, Chatham, ADM 98/224, TNA.

26. Board to Shortland, 11 August and 31 December 1814, 11 January and 16 January 1815, ADM 98/228, TBOL. Elisha Clark was no. 1963 in the Dartmoor register: GEBA, ADM 103/88.

27. Jonathan Paul was no. 1998 in the Dartmoor register: GEBA, ADM 103/88; he was murdered by another prisoner in March 1815. Four men with the surname Ray appear in the register: three (nos. 2578, 3584, and 4183) served on Royal Navy ships before they were 'delivered up' to Dartmoor between August and October 1814; GEBA, ADM 103/89 and 103/90. Board to Shortland, 15 February 1815, ADM 98/228, TBOL. Sankey was no. 5371: GEBA, ADM 103/90.

28. 'Dartmoor Prisoners of 1812' (taken 1853), Early Brooklyn and Long Island Photograph Collection, Brooklyn Public Library. George D. Small was no. 4180 at Dartmoor, GEBA, ADM 103/90; and no. 1881 at Chatham, General Entry Book of American Prisoners of War, Chatham, ADM 103/57, TNA. Small was captured in March 1813 in the Bay of Biscay, then held at Portsmouth before being transferred to Chatham on 7 July 1813. The board's search for a wet nurse (see note 25 above) took place a few weeks later, so it remains a possibility that Small's wife was heavily pregnant and followed him from the south coast to Chatham (and then to Dartmoor).

29. 'Description of the New Prison of War, Dartmoor, Devon', 162; Morieux, *Society of Prisoners*, 185, 225–227, 286–287.

30. *Report from the Committee on the Prisons Within the City of London and Borough of Southwark*, 8 May 1818, *Parliamentary Papers* 392 (1818): 181; Board to Cotgrave, 22 July, 22 September, and 18 November 1809, ADM 98/225, TBOL.

31. Board to Cotgrave, 29 November 1810, ADM 98/226; Board to Shortland, 7 November 1814, ADM 98/228. George Dennison, no. 940, escaped on 13 March 1815: GEBA, ADM 103/87. Basil Thomson, *The Story of Dartmoor Prison* (London: William Heinemann, 1907), 23; Morieux, *Society of Prisoners*, 221–223.

32. Louis Vanhille, no. 8496, GEBF, ADM 103/95; M. Georges Pariset, *Les Aventures de Louis-François Vanhille, Prisonnier de Guerre Chez Les Anglais* (Nancy: Berger-Levrault etc., 1905); Louis Vanhille, no. 14,933, Register of Prisoners of War at Chatham, Kron Prinds prison ship, ADM 103/218, TNA; Thomson, *Story of Dartmoor Prison*, 35–44.

33. Cynthia Neal Rentoul, ed., *East by Sea and West by Rail: The Journal of David Augustus Neal of Salem, Mass., 1798–1861* (Toronto: Elvidge, 1979), 97–107; BFB, 5:463–464; DBFP, 102; 'Portsmouth, August 7', *London Morning Post*, 9 August 1814, 4. Neal (listed as David A. Neil) was no. 3911, GEBA, ADM 103/90. Francis G. Selman, 'Extracts from the Journal of a Marblehead Privateersman', in *The Marblehead Manual*, ed. Samuel Roads Jr. (Marblehead, MA: Statesman Publishing Company, 1883), 29–71, 60; JB, 61–70.

34. Richard Philen, no. 293, GEBA, ADM 103/87; TPM, 64–65; Board to Shortland, 26 January 1814, TBOL, ADM 98/228; Thomson, *Story of Dartmoor Prison*, 112.

35. James McDadon, no. 929, and John Langford, no. 774, GEBA, ADM 103/87; 'Breach of Parole of Honour', *London Morning Chronicle*, 7 February 1815, 1; Henry Allen, no. 1684 and no. 6153, GEBA, ADM 103/88 and ADM 103/91; George Coggeshall, *History of the American Privateers and Letters-of-Marque* (New York: Published By and For the Author, 1856), 253–263; JV, 26.

36. Thomas Swaine, no. 2971, GEBA, ADM 103/89; Faye M. Kert, *Privateering: Patriots and Profits in the War of 1812* (Baltimore: Johns Hopkins University Press, 2015), 104.

37. TPM, 127–128.

38. DBFP, 104, 106; JNP, 33.

39. LPC, 3:518.

PART III. KING DICK AT DARTMOOR

1. Richard Crafus, no. 3711, General Entry Book of American Prisoners of War at Chatham, Admiralty Records (ADM) 103/59, TNA. At Dartmoor, Crafus was no. 4603: GEBA, ADM 103/90.

2. BW, 164; JC, 2:43–44; BFB, 3:210.

3. BW, 164; BFB, 3:212.

4. BFB, 3:210–211; BW, 164.

5. JC, 2:44; BW, 164–165.

6. BFB, 4:361–362, 3:211; BW, 165–166.

7. JC, 2:44; BFB, 3:210.

CHAPTER 9. PRISON FOUR

1. DBFP, 108.

2. Katherine Astbury, "'Whole Shew and Spectacle": French Prisoner-of-War Theatre in England During the Napoleonic Era', *Journal of War and Culture Studies* 14, no. 2 (2021): 194–210.

3. DBFP, 108–109.

4. Jeffrey Richards, *Sir Henry Irving: A Victorian Actor and His World* (London: Bloomsbury, 2006), 34; Tony Tanner, *The American Mystery: American Literature from Emerson to DeLillo* (Cambridge: Cambridge University Press, 2000), 84–85.

5. DFBP, 109.

6. GEBA, Admiralty Records (ADM) 103/87–103/90. (James Johnson was no. 3608, ADM 103/89. Scipio Bartlett was no. 4256, ADM 103/90.) Given the fuzziness of the 'complexion' field in the Dartmoor register, we'll never know exactly how many people of colour were in Dartmoor. My figure here represents a conservative reading of the register's race-making categories.

7. John Newell, no. 22, GEBA, ADM 103/87; William Spince, no. 10,763, GEBF, ADM 103/97; William Spince, no. 1191, GEBA, ADM 103/88.

8. 'Thomas Wilson', box 11, RIS; Samuel Turner to James Monroe, 20 March 1814, 'Charles White', box 11, RIS; Francis Johnston to James Madison, 4 October 1808, 'George Jamieson', box 6, RIS.

9. Appene, no. 590, GEBA, ADM 103/87; Edgardo Pérez Morales, *No Limits to Their Sway: Cartagena's Privateers and the Masterless Caribbean in the Age of Revolutions* (Nashville, TN: Vanderbilt University Press, 2018); Aline Helg, 'The Limits of Equality: Free People of Colour and Slaves During the First Independence of Cartagena, Colombia, 1810–1815', *Slavery and Abolition* 20, no. 2 (1999): 1–30. The note in the register insisting that the *President* was American is beside the name of James Knabbs, no. 4798, GEBA, ADM 103/90. Ira Dye believes that Appene was servant to the captain of the

US Navy vessel on which he was captured: Dye, *The Fatal Cruise of the* Argus: *Two Captains in the War of 1812* (Annapolis: Naval Institute Press, 1994), 135.

10. James Marthy, no. 4831, GEBA, ADM 103/90; 'Barbados, March 7', *National Intelligencer*, 7 May 1814, 3.

11. In thinking about the Black experience at Dartmoor, and both the absences and the misdirection of the archive, I've been particularly influenced by Saidiya Hartman, 'Venus in Two Acts', *Small Axe*, 26 (June 2008): 1–14; Marisa J. Fuentes, *Dispossessed Lives: Enslaved Women, Violence, and the Archive* (Philadelphia: University of Pennsylvania Press, 2016); and Jessica Marie Johnson, *Wicked Flesh: Black Women, Intimacy, and Freedom in the Atlantic World* (Philadelphia: University of Pennsylvania Press, 2020).

12. St George Tucker, *A Dissertation on Slavery, with a Proposal for the Gradual Abolition of It, in the State of Virginia* (Philadelphia: Mathew Carey, 1796), 89; Nicholas Guyatt, *Bind Us Apart: How Enlightened Americans Invented Racial Segregation* (New York: Basic Books, 2016), 17–38.

13. Guyatt, *Bind Us Apart*, 79–86.

14. Eric Burin, *Slavery and the Peculiar Solution: A History of the American Colonization Society* (Gainesville: University Press of Florida, 2006), 6–19; Brandon C. Mills, *The World Colonization Made: The Racial Geography of Early American Empire* (Philadelphia: University of Pennsylvania Press, 2021), 48–57; Guyatt, *Bind Us Apart*, 262–275.

15. Maya Jasanoff, *Liberty's Exiles: American Loyalists in the Revolutionary World* (New York: Knopf, 2011), 279–309; Guyatt, *Bind Us Apart*, 197–205.

16. Olaudah Equiano, *The Interesting Narrative and Other Writings* (London: Penguin, 2003), 226–230; Padraic X. Scanlan, *Freedom's Debtors: British Antislavery in Sierra Leone in the Age of Revolution* (New Haven, CT: Yale University Press, 2017); Cassandra Pybus, *Epic Journeys of Freedom: Runaway Slaves of the American Revolution and Their Global Quest for Liberty* (Boston: Beacon Press, 2006), 139–155, 169–202.

17. Lamont D. Thomas, *Rise to Be a People: A Biography of Paul Cuffe* (Urbana: University of Illinois Press, 1986), 46–106; Bronwen Everill, *Abolition and Empire in Sierra Leone and Liberia* (Houndmills, UK: Palgrave, 2013), 23–24; Guyatt, *Bind Us Apart*, 259–262.

18. Scanlan, *Freedom's Debtors*, 200–201; James Sidbury, *Becoming African in America: Race and Nation in the Early Black Atlantic* (Oxford: Oxford University Press, 2007); Patrick Rael, *Black Identity and Black Protest in the Antebellum North* (Chapel Hill: University of North Carolina Press, 2002), 209–236.

19. Johnhenry Gonzalez, *Maroon Nation: A History of Revolutionary Haiti* (New Haven, CT: Yale University Press, 2018), 1–48; Sara Fanning, 'The Roots of Early Black Nationalism: Northern African Americas' Invocations of Haiti in the Early Nineteenth Century', *Slavery and Abolition* 28, no. 1 (2007): 61–85; Michael O. West and William G. Martin, 'Haiti, I'm Sorry: The Haitian Revolution and the Forging of the Black International', in *From Toussaint to Tupac: The Black International Since the Age of Revolution*, ed. Michael O. West, William G. Martin, and Fanon Che Wilkins (Chapel Hill: University of North Carolina Press, 2009), 72–104.

20. 'The return of prisoners of war on this day', unsigned and undated note (c. October 1814), Statements of the Staff . . . Prepared for the Admiralty Board Visitation, ADM 1/5122/16, TNA; BFB, 3:208. The board's inspector visited Dartmoor on 3 November 1814; on the basis of this and an accompanying estimate of the prison's population, we

can confidently date the unsigned note to October 1814. This note also claimed that white American prisoners had 'persecuted the poor blacks to such a degree that they had begged to be removed into a separate prison'—an inversion of Charles Andrews's insistence that it was white Americans who had insisted on segregation. I have found no evidence to corroborate this claim, though the idea of 'persecution' supports my argument that white sailors' refusal to share political power with Black sailors offers a better explanation for the segregation request than Andrews's insistence that Black sailors were inveterate thieves.

21. BFB, 3:210.

22. BFB, 3:210–211.

23. I have identified twenty-one Black sailors from the USS *Argus* in the Dartmoor register; seventeen were captured on the *Argus* itself, and four were seized on prizes which had previously been taken by the American ship. One of these men died of pneumonia in the prison; the rest were given priority release (in recognition of their US Navy status) on 30 September 1814. The men can be found in the range of register entries from no. 586 to no. 686, GEBA, ADM 103/87; and no. 2913 and no. 2914, ADM 103/89.

24. DBFP, 44; JV, 16; JNP, 33–34.

25. BW, 170; BFB, 5:461.

26. BFB, 461–462.

27. JNP, 53. Intriguingly, the only Thomas Cutler in the register gave his birthplace as Exeter (around twenty miles from Newburyport) but was described as 'fair' in complexion; Pierce was clearly convinced that Cutler was Black, so did the clerk make an error on entering Cutler into the register? (The same page of the register contained four Black sailors.) No. 4736, GEBA, ADM 103/90. Cutler won £16/19 at the gaming table in Four, which equated to roughly four months of earnings for a skilled tradesman in 1815.

28. BFB, 3:212.

29. BFB, 5:461, 458.

30. JB, 73; JNP, 34; JV, 18, 20; BFB, 4:360. Comparing the various accounts of Simon to the register's Black population, the closest match is Simon Harris, no. 4199, GEBA, ADM 103/90. On prison agents encouraging the evangelization of prisoners of war, see Renaud Morieux, *The Society of Prisoners: Anglo-French Wars and Incarceration in the Eighteenth Century* (Oxford: Oxford University Press, 2019), 121–125.

31. Charles F. Irons, *The Origins of Proslavery Christianity: White and Black Evangelicals in Colonial and Antebellum Virginia* (Chapel Hill: University of North Carolina Press, 2008), 81–83; Albert J. Raboteau, *Slave Religion: The 'Invisible Institution' in the American South*, updated edition (Oxford: Oxford University Press, 2004), 134; Richard J. Boles, *Dividing the Faith: The Rise of Segregated Churches in the Early American North* (New York: New York University Press, 2020), 176–193.

32. JV, 19, 17.

33. DBFP, 140; JNP, 34.

34. BFB, 4:361.

35. BW, 167.

36. Hosea Easton, *A Treatise on the Intellectual Character and Civil and Political Condition of the Colored People of the U. States* (Boston: Isaac Knapp, 1837), 39–40.

37. Easton, *Treatise on the Intellectual Character*, 43.

CHAPTER 10. HOPE DEFERRED

1. TPM, 133; LPC, 3:520; JV, 16; no. 1060, GEBA, Admiralty Records (ADM) 103/87.

2. DBFP, 111.

3. TPM 134–135; DBFP, 124.

4. DBFP, 134–135, 160–162.

5. Register of Deaths of Prisoners of War, Dartmoor, ADM 103/623, TNA; Matthew Kelly, *Quartz and Feldspar: Dartmoor, a British Landscape in Modern Times* (London: Jonathan Cape, 2015), 134–136, 140; *Report from the Committee on the Prisons Within the City of London and Borough of Southwark*, 8 May 1818, *Parliamentary Papers* 392 (1818): 175–177; Kevin Siena, *Rotten Bodies: Class & Contagion in 18th Century Britain* (New Haven, CT: Yale University Press, 2019), 124–153.

6. *Report from the Committee on the Prisons*, 194; TPM, 123; BFB, 5:460; Lawrence Brockliss, John Cardwell, and Michael Moss, *Nelson's Surgeon: William Beatty, Naval Medicine, and the Battle of Trafalgar* (Oxford: Oxford University Press, 2005), 95–96.

7. BFB, 5:460; TPM, 140; JV, 13–14.

8. Andrew Baird to Transport Board, 7 November 1814, Transport Board Medical Committee In-Letter Book, ADM 105/21, TNA; Board to Shortland, 22 February 1815 (two letters), 6 March 1815, TBOL, ADM 98/228.

9. *Report from the Committee on the Prisons*, 177, 201–202. See also George Magrath, 'On the Sanitary Condition of Dartmoor', in *A Perambulation of the Antient and Royal Forest of Dartmoor*, ed. Samuel Rowe (Plymouth: J. B. Rowe, 1848), 251–253, 252.

10. GL, 236–239.

11. TPM, 110–114.

12. TPM, 115–116.

13. The only Black escapee was Caleb Richmond, who fled Dartmoor on 1 June 1815: no. 6523, GEBA, ADM 103/91. Norma Myers, *Reconstructing the Black Past: Blacks in Britain, 1780–1830* (London: Frank Cass & Co., 1996), 35.

14. TPM, 117–120.

15. Basil Thomson, *The Story of Dartmoor Prison* (London: William Heinemann, 1907), 161–162; Board to Shortland, 12 September 1814, TBOL, ADM 98/228; TPM, 119.

16. GL, 238; no. 369 and no. 6143, GEBA, ADM 103/87 and 103/91.

17. No. 2600, GEBA, ADM 103/89.

18. TPM, 95–96; Thomson, *Story of Dartmoor Prison*, 123–124.

19. Ira Dye, *The Fatal Cruise of the Argus: Two Captains in the War of 1812* (Annapolis: Naval Institute Press, 1994), 134–145, 263–275.

20. Dye, *Fatal Cruise*, 276–290.

21. Dye, *Fatal Cruise*, 284–285, 289; TPM, 164; no. 592, GEBA, ADM 103/87. Thomson, *Story of Dartmoor Prison*, 159, claims that Bradt was returned to Dartmoor on 1 April 1815. If so, there is no mention of his return in the register; the final American prisoner was entered into ADM 103/91 on 26 March 1815.

22. Nos. 5719–5723, no. 5786, GEBA, ADM 103/90; TPM, 138; DBFP, 127.

23. TPM, 141–142.

24. DBFB, 145; TPM, 150–151; BFB, 5:462–463; JV, 18; JNP, 27. The four indicted men were John Hogabets (no. 338), Joseph Jackson (no. 1536), Cornelius Saunders (no. 1738), and Samuel Robinet (no. 2113). Their victims were named in the court record as John McMahon and John Holston, though neither of those names appears in the Dartmoor register. Calendar of the Prisoners for Trial, Western Circuit Assizes, Lent 1815, ASSI 25/11/8, TNA.

25. DBPF, 138–139; JV, 19.

26. No. 1671, GEBA, ADM 103/88; TPM, 129–130, 147, 153–154; Cynthia Neal Rentoul, ed., *East by Sea and West by Rail: The Journal of David Augustus Neal of Salem, Mass., 1798–1861* (Toronto: Elvidge, 1979), 115; BW, 188. Thomas Shortland later testified that he had closed the market 'in consequence of the escape of Simon Hayes . . . and his taking refuge among the prisoners'. MDP, 46.

27. No. 121, GEBA, ADM 103/87; DBFP, 149–153; BFB, 6:143–144.

28. DBFP, 149; BFB, 5:144.

29. BFB, 5:457–458; BW, 162, 172, 180; DBFP, 152.

30. TPM, 130–131; DBFP, 118–119.

31. DBFP, 125–126; TPM, 135; GL, 239–240; BFB, 6:143.

32. DBFP, 163.

33. Beasley to Alexander McLeay, 18 January 1815, McLeay to Beasley, 21 January 1815, Beasley to John Mason, 10 February 1815, box 2, folder 1, RAG.

34. GL, 240–241; Beasley to the Committee of American Prisoners of War at Dartmoor, 31 March 1815, box 9, folder 4, RAG. Beasley's letters to the board on behalf of individual prisoners seeking release are in Letters from the Office of the Commissioners of Sick and Wounded Seamen to the US Agent in Britain, 1812–1815, ADM 98/291, TNA. In one of the board's replies, Beasley was told that the men he had proposed for early release were 'unable for want of money to avail themselves of their discharge'. Board to Beasley, 20 March 1815, ADM 98/291, TNA.

35. Beasley to the American Committee, 22, 23, and 31 March 1815; Beasley to Thomas Shortland, 25 March 1815, box 9, folder 4, RAG. (Beasley had commissioned a fourth vessel by the end of March.) Beasley to Mason, 13 April 1815, in Records Relating to War of 1812 Prisoners of War, M2019, USNA; Roger Knight, *Britain Against Napoleon: The Organisation of Victory, 1793–1815* (London: Allen Lane, 2013), 455–456; Rory Muir, *Britain and the Defeat of Napoleon, 1807–1815* (New Haven, CT: Yale University Press, 1996), 345–357.

36. TPM, 152; JNP, 37; DBFP, 171.

37. TPM, 156–161; UJN, 23; LPC, 4:459; JB, 76.

38. JV, 25; DBFP, 172; JNP, 37.

CHAPTER 11. THE DEAD HOUSE

1. DBFP, 174–175.

2. JNP, 38–39; Register of Deaths, Admiralty Records (ADM) 103/623, TNA.

3. John Burke, *A Genealogical History of the Commoners of Great Britain and Ireland*, 4 vols. (London: Henry Colburn, 1834), 1:517–518; 'The First Somerset Regiment', *Royal Cornwell Gazette*, 12 November 1814, 4.

4. Testimony of Neil McKinnon, MDP, 37; BFB, 6:144. The Derbyshire militia rotated into Dartmoor early in 1815, and then Jolliffe and the Somerset militia returned (for a sixth spell guarding the prison) early in March: 'The First Somerset Regiment', *Hampshire Telegraph*, 6 March 1815, 4.

5. JB, 78.

6. Testimony of Neil McKinnon, MDP, 37; JNP, 40.

7. DBFP, 176–177; TPM, 167–169; 'Report of Messrs Larpent and King upon the Occurrence at Dartmoor Prison', 26 April 1815, MDP, 21.

8. TPM, 167–169; DBFP, 176.

9. DBFP, 177; JNP, 39.

10. TPM, 169–172; DBFP, 178.

11. DBFP, 179; BFB, 6:144; Testimony of James N. Bushfield, MDP, 38.

12. LPC, 4:460–461; JNP, 40; BFB, 6:147; Testimony of Stephen Hall, MDP, 42.

13. 'Report of Messrs Larpent and King', MDP, 21; JNP, 40; Testimony of Samuel White, MDP, 25–26; BFB, 6:147; DBFP, 179; UJN, 28–29.

14. 'A Tale of Dartmoor Prison', *New Hampshire Statesman and Register*, 15 September 1827, 1; LPC, 4:145; Testimony of Thomas Mott, John Rust, and John Trowbridge, MDP, 31, 33.

15. Testimony of Thomas Shortland, William Clements, and Samuel White, MDP, 45, 38, 25; BFB, 6:147.

16. Testimony of Neil McKinnon, John Mitchell, John Odiorne, James Carley, MDP, 37, 26, 28–29, 41; TPM, 174–175; 'Report of Messrs Larpent and King', MDP, 21; JB, 79.

17. TPM, 173–174; Testimony of Thomas Shortland, John Collard, John Clement, James Bushfield, MDP, 45, 43, 47, 39; DBFP, 179.

18. John Arnold, John Odiorne, Thomas Shortland, George Magrath, MDP, 29, 28, 45, 28.

19. George Magrath, Thomas Shortland, John Bennett, John Collard, John Saunders, Joseph Manning, John Soathern, MDP, 28, 45, 42, 43, 33, 44.

20. James Reeves, Richard Arnold, Stephen Laphorn, MDP, 39, 42, 42.

21. John Collard, Thomas Shortland, Amos Wheeler, MDP, 42, 45, 33; TPM, 175–176.

22. Richard Crafus, MDP, 27–28; no. 2719, GEBA, ADM 103/89. There were two John Haywoods in the register: both were Black, both were from Maryland, both were twenty-five years old, and both had been serving in the Royal Navy (though on different vessels). On the basis of descriptions from the casualty reports and comparisons with the Chatham register, I believe the Dartmoor clerks recorded Haywood's death against the wrong man; Haywood was no. 2719, not no. 3134 as noted in the register.

23. George Magrath, William Dewetter, John French, Samuel Morgan, William Wakelin, Addison Holmes, MDP, 28, 45, 41, 29; 'Report of Messrs Larpent and King', MDP, 22; 'Description of Death Wounds Inflicted on the Evening of April 6, 1815', MDP, 53; JV, 27.

24. 'A Tale of Dartmoor Prison', *New Hampshire Statesman and Register*, 15 September 1827, 1; James Reeves, Stephen Hall, MDP, 39, 27; JV, 27; JNP, 41.

25. John Gatchell, James Reeves, Andrew Davis, William Wakelin, MDP, 37, 39, 38, 42; TPM, 180.

26. Hardie to Wilson, Robert Hardie Papers, box 1, folder 2, Historical Society of Pennsylvania; Testimony of Neil McKinnon, MDP, 37.

27. No. 6520, GEBA, ADM 103/91. (The register lists him as 'Thomas Jack'.) McKinnon, MDP, 37; 'Description of Death Wounds', MDP, 53.

28. DBFP, 181.

29. JNP, 41; BFB, 7:209–217, 209–210; John Clement, MDP, 47; DBFP, 181–182; TPM, 183, 199–206; J. W. Croker to J. P. Morier, 10 April 1815, MDP, 50.

30. 'From the Committee Appointed to Investigate the Circumstances Attending the Massacre at Dartmoor', MDP, 51–52. On the numbers of men at Dartmoor who had experienced impressment/Royal Navy service, see Chapter 7, note 19.

31. John Clement, MDP, 47; TPM, 190–192; BFB, 7:210; Board to Shortland, 18 April 1815, TBOL, ADM 98/228; 'Minute of a Conversation Between Lord Castlereagh and Messrs Clay and Gallatin on 16 of April 1815', MDP, 29; Henry Clay to William Bayard, 28 April 1815, in Elizabeth Donnan, ed., *Annual Report of the American Historical Association for the Year 1913 in Two Volumes, Volume II: Papers of James Bayard, 1796–1815* (Washington, DC: American Historical Association, 1913), 380–381.

32. Clay to Bayard, *Annual Report of the American Historical Association*, 381; Henry Clay and Albert Gallatin to Reuben Beasley, 18 April 1815, Reuben Beasley to John Mason, 17 April 1815, MDP, 20, 52; Beasley to Mason, 19 April 1815, box 9, folder 4, RAG.

33. LPC, 4:462–463; DBFP, 196, 198; W. A. J. Archbold, revised by M. C. Curthoys, 'Francis Seymour Larpent', *Oxford Dictionary of National Biography*, 23 September 2004, accessed 14 June 2021.

34. JNP, 41, 43; William West et al. to James Madison, 28 March 1815, FO; Board to Shortland, 17 and 21 April 1815, TBOL, ADM 98/228.

35. JNP, 46; TPM, 203; Shortland to Transport Board, 27 April 1815, Minutes, Prisoners of War, ADM 99/260, TNA.

36. 'Report of Messrs Larpent and King', MDP, 22–23.

37. Charles King to John Quincy Adams, 26 April 1815, MDP, 20.

38. Castlereagh to Henry Clay and Albert Gallatin, 22 May 1815, MDP, 23.

CHAPTER 12. GOING HOME

1. 'Disturbances at Dartmoor Prison', *London Morning Chronicle*, 11 April 1815, 3; Beasley to the Committee of the American Prisoners of War at Dartmoor, 12 April 1815, in 'Dartmoor Massacre', *Niles' Weekly Register*, 8 July 1815, 325.

2. Prisoners' Committee to Beasley, 14 April 1815, in 'Dartmoor Massacre', *Niles' Weekly Register*, 8 July 1815, 325–326; Beasley to John Mason, 15 February 1815, box 9, folder 4, RAG.

3. DBFP, 193–194.

4. DBFP, 194, 198, 202, 213; JNP, 49, 48.

5. Alexander McLeay to Beasley, 19 April 1815, box 9, folder 4, RAG; DBFP, 195; LPC, 5:519–5:524, 5:519–5:520.

6. DBFP, 199; JV, 27.

7. Charles Carrol and Benjamin F. Palmer, no. 1079 and no. 3944, GEBA, Admiralty Records (ADM) 103/88 and 103/90; DBFP, 199.

8. DBFP, 201.

9. JB, 84–85; BFB, 7:213.

10. DBFP, 203.

11. DBFP, 203–204.

12. Nathaniel Ingraham to John Mason, 4 May 1815, box 10, folder 4, RAG; Ingraham to Beasley, 29 August 1815, box 13, folder 2, RAG. Beasley told the board in May that prisoners were leaking from Ingraham's charge at Plymouth and that 'it would only be prevented by a guard being placed over them': Beasley to Transport Board, 3 May 1815, Board Minutes, ADM 99/260, TNA.

13. Ingraham to Mason, 28 and 29 April 1815, box 10, folder 4, RAG. Partial notes on the cartel ships and their captains are in RAG, box 1, folders 3 and 4.

14. 'Disturbances at Dartmoor Prison', *New York Evening Post*, 24 May 1815, 2; 'Salem, May 24', *New York Evening Post*, 26 May 1815, 2.

15. Donald R. Hickey, *The War of 1812: A Forgotten Conflict, Bicentennial Edition* (Urbana: University of Illinois Press, 2012), 312–316; Alan Taylor, *The Civil War of 1812: American Citizens, British Subjects, Irish Rebels, & Indian Allies* (New York: Knopf, 2010), 420–424.

16. 'Arrived', *Long-Island (NY) Star*, 7 June 1815, 2; 'The Horrible Tragedy at Dartmoor', *National Intelligencer* (Washington, DC), 15 June 1815, 2.

17. Madison to James Monroe, 12 June 1815, FO.

18. Adams to James Monroe, 23 June 1815, MDP, 23; *The Diaries of John Quincy Adams, Digital Collection*, Massachusetts Historical Society, 29:257–261.

19. *Diaries of John Quincy Adams*, 261–265.

20. JB, 86, 88–89; DBFP, 207; Beasley to John Mason, 18 April 1815, box 9, folder 4, RAG.

21. JB, 88–89; DBFP, 219–220.

22. Testimony of William Hobart to Jed Huntington, New London Customs Collector, 10 June 1815, box 2, folder 4, RAG; Deposition of Andrew Carr, 9 June 1815, box 5, folder 2, RAG; DBFP, 220; Renaud Morieux, *The Society of Prisoners: Anglo-French Wars and Incarceration in the Eighteenth Century* (Oxford: Oxford University Press, 2019), 174–175.

23. Beasley to John Mason, 10 April 1815, box 9, folder 4, RAG; Beasley to Mason, 15 April 1815; TPM, 220–222; BFB, 7:215–216.

24. Board to Shortland, 23 June 1815, TBOL, ADM 98/228.

25. JNP, 46, 55.

26. JNP, 57; JC, 2:255–257.

27. JNP, 54; Shortland to the Board, 2 June 1815, Board Minutes, ADM 99/260.

28. 'Dartmoor Prisoners', *Lancaster (PA) Intelligencer*, 8 July 1815, 3; 'Fellow Feeling', *Columbian*, 4 August 1815, 2; 'Domestic Intelligence', *Boston Repertory*, 1 August 1815, 2.

29. Jacob Radcliff to Alexander Dallas, 3 August 1815, James Madison to Dallas, 13 August 1815, in George Mifflin Dallas, *Life and Writings of Alexander James Dallas*

(Philadelphia: J. B. Lippincott, 1871), 437–438, 441; Dallas to Madison, 28 August 1815, FO.

30. LPC, 5:522–523.

31. 'The Dartmoor Tragedy', *New York Examiner*, 15 January 1816, 84.

32. *Diaries of John Quincy Adams*, 29:267–268; Beasley to Adams, 7 December 1815, box 10, folder 4, RAG; Sara Caputo, 'Foreign Seamen and the British Navy' (PhD diss., University of Cambridge, 2019), 287–291.

33. 'Ex parte Dunlop—In the Matter of Beasley', in J. W. Buck, *Cases in Bankruptcy . . . From Michaelmas Term 1816 to Michaelmas Term 1820* (London: Henry Butterworth, 1820), 253–255; 'The Creditors of Reuben Gaunt Beasley', *London Gazette*, 23 March 1816, 564. Thanks to Julius Grower for (pro bono) legal advice on Beasley's predicament.

34. Beasley to James Madison, c. July 1816, FO; 'R.G. Beasley', *New York Evening Post*, 5 March 1815, 2.

35. LPC 5:524; JB, 97; *The Travels and Adventures of David C. Bunnell* (Palmyra, NY: J. H. Bortles, 1831), 141; Benjamin Morrell Jr., *A Narrative of Four Voyages* (New York: J. & J. Harper, 1832), xviii.

36. According to the register, 206 Black sailors were evacuated in July 1815, but this number does not include those who sold their place in line to white sailors like Frank Palmer and Joseph Valpey.

37. 'For the Journal', *Georgia Journal*, 2 March 1819, 3; 'Chronicle', *Niles' Weekly Register*, 24 April 1819, 158; 'Napoleon', *Philadelphia Album*, 20 August 1831, 271; Daniel Ballace, no. 6129, GEBA, ADM 103/91.

PART IV. KING DICK AT BOSTON

1. 'Reminiscences of Old Boston', *Boston Commercial Bulletin*, 21 June 1873, 1; Joanne Lloyd, 'Beneath the "City on the Hill": The Lower Orders, Boston, 1700–1850' (PhD diss., Boston College, 2007), 148–178.

2. 'Big Dick', *New England Galaxy*, 21 December 1821, 3.

3. 'The English and American Character for Humanity, Compared', *Boston Patriot*, 24 June 1819, 2; Elliott J. Gorn, *The Manly Art: Bare-Knuckle Prize Fighting in America*, updated edition (Ithaca, NY: Cornell University Press, 2010).

4. 'The Fancy', *New England Galaxy*, 18 March 1825, 3.

5. 'King Dick', *New England Galaxy*, 25 January 1822, 2; Mark Peterson, *The City-State of Boston: The Rise and Fall of an Atlantic Power, 1630–1865* (Princeton, NJ: Princeton University Press, 2019), 542–545.

6. 'Reminiscences', 1; *The Boston Directory* (Boston: John H. A. Frost and Charles Stimpson Jr., 1825), 297.

7. Shane White, '"It Was a Proud Day": African Americans, Festivals, and Parades in the North, 1741–1834', *Journal of American History* 81, no. 1 (1994): 13–50.

8. George Hugh Crichton, 'Old Boston and Its Once Familiar Faces', chap. 3, Boston Athenaeum; W. Jeffrey Bolster, *Black Jacks: African American Seamen in the Age of Sail* (Cambridge, MA: Harvard University Press, 1997), 108; Joanne Pope Melish, *Disowning Slavery: Gradual Emancipation and 'Race' in New England, 1780–1860* (Ithaca, NY: Cornell University Press, 1998), 172–183.

9. 'Reminiscences', 1; 'Riot', *Boston Statesman*, 15 July 1825, 3; Lloyd, 'Beneath the "City on the Hill"', 389–393; Jack Tager, *Boston Riots: Three Centuries of Social Violence* (Boston: Northeastern University Press, 2001), 76–88.

10. 'Reminiscences', 1; Peterson, *City-State of Boston*, 581–585.

11. Harry Hazel (Justin Jones), *Big Dick, the King of the Negroes* (New York: Star Spangled Banner Office, 1846); Thomas Lipke, 'The Strange Life and Stranger Afterlife of King Dick' (MA diss., University of South Florida, 2013), 27–38.

12. 'Police Court', *New York Evening Post*, 21 June 1824, 3; 'Police Court', *Boston Traveler*, 16 December 1828, 2.

13. Edward H. Savage, *Police Records and Recollections* (Boston: John P. Dale & Company, 1873), 69; 'Deaths Registered in the City of Boston . . . from 1801 to 1848 inclusive', Boston City Records; 'Deaths', *Liberator*, 12 February 1831, 27.

CHAPTER 13. REMEMBERING AND FORGETTING

1. DBFP, 226. 'Palmer's Journal', *New York Columbian*, 17, 19, 29, 21 June 1815, 2.

2. 'Dartmoor Memoirs', *New York Columbian*, 24 June 1815, 3; 'Prospectus: The Prisoners' Memoirs', *New York Columbian*, 26 September 1815, 3; 'The Prisoners' Memoirs', *New York Columbian*, 16 November 1815, 4.

3. 'Proposal by Rowe & Hooper, Printers', *Providence Patriot*, 10 February 1816, 3.

4. Philip Cash, *Dr Benjamin Waterhouse: A Life in Medicine and Public Service* (Sagamore Beach, MA: Boston Medical Library and Science History Publications, 2006); Robin Agnew, 'Benjamin Waterhouse and the Riddle of Amos Babcock', *Journal of Medical Biography* 22, no. 1 (2014): 9–15.

5. Agnew, 'Benjamin Waterhouse', 12–13.

6. Waterhouse to Thomas Jefferson, 17 February, 26 March, 1 May 1813, FO.

7. Waterhouse to James Madison, 18 June 1816, FO. On the confusion over the original source for Waterhouse's embellished narrative, see Agnew, 'Benjamin Waterhouse', 10–11, 13–14; and Ira Dye, 'American Maritime Prisoners of War, 1812–1815', in *Ships, Seafaring and Society: Essays in Maritime History*, ed. Timothy J. Runyan (Detroit: Wayne State University Press, 1987), 315–316.

8. BW, 164–165. For a sense of Waterhouse's indulgent views on enslavers, see Edward Peterson, *History of Rhode Island* (New York: John S. Taylor, 1853), 104–105.

9. Donald R. Hickey, *The War of 1812: A Forgotten Conflict, Bicentennial Edition* (Urbana: University of Illinois Press, 2012), 261–283, 314–315.

10. BW, 228, 218–219.

11. Jefferson to Waterhouse, 20 July 1816; Madison to Waterhouse, 16 March 1817, FO.

12. 'The Dartmoor Affair', *New York National Advocate*, 27 October 1823, 2; 'The Dartmoor Party', *New York National Advocate*, 7 November 1823, 3. 'Mr Randolph's Speech', *Boston Statesman*, 16 March 1826, 2; 'Mr Charles King', *Daily National Intelligencer*, 8 November 1849, 3.

13. Louis Catel, *La Prison de Dartmoor*, 2 vols. (Paris: Chez Les Principaux Libraires, 1847), 2:143.

14. Catel, *La Prison*, 2:138–142.

15. Beasley to Jefferson, 29 September 1817, FO.

16. Washington Irving to William Irving, 22 September 1820, Washington Irving to Peter Irving, 9 July 1832, in Pierre M. Irving, ed., *The Life and Letters of Washington Irving*, 4 vols. (London: R. Bentley, 1862–64), 2:14–15, 3:26–27; 'The American Consul at Le Havre', *New Orleans Times-Picayune*, 18 October 1842, 2. Jenny Guestier Beasley died on 23 January 1829: 'Mortuary Notice', *New York Commercial Advertiser*, 28 March 1829, 2; Michael Stephen Smith, *The Emergence of Modern Business Enterprise in France, 1800–1930* (Cambridge, MA: Harvard University Press, 2006), 38, 40–41.

17. 'The Later Murders at Sea', *London Observer*, 23 May 1841, 3.

18. 'The William Brown', *London Morning Post*, 18 May 1841, 5.

19. 'The Ship William Brown', *Massachusetts Spy*, 9 June 1841, 2; Hugo Adam Bedau, *Making Mortal Choices: Three Exercises in Moral Casuistry* (Oxford: Oxford University Press, 1997), 5–35.

20. JV, vii; JNP, 24; DBFP, xix–xxiii; Charles Andrews, *The Prisoners' Memoirs, or, Dartmoor Prison* (New York: Printed for the Author, 1852). The 'certificate' of authenticity accompanying the 1815 edition was reprinted in full, with a note that 'out of the above list' of Dartmoor prisoners 'there are, at this time, only nine survivors, as far as can be ascertained.'

21. JB, 178–180, 243–244, 276–306.

22. Mira Wilkins, *The History of Foreign Investment in the United States to 1914* (Cambridge, MA: Harvard University Press, 1989), 49–66; Elisa Tamarkin, *Anglophilia: Deference, Devotion, and Antebellum America* (Chicago: University of Chicago Press, 2007).

23. 'Memoir of Lewis P. Clover', *United States Magazine and Democratic Review*, March 1850, 260–265; 'Memoir of Benjamin Frederick Browne', *Historical Collections of the Essex Institute* 13, no. 2 (1875): 81–89.

24. Nathaniel Hawthorne to Evert A. Duyckinck, 24 January 1846, in Joel Myerson, ed., *Selected Letters of Nathaniel Hawthorne* (Columbus: Ohio State University Press, 2002), 120–121; Margaret B. Moore, *The Salem World of Nathaniel Hawthorne* (Columbia: University of Missouri Press, 1998), 187–190.

25. *The Yarn of a Yankee Privateer*, edited by Nathaniel Hawthorne (New York: Funk and Wagnalls Company, 1926), 89–138.

26. James Monroe to Anthony St John Baker, 11 December 1815, MDP, 24; Richard Peters, ed., *The Public Statutes at Large of the United States of America, Volume VI*, (Boston: Charles C. Little and James Brown, 1846), 160; Robert L. Clark, Lee A. Craig, and Jack W. Wilson, *A History of Public Sector Pensions in the United States* (Philadelphia: University of Pennsylvania Press, 2003), 60–61; Faye M. Kert, *Privateering: Patriots and Profits in the War of 1812* (Baltimore: Johns Hopkins University Press, 2015), 108–109.

27. 'Coroner's Office', *Long-Island (NY) Star*, 2 August 1820, 2; Samuel B. Parsons, no. 492, GEBA, Admiralty Records (ADM) 103/87; John Stone, no. 5888, GEBA, ADM 103/91; 'Congress', *United States Telegraph*, 19 December 1833, 64; *Army and Navy Pension Laws, and Bounty Land Laws . . . from 1776 to 1852* (Washington, DC: Jno. T. Towers, 1852), 265.

28. 'Progress of the President', *Massachusetts Ploughman*, 17 June 1843, 2; 'Dartmoor Prisoners—Attention', *Philadelphia Public Ledger*, 7 December 1843, 4; 'Programme of Arrangements', *Philadelphia North American*, 26 June 1845, 3; 'The Obsequies of General Taylor', *Philadelphia North American*, 1 August 1850,132.

29. Charles W. Upham to Glover Broughton, 12 February 1855, Glover Broughton to George R. Williams, 17 January 1857, Broughton Family Papers, GBP.

30. 'Memorial, Privateersmen of Marblehead', 10 December 1861, GBP.

31. 'Address on Privateering', [1871], GBP.

32. 'Address on Privateering', [1871], GBP.

33. Board to Shortland, 25 March 1816, TBOL, ADM 98/229; *Oxford Dictionary of National Biography*, Online Edition, s.v. 'Thomas George Shortland', by J. K. Laughton, revised Andrew Lambert.

34. 'Devon', *New Monthly Magazine*, June 1814, 490; Transport Board to Lord Viscount Sidmouth, 18 February 1815, *Report from the Committee on the Prisons Within the City of London and Borough of Southwark*, 8 May 1818, *Parliamentary Papers*, 392 (1818): 238.

35. 'Cultivation of the Forest of Dartmoor', *Yorkshire Herald*, 22 January 1820, 2; 'The Severity of the Weather', *Jackson's Oxford Journal*, 22 January 1820, 2; 'Agricultural Employment of the Poor', *London Morning Post*, 28 January 1820, 2; 'Metropolitan School of Industry', *London Morning Post*, 5 May 1820, 2; 'Plymouth and Dartmoor Railway', *Exeter Flying Post*, 2 October 1823, 4.

36. N. T. Carrington, *Dartmoor: A Descriptive Poem* (London: John Murray, 1826), 15, 46; Joanne Parker, '"More Wondrous Far than Egypt's Boasted Pyramids": The South West's Megaliths in the Romantic Period', in Nicholas Roe, ed., *English Romantic Writers and the West Country* (Houndmills, UK: Palgrave Macmillan, 2010), 15–36, 28–30; Matthew Kelly, *Quartz and Feldspar: Dartmoor, a British Landscape in Modern Times* (London: Jonathan Cape, 2015), 57–69.

37. Rachel Evans, *Home Scenes: Or, Tavistock and Its Vicinity* (London: Simpkin and Marshall, 1846), 143; Joshua Jebb, *Report on the Discipline and Management of the Convict Prisons, 1850* (London: W. Clowes & Sons, 1851), 20–22; Philip Harling, 'The Trouble with Convicts: From Transportation to Penal Servitude, 1840–67', *Journal of British Studies* 53, no. 1 (2014): 80–110.

38. 'How Closing Dartmoor Prison Could Be Transformed into a Hotel', *Plymouth Herald*, 3 February 2020.

CHAPTER 14. THE TWO MASSACRES

1. 'To the Men of Color', *National Intelligencer*, 21 January 1815, 3.

2. David Walker, *Walker's Appeal . . . To the Colored Citizens of the World* (Boston: Printed for the Author, 1829), 66; Nicholas Guyatt, *Bind Us Apart: How Enlightened Americans Invented Racial Segregation* (New York: Basic Books, 2016), 197–224, 247–280.

3. James T. Campbell, *Middle Passages: African American Journeys to Africa, 1787–2005* (New York: Penguin Press, 2006); James Sidbury, *Becoming African in America: Race and Nation in the Early Black Atlantic* (Oxford: Oxford University Press, 2007); Ousmane K. Power-Greene, *Against Wind and Tide: The African American Struggle Against the Colonization Movement* (New York: New York University Press, 2014); Chris Dixon, *African America and Haiti: Emigration and Black Nationalism in the Nineteenth Century* (Westport, CT: Greenwood Press, 2000); Beverly C. Tomek, *Colonization and Its Discontents: Emancipation, Emigration, and Antislavery in Antebellum Pennsylvania* (New York: New

York University Press, 2011); Tunde Adeleke, *UnAfrican Americans: Nineteenth Century Black Nationalists and the Civilizing Mission* (Lexington: University Press of Kentucky, 1998).

4. Guyatt, *Bind Us Apart*, 259–263; Rosalind Cobb Wiggins, ed., *Captain Paul Cuffe's Logs and Letters, 1808–1817: A Black Quaker's 'Voice from Within the Veil'* (Washington, DC: Howard University Press, 1986), 326–398.

5. Guyatt, *Bind Us Apart*, 262–263.

6. 'Henry Van Meter: Death of a Black Hero of the Revolution', *New National Era*, 23 February 1871, 3; 'A Centenarian', *Bangor (ME) Whig*, 4 October 1867.

7. Richard Archer, *Jim Crow North: The Struggle for Equal Rights in Antebellum New England* (Oxford: Oxford University Press, 2017), 35–36.

8. 'A Case of Distress', *Liberator*, 24 April 1835; 'New Goods', *Bangor (ME) Weekly Register*, 22 October 1818, 3.

9. 'A Case of Distress', *Liberator*, 24 April 1835.

10. 'A Case of Distress', *Liberator*, 24 April 1835; 'Henry Vanmeter', *Liberator*, 25 April 1835; 'Mr Vanmeter's Lecture', *Boston Transcript*, 20 July 1839.

11. 'I, Henry Vanmeter', *Liberator*, 27 June 1835; 'A Case of Distress', *Liberator*, 24 April 1835.

12. 'Notice', *Bangor (ME) Daily Whig*, 22 May 1844, 2; 'Scenes in the War of 1812', *Harper's New Monthly Magazine*, October 1864, 596–607, 606.

13. 'Henry Van Meter', *Liberator*, 7 July 1865, 2; 'A Centenarian', *Bangor (ME) Whig*, 4 October 1867; 'Henry Van Meter,' *Bangor (ME) Whig*, 14 February 1871, 2; 'Henry Van Meter: Death of a Black Hero of the Revolution', *New National Era*, 23 February 1871, 3.

14. Charles Black, no. 6176, GEBA, Admiralty Records (ADM) 103/91.

15. 'A Riot in Philadelphia', *National Intelligencer*, 3 August 1842, 2; 'More of the Philadelphia Riots', *Emancipator*, 25 August 1842, 3; Margaret Hope Bacon, *But One Race: The Life of Robert Purvis* (Albany: State University of New York Press, 2007), 98–100.

16. 'Afflictions of Our Colored Population', *Liberator*, 9 September 1842, 142.

17. 'Afflictions of Our Colored Population', *Liberator*, 9 September 1842, 142.

18. Michael A. Schoeppner, *Moral Contagion: Black Atlantic Sailors, Citizenship, and Diplomacy in Antebellum America* (Cambridge: Cambridge University Press, 2019); W. Jeffrey Bolster, *Black Jacks: African American Seamen in the Age of Sail* (Cambridge, MA: Harvard University Press, 1997), 190–214.

19. George Wilson, no. 5712, GEBA, ADM 103/90. (NB that this register entry is missing a number of fields, though by process of elimination I believe this entry to correspond to the George Wilson who would reappear in 1841.) Michael A. Schoeppner, 'Status Across Borders: Roger Taney, Black British Subjects, and a Diplomatic Antecedent to the Dred Scott Decision', *Journal of American History* 100, no. 1 (2013): 46–67, 66.

20. David Roberts, no. 2038, GEBA, ADM 103/88; 'Imprisonment of Colored Seamen', *National Anti-Slavery Standard*, 30 December 1841, 118.

21. 'Imprisonment of Colored Seamen', *National Anti-Slavery Standard*, 30 December 1841, 118.

22. 'The Duty of Colored Americans', *Emancipator*, 31 March 1842, 191.

23. 'An Important Subject Mooted', *Maryland Colonization Journal*, 15 April 1842, 173–176.

24. 'An Important Subject Mooted', 173.

25. Stephen Kantrowitz, *More Than Freedom: Fighting for Black Citizenship in a White Republic, 1829–1889* (New York: Penguin Press, 2012), 41–43; Dorothy Porter Wesley, 'Integration Versus Separatism: William Cooper Nell's Role in the Struggle for Equality', in *Courage and Conscience: Black and White Abolitionists in Boston*, ed. Donald M. Jacobs (Bloomington: University of Indiana Press, 1993), 207–224.

26. Frederick Douglass to Harriet Beecher Stowe, 8 March 1853, in John R. McKivigan, ed., *The Frederick Douglass Papers, Series Three: Correspondence*, Vol. 2 (New Haven, CT: Yale University Press, 2018), 10–17; William Watkins, 'Frederick Douglass in Boston', *Frederick Douglass' Paper*, 12 August 1853, 3; Kantrowitz, *More Than Freedom*, 58–64, 62, 139–157; Patrick T. J. Browne, '"To Defend Mr. Garrison": William Cooper Nell and the Personal Politics of Antislavery', *New England Quarterly* 70, no. 3 (1997): 415–442, 438–441; Manisha Sinha, *The Slave's Cause: A History of Abolition* (New Haven, CT: Yale University Press, 2016), 491–493.

27. William Cooper Nell, *The Colored Patriots of the American Revolution* (Boston: Robert F. Wallcut, 1855), 5; Scott Hancock, '"Tradition Informs Us": African Americans' Construction of Memory in the Antebellum North', in *Slavery, Resistance, Freedom*, ed. Ira Berlin, Gabor S. Boritt, and Scott Hancock (New York: Oxford University Press, 2007), 40–69; Kantrowitz, *More Than Freedom*, 219–221; Margot Minardi, *Making Slavery History: Abolitionism and the Politics of Memory in Massachusetts* (New York: Oxford University Press, 2010), 94–95.

28. William Cooper Nell, *Services of Colored Americans in the Wars of 1776 and 1812* (Boston: Prentiss and Sawyer, 1851); Nell, *Colored Patriots*, 166–181, 64–91.

29. Serena Zabin, *The Boston Massacre: A Family History* (Boston: Houghton Mifflin Harcourt, 2020), 215–221; Eric Hinderaker, *Boston's Massacre* (Cambridge, MA: Harvard University Press, 2017), 159–220.

30. Zabin, *Boston Massacre*, 218.

31. Nell, *Colored Patriots*, 14–15; Stephen Kantrowitz, 'A Place for "Colored Patriots": Crispus Attucks Among the Abolitionists, 1842–1863', *Massachusetts Historical Review* 18 (2016): 190–212; Hinderaker, *Boston's Massacre*, 263–275.

32. Nell, *Colored Patriots*, 191–192.

33. Nell, *Colored Patriots*, 27–28.

34. Nell, *Colored Patriots*, 367–368; Watkins, 'Frederick Douglass in Boston'. On improvised and grassroots assertions of Black citizenship and belonging, see Christopher James Bonner, *Remaking the Republic: Black Politics and the Creation of American Citizenship* (Philadelphia: University of Pennsylvania Press, 2020) and Koritha Mitchell, *From Slave Cabins to the White House: Homemade Citizenship in African American Culture* (Urbana: University of Illinois Press, 2020).

INDEX

Vic Leung

Nicholas Guyatt is Professor of North American history at the University of Cambridge and the author of five previous books, including *Bind Us Apart: How Enlightened Americans Invented Racial Segregation*. He lives in Cambridge, UK.